PRACTICAL CODE GENERATION IN .NET

COVERING VISUAL STUDIO®
2005, 2008, AND 2010

Peter Vogel

✦ Addison-\

Upper Saddle River, NJ • Boston • Indianapolis • San Francisco
New York • Toronto • Montreal • London • Munich • Paris • Madrid
Capetown • Sydney • Tokyo • Singapore • Mexico City

Many of the designations used by manufacturers and sellers to distinguish their products are claimed as trade-marks. Where those designations appear in this book, and the publisher was aware of a trademark claim, the designations have been printed with initial capital letters or in all capitals.

The author and publisher have taken care in the preparation of this book, but make no expressed or implied warranty of any kind and assume no responsibility for errors or omissions. No liability is assumed for inciden-tal or consequential damages in connection with or arising out of the use of the information or programs con-tained herein.

The publisher offers excellent discounts on this book when ordered in quantity for bulk purchases or special sales, which may include electronic versions and/or custom covers and content particular to your business, training goals, marketing focus, and branding interests. For more information, please contact:

U.S. Corporate and Government Sales
(800) 382-3419
corpsales@pearsontechgroup.com

For sales outside the United States please contact:

International Sales
international@pearson.com

Visit us on the Web: informit.com/aw

Library of Congress Cataloging-in-Publication Data:

Vogel, Peter, 1953-
  Practical code generation in .NET : covering Visual Studio 2005, 2008, and 2010 / Peter Vogel.
    p. cm.
  Includes bibliographical references and index.
  ISBN 978-0-321-60678-5 (pbk. : alk. paper)
  1. Microsoft Visual studio. 2. Code generators. 3. Microsoft .NET Framework. I. Title.
  QA76.76.G46V65 2010
  006.7'882--dc22

                          2010003301

ISBN-13: 978-0-321-60678-5

ISBN-10: 0-321-60678-7

Text printed in the United States on recycled paper at RR Donnelly in Crawfordsville, Indiana.

First printing April 2010

For Jan. Always.

CONTENTS

FOREWORD

"I believe raising the level of abstraction is fundamental in all practical intellectual endeavors."

—*Bjarne Stroustrup, 2004*

The story of software engineering has been the story of increasing the level of abstraction at which we as programmers work, from logic encoded in hardware to toggle switches representing binary digits, through machine code, assembly language, low-level languages, and high-level languages both procedural and functional. More recently, we have declarative models of business processes that can be shared and discussed with folks who have no formal training in computer science at all. I'd wager that most readers were nodding along with my list above until I got to the last item. Has abstract modeling become a proven mainstream technique yet, accepted and used by all in the industry? No, of course not; this is the abstraction increase that we're currently involved in working out, and doubts and skepticism still abound. It's hard to remember now, but all earlier progressions were surrounded by doubt as to their value as well. In the infancy of each new technique, programmers wanted detailed access to the previous layer, not fully trusting the new tool to meet their needs, but as tools and understanding matured, this requirement slipped away. Today, few developers feel the need to examine the IL or bytecode produced by their C# or Java compiler, and fewer still the assembly code produced by the JIT compiler underlying their runtime.

Code generators bridge the gap from nascent abstractions to their well understood predecessor technologies. They facilitate working on a problem at a higher, more productive level and translate that to a practical solution based on best practices at a lower level. Of course, all this talk of raising abstraction levels implies some sort of grandiose vision of defining your application with metadata and generating the whole thing. This book demonstrates clearly that nothing is further from the truth and that starting small is where the value is at when it comes to code generators.

As our abstractions get closer to our problem space, as opposed to being merely refinements in the solution space, we're inevitably going to use more granular, more fragmented tools that are specialized for the task at hand. Alongside a gradual easing of the difficulty of building such tools, we have the ingredients for a productivity explosion, driven by the creation of small tools to help with the distinct tasks in our day-to-day jobs. Unix command-line developers have known this truth since the 1980s with their chaining of small scripts; now it's becoming a reality for the IDE generation.

Whether your design-time metadata is a simple list of settings and their default values in Visual Studio, or the set of tables and stored procedures to be accessed in your relational database, there's ample opportunity for using that data to generate reliable code that conforms to proven patterns. Look for metadata that's already present in your application design, and surface it to drive tools. Look for repetitive patterns in your code and determine which pieces are fixed and where the variability is. Make creating tools and increasing task repeatability part of your normal approach to problem solving to ease your working life.

Once these skills are within your everyday comfort zone, your productivity will get a boost and your value to your team will increase. Spreading the use of such tools to make your peers more productive is an important step in the transition of our industry from one dominated by software artisans to one driven by engineering practices that provide predictable results at scale.

I encourage you to add the techniques outlined in this book to your toolset and to use them to develop your own workbench of generative tools. In doing so, I'm confident you'll improve your capabilities, and what's more, have fun doing so.

—*Gareth Jones,*
Developer Architect, Visual Studio
Issaquah, WA
March 2010

PREFACE

Whenever you're looking at buying a book, it seems to me there's only one question that should be asked: "Why should I invest my hard-earned money in this book?"

This book is designed to make you, as a software developer, more productive. It does that by giving you all the tools you need to incorporate code generation into your standard development practices. Why would you buy this book? Because letting Visual Studio and .NET write the boring code lets you work on the important stuff.

All the code-generation tools you need are already available to you because you're already using code generation. As soon as you start working in .NET and any version of Visual Studio, an enormous amount of code is being created for you. For instance, if you've ever created a DataSet then you've been using a Visual Studio custom tool that generates the code class file for your DataSet—and that's just some of the code that's easy to see. There's a great deal more generated code hidden away where you can't find it. In addition to making you more productive, those code-generation tools have taken over creating some of the repetitive and error-prone parts of building applications, thereby also increasing the quality of your code. The next step is for you to start using those tools to create solutions that you—rather than the .NET team—want solved.

But the problem is that there is no single point of reference for this material. Code generation requires several tools, and there is no one place where all those tools are discussed. And, even when you find resources for those tools, a comprehensive reference that shows you how to apply them is missing. So part of the answer to the question "Should I buy this book?" is that the book provides "one-stop shopping" for all the tools you need to implement code generation. I've put all the tools in one book and covered all the parts of each tool that are relevant to code generation.

I've been building Visual Studio add-ins that created code for me since .NET 1.1. As I worked with various clients, I found that they were also adopting code-generation solutions—and I got to help them do it. So, in this book, I wanted to show how those tools could be used in a practical way—and how they would work together. As a result, almost a third of this book is taken up with three case studies that show how to coordinate these tools to create useful, reliable code-generation solutions for common problems.

To put it another way: I wrote this book because I believe that the code-generation tools built into .NET and Visual Studio 2005/2008/2010 will make you a better, more productive developer. And I believe that more developers would develop more code-generation solutions if the tools were more accessible to them.

And, of course, I wrote this book because it's cool technology. Several years ago, I stumbled across a great quote from Dick Sites (one of the designers of Digital Equipment Corporation's Alpha architecture): "I'd rather write programs that help me write programs than write programs." That seemed right.

One caveat: If you're looking for a book that shows you how to create enormous frameworks that will generate thousands of lines of code from a single XML document that describes an application—this is not that book. Certainly, all the tools you'll need are in here, but that's not my focus. I don't want to describe how to spend three years building your very own "application generator." Instead, I want to give you the tools that will let you solve a problem in your life and do it in a morning—a solution that you'll never have to think about again because it will just work.

The first case study in this book (in Chapter 9) is a good example: This solution generates a class that simplifies access to the connection strings specified in the connectionStrings element. It took me about a morning to write, it works in every application, it reduces the amount of code I write, and it eliminates errors in my applications. The second case study (Chapter 10) is similarly focused: It generates the code for an ASP.NET validator that checks that data entered by the user is a valid entry in a table. Like my connection string generator, this is something I use in almost every ASP.NET application I write. The final case study (Chapter 11) took a full day to write, but it allows nonprogrammers to use a visual designer to generate the code necessary to integrate their software into one of my applications—and to do it reliably and without requiring my intervention.

Here's a breakdown of the topics covered in this book:

- Chapter 1, "Introducing Code Generation," is the "theory and practice" chapter. It discusses the structure of code-generation solutions and covers best practices in architecting solutions.

- Chapter 2, "Integrating with Visual Studio," gives you enough information about creating Visual Studio add-ins for you to integrate code generation into your standard activities. The connection string generator, for instance, generates code whenever the developer closes the web.config file; the validator example generates code whenever the developer closes an .aspx file containing a specific tag.
- Chapter 3, "Manipulating Project Components," covers the objects and methods that you need to add (or remove) components to a project: code files, folders, and so on.
- Chapter 4, "Modifying Code in the Editor," gives you the tools you need to insert text into files. This allows you to generate code using any tool you want (even standard string-handling functions) and then insert that code into a file in your project.
- Chapter 5, "Supporting Project-Specific Features," provides support for working with specific types of projects: C#, Visual Basic, and ASP.NET websites. Each of these project types have special features that aren't available through the objects covered in Chapter 4.
- Chapter 6, "Generating Language-Neutral Code," contains full coverage of the CodeDom, which allows you to generate code without having to commit to producing Visual Basic or C# until it's time to insert text into files.
- Chapter 7, "Generating Code from Templates with T4," covers a new technology in .NET: Text Template Transformation Toolkit (T4), which uses a template-based approach to code generation that reduces the amount of code required in a solution.
- Chapter 8, "Other Tools: Templates, Attributes, and Custom Tools," has three technologies you can use in creating code-generation solutions: Visual Studio templates, attributes, and custom tools. Visual Studio templates reduce the code that must be generated from your code; attributes provide a way for developers to insert information into a file to specify the code to be generated; custom tools are standalone programs that, when associated with a file, read the file's contents and create a file of generated code.
- Chapter 9, "Case Study: Generating a Connection String Manager," Chapter 10, "Case Study: Generating Validation Code," and Chapter 11, "Case Study: Generating Data-Conversion Code," are the three case studies included in this book.

When I wrote this book, I assumed that you're an experienced developer with a solid command of your programming language. I also assumed that you have several years of experience in creating complex applications.

You can find code samples for this book and all three of the case studies on www.informit.com and on my website at www.phvis.com.

I hope you find this book useful and enjoyable to read.

—*Peter Vogel*
March 2010

ACKNOWLEDGMENTS

I get to put my name on the cover of this book. However, there are many more people involved. I'd like to especially thank the two people at Pearson who I worked with most closely: Joan Murray and Olivia Basegio (two of the most patient people in the world). Joan and my agent Neil Salkind of StudioB thought there was a future in this book when no one else (in their right minds) would have. Finally, the material on T4 is immeasurably better because of the involvement of Gareth Jones. (You should read his book on domain-specific development.)

About the Author

Peter Vogel began working in information technology in 1984 and by 1994 was the head of the IT department for a multinational heavy equipment manufacturer. While working for Imperial Oil, Peter served on their software management counsel and was given the President's award for excellence, marking only the second time the award had been given to Imperial Oil's IT department. While working for Bayer AG, Peter won the company's quality in IT award.

Peter branched out as an independent consultant in 1997, founding PH&V Information Services. PH&VIS specializes in system design and development for systems that use Microsoft tools. PH&VIS has consulted for, designed, built, and/or installed n-tier and service-based applications for Volvo, Schumaker and Associates, Stemco, Service Brands International, Microsoft, and the Canadian Imperial Bank of Commerce. PH&VIS's focus on database design, middle-tier object development, user interface design, XML, and Service Oriented Architecture allows the company to consult on end to end solutions.

Peter also teaches .NET development throughout the world, primarily for Learning Tree International. He has written four courses for Learning Tree International, including two on ASP.NET and one on technical writing. He's also acted as a technical editor or subject matter expert on an equal number of courses.

In addition to providing software development services, Peter has had a flourishing career as a technical writer and consultant on effective communication. He was the editor of the Smart Access newsletter, the founding editor of the XML Developer newsletter, and the editor of *Adivsor* magazine. He currently edits Learning Tree International's Management Insights newsletter. He also wrote the Contractor Skills column for *Contract Professional* magazine. In addition to this book, Peter has had three books published. (His *Visual Basic Object and Component Handbook* was called "the definitive guide to 'thinking with objects.'") He recently self-published *rtfm**, a book on creating effective user manuals, and he blogs on technical writing topics at http://rtfmphvis.blogspot.com/. Currently, Peter is the Products editor for *Visual Studio* magazine, writes the online column *Practical ASP.NET* (read by thousands of developers every month), and contributes feature articles. You can find many of the whitepapers he has written for Microsoft on Microsoft's MSDN site.

Peter has a BA from the University of Western Ontario, an MBA from Wilfrid Laurier University, has been a Microsoft MVP, and was one of the first Microsoft Certified Solution Developers.

Peter lives in Goderich, Ontario, Canada—officially, the "prettiest town in Canada."

CHAPTER 1

INTRODUCING CODE GENERATION

In this chapter:

- Repetitive Code: Your History
- Benefits of Code Generation
- When to Use Code Generation
- Best Practices in Code-Generation Solutions
- Code-Generation Process
- Code-Generation Tools
- Model-Driven Architecture, Declarative Programming, and Code Generation

You're already using code generation. A lot. You just don't know it.

If you've ever dragged a control onto a form then you've been letting Visual Studio and .NET generate code for you. If you've ever added a DataSet to an application (or, for the more up to date, added an ADO.NET Entity Data Model to an application) then you've been using code generation. For both DataSets and Entity Data Models, Visual Studio has used the tools built into .NET to create the class files associated with your data design. If, in ASP.NET, you've defined personalization properties and then found those properties waiting for you on the Profile object, it's because .NET used code generation to create a Profile class for you.

Code generation is used throughout the .NET Framework for the same reasons you should be using it throughout your application development process: Code generation makes you more productive, reduces errors, and increases the quality of your code. And all the tools you need are already built into the .NET Framework and Visual Studio—they're just waiting for you to start using them.

Repetitive Code: Your History

As a programmer, you know that much of the code you write is repetitive, ranging from creating simple constructs (looping through a set of records) to more complex structures (creating a business entity class). Much of the history of development tools can be written in terms of reducing the amount of repetitive code that developers are obliged to write. (There's even a three-letter acronym that describes the related best practice: DRY—Don't Repeat Yourself.).

Writing repetitive code—code with only minor variations from one version to another—drives programmers crazy. The primary reason is, of course, that it's boring. But the worst part of creating repetitive code is that if you don't repeat the code precisely then the only variation from one version to another is the number of errors you introduce (and then get to track down). This is one of the reasons that DRY is considered a best practice: It's unlikely that human beings can successfully implement repetitive code, so repeating yourself is just an accident waiting to happen.

Over the years, developers have developed a number of strategies for dealing with repetitive code.

Copy-and-Paste

The most obvious alternative to writing the same code again is to copy and paste existing code into your current application. However, the new environment that the code is pasted into usually requires that you modify the code in some way, if only to replace the names of the variables in the copied code. Because even the simplest copy-and-paste solution is time consuming (you must find a version of the code and then modify it to fit the new environment), when the amount of code is small most developers just type in a new version. Even where the amount of code being copied is large, because of the time required to determine the necessary changes and then to implement them (and the danger that not all of those changes will be made correctly), most developers type in repeated code.

As a result, developers tend to use copy-and-paste solutions in a narrow range of cases: "not too small" to "not too big." In practice, many developers only use the copy-and-paste solution when they aren't really sure what code is needed but know they've figured out this problem before and can use that code as a template in their current application. If they can remember the solution, developers will often choose to type in the code rather than copy an earlier version.

It's not that Microsoft hasn't tried to make the copy-and-paste solution work. Visual Studio 2005 introduced code snippets, which supported inserting parameters into recycled code, to speed the copy-and-paste process. But, even with Visual Studio's support, using copy-and-paste code has never caught on as a popular solution. The primary reason was that the code snippets provided with Visual Studio often weren't large enough: It was easier for the developer to just type in a new solution rather than incur the overhead of keeping track of what was in the library of code snippets and work through entering all the parameters (assuming that the developer could remember what each parameter did).

General-Purpose Code

The next solution that developers turn to in reducing repetitive code is to create methods or objects that can handle a variety of scenarios. There is a variety of names for this kind of solution: "general-purpose code," "helper functions," and "utilities" are three of them.

The major problem with this solution is in writing a utility that can handle enough scenarios to make the utility worthwhile without making the utility too complex to maintain. Typically, as the number of scenarios that the utility handles increases, the complexity of the utility's code increases exponentially. This is because complexity in the utility is of the worst kind: The number of `If` and `Select...Case` statements increases, driving up the number of execution paths through the code, making testing the utility increasingly difficult.

In addition, as the number of scenarios increases, the utility's interface also becomes more complex. To support more scenarios, the developer tends to add more properties and overloaded methods. To use the resulting utility, developers either find themselves having to set multiple properties before calling any method or having to pass multiple parameters to each method. Effectively, developers find that they have to understand too much about how the utility works in order to control it. In effect, the developer moves from programming in some language to programming with the utility.

This creates a paradox: Had the developer just written the code to handle the scenario, the resulting code might be relatively simple and easy to maintain or extend. The utility that handles the scenario, however, is complex and hard to maintain or extend.

The developers who build these utilities face equally challenging hurdles. As the differing expectations from the developer community force the utility to handle more and more scenarios, the utility not only becomes more complex but also more self-reflexive. The code frequently has to keep track of how many variables it is working with, their data types, and mappings between those variables and other external values (the fields in a database, for instance). It's not unusual, for instance, for a utility to require that a developer pass not only the values that are to go into a database but also the names of fields those values are to go into so that the utility can then construct the appropriate SQL statement.

In addition, general-purpose utilities that handle a wide variety of scenarios generally give poor performance. In order for the utility to determine what scenario it's handling and to deal with all possible problems, the utility often has to go through many steps that wouldn't be required if the developer had just written the dedicated code required to solve the problem. For instance, to handle a variety of data types the utility often has to either declare variables as objects or turn everything into a string. The result is not only "self-reflexive" code that is constantly checking data types but also added code that casts from the object or string data types to the data type required by the application. In the bad old days, these utilities often incorporate `Select...Case` statements that check the data type of the incoming data and select the correct method for each data type. Modern code tends to use reflection, making the code harder to read and understand—and, as a result, harder to debug and maintain.

Finally, utilities often impose unnecessary standardization on the applications that use them. In order to control the utility, developers are forced to solve problems a specific way, to adopt specific naming conventions or to incorporate specific flags in the data that the utility will recognize and react to. For instance, utilities that work with relational databases often need a mechanism to identify primary or foreign keys and, as a result, oblige the developer to use a naming convention for those fields—or even force the developer to add the tables that the utility requires to the application's database.

Not surprisingly, many utilities have a common history: The original version handles a few scenarios and does it well. The developer, buoyed by early success, extends the utility (at the request of other developers) to handle more scenarios. Performance begins to suffer and bugs start to appear. Developers new to the utility find it difficult to use and avoid it. Eventually, something in the environment changes that would force the utility to be rewritten. However, rather than rewrite the utility, developers simply abandon it and go back to writing the dedicated code.

Benefits of Code Generation

Code generation eliminates the problems associated with both the copy-and-paste solution and the general-purpose code solution:

- Unlike copy-and-paste solutions, code generation can be integrated with the development environment. Often code generation can be triggered by events fired by Visual Studio so that the code generation happens without the developer being aware of it. (This is how the code generated for DataSets is handled, for instance.)
- Unlike copy-and-paste solutions, code generation can dynamically modify the code as it is created and without intervention from the developer.
- Unlike general-purpose utilities, which may not be maintainable, the code produced by code-generation solutions is part of the application and can be altered or extended just like the rest of the code in the application—even if the code-generation solution is disabled.
- Unlike self-reflexive utilities, code generation creates just the code required for the scenario specified at design time. No additional overhead is required to deal with any scenario except the one specified by the developer.
- Code generation eliminates many of the problems associated with distributing utilities. When a new version of a utility is released, developers must either incorporate the utility into every project or— if the utility is installed in the Global Assembly Cache (GAC)— ensure that the correct version of the utility is installed both in the development and production environments. Code-generation solutions are implemented only when the project is recompiled—usually when the project is being modified/enhanced/fixed and will be retested. For most code-generation solutions, all the components of the solution (typically, just more code) are contained within the project.
- A code-generation solution—because it executes at design time— can perform activities that aren't practical at runtime because of the overhead involved (examining the database structure to determine the data types of the fields to be updated, for instance).

But just because code generation eliminates the problems associated with the alternatives, that doesn't necessarily mean you should you invest your time in implementing code-generation solutions. You could, after all, still type in the necessary code. However, in addition to avoiding the problems associated with the other solutions, there are several positive benefits to incorporating code generation into your application development toolkit:

- Improved productivity is the most obvious reason for using code generation. Provided that creating the inputs for a code-generation solution takes less time than writing the code, code generation makes you more productive.

- Reliability is improved through the use of code generation. As I said earlier, the reason that DRY is a best practice is that, when you fail to repeat yourself exactly, you are more likely to introduce a bug than an enhancement. Code generation ensures that the accepted solution is applied every time the code-generation tool is used.

- Debugging is simplified with code generation. When a general-purpose utility doesn't perform as expected, trying to figure out what the relatively abstract code is doing is harder than figuring out dedicated code. Modifying general-purpose code to perform correctly—and then doing the regression testing required to ensure that all previous implementations are unaffected—is even harder. In generated code, deducing the problem is often no harder than it would be to spot the same problem with dedicated code. In most cases, modifying the code-generation process is simpler than modifying general-purpose code. But the developer also has the option to disconnect the generated code from the code-generation process and just treat the code as dedicated code.

- Programmer support is enhanced. Code generation adds new code to the current project. Where that code adds new classes or members (e.g., methods, properties, or events), those classes and members appear in IntelliSense. Unlike a general-purpose utility that has all the methods and properties to handle any scenario with indeterminate data types, code-generation solutions can be parsimonious: They add only the necessary methods and properties with the right data types.

- Uniformity is improved. In addition to being consistent in generating the same solution to the same problem, code generation is also consistent in ensuring that naming conventions, code formatting, and other tools for making code "look alike" are applied automatically. Making similar code "look the same" improves productivity by making it easier for developers to read each other's code.

- Quality improves under code generation. When creating a code generation solution, developers implement the current best-known solution. As a result, the expertise of the developer building the code-generation solution is embedded in all other developers' applications. If a better solution is found and incorporated into the code-generation tool, the next time the application is modified, the new solution is automatically generated without any work required by the developer. The quality assurance department may have less to do because, once they have tested one set of generated code, they may not have to test every repetition of the same code because it's guaranteed to be identical.

- Dealing with change is also better supported by code generation. In most IT shops, many of the changes to code are generated by changes in the environment: new regulations, new programming standards, changes in the business, or adoption of new development tools. Rather than having to revise the code in each affected application, the changes can be made to the code-generation tool. The changes will be incorporated into each application the next time the application is compiled.

One problem that developers of code-generation solutions and utilities share is complexity: It's possible to create a code-generation solution that, although it generates relatively simple code, is so complex that it's impossible to maintain, extend, or even test. There is, of course, no substitute for good application design: Ambitious code-generation solutions need to be architected as carefully as ambitious business applications.

Some approaches to code generation are necessarily more complex than others, however. Any solution that aims to generate code in multiple programming languages will use the CodeDom (covered in Chapter 6, "Generating Language-Neutral Code," and used in the case study in Chapter 10, "Case Study: Generating Validation Code") and will, at the very least, contain a lot of code. On the other hand, a template-based solution using T4 (covered in Chapter 7, "Generating Code from Templates with T4," and used in the case study in Chapter 11, "Case Study: Generating Data-Conversion Code") typically results in less-complex solutions though these solutions will typically only support generating code in a single language. You need to be familiar with all the tools available for code generation so that you pick the right tool for the job.

When to Use Code Generation

I'm not, however, going to suggest that code generation is a panacea that can be applied to every problem in application development. Code generation handles a subset of the problems faced by developers who would otherwise create general-purpose utilities. Specifically, code generation handles those scenarios where all the parameters are known at design time and there is a single solution for the problem. In those scenarios—where all (or most) of the information required by the utility is known at design time and a standard solution exists—code generation can be used to generate that standard solution. For instance, whenever SQL statements are being assembled in code at runtime, it's worth investigating whether enough information exists at design time so that a code-generation solution could create the correct SQL statement before the application is even compiled.

The design time information required by the code generator may be available in the existing Visual Studio project without any additional effort by the developer (e.g., the solution can gather the information it needs by reading the application's configuration file). Alternatively, required information can be provided by the developer through some customized input process (e.g., decorating code with attributes—discussed in Chapter 8, "Other Tools: Templates, Attributes, and Custom Tools"—or using a visual designer to create a specification file—discussed as part of the case study in Chapter 11).

To be useful (and learning from the problems with cut-and-paste solutions), code-generation solutions should normally handle problems that stretch beyond a few lines of code. The obvious opportunities for code-generation solutions are those cases where the developer would otherwise have to write many lines of code.

However, frequency can also make code generation attractive: Code-generation solutions are also a good idea when they make life easier for developers if the problem happens often enough and if the developer has to write a lot of related code. For instance, dragging a control onto a form generates only a few lines of code—but it's an activity that a developer performs frequently. Furthermore, there are many follow-on benefits to generating the code: The code that is generated makes it easier for the developer to both access and configure the control. Here, the benefits accrue not just to the code generated by the solution but all the subsequently created hand-written code that uses the generated code.

If I were to write a formula for calculating the value of a code-generation solution, it would be something like:

B (Benefit) = N (number of lines generated) * F (frequency of code being generated) + T (time saved in follow-on activities)

And that formula ignores the harder-to-measure benefits I mentioned before: improved code quality, improved standardization, and so on.

BEST PRACTICES   Although it may be obvious to say, it's worth mentioning because so many general-purpose solutions have violated this rule: A code-generation solution should always be easier for developers to use than writing the code themselves. In addition, the generated code should be no more complicated than the code that the developer would have written to solve the problem.

As an example of a typical code-generation solution, consider an application that must support various business objects that need the ability to delete records in a database. There is a wide variety of scenarios that the code in the objects will need to be able to handle, including the following:

- Deleting a single row in a table
- Deleting multiple rows in a single table
- Deleting multiple rows in multiple tables
- Copying records to an archive table before removing them from their original table

In other cases, depending on the scenario, the business object shouldn't delete any records (e.g., if related child records exist). For all of these scenarios, the solution is well understood and the code to handle the scenario is well known.

You could handcraft a solution for each of your business objects, including copying and pasting related code from one object to another. There is the constant danger that, as you copy the code from one object to another, you will miss one of the required changes needed to customize the code for the new object. In the worst possible scenario, you could end up with a business object deleting the records for the object the code was copied from.

Alternatively, you could create a "delete utility" that, when passed a business entity and some parameters, would delete the right records. The code inside the utility would be complex and the resulting interface would be "feature rich" (a synonym for "also complicated").

Or you could create a code-generation solution that would write out, for each class, exactly the right code. Much of the information that the code-generation solution needs could be retrieved by accessing the database and analyzing the files currently in the application. In addition, the developer could specify what code is to be generated by adding an XML document to the project that specifies what classes are to be extended in which ways (a visual designer could be provided to support creating this document). Alternatively, the developer could add attributes to the business object's class files that specify what delete actions to take. The code could be generated when the developer requests it, when the application is built, whenever a change is made to any of the files in the application, or just when changes are made to the classes that are being extended.

With the code-generation solution, the developer gets the right code for the job (and only the right code). Furthermore, that code is quietly generated by Visual Studio as the developer carries on with the normal tasks involved in building the application. Once the code is generated, any new methods appear in the IntelliSense list for the class that the code extends.

Best Practices in Code-Generation Solutions

It is, of course, possible to create bad code-generation solutions—solutions that developers either won't or can't use. Developers won't use a code-generation solution for many reasons, but the most common reasons are because the solution is too hard to use, because it's too inflexible, or because developers just don't trust the generated code. Developers don't trust a code-generation solution unless they are sure that generating code won't harm their own code or their application.

I follow five principles when designing a code-generation solution to ensure that the solution is easy to use, that the developer can extend my solution, that the developer can see what my code-generation solution has done, and that the developer's code is preserved through the code-generation process. Those principles are as follows:

- **Simple inputs**—Developers shouldn't have to enter more information to support the code-generation solution than would be required if they just wrote the code.
- **Integrated with Visual Studio and .NET projects**—Code-generation solutions should integrate seamlessly with the developer's environment. Ideally, the developer can provide any required inputs by using tools already built into Visual Studio (e.g., by adding to the application's configuration file or using attributes to decorate existing code). Effective code-generation solutions accept options through Visual Studio's Tools | Options dialog, use Visual Studio task panels, display progress messages in the Output window or the status bar, and display fixable error conditions in the Task List.
- **Visible**—All the generated code should be visible to the developer so that the code can be reviewed for quality and compatibility (and be disconnected from the code-generation process and handled manually). The developer should be able to step through the code during debugging to see what the code does.
- **Extensible**—The developer should be able to build on the generated code either to add functionality or to customize what the generated code does. This can be handled either by generating classes that developers can inherit from, by using partial classes, or by having generated code call out to methods (or event procedures) that the developer can customize.
- **Separation of generated code and developer code**—Code is usually generated several times over the life of the project. Developers should be free to regenerate the code at any point without fear of losing any of their own code. To support this, any code

that the developer writes should be kept separate from generated code—ideally, the two kinds of code should be kept in separate files. Rather than modifying code in the developer's files, code-generation solutions should generate new files containing new classes (or interfaces, etc.). By keeping generated code separate from the developer's code, code-generation solutions can just delete any files associated with previous executions of the code generator.

Following these five principles will ensure that you create code-generation solutions that are genuinely useful to developers. More importantly, you will create solutions that developers will trust.

Code-Generation Process

Based on the preceding principles, the code-generation process consists of these steps:

1. **Read inputs.** The first step in generating code is to determine if the necessary inputs to the code-generation process exist. If they don't, the code generator should either silently quit (the appropriate solution if the tool is automatically triggered by some event in the Visual Studio environment) or display an error message (the appropriate solution if the developer triggered code generation by, for instance, selecting a menu choice). Error messages should be displayed in Visual Studio's status bar, Output window, or Task List.

2. **Create space in the project.** Wherever possible, generated code should be kept in separate files from the developer's code. Creating separate files for generated code keeps the code visible to the developer while protecting the developer's code from the code-generation process. Therefore, the next step in generating code is to create the files that will hold the generated code. (I typically create a separate folder within the project for the files holding generated code.) At this step, if the files for generated code already exist (from a previous run of the code-generation solution), they should be deleted and re-created.

3. **Add the base code.** The output from a code generator often contains code that never changes from one code generation to another. The third step in the code-generation process is to add that common code. You can either generate this code or use a Visual Studio template as the starting point.

4. **Customize.** After the base code is created, the second-to-last step is to generate the code that varies from one code generation to another and then insert it into the files created earlier in the process.
5. **Save the results to the project, if necessary.**

Code-Generation Tools

When building an application in .NET, you use a variety of tools. Building an ASP.NET or Windows Forms application, for instance, also requires that you use ADO.NET (or LINQ/Entity Framework). In the same way, you need a variety of tools to implement code-generation solutions. This book covers the following:

- **Integrating with Visual Studio**—In order to integrate your code-generation solutions with your development environment, you need to create Visual Studio add-ins. Chapter 2, "Integrating with Visual Studio," covers all of the aspects of Visual Studio object model that you need for code-generation solutions. You can also integrate your code-generation solution with Visual Studio by using T4, as discussed in Chapters 7 and 11, or by creating a custom tool, as discussed in Chapter 8 in the section on custom tools.
- **Adding components to projects**—The second and third steps in the code-generation process require that you add components (files, references, etc.) to an existing project. The `FileCodeModel` objects (covered in Chapter 3, "Manipulating Project Components") allow you to add components to a project in Visual Studio, regardless of the project type. Using the `FileCodeModel`, you can also generate code (primarily in C#) for a limited number of code structures (class declarations, `If...Then` structures, etc.)
- **Defining the base code for your solution in Visual Studio templates**—Visual Studio Templates (Chapter 8) provide an efficient way of creating the "starting point" for the code you generate.
- **Providing inputs**—One way to provide input to a code-generation solution is to allow developers to embed information in their code. Attributes (also covered in Chapter 7) provide an easy, structured way for developers to embed information in their code that your code-generation solution can read. Creating a visual designer is another option (covered as part of the T4 case study in Chapter 11). Custom tools (Chapter 8) allow you to define your own input format

and process to generate code. Custom tools can also be used with visual designers if you don't want to use them with T4.

- **Generating code**—You can create the code to put in your files in a variety of ways, ranging from concatenating strings to replacing tokens in template files to using XSLT transforms. You can also use the CodeDom objects (discussed in Chapter 6) to describe your code and then generate your code in the .NET language of your choice. T4 (Chapter 7) provides a way to limit the amount of "code-generation code" that you have to write by allowing you to enter the code that doesn't change from one generation to another as plain text.

- **Inserting code into files**—Once you've generated the files that will hold your code and the code you want to put into the file, the Code Editor objects (Chapter 4, "Modifying Code in the Editor") give you the ability to insert text into a file. You can also use the Code Editor objects to retrieve text in a file and use that information as part of the inputs to your code-generation process. Not all solutions require this step: If you use a custom tool (Chapter 8), the code file holding your generated code is automatically added to the project for you; creating a visual designer (Chapter 11) also allows you to skip this step because the code file is created for you automatically.

- **Handling special features of Visual Studio projects**—Although the FileCodeModel provides a language-neutral and project-neutral way to manage project components, there are special features of the Visual Studio project types that it does not support. The VsLangProject and VsWebSite objects (Chapter 5, "Supporting Project-Specific Features") give you the ability to manage the project features unique to C#, Visual Basic, and ASP.NET websites.

Whereas Chapters 2 through 8 provide you with the tools for your code-generation toolkit, Chapters 9 through 11 are three case studies that show how the tools can be used in a complete solution. Chapter 9's case study is a solution that generates a small amount of code: This case study creates a Visual Studio add-in that uses the FileCodeModel and a little bit of the Code Editor objects to create a class that provides access to an application's connection strings. Chapter 10 goes beyond that example to use a custom Visual Studio template and the CodeDom objects to create a more "code-intensive" solution than the case study in Chapter 9. Chapter 11 shows how to create a visual designer and integrate it with a custom tool and T4 to generate new classes for a project.

Model-Driven Architecture, Declarative Programming, and Code Generation

I've tried to make this book as practical as possible. My goal in writing this book is to provide the tools for developers to create solutions that will make them more productive. As I said in the Introduction, to support that goal the examples in this book are focused on "small-scale problems": code-generation solutions that automate generating part of the code for a full application. In this book I won't discuss code-generation solutions that would generate a full application (or even large parts of it). One of the primary reasons that the three case studies focus on small-scale solutions is that I expect most programmers won't be able to spend weeks or months building large, complex code-generation solutions—but I do expect developers will find value in being able to spend hours or days on building a tool that will make them more productive.

Having said that, all the tools you would need for a large, complex code-generation solution are in this book. So it wouldn't be fair not to discuss what those large, complex code-generation solutions look like. This, therefore, is the *im*practical part of the book—a "theory of code generation."

Model-Driven Architecture

Many developers would consider the ultimate goal of code generation to be Model-Driven Architecture (MDA). The goal of MDA is to, ideally, eliminate the need for code to be written by developers at all. Instead, developers would design an application in some high-level tool and have all the application code generated for them. One of the mutual goals of MDA and the Unified Modeling Language (UML), for instance, is to use UML as the graphical notation to support MDA.

Why MDA?

There are three compelling reasons for moving to an MDA-based solution: agility, transferability, and productivity. Agility allows developers to generate simple applications at an early stage in the process—ideally, at the requirements gathering stage—so that the application stakeholders can start evaluating the application before much time and resources have been committed to it. This creates a shorter feedback loop between the design phase and the delivery phase and would allow developers to deliver higher quality applications.

Transferability addresses a different problem: the cost of moving from one development platform to another. Most organizations move their developers to a new development platform every five to ten years. The costs of moving existing applications to new platforms has been estimated to be as high as $300 billion per year. An MDA approach would allow developers to build their applications in a platform-neutral way and then transfer that application to a new platform by rewriting their code-generation tool, rather than having to migrate each application.

And agility plus transferability equals productivity.

Stumbling Blocks

Although the ultimate goal of MDA is to generate all the code for an application, proponents of MDA recognize that some code will always have to be written—at least with the current set of tools. However, many parts of that ideal, write-no-code solution do already exist. The various Object Relational Modeling (ORM) tools (including Microsoft's Entity Framework) have already automated large parts of generating an application's data access layer. In addition, developers can customize the generated code by modifying an ORM model rather than by writing code.

There are, however, at least three major stumbling blocks on the road to complete application generation: requirements, user interface, and complexity.

Ideally, for instance, it would be possible to generate an application from the application's requirements. That goal, however, requires some tool for modeling requirements in a structured way. Without that front end, developers must still read the requirements and create a model of the application—effectively, instead of programming in code, the developer programs in some modeling tool. While a structured requirements language doesn't yet exist, ORM tools suggest that they are possible. Effectively, either the relational database design for an application forms the requirements document used by the ORM code-generation process to create objects, or the object model forms the requirements document for the tables that are created by the ORM tool.

Even though code-generation solutions exist for the data access layer of the application, the further you move away from the data access layer, the fewer solutions exist. The furthest point in the application from the database—the user interface—forms the second stumbling block in MDA. There is not yet a fully robust solution for generating user interfaces, especially for desktop applications (though Ruby On Rails and Microsoft's Dynamic Data show what can be done in the more limited web environment). An effective way to model rich user interfaces that is more productive than the current suite of code-oriented development tools doesn't yet exist.

To a certain extent, this reflects the inherent demands of the user interface. Great user interfaces reflect the user's workflow and the demands of the organization. Poor user interfaces reflect the table design (driven by the rules for normalization) or the object model (driven by the requirements of business entity design). Unlike ORM tools, which use the database design as their initial inputs, there isn't an effective tool for specifying the user interface except to create one in some programming environment.

The final stumbling block on the way to complete application generation is the diversity and flexibility that users require from applications. As noted before, with the present tools, MDA tools still require some code to be handwritten—typically the code in the business layer.

However, in many ways, code generation has already succeeded in the business layer. The applications that developers currently create are several orders of magnitude more complicated than the applications that were being created 50 years ago at the dawn of the business-computing era. That complexity is possible only because the current set of development tools do generate multiple lines of machine code from a single line of code written in a third-generation programming language such as Visual Basic. From the point of view of the earliest programmers, working directly in machine code, the move to assemblers and on to the third-generation languages can be seen as better and better tools for "machine code generation."

Extending this idea, the MDA solution for implementing business logic may be domain-specific languages (DSLs; also called domain-specific modeling languages), especially when extended with additional tools. Whereas a general-purpose language such as C# or Visual Basic can't have a simple construct for every potential need, a DSL can contain all the constructs for a specific business environment. An effective DSL forms a shorthand for specifying the business code to be generated. The tools discussed in Chapter 7 (T4) and the case study in Chapter 11 use Microsoft's tools for creating domain-specific languages in Visual Studio.

Assuming that it is possible to create DSLs, the problem they create is an increased specialization of developers: Developers who become experts in one DSL may not be able to transfer their skills to another DSL. This discourages developers from becoming experts and makes it difficult to transfer resources among projects using different DSLs.

Declarative Programming

Looking at the current state of code generation, although great strides have been made toward generating whole applications, it's plain that the real power of code generation is in incremental solutions using existing languages. Or, to put it another way, the immediate future of code generation is in the hands of developers like you who can implement real solutions to the problems you face every day. Someday, MDA may become a reality. Today, code generation solutions can solve enumerable problems within the range of a single developer.

Even if the MDA tools never generate all the code required for an application, .NET has shown that the real benefits in code generation have come from the partial solutions—from the small-scale solutions used in this book up to the medium-scale solutions represented by the ORM tools. Existing code-generation packages are already reducing the amount of code that has to be managed to a small percentage of the total lines of code in the application. And every new code-generation tool reduces the amount of code you don't need to write (or maintain). More importantly, you have, on your desktop, all the tools you need to further reduce that percentage.

It's the middle ground between hand-coding every line of code you write and a full-scale MDA solution where you can use code generation to make yourself more productive while generating more reliable code. There's even a name for this middle ground: declarative programming.

If you use SQL, you're already familiar with the idea behind declarative programming. In SQL you specify the data that you want and the Relational Database Management System figures out how to get it. In SQL you ask for "All the customers in Canada who purchased more than $10,000 worth of product"; you don't specify what order to process the tables in or what indexes to use—that's the responsibility of the RDBMS.

Most of the code you write isn't like SQL. Most of the code you write is procedural: Do this, then do this, then do that. SQL, on the other hand, is declarative: You just specify what data you want and the RDBMS figures out the procedure for retrieving it. Declarative programming carries that concept to application development: You tell your development environment what you want and it takes care of it.

Microsoft has been incorporating declarative programming into .NET since its inception. Many of the .NET attributes that you can use to decorate your code provide ways for you to declare what you want your program to do—the Windows Communication Foundation attributes that make your classes available to remote clients are just one example. In the business tier, LINQ is a declarative way of accessing data from within procedural code. And, in the presentation tier, XAML is a language for declaring user interfaces. Microsoft Workflow Foundation allows the developer to implement many standard functions declaratively.

When you create a code-generation solution, you often have to specify a format for developers to provide the inputs that your code-generation solution needs. Effectively, those input formats allow developers to declare what they want their program to do. Your code generator then uses those inputs to generate the procedural code that the application requires. You're not doing "code generation"—you're "implementing declarative programming."

This book will give you the tools to start doing that. Today.

TOOLS

CHAPTER 2

INTEGRATING WITH VISUAL STUDIO

In this chapter:

- Design-Time Integration
- Starting Your Visual Studio Add-In
- Creating a Menu-Driven User Interface
- Working with Visual Studio Windows
- Responding to Events
- Accepting Input
- Integrating with Visual Studio

When you solve a problem with code generation, you'll end up creating a solution with many components that may be spread over two or more projects. Your code-generation "solution" may be a solution in two senses of the word: something that solves your problem and a Visual Studio Solution that consists of multiple projects. For most code-generation solutions, one of the components that you'll want to consider including is an add-in that integrates your solution with Visual Studio. The first two case studies in this book (Chapter 9, "Case Study: Generating a Connection String Manager," and Chapter 10, "Case Study: Generating Validation Code") both use Visual Studio add-ins to trigger code generation.

Using an add-in allows you to integrate your code-generation solution into Visual Studio, so that your generated code is created as part of your standard application development process rather than being performed by, for instance, an external package. Integrating code generation into Visual Studio often means that code will be generated without the developer having to take any action at all. If you tie your code generation to events fired by Visual Studio, code can be generated whenever the developer makes a change to the code. In addition to reducing the demands that your solution makes on the developer, it means that any public classes, methods, or fields generated by your solution immediately become available to the developer and appear in Visual Studio's IntelliSense lists.

This chapter covers the tools you'll need to create a Visual Studio add-in that runs your code-generation solution in any version of Visual Studio, beginning with Visual Studio 2005 (although later versions of Visual Studio will have more functionality than earlier versions).

Because this chapter focuses on the tools you'll use in writing an add-in, it doesn't discuss the other components of a code-generation solution (that happens in Chapters 3 through 8). It's also not my intention to explain the full object model used by Visual Studio add-ins—that's the topic for another book. However, this chapter discusses all the options you need for integrating code-generation solutions into Visual Studio, concentrating on the features available in every version of Visual Studio from 2005 on. I provide you with the code to enable you to integrate your code-generation solution into Visual Studio. To put it another way: This chapter gives you just enough add-in information to be dangerous.

Unlike other code in this book, where you are primarily interested in the tool or technique and not my particular solution, much of the integration code in this chapter is code you'll want to use "as is." Rather than attempting to understand the code in this chapter, you may prefer to just copy it. Although you can copy the code from this book, it's probably easier to download the code for the case studies in Chapters 9 and 10 from the InformIT website (www.informit.com/aw) or from my website at www. phvis.com.

Design-Time Integration

I'm going to take an evolutionary approach to these solutions. I start with simple scenarios (running code by clicking a menu choice) and work up to more sophisticated approaches (running code automatically in response to Visual Studio events).

The simplest solution—adding a menu item to Visual Studio's menu bar—is the appropriate solution if one of these two conditions is true for the inputs for your code generation:

- It's always held in the same file in the project (for example, the web.config file of an ASP.NET project).
- It's scattered through many files in your project, but you want to generate all your code at once.

In either case, the developer doesn't need to select a specific file before starting code generation.

The next evolutionary step is to add a menu item to a context menu that appears only in, for instance, the editing window or the Solution Explorer window. You can also use a context menu in the code editor window to process the currently selected text. Adding a context menu choice is a good idea for these scenarios where the inputs to your code-generation process are held either in a single file or in many files but you want to be able to selectively generate code on a file-by-file basis. For instance, using a context menu would enable a developer to select a specific table in Server Explorer to use as the input for generating support code.

In the next step of the evolutionary ladder, rather than triggering code generation by clicking a menu item, you may want to have your code automatically generated when a specific event occurs in Visual Studio—for example, when the developer switches away from a specific file type or closes a file. The section "Responding to Events" in this chapter shows you how to wire your code generation up to specific events in Visual Studio.

On occasion, your code-generation process may require the developer to provide inputs that aren't stored in a file. The first time you generate a piece of code you may need to pop up a dialog that enables the developer to enter options for this task. The section "Accepting Input" later in this chapter shows you how to capture that information the first time you generate code and bypass the process for subsequent generations. However, developers must be able to change those options if it turns out that their first choices weren't the ones they want to live with. Your choices for accepting inputs include dialogs, task panes, and additions to Visual Studio's Tools | Options dialog.

Starting Your Visual Studio Add-In

Appropriately enough for this book, the initial code for your add-in is generated for you by a wizard. I recommend that you make as few changes in that generated code as possible, and instead put much of your "code-generation code" as possible in a different file. Appendix C, "Case Study: A Code-Generation Add-In," describes a basic Visual Studio add-in that can be easily extended to incorporate most code-generation projects that require integration with Visual Studio.

Laying the Foundation

You start creating your add-in by selecting the Add-In template in Visual Studio. This template is in the Other Project Types section under the Extensibility heading (see Figure 2-1) in the Add New Item dialog you get when you create a project using the File | New Project choice.

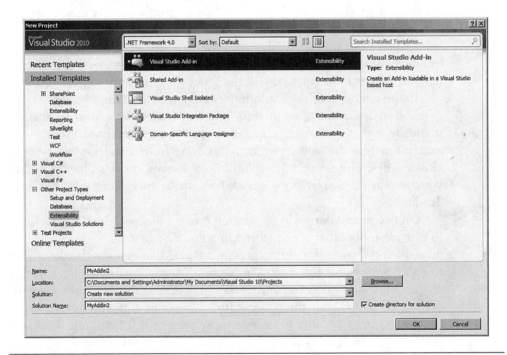

FIGURE 2-1   Add-ins are just another project type that Visual Studio can work with.

After you've created your project, you are greeted by the Add-In Wizard (see Figure 2-2). Use the wizard! There are a number of required pieces of code that your application needs in order to load and hook into Visual Studio. The wizard takes care of that code for you. (Where the default code doesn't match your needs, it's easier to modify the default code than to write your own.)

As you work your way through the wizard, you're asked the following:

- Do you want your Visual Studio add-in framework to be generated in Visual Basic or C#?
- Which host do you want to have load your add-in? Visual Studio provides two: Visual Studio and Visual Studio Macros. (I don't pick the Visual Studio Macros option, as you'll see in the screenshots.)

FIGURE 2-2 Visual Studio's Add-In Wizard handles creating much of the utility code that your add-in requires.

- What name and description do you want to use with this add-in? The name and description you provide are used in the menu item that calls your add-in as the menu item's name and tooltip, so enter meaningful values (you can change these later). Although spaces are eliminated from your name where they're not allowed, characters that aren't valid in class names (for example, the hyphen in "add-in") aren't always fixed. If, during testing, you get the message "The Add-in '*add-in name*' failed to load," you should check your name for invalid characters.
- Will your add-in add a menu item to the Tools menu? Pick Yes. Later in this chapter you'll see how to move the choice to some other menu or tie code generation to an event.
- Will your add-in load when Visual Studio starts? Pick the "always load" option.
- Will your add-in ever stop Visual Studio processing by putting up a modal dialog? Choose No.
- What information do you want to be displayed in the About dialog? Providing a release number and date is essential to enable you to determine what version of your code you're running. If you're going to let other people run your solution, providing your e-mail address so that those developers can contact you is the decent thing to do.

In Visual Studio 2005, you also have an opportunity to decide if you want your add-in to be installed for all users or just for you.

Best Practices for Creating Your Add-In

Menu option: Pick the option that adds an item to the Visual Studio menu for your add-in. Having a menu item added to the Tools menu is the simplest way to test your add-in.

Load option: Initially, you will be testing your add-in frequently so also pick the "always load" option. If your add-in is rarely used and you're willing to load it from the Tools | Add-In Manager dialog before using it, you can change this option from Visual Studio's Tools | Add-In Manager after your add-in is created (or in the project's Addin file, discussed later).

Modal dialog option: Don't plan on popping up a dialog every time you generate code—there are better ways to gather the information you need for code generation, as discussed in this book (and you'll just annoy developers using your solution). Also, popping up a dialog prevents your add-in from being loaded when Visual Studio is used from the command line. If you do need to pop up a dialog, you can change this option from Visual Studio's Tools | Add-In Manager after your add-in is created.

After you finish working through the wizard, you have a new project similar to the one in Figure 2-3 if you picked the options I suggested. (You'll have to provide your own name for your generator, though.) Here are the files in the project that are unique to add-in projects:

- **Connect.cs or Connect.vb**—Holds the code to wire your add-in up to Visual Studio.
- **.AddIn files**—The XML that describes your add-in to Visual Studio. The file marked "- For Testing.AddIn" holds the settings that are used when you're debugging your add-in in Visual Studio.
- **CommandBar.resx**—A resource file, which you can use to support multiple languages in the menus for your user interface (this file isn't included the Visual Studio 2010 template and isn't required).

Now that your project has been created, open the Project Properties dialog and set Assembly Name to the name of your project (the default name is Project1). You'll also need to change the name of the DLL in the `<AssemblyName>` tag in both .AddIn files in the project.

To see what you've accomplished, press F5 to test your add-in. A new copy of Visual Studio launches and your add-in is listed on the Tools menu with the default smiley face icon (see Figure 2-4).

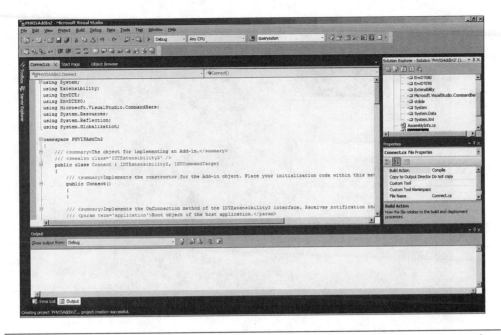

FIGURE 2-3   The Connect.vb or Connect.cs file of your add-in project is where you put the code to start your add-in.

The rest of this chapter covers the objects you can use within your add-in. I've organized the material by task: If you want to do this, here are the objects (and code) that you need. For a walkthrough of a complete Visual Studio add-in, see the case studies in Chapters 9 and 10.

Integrating with Visual Studio

Just putting a menu item on your toolbar isn't sufficient—you want your add-in to call the methods that will generate your code. The Exec method in Connect.cs is automatically called from the menu item added to the Tools menu, so this is where you'll want to call your code-generation solution. You'll find this code already present in your Exec method:

```
public void Exec(string commandName,
    vsCommandExecOption executeOption,
    ref object varIn, ref object varOut,
    ref bool handled)
{
  handled = false;
  if(executeOption == vsCommandExecOption.vsCommandExecOptionDoDefault)
```

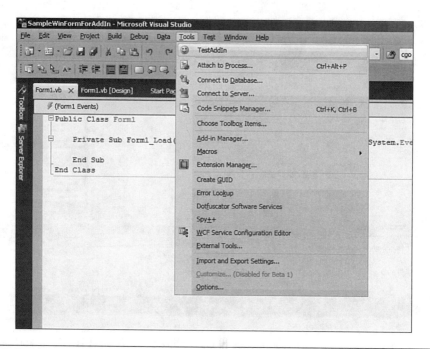

FIGURE 2-4   The standard settings for an add-in puts a menu choice on Visual Studio's Tools menu with a default icon of a smiley face.

```
{
    if(commandName ==
            "ConnectionStringGenerator.Connect")
    {
      handled = true;
      return;
    }
  }
}
```

This default code checks the parameters passed to the Exec method to see which option is being requested (in this case, the DoDefault option) and which command has been selected (in this case, the Connect method on the ConnectionStringGenerator). Once the add-in finishes executing, the code sets the handle parameter passed to the method to True to indicate that the add-in finished correctly.

As this code suggests, a single add-in can respond to multiple menu commands by checking the command name parameter passed to this method when Visual Studio calls it. Extending your add-in to handle multiple commands consists, in part, of adding additional menu items and associating each with a different command (you'll see how to add additional menu commands in the section "Creating a Menu Driven-User Interface" later in this chapter).

You're now ready to write the code for your add-in. For these examples, I've placed my code in a class called CreatePartialClasses (I'll refer to it as the "generation class" in this chapter) in a file separate from Connect.cs. When this class is instantiated, I pass it the name of a class file to be created. Within the generation class, I add a method that adds a .vb file containing a partial class declaration using the name passed when the class was created. I've named this method CreateVBClass. (The objects you need to add components such as files and project references to your application are discussed in Chapter 3, "Manipulating Project Components.")

BEST PRACTICE   Put your code-generation code in a separate project from your add-in and add a reference to that project to your add-in project. By putting your code in a separate project, you can potentially share components of your code-generation solution among multiple add-ins. This strategy also reserves the Connect file for the code that creates menu choices and responds to developer actions in the Visual Studio.

You communicate with Visual Studio through the DTE2 class passed to the OnConnection method as its first parameter and held in the _applicationObject field (the DTE class in Visual Studio 2005). The default code added to the OnConnection method by the wizard sets the _applicationObject field.

BEST PRACTICE   The simplest way to wire your generation class into Visual Studio is to pass the _applicationObject field to your generation class when you create it.

The Exec routine that creates my generation class and passes the name of the class to be created and the reference to the DTE2 object in the _applicationObject field looks like this:

```
if (commandName == _addInInstance.Name + ".CodeGenerateManager")
{
   CreatePartialClass cpc;
   cpc = new CreatePartialClass("MyClass", _applicationObject);
   cpc.CreateVBClass();
   handled = true;
   return;
}
```

You still need to put some code in the methods your Exec routine calls before you can justifiably claim that your add-in "does something."

Writing a Generation Class in Visual Studio

The start of your generation class looks much like any other class, except that, to save some typing, you should import the namespaces that contain the objects you will use for managing Visual Studio. For instance, if you created a class called CreatePartialClass, the start of your class would look like this:

```
using EnvDTE;
using EnvDTE80;
using EnvDTE90;

public class CreatePartialClass
```

The first code in your generation class is the constructor that catches the reference to the DTE2 object (along with whatever other data you want to pass to the class's constructor). I typically call this parameter ApplicationObject. Because, for this example, I'm also passing the name of the class file to be created, my constructor looks like this (for Visual Studio 2005, replace the references to DTE2 with DTE):

```
private string className;
private DTE2 applicationObject;

public CreatePartialClass(string ClassName, DTE2 ApplicationObject)
{
  className = ClassName;
  applicationObject = ApplicationObject;
}
```

As you can see, all I do in this routine is capture the parameters passed to the constructor and store them in some fields declared at the top of the class file.

Before investing a lot of time in your code, it's a good idea to see if your add-in is working. The easiest way to do this is to add a single line of code to a method in the class that does something obvious to Visual Studio. For instance, the initial version of my CreateVBClass method might look like this:

```
public void CreateVBClass()
{
   applicationObject.Documents.CloseAll(
                        vsSaveChanges.vsSaveChangesPrompt);
}
```

As you might guess, this method closes all the open windows in Visual Studio. You can now press F5, open a project, open some files in the project, and then click your add-in's menu item in the Tools menu to see if your add-in closes all the open windows. If the windows close, you know your add-in is loading correctly and communicating with Visual Studio. (Typically, if anything goes wrong in an add-in, nothing at all will happen except that you might get a message in Visual Studio's status bar.) Once you've confirmed that your add-in is working, you can replace this line with code that does something you actually want.

Working with COM

You need to be aware that Visual Studio is *not* a .NET application (at least not yet). Visual Studio is a COM application, which you're manipulating from your .NET add-in. You are made aware of this fact whenever you access a collection. C# and Visual Basic programmers won't be able to access the first member of the `Projects` collection just by supplying an index value of 0. This code won't work:

VB: `_applicationObject.Solution.Projects(0)`

C#: `applicationObject.Solution.Projects[0];`

Instead, you must explicitly use the `Item` method and, to get the first member in a collection, pass 1 as the parameter to the method. This code will work. (Notice that, in C#, parentheses are used instead of brackets, because you're passing a parameter to a method rather than a position to an indexer.)

VB: `_applicationObject.Solution.Projects.Item(1)`

C#: `applicationObject.Solution.Projects.Item(1);`

You are also going to be doing a lot of type conversions to convert the COM objects used by Visual Studio to the appropriate .NET data type you use in your code.

BEST PRACTICE If you process a large number of objects (while iterating through a collection of Visual Studio objects, for instance), you can build up a large number of COM objects being held in memory. Because the .NET garbage collection process doesn't necessarily have visibility to COM resources, you can run out of memory. The solution is to call the Marshal object's `FinalReleaseCOMObject` before setting the object variable to null.

```
System.Runtime.InteropServices.Marshal.
                    FinalReleaseComObject(cm);
cm = null;
```

Debugging Issues in Visual Studio 2005/2008

Unfortunately, if you close Visual Studio, reopen it, and try to debug your add-in, you may find that you get an error message that says your add-in's DLL cannot be copied. The reason you can't test your add-in again is because when you restarted Visual Studio, it loaded your add-in. When you press F5 to test your application, Visual Studio attempts to copy your DLL to a new location before launching the second instance of Visual Studio that your add-in will be debugged in. However, because your add-in is already being used by the existing copy of Visual Studio, that copy will fail.

There are two solutions:

- Don't have your add-in load with Visual Studio.
- Add code to the pre-build event of your add-in project that resolves the problem.

Having your add-in load with Visual Studio is one of the options available in the Add-In Wizard when you first created your add-in. If you selected the recommended "always load" option when you created your add-in, you can turn that off in your project's .Addin file by setting the `<LoadBehavior>` tag to 0 (Disconnected) or 4 (Load only when run from the command line). This example specifies the command line option:

```
<LoadBehavior>4</LoadBehavior>
```

You only need to make this change in the .Addin file that has the "- For Testing" suffix in its name. After making the change, shut down Visual Studio and restart it to pick up the change.

I feel obliged to mention that my experience with setting `LoadBehavior` has been problematic. With 0, I've sometimes found that after pressing F5 to start debugging, I had to select my add-in from Tools | Add-In Manager in order to test it, and sometimes have not. When I set `LoadBehavior` to 4, I didn't have to select my add-in from Add-In Manager, but my add-in didn't appear as loaded in Add-In Manager either. Testing these settings was made more difficult because changes made to the `LoadBehavior` tag often didn't become apparent until I did a rebuild rather than a build.

I've found that adding two lines of code to my project's pre-build event is more reliable than using `LoadBehavior`. The code I add to the event checks to see if the DLL is locked, and if it is, removes it while substituting a file that isn't locked. To add this code, open your project's Properties dialog and do the following:

- For Visual Basic: Switch to the Compile tab and click the Build Events button near the bottom of this form.
- For C#: Click the Build Events tab.

A dialog that enables you to enter pre- and post-build commands appears (see Figure 2-5). In the text box labeled "Pre-build event command line," enter these two lines of code:

```
if exist "$(TargetPath).locked" del "$(TargetPath).locked"
if exist "$(TargetPath)" if not exist "$(TargetPath).locked" move
         "$(TargetPath)" "$(TargetPath).locked"
```

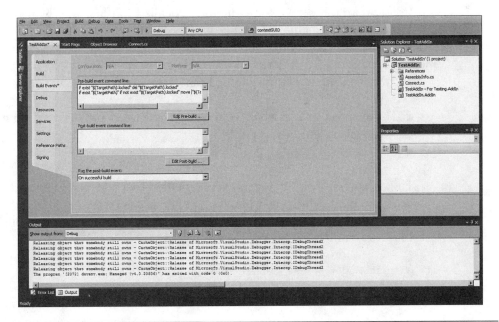

FIGURE 2-5 The Build Events dialog lets you enter the commands that free your add-in for debugging.

This code appears on three lines here because the code is being wrapped to fit on the page. The third line in this example must be at the end of the second line.

BEST PRACTICE   Use a pre-build event rather than `LoadBehavior` when debugging your add-In.

The OnConnection Method

Finally, a word on the `OnConnection` method and how debug mode may mislead you about how this method is called. `OnConnection` is called the first time your add-in is loaded by Visual Studio to allow you to execute any code required to set up your add-in. (I'll refer to this as calling your add-in in "setup mode.") For instance, you would normally add any new menu items when the `OnConnection` method is called in setup mode. Visual Studio would then "remember" and continue to display the menu items you added. Even if you picked the option to load your add-in when Visual Studio starts, your `OnConnection` method will only be called in setup mode the very first time it's loaded.

In addition, the `OnConnection` method is called the first time you run one of your methods after restarting Visual Studio—it's just not called in setup mode. To distinguish between the two modes, the `OnConnection` method is passed a flag in its `connectMode` parameter.

So, for the purposes of this chapter, I can distinguish between two modes:

- The first call made when your add-in is loaded for the first time (what I've called "setup mode")
- All other calls

The default code in the `OnConnection` method that adds menu items to Visual Studio is executed only when the method is passed the flag that indicates the add-in is in setup mode. This is the code you see in your `OnConnection` method to check for setup mode:

```
if (connectMode == ext_ConnectMode.ext_cm_UISetup)
{
}
```

When debugging your add-in, however, you'll see that the OnConnection method is called in setup mode every time. The add-in is always called in setup mode during debugging because of a setting on the Debug tab of your add-in project's property pages. This option clears out any settings you made on previous tests of your add-in and ensures that every execution happens in setup mode:

```
/resetaddin <namespace.classname of your Add-In>.Connect
```

This option removes the record that Visual Studio has kept flagging your add-in as having been loaded at least once. This causes Visual Studio to call the OnConnection method in setup mode repeatedly (and to remove any menus that were added when your add-in loaded—this keeps your menus from appearing multiple times). In the unlikely event that you change the name of your add-in, you'll need to change the name passed to the resetaddin parameter on the Debug tab of the Project Properties dialog.

Summing up: Don't expect the OnConnection method to be called in setup mode every time your add-in is loaded because that's what you see when debugging. Rather than deal with checking whether the add-in is starting in setup mode, when I write an add-in, I use a different mechanism for determining whether to add menus.

Removing Add-In Menus

If you start Visual Studio from the command line, you can use the resetaddin utility to remove Visual Studio's record that had called the add-in before. This will cause your add-in's menus to be removed from the Visual Studio menuing system (and, should you ever load your add-in again, cause Visual Studio to execute your add-in's initialization code again). Passing * to resetaddin causes all add-ins to be reset. If using resetaddin * doesn't eliminate your add-ins, you can delete your add-in's DLLs and "- For Testing.AddIn" files from the "*documents*\Visual Studio *version*\Addins" folder. After starting Visual Studio, you can then remove your add-in's menu items just by clicking them. (You'll have to respond to a dialog asking if you want to remove the menu item because the add-in couldn't be found.)

Creating a Menu-Driven User Interface

This section discuses how to tie your add-in to a menu in the Visual Studio interface. (Later in the chapter you'll see how to have your add-in execute when events fire in the Visual Studio interface.) Even if you intend to tie your add-in to events in the Visual Studio interface, adding a menu item to execute your add-in is a good idea for two reasons: It makes it easier to test your add-in (just click the menu item), and it allows the developer to execute your add-in whenever the developer wants.

Extending Your Menus

In the default code generated by the Add-In Wizard and placed in the Connect.cs file, the key line that adds menu items to Visual Studio is the one that creates a `Command` that can be associated with a menu item:

```
Commands2 cmds = (Commands2) _applicationObject.Commands;
object[] contextGUIDS = new object[] { };
Command command = cmds.AddNamedCommand2(
                _addInInstance,
                "Code Generation",
                "Code Generation",
                "Add a partial class",
                true,
                59,
                ref contextGUIDS,
                (int) vsCommandStatus.vsCommandStatusSupported  +
                (int) vsCommandStatus.vsCommandStatusEnabled,
                (int) vsCommandStyle.vsCommandStylePictAndText,
                vsCommandControlType.vsCommandControlTypeButton);
```

In Visual Studio 2005, the command uses the `Commands` class rather than `Commands2` and the `AddNamedCommand` method rather than `AddNamedCommand2`. The `AddNamedCommand` method is missing some parameters compared to `AddNamedCommand2`. Here's a typical example of the code in Visual Studio 2005:

```
Object[] contextGUIDS = {};
Command command = cmds.AddNamedCommand(
                _addInInstance,
                "CodeGeneration",
```

```
       "Code Generation",
       "Generate a partial class",
       true,
       59,
       ref contextGUIDS,
(int) vsCommandStatus.vsCommandStatusSupported) +
       (int) vsCommandStatus.vsCommandStatusEnabled,;
```

Although you can modify all the parameters (except for `AddInInstance`), typically you only want to change these four. (IntelliSense will show you where these parameters fall.)

- **Name**—The name of your command. Each command must have a unique name. Do not include special characters in this name. (For example, don't give your command the name "C#Class." Instead, name it "CSClass.")
- **ButtonText**—The caption for your menu item.
- **Tooltip**—The tooltip for your menu item.
- **BitMap**—This enables you to select from a list of available icons. (The default setting of 59 picks the smiley face icon.)

Just to make my code a little easier to read, I'll call my commands "`NamedCommand`" in the rest of this chapter.

Adding Additional Menus

If you want to perform multiple actions from a single add-in, you have two choices:

- Have your add-in check the current context (for example, if text is selected) and call different methods on your generation class, depending on the context.
- Add additional menu items, associate them with a `Command`, and (in the `Exec` method in the Connect.cs file) call different methods on the generation class.

As you add menu items, consider adding all your menu items to the Tools menu. The code that the wizard adds to your `OnConnection` method automatically finds the Tools menu for you, so this strategy piggybacks on the wizard's code. Later in this chapter, you'll see how to create a submenu and add menu items to it; this will allow you to keep your new menu items off the main Tools menu and keep the menu from growing too long to be easily used.

If you want to use some other menu than the Tools menu, you must first find that menu. Finding a menu fundamentally comes down to searching for a menu with a particular caption. As a result, finding a menu in Visual Studio in a way that works across multiple languages isn't trivial (at least in Visual Studio 2005 and 2008—Visual Studio 2010 simplifies this process). If you look at the menu-related code in the OnConnection method, you see that much of it is devoted to just retrieving a reference to the Tools menu in a language-neutral way. (Even then, the last line in the routine just gives up and asks for the menu named "Tools.")

If you would prefer to add your menu item to some other menu, change the word Tools in the default code in the three places it appears to the name of the menu you would prefer.

You should always add new menus in the OnConnection method of your add-in. To avoid adding any permanent menu items twice, you could add new menus only when the OnConnection method is called in setup mode. However, good defensive programming mandates that before adding the menu item you should check that it doesn't already exist.

BEST PRACTICE Don't depend on checking to see if your add-in is being called in setup mode. Instead, always check to see if a menu item already exists before adding it: If your menu item is missing, add it; if your menu item is present, skip adding it. This ensures that you don't add a menu item with a name that duplicates an existing menu item (and that you don't add multiple copies of your menu item).

Finding the Menu

The first step in adding a menu item to an existing Visual Studio menu is to find the menu you want to add to.

BEST PRACTICE In versions of Visual Studio prior to Visual Studio 2010, when searching for menu items you should take advantage of the Resource file added to your application to handle language differences in the user interface as the following code does.

You can find much of the following code, tailored to work in your add-in, already in the OnConnection method generated for your add-in. This code finds the Tools menu in Visual Studio 2005 and 2008; however, unlike the code generated by the Add-In Wizard, this code has a few small changes to make it easy to modify to work with a different menu (changed code is in bold):

```
string FoundMenuName;
string MenuName = "Tools";

try
{
 System.Resources.ResourceManager resourceManager  =
        new System.Resources.ResourceManager(
              _addInInstance.ProgID + ".CommandBar",
              System.Reflection.Assembly.GetExecutingAssembly());
 System.Globalization.CultureInfo cultureInfo =
      new System.Globalization.CultureInfo(_applicationObject.LocaleID);
 if (cultureInfo.TwoLetterISOLanguageName == "zh")
 {
   System.Globalization.CultureInfo parentCultureInfo
                              = cultureInfo.Parent;
   FoundMenuName =
           resourceManager.GetString(
              String.Concat(parentCultureInfo.Name, MenuName));
 }
 else
 {
   FoundMenuName =
           resourceManager.GetString(
               String.Concat(
               cultureInfo.TwoLetterISOLanguageName, MenuName));
 }
}
catch (Exception e)
{
 FoundMenuName = MenuName;
}

if (FoundMenuName == "")
{
        FoundMenuName = MenuName;
}
```

This code isn't required in Visual Studio 2010 because searching the various menu collections is no longer language dependent. The wizard omits the previous code (and so should you). However, the code that actually finds the menu is slightly different in Visual Studio 2010 compared to earlier versions of Visual Studio. The code for earlier versions of Visual Studio (2005/2008) is relatively simple. (This code assumes that the name of the menu you're looking for is in the variable FoundMenuName.)

```
CommandBars cbs;
CommandBar cb;

cbs = (CommandBars) _applicationObject.CommandBars;
cb = cbs[FoundMenuName];
```

In Visual Studio 2010, you must distinguish between menus on the main menu bar (e.g., the Tools menu) and other menus (e.g., context menus). To keep the code flexible (and allow me to copy it from one add-in to another), I added a Boolean variable and a string variable, which I use to control where I look for the menu. If the Boolean variable MainMenu is set to True, I retrieve the main menu bar and find the menu on it; if the variable is set to False, I assume that I'm looking for a context menu and skip searching the menu bar:

```
CommandBar cb;
bool MainMenu = true;
string MenuBarName = "Menubar";

if (MainMenu)
{
 cb = ((CommandBars)_applicationObject.CommandBars)[MenuBarName];
 cb = ((CommandBarPopup)cb.Controls[FoundMenuName]).CommandBar;
}
else
{
 CommandBars cbs = (CommandBars)_applicationObject.CommandBars;
 cb = cbs[FoundMenuName];
}
```

Adding the Menu Item

With the menu found and held in the cb variable, it's time to create your Command and add it to a menu. This code checks whether the Command already exists by seeing if an error is raised while retrieving the Command from the Commands collection. If an error is raised, indicating that the Command doesn't exist, the code creates the Command:

```
Command NamedCommand;
string commandId = "CrVBPartial";
string commandCaption = "Create a VB Partial Class";
string commandDesc = "Creates a partial class in VB";

object[] obj = {};
try
{
 NamedCommand = _applicationObject.Commands.Item(
                _addInInstance.ProgID + "." + commandId,1);
}
catch
{
 NamedCommand = cmds.AddNamedCommand2(
                _addInInstance,
                commandId, commandCaption, commandDesc,
                true, 59, ref obj,
                (int) vsCommandStatus.vsCommandStatusSupported +
                (int) vsCommandStatus.vsCommandStatusEnabled,
                (int) vsCommandStyle.vsCommandStylePictAndText,
                vsCommandControlType.vsCommandControlTypeButton);
}
```

With the Command created, you can add it to the menu you retrieved. This code first checks to see if the Command is already on the menu by looking for its caption. If the menu item isn't present, the menu is added to the Command, thereby creating the menu item:

```
try
{
   CommandBarControl cbc = cb.Controls[commandCaption];
}
catch (Exception ex)
{
   NamedCommand.AddControl(cb, 1);
}
```

The second parameter to the `AddControl` method specifies the position on the menu where the `Command` will be added. In this example, the menu item will appear in the first position, at the top of the menu.

Supporting Multiple Menu Items

There's one wrinkle, however: Any `Command` that doesn't match the string `AddInName.Connect.AddInName` (for example, `"ConnectionStringGenerator.Connect.ConnectionStringGenerator"`) will disappear from your menus. This is caused by code that the wizard adds to the `QueryStatus` method of your add-in. The `QueryStatus` method is called by Visual Studio to give your add-in the opportunity to enable and disable your menu choices. By default, this code checks for `Command`s in the format I just described and disables any `Command` with a different name.

The code that I've shown for creating `Command` will produce commands that begin with the `AddinName.Connect` but will change the last part of the command name (that is, `AddinName.Connect.???`). So, to keep your menus from disappearing you need to make the `QueryStatus` event more broad-minded by having it just check for commands that begin with the name of your add-in. This is the enhanced version that does just that (the modified code is in bold):

```
public void QueryStatus(string commandName,
    vsCommandStatusTextWanted neededText, ref vsCommandStatus status,
    ref object commandText)
{
  if (neededText ==
          vsCommandStatusTextWanted.vsCommandStatusTextWantedNone)
  {
    if (commandName.StartsWith(_addInInstance.Name +
                              ".Connect"))
    {
      status = (vsCommandStatus)vsCommandStatus.
        vsCommandStatusSupported | vsCommandStatus.vsCommandStatusEnabled;
      return;
    }
  }
}
```

When you click a menu item, the Exec method in your Connect class will be called. The name of the Command whose menu item has been clicked is passed in through the Exec method's commandName parameter. You need to check to see which Command was clicked and call the appropriate method on your generation class. This example checks for names ending with either "CrVBPartial" or "CrCSPartial" (_addInInstance.Progid returns the first part of the command names):

```
handled = false;
if (executeOption ==
    vsCommandExecOption.vsCommandExecOptionDoDefault)
{
 switch (commandName)
 {
  case _addInInstance.ProgID + "." + "CrVBPartial":
       //...code to call a method on the Generation Class
       break;
  case _addInInstance.ProgID + "." + "CrCSPartial":
       // ...code to call a method on the Generation Class
       break;
 }
 handled = true;
 return;
}
```

Creating Submenus

If you have multiple menu items you may want to organize your menu items into a submenu. Once you've created a submenu, you can add a Command to it.

A Command is a permanent item that survives shutting down and restarting Visual Studio. Submenus, unlike Commands, are temporary items and won't survive a shutdown and restart. When your submenu disappears, all of its associated items will disappear unless you re-create the submenu item every time the add-in is loaded. The code to add your submenu, therefore, shouldn't be added when the OnConnection method is called in setup mode because setup mode happens only once in the life of the add-in.

Rather than distinguish between temporary and permanent menu items, as I've suggested before, the simplest solution is to add your menu items on each call to the OnConnection method. As before, when adding any item, you should first check whether the item already exists and only add it if the item isn't already present.

Adding Submenus

As with adding a menu item, the first step in adding a submenu is to find the menu you want to add your submenu to. The next step is to check to see whether the submenu header (a CommandBarPopup) already exists on the menu and, if it doesn't, add it. Once the submenu header is added, you can set its caption.

This code adds a submenu header to the menu held in cbMain, giving the submenu header the caption "Code Generation." The resulting header is held in the cbp variable:

```
CommandBarPopup cbp
try
{
  cbp = (CommandBarPopup) cbMain.Controls["Code Generation"];
}
catch
{
  cbp = (CommandBarPopup)cbMain.Controls.Add(
    MsoControlType.msoControlPopup,
                              System.Type.Missing,
                              System.Type.Missing,
                              System.Type.Missing,
                              System.Type.Missing);
  cbp.Caption = "Code Generation";
}
```

With the submenu's header held in the cbp variable, you can create your submenu by adding your Command to the header:

```
NamedCommand.AddControl(cbp.CommandBar, 1);
```

Context Menus

In addition to adding your menu items to the existing menus in the Visual Studio main menu bar, you can also add Commands and submenus to the various Visual Studio context menus (the pop-up menus available when you right-click). The good news is that the context menus are just another set of menus in Visual Studio, and you work with them in the same way as the menus I've already discussed. For instance, to add items to the context menu for the code window shown in Figure 2-6, you would search for the menu called "Code Window" instead of the menu called "Tools."

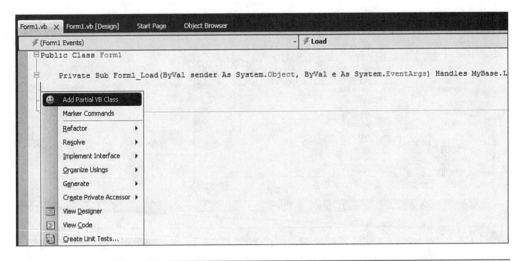

FIGURE 2-6   You can add menus to the context menu for the code window just by asking for the "Code Window" menu.

In versions of Visual Studio prior to Visual Studio 2010, you can get a list of the menu names for the menus on the menu bar by looking in the Value column of the CommandBar.resx file included in your add-in project (see Figure 2-7). However, not all of Visual Studio's menus are listed there (including, for instance, the "Code Window" menu).

You can generate a list of menus in Visual Studio's Output window with this code in an add-in:

```
cbs = (CommandBars) _applicationObject.CommandBars


for(int ing = 0; ing < cbs.Count; ing++)
{
   System.Diagnostics.Debug.WriteLine(cbs[ing].Name);
}
```

Appendix A, "Case Study: Generating Menu Names," provides code you can use to generate a list of top level menus in Visual Studio. (There's well over 300 menus on my last count.) Typically, you'll want to update the context menus used in Solution Explorer. Most (if not all) of the context

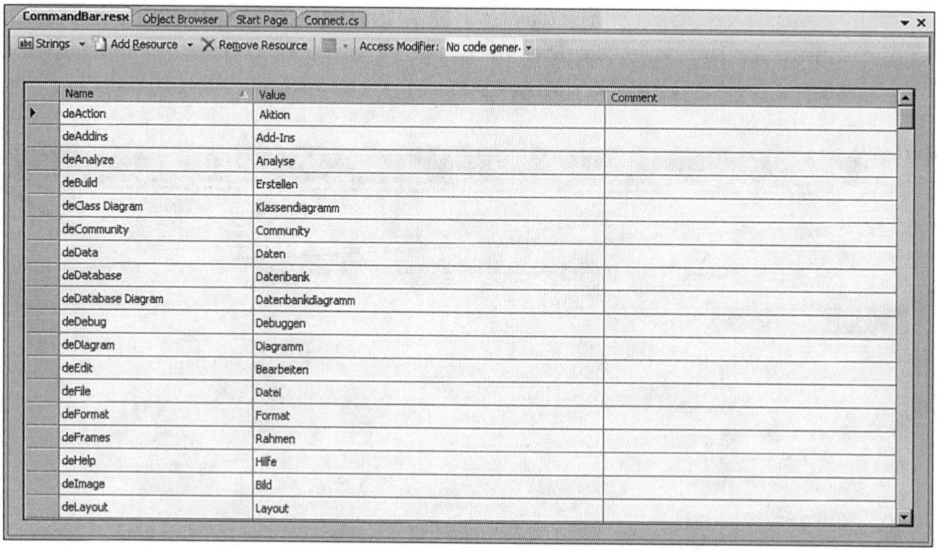
CommandBar.resx
Object Browser
Start Page
Connect.cs
Strings
Add Resource
Remove Resource
Access Modifier: No code gener.
Name
Value
Comment
deAction
Aktion
deAddins
Add-Ins
deAnalyze
Analyse
deBuild
Erstellen
deClass Diagram
Klassendiagramm
deCommunity
Community
deData
Daten
deDatabase
Datenbank
deDatabase Diagram
Datenbankdiagramm
deDebug
Debuggen
deDiagram
Diagramm
deEdit
Bearbeiten
deFile
Datei
deFormat
Format
deFrames
Rahmen
deHelp
Hilfe
deImage
Bild
deLayout
Layout

FIGURE 2-7 The CommandBar resource file in your project lists many of the menu names available in Visual Studio.

menus for Solution Explorer are grouped onto the "Project and Solution Context Menus" menu in Visual Studio. (Appendix A includes sample code for generating the list of menu items in this group.) Here are the context menus in that group you're most likely to use:

- **Solution**—Visual Studio Solution
- **Project**—Most non-ASP.NET projects
- **Folder**—Folders in non-ASP.NET projects
- **Item**—Most items in a non-ASP.NET project
- **Web Project Folder**—ASP.NET projects
- **Web Folder**—Folders in an ASP.NET project
- **Web Item**—Most items in an ASP.NET project

Accessing the Context

Putting items on context menus makes sense if you intend to take the context of the menu item into account when generating code. Typically, for these windows, you'll want to know these questions:

- In Solution Explorer: Which code file did the developer click?
- In the Code window: What is the current file?

- In Server Explorer: Which is the currently selected table?

Information about what's currently going on in Visual Studio can be retrieved through objects in the EnvDTE2 namespace. In my generation class, I typically hold this object in a field called _applicationObject as you'll see in the code in this chapter and the case studies. Typically, the first context-related information you'll want to know is what project the developer is working on so you can add your code to the right project. Visual Studio doesn't have a concept of a "current project," but you can determine the project for the current item open in the editor window. For instance, you can retrieve the project for the currently open document with this code:

```
Project pr;
pr = _applicationObject.ActiveDocument.ProjectItem.ContainingProject;
```

Of course, it's possible that your menu item may be clicked without any document being open. In that case, you shouldn't call any method that needs to know which project is to be updated. In your Exec method, you would use code like this to handle calling a method that needs to know the current project when no document is open:

```
if (_applicationObject.ActiveDocument != null)
{
 Project pr;
 pr = _applicationObject.ActiveDocument.ProjectItem.ContainingProject;
    ...code to call Add-In method...
 handled = true;
}
```

BEST PRACTICE Only set the handled parameter in the Exec method to True if you successfully process the menu click.

Instead of looking at the currently opened document to determine the project, you could look at the currently selected item in Solution Explorer (see Figure 2-8). You can determine which items have been selected in

Solution Explorer through the _applicationObject's SelectedItems collection. If you attempt to access items in this collection when nothing has been selected, however, you'll get a "Catastrophic Error."

FIGURE 2-8   You can use the **SelectedItems** collection to retrieve the items currently selected in Solution Explorer.

This code safely retrieves the selected item in Solution Explorer by first checking that some item is selected. It then checks to see if the current item is a Visual Basic code file:

```
if (_applicationObject.SelectedItems.Count > 0)
{
  if (_applicationObject.SelectedItems.Item(1).Name.EndsWith(".vb"))
  {
        ...code to process the selected file
  }
}
```

As with the ActiveDocument, you can retrieve the Project for the selected item by using the ContainingProject property of a SelectedItem's ProjectItem property:

```
pr = _applicationObject.SelectedItems.Item(1).
                ProjectItem.ContainingProject;
```

Working with Visual Studio Windows

You may want to work with windows other than Solution Explorer. Some windows are easy to get to in some versions of Visual Studio: In Visual Studio 2008 and 2010, the DTE2 object (referenced by the _applicationObject field) has a ToolWindows property that provides access to these windows:

- Solution Explorer
- OutputWindow
- CommandWindow
- ErrorList
- TaskList
- Toolbox

Using the Task List Window

This code in Visual Studio 2008/2010 would retrieve the TaskList:

```
TaskList tl;
tl = _applicationObject.ToolWindows.TaskList;
```

BEST PRACTICE   Use the Task List window when you want to report an error in code generation that's specific enough to direct the developer to the source of the error. For more general errors, write to the Output window.

In Visual Studio 2005 the ToolWindows property isn't available. (Visual Studio 2005 uses the older DTE class.) However, you can retrieve a Window object from the _applicationObject's Windows collection by passing one of the EnvDTE.Constants. to the Item method of the Windows collection. Once you've retrieved the Window object, you can pull a type-specific reference from the Window's Object property. This code in Visual Studio 2005 retrieves the Task List window:

```
TaskList tl;
tl = (EnvDTE.TaskList)_applicationObject.Windows.Item(
            EnvDTE.Constants.vsWindowKindTaskList);
```

In Visual Studio 2008/2010, if a `Window` isn't available through the `ToolWindows` object, you can also use the `_applicationObject`'s `Windows` collection to retrieve the window. For instance, this code retrieves a reference to the Server Explorer window, which isn't available from the `ToolWindows` object, as a generic `Window` object:

```
Window se;
```

```
se = _applicationObject.Windows.Item(
            EnvDTE.Constants.vsWindowKindServerExplorer);
```

Retrieving Selected Items

If you've created a context menu for the Server Explorer window that allows developers to click an item in the window and pick one item to generate code for, you'll want to know which item the developer has selected. As with many windows in Visual Studio, the Server Explorer window can be accessed as a `UIHierarchy` object. To find out which item in the hierarchy is currently selected, you need to extract the array of objects that represents the `SelectedItems` in the hierarchy. Once you've retrieved that collection, you can convert each item in the array into a `UIHierarchyItem`. The `Name` property on the `UIHierarchyItem` will give you the name of the selected item.

This code would retrieve the currently selected item from the Server Explorer window. Because this code is run from a context menu, I've assumed there will always be a selected item:

```
se = _applicationObject.Windows.Item(
            EnvDTE.Constants.vsWindowKindServerExplorer);
```

```
UIHierarchy uih;
UIHierarchyItem uihi;
```

```
    uih = (UIHierarchy) se.Object;
    objs = (Object[]) uih.SelectedItems;
    uihi = (UIHierarchyItem) objs[0];
    string DatabaseName = uihi.Name;
```

BEST PRACTICE   The Server Explorer lists many types of resources and there's no way to determine the type of a `UIHierarchyItem`: Check what kind of item you've retrieved before using it (for instance, that it really is the name of a database).

Not all selected items are so difficult to access. For instance, to retrieve the currently selected text in the code window, you can use the `ActiveDocument`'s `Selection` property. The `Selection` property returns a `TextSelection` object whose `Text` property contains the currently selected text. This code retrieves whatever text is selected into a string variable named `SelectedText`:

```
TextSelection ts;
string SelectedText;

ts = (TextSelection) _applicationObject.ActiveDocument.Selection;
SelectedText = ts.Text;
```

If nothing is selected, the `Text` property returns an empty string. The `TextSelection` class has many other properties I'll be using in Chapter 4, "Modifying Code in the Editor," when discussing adding code to the current file.

Writing Messages to the Output Window and the TaskList

If you intend for your add-in to be used when Visual Studio is run with its user interface suppressed (e.g., during builds executed from the command line), you should avoid displaying dialogs. Rather than using pop-up dialogs, you should write status messages (and any messages to support debugging) to the Output window. This code, for Visual Studio 2008/2010, updates the pane in the Output window that's currently being displayed (the "active pane") with the message "Generation complete" (I'll discuss Visual Studio 2005 in the next section):

```
OutputWindow ow;
ow = _applicationObject.ToolWindows.OutputWindow;
ow.ActivePane.OutputString("Generation complete");
```

The Output window can have multiple panes that can be selected from the drop-down list at the top of the window (see Figure 2-9). Rather than randomly writing to whatever pane is active, you should pick the pane you want to write to. This code explicitly selects the Build pane (which Visual Studio adds after the project is built for the first time) and writes to it:

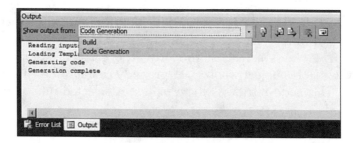

FIGURE 2-9   Although the Output window has only a single pane initially, you can add additional panes.

```
OutputWindow ow;
OutputWindowPane owp;


ow = _applicationObject.ToolWindows.OutputWindow;
owp = ow.OutputWindowPanes.Item("Build");
owp.OutputString("Generation complete");
```

You can keep your messages separate from other messages in the Output window by adding a pane for your messages. This code creates a pane called "Code Generation" (if the pane isn't already present), clears the pane of any previous messages, and then writes a message to it, appending a carriage return to the end of the message to ensure that the next message starts on a new line:

```
OutputWindow ow;
OutputWindowPane owp;


ow = _applicationObject.ToolWindows.OutputWindow;
try
{
  owp = ow.OutputWindowPanes.Item("Code Generation");
}
catch
{
  owp = ow.OutputWindowPanes.Add("Code Generation");
}
```

```
owp.Clear();
owp.OutputString("Generation complete\n");
```

BEST PRACTICE Write your messages to your own pane of the Output window. It keeps the messages from the code-generation process separate from messages generated when building your application. When you write to your pane, make your pane the active page—odds are that if your code generation fails, the developer's project won't have compiled and the messages in the other Output windows aren't relevant.

The last pane written to will be the pane being displayed when processing is complete. However, you can force a pane to the active pane by calling its `Activate` method. This code makes the Code Generation pane the active pane:

```
OutputWindow ow;
ow.OutputWindowPanes.Item("Code Generation").Activate();
```

Unlike with status and debugging messages, you might want to add error messages to the Error List. If you do, give up—the Error List is reserved for compiler errors and is a read-only object from an add-in. Your next best choice is to add any error messages to the Task List. Like the Output window's panes, the Task List has multiple categories. Again, though, you don't get to choose—any errors generated by your add-in will always be added to the Add-ins and Macros category (see Figure 2-10).

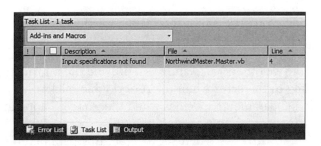

FIGURE 2-10 Messages added to the Task List from your add-in are displayed in the Add-ins and Macros category.

This code accesses the `TaskList` and adds a `TaskItem` with the description "Input specification not found" (as shown in Figure 2-10). This will only work in Visual Studio 2008/2010 (the Visual Studio 2005 code is covered in the next section):

```
TaskList tl = _applicationObject.ToolWindows.TaskList;
TaskItems2 tis = (TaskItems2) tl.TaskItems;
TaskItem  ti = tis.Add2("",
            "",
            "Input specifications not found",
            (int) vsTaskPriority.vsTaskPriorityHigh,
            (int) vsTaskIcon.vsTaskIconCompile,
            true,
            @"C:\Projects\MyProject\NorthwindMaster.Master.vb",
            4,
            true,
            true,
            true);
```

The first two parameters (Category and SubCategory) have no effect on how the task is displayed in Visual Studio. Visual Studio doesn't use SubCategory at all, and the Category column in the user interface is actually used to display the icon for the taskv.

BEST PRACTICE Just because Visual Studio doesn't use the information in the Category and SubCategory columns doesn't mean that you should omit them—they can be useful in Visual Studio 2005 if you intend to give the developer the ability to go to the file containing the error by double-clicking the task item (discussed later in the section "AutoNavigate in Visual Studio 2005").

The `Description`, `Icon`, and `Priority` parameters affect the display of the task item in the Task List. Three parameters (`Checkable`, `CanUserDelete`, and `AutoNavigate`) control what actions the developer can perform with the `TaskItem`. Two others (`File` and `Line`) provide the information that supports navigating to the error when the user double-clicks on a `TaskItem`. A sixth (`FlushItem`) parameter specifies when the `TaskItem` appears on the menu:

- **Checkable**—When set to True, this parameter allows the developer to check off the item in the `TaskList`. Checking off an item causes Visual Studio to draw a line through the description.
- **CanUserDelete**—This parameter defaults to True, allowing the developer to delete the item. Because this is probably the setting you want, you can omit it.

- **AutoNavigate**—When the developer clicks the item in the TaskList, the developer will be taken to the file and line in error.
- **File and Line**—These are the line number and the filename used to support AutoNavigate.
- **FlushItem**—This parameter controls when the item will appear on the TaskList. If you set this parameter to False, the item will appear in the TaskList only when your code finishes running (the default value of True causes the message to appear as soon as you add the TaskItem to the TaskList). If you may add a large number of messages during processing, then passing False in this parameter will speed up execution.

In addition to supporting AutoNavigate, the File and Line parameters also appear in the developer interface. When AutoNavigate is set to True, these parameters are used to open the referenced file and highlight the line when the developer double-clicks the task item. To support this feature, you must provide the full pathname to your file when adding the TaskItem.

AutoNavigate in Visual Studio 2005

Unfortunately, Visual Studio 2005 doesn't support the AutoNavigate parameter as part of adding an item to the Task List. If, in Visual Studio 2005, you want to give the developer the ability to go directly to an error, you must provide code in the TaskNavigate event of the TaskItem.

To support going to the file, you must first declare a field of type TaskListEvents at the top of your Connect class (Visual Studio events are discussed in more detail later in this chapter):

```
EnvDTE.TaskListEvents tle;
```

Then, in the OnConnection method, you need to wire up an event handler to the TaskNavigated event available from the field you just declared. Supplying a Category name when creating a TaskItem has a payoff here: You can use the Category to limit the events received by your add-in to just those tasks with your Category name. The following code, for instance, specifies that only TaskListEvents for the category "Code Generation" are to be passed to the tle variable. The code then wires up a method named CodeGeneration_Navigate to tle's TaskNavigated event:

```
TaskListEvents tle;

if ( tle == null)
```

```
{
  tle = (EnvDTE.TaskListEvents)
     _applicationObject.Events.get_TaskListEvents("Code Generation");
  tle.TaskNavigated +=
        new _dispTaskListEvents_TaskAddedEventHandler(
                                    this.CodeGeneration_Navigate);
}
```

BEST PRACTICE   As with adding menus, in your code check to see if you've already wired up the event: If the variable is null, add your event; if the variable isn't null, skip adding your event.

The event handler itself looks like the following example (much of this code will be explained in Chapter 3, which discusses the `FileCodeModel`). If you do successfully navigate to the error file, you should set the `NavigateHandled` parameter that's passed to the handler to True:

```
void CodeGeneration_TaskNavigated(
                TaskItem TaskItem,
                ref bool NavigateHandled)
{
  EnvDTE.Window fw;
  EnvDTE.TextWindow tw;
  EnvDTE.TextPane tp;

  fw = _applicationObject.ItemOperations.OpenFile(
            TaskItem.FileName, EnvDTE.Constants.vsViewKindTextView);
  tw = (EnvDTE.TextWindow) fw.Object;
  tp = (EnvDTE.TextPane) tw.ActivePane;
  tp.Selection.MoveTo(TaskItem.Line, 1, false);
  tp.Selection.SelectLine();

  NavigateHandled = true;
}
```

Final Touches

If you do, add an error to the Task List, you should bring up the Task List so that you can see your error. This code is the same in all versions in Visual Studio:

```
_applicationObject.Windows.
        Item(EnvDTE.Constants.vsWindowKindTaskList).Activate();
```

Unfortunately, there currently isn't a way to ensure that the pane with your errors (Add-ins and Macros) will be the current pane.

If you are supporting navigating to the error code, you also can make life a little easier for the developer tracking down the error by navigating to the file with the error as soon as you add it to the TaskList (rather than forcing the developer to click it in the TaskList). You can do this by calling the Navigate method on your TaskItem immediately after adding to the TaskList:

```
TaskItem ti;
ti = tl.TaskItems.Add("Code Generation",
                "",
                "Input specifications not found",
                vsTaskPriority.vsTaskPriorityHigh,
                vsTaskIcon.vsTaskIconCompile,
                true,
                @"C:\MyProject\NorthwindMaster.Master.vb",
                4,
                true,
                false);
        ti.Navigate();;
```

BEST PRACTICE If all you need to do is to let the developer know about the condition of your application, the Task List window may be overkill. It may just be easier to just update the text in Visual Studio's status bar:

```
applicationObject.DTE.StatusBar.Text =
                        "Code generated.";
```

Responding to Events

Rather than triggering code generation by clicking a menu choice, you may want to have your code generated automatically when some event takes place in Visual Studio. For instance, the input to your code generation might be a set of tags in the application's config file. When the developer closes the config file (or even just switches away from it), you may want to scan the config file for your tags and, if you find them, generate your code.

BEST PRACTICE   From the developer's point of view, your code-generation solution is more tightly integrated with Visual Studio when code generation happens automatically and in response to events in Visual Studio.

Visual Studio organizes events into packages. The packages containing key events for code generation are shown in Table 1-1.

Some of the events can accept a filter that limits an event to being called only under specific conditions. For instance, with the Task List you can limit the events you receive to `TaskItems` with a specific Category. With `DocumentEvents`, `WindowEvents`, and `ProjectItemsEvents`, you can limit events to a specific document, window, or type of project.

As that suggests, there are three different classes of events in a Visual Studio add-in and you wire up your code to each class differently. What I'll refer to as "simple events" use the same wire up process that you're familiar with from building applications in Visual Studio; a second class of events are "filtered"—you can specify the object whose events you will accept as part of defining and wiring up the event; the third class of events are tied to opening and closing documents in the Visual Studio editor window.

Simple Events

Some events can be wired up to methods using the syntax you're familiar with from working with events in other environments—the `Opened` event of `SolutionEvents` is a good example of this kind of event. The `Opened` event is useful because it provides a convenient place to wire up any other events you need. Rather than dump additional code into your `OnConnection` method, you can use the `SolutionEvents` package's `Opened` event, which fires after a solution is opened, to hold the code that wires up additional events. (This is the strategy used in the case study in Chapter 10, for instance.)

Table 1-1 Event Interfaces and "Packages" Available to Add-Ins

Event Object	Events	Filter Available?
DTEEvents	Visual Studio startup, shutdown, and mode changes	No
DocumentEvents	Documents open and closing	Yes
WindowEvents	Windows created, activated, opened, and moved	Yes
SelectionEvents	Selection changed	No
BuildEvents	Build begun, ended, and configured	No
SolutionEvents	Solutions opened, closed, renamed; also projects added to and removed from solutions	No
ProjectItemsEvents	Items in projects added, removed, and renamed	No
WebSiteItemsEvents	Items in web projects added, removed, and renamed	No
TaskListEvents	Task items added, deleted, modified, and navigated to	Yes

To use SolutionEvents, you'll need a field declared at the top of your class module to hold a reference to the SolutionEvents object (Visual Basic programmers will need to use the WithEvents keyword):

```
EnvDTE.SolutionEvents slnE;
```

In the OnConnection method, you must initialize that field with this code:

```
slnE = _applicationObject.Events.SolutionEvents;
```

If you're a Visual Basic programmer, you can now select SlnE from the drop-down list at the top of the editing window to generate the skeleton of

Opened event, just as you would with any other event; C# programmers can use the standard += syntax to wire up an event handler:

```
slnE.Opened += new _dispSolutionEvents_OpenedEventHandler(slnE_Opened);
```

With that, you're done—at least for simple events such as SolutionEvents.

Filtered Events

You can now use the SolutionEvents Opened handler to wire a handler to one of Visual Studio's "filtered" events such as the WindowEvents. Filtered events allow you to limit which events you will capture in your add-in. For instance, for WindowEvents you can pick which window you want to catch events from.

As an example, to capture the Solution Explorer window's WindowActivated event, you should first declare a field to hold a reference to WindowEvents:

```
EnvDTE.WindowEvents winE;
```

Then, in the SolutionEvents Opened event, you can add code to check to see if you've set that variable. If you haven't, you'll need to use the window's identifier to retrieve the window from the Windows collection (you can't use the ToolWindows collection for this). This code retrieves the Solution Explorer window:

```
if (winE == null)
{
    Window win;
    win = _applicationObject.Windows.Item(
                EnvDTE.Constants.vsWindowKindSolutionExplorer);
```

Now that you've accessed the window, you can pass that reference as a filter to the WindowsEvents object when you set the winE field:

```
winE = (EnvDTE.WindowEvents)
                _applicationObject.Events.get_WindowEvents(win);
```

Because the winE variable now references the WindowEvents object, you can wire up a handler to the event:

```
winE.WindowActivated += new
   _dispWindowEvents_WindowActivatedEventHandler(winE_WindowActivated);
```

The simplest version of the handler would look like this and will run when the Solution Explorer is opened or the developer switches to it from another window:

```
void winE_WindowNavigated(Window GotFocus, Window LostFocus)
{

}
```

If you want, you can accept references both to the window being activated and the window that is losing the focus so that you can generate code when a developer leaves or enters a window (these parameters are optional and will be omitted in Visual Basic if Visual Studio generates the handler's skeleton):

```
void winE_WindowNavigated(Window GotFocus, Window LostFocus)
{
  string WindowName;
  WindowName = winGetFocus.Caption;
}
```

Working with Document Events

A slightly more complicated process is required to capture document events such as opening and closing a document. The problem is that, for any item in your project, the corresponding document doesn't exist until it's opened. So the first step is to create an unfiltered "master" document Opened event that catches every document opening event. In this "master" event you can check for a particular document and wire up a second event to monitor that document.

Begin by declaring fields both for the "master" event and for the document you actually want to monitor at the top of your add-in:

```
EnvDTE.DocumentEvents docMaster;
EnvDTE.DocumentEvents docE;
```

Then, in the SolutionEvents Opened event, you can wire up the DocumentOpened event to the "master" field. For this event, you shouldn't pass anything as the filter because you want all document openings to go through the event:

```
if (docMaster == null)
{
 docMaster =
(EnvDTE.DocumentEvents) _applicationObject.Events.get_DocumentEvents(
                                                    null);
 docMaster.DocumentOpened +=new
                _dispDocumentEvents_DocumentOpenedEventHandler(
                                        docMaster_DocumentOpened);
}
```

In the DocumentOpenMaster event, you can check for the document that you're interested in being opened. The code is similar to the code for wiring up the "master" event but this time, you'll pass a reference to the document you want to monitor. Since the DocumentOpened event is passed a reference to the document that was just opened, you can use that reference both to check the document's name and to filter the event when wiring it up.

This code checks to see if the app.config file was opened and, if so, wires up a handler to run when that file is closed:

```
void docMaster_DocumentOpened(Document Doc)
{
 if (docE == null && Doc.Name.Contains("app.config"))
 {
  docE = (EnvDTE.DocumentEvents)
            _applicationObject.Events.get_DocumentEvents(Doc);
  docE.DocumentClosing +=new
                _dispDocumentEvents_DocumentClosingEventHandler(
                                    docE_DocumentClosing);
 }
}
```

In the docE_Closing handler you could check the file for any code-generation input values and generate your code. Once the Closing event fires, you should disconnect the event because the document no longer exists:

```
void docE_DocumentClosing(Document Doc)
{
  ...call code generation...
 docE.DocumentClosing -=
          new StartEventHandler(docE_DocumentClosing);
 docE = null;
}
```

Extracting Event Packages

Another set of events can have their corresponding event objects extracted using the _applicationObject's GetObject method. These event packages include the following:

- BuildManagerEvents
- ProjectItemsEvents
- ProjectsEvents
- ReferencesEvents
- WebSiteItemsEvents
- WebSiteEvents

As before, you'll need fields to hold the event objects. To capture events fired as items are added and removed from a project, you'd use ProjectItemsEvents:

```
EnvDTE.ProjectItemsEvents PrjItmE;
```

Again, in the solution's Opened event you retrieve the event and wire up a handler. To get the event object for VB projects, you use GetObject, passing the string "ProjectsEvents" prefixed with the language. This code, in the solution's Opened event, retrieves the event object for VB project items:

```
if (PrjItmE == null)
(
   PrjItmE = (EnvDTE.ProjectItemsEvents)
         _applicationObject.Events.GetObject("VBProjectItemsEvents");
   PrjItmE.ItemAdded += new
      _dispProjectItemsEvents_ItemAddedEventHandler(PrjItmE_ItemAdded);
}
```

In some versions of Visual Studio, you can also reference event packages directly by casting the Events object to the Events2 interface. This example does the cast and then uses the Events2 object's ProjectItemsEvents property to get the event package:

```
EnvDTE80.Events2 objEvents2;
EnvDTE.ProjectItemsEvents objProjectItemsEvents;

objEvents2 = (EnvDTE80.Events2) EnvDTE.Events;
objProjectItemsEvents = objEvents2.ProjectItemsEvents;
```

For C# projects you would use CSharpProjectItemsEvents.

The event handler that will fire when an item is added will be passed a reference to the item being added. This handler retrieves the project of the item being added:

```
void PrjItmE_ItemAdded(ProjectItem pi)
{
   Project pr;
   pr = pi.ProjectItems.ContainingProject;
}
```

Finishing Events

You can disconnect any event objects that you wired up in the solution's Open event in the solution's AfterClosing event by setting the event object to null:

```
void Sub SlnE_AfterClosing()
{
 docMaster.DocumentOpened -= new
             _dispDocumentEvents_DocumentOpenedEventHandler(
                                     docMaster_DocumentOpened);
 docMaster = null;
 ...handle disconnecting SlnE and PrjItemE...
}
```

BEST PRACTICE You should always disconnect your events when you're done, even though all events will be automatically disconnected for you when you change projects or shut down Visual Studio.

Accepting Input

In many code generation scenarios, all the information you need to generate code will be found in the files in the project. In some cases, however, you will need to provide mechanisms for the developer to provide additional information. This section discusses those scenarios and the tools available to your add-in for interacting with the developer.

Options

Not all the inputs to code generation may be embedded in files in the project—some of your inputs may have to come from the developer. Methods in your code-generation class can pop up a dialog each time you run your solution, which makes sense if the developer's choices will change every time code is generated. However, if that strikes you as tiresome, there's a better solution. You can do either of the following:

- Have a menu choice open a dockable window where the developer can enter data to be used in generating code. For inputs that change frequently, this is a good solution because it allows the developer to review the current settings and change them before generating code (see Figure 2-11). A button on the `ToolWindow` can be used to trigger code generation so that the developer can get the code without having to wait for some Visual Studio event to trigger generation.
- Add a new tab to Visual Studio's Options dialog. This is a good solution for inputs that don't change often (e.g., the location to put temporary files). Because it takes more mouse clicks to get to the Options dialog (see Figure 2-12), you don't want to put inputs that change frequently in this dialog.

Creating a Dockable Window

To create a dockable window, you must first add a `UserControl` to your project. Once the `UserControl` is added, you can design it as you would any other form:

- Add a button to trigger code generation. Typically you'll use this button's `Click` event to call a method on your code-generation class.
- Optionally, add public properties to allow your add-in code to set and retrieve options entered on the form. Your code-generation class will need, for instance, a reference to the `_applicationObject`,

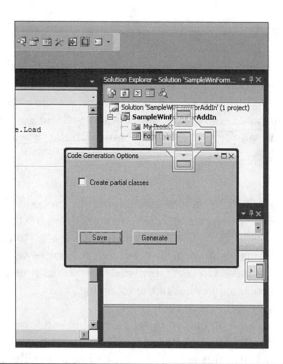

FIGURE 2-11 UserControls opened as Tool windows have all the docking features associated with other windows in Visual Studio.

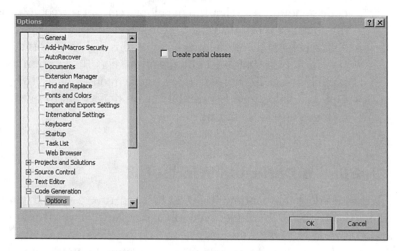

FIGURE 2-12 UserControls can also be used to add new tabs to Visual Studio's Options dialog.

so you should create a property that accepts the object. The next code sample demonstrates this technique.

- Optionally, add a button to save the developer's entries.

Here's the general pattern for a `UserControl` in an add_in:

1. The `Click` event of a menu opens the `UserControl`.
2. In the `UserControl`'s `Load` event, check if the values exist in whatever datastore you'll use for the information the developer enters. If the values do exist, retrieve them and use them to set the form's user interface; if the values don't exist in the datastore, set the form's user interface using default values.
3. When the developer clicks the button to run code generation, save the values from the form (alternatively have a Save button on the form to let the developer save the current settings independently of generating code).

It's your responsibility to save any values the developer enters. Later in this chapter I'll discuss some of your alternatives for saving the values.

To display the `UserControl` you use the `CreateToolWindow2` method of the `Windows2` object. That object can be retrieved from the `_applicationObject`'s `Windows` property. The `CreateToolWindow2` method must be passed six parameters:

- The `_addInInstance` object.
- The full path name to the add-in's DLL. This can be retrieved through reflection.
- The full name of the `UserControl`, consisting of the name of the add-in and the `UserControl` (this *must* be spelled correctly, including matching any upper/lowercase letters).
- The caption for the window.
- A GUID that allows Visual Studio to ensure that the form opens in the location where the developer left it (*don't* regenerate this value each time). You can create a GUID either by running the guidgen utility in Visual Studio 2005 or by selecting the Create GUID choice on the Tools menu in Visual Studio 2008/2010. Use the GUID in registry format that's generated by the utility.
- A variable of type `Object`, which is used to return a reference to the tool window.

Typical code for opening a Tool window looks like this:

```
Object obj = null;
EnvDTE.Window win;
EnvDTE80.Windows2 win2;
string AssemblyLocation;
string WinGUID;

win2 = (EnvDTE80.Windows2) _applicationObject.Windows;
AssemblyLocation =
        System.Reflection.Assembly.GetExecutingAssembly().Location;
WinGUID = "{0d3619e3-b0b4-4af3-9053-95a29222159b}";
win = win2.CreateToolWindow2(_addInInstance,
                        AssemblyLocation,
                        typeof(MyUserControl).FullName,
                        "My Tool Window", WinGUID, ref obj);
```

After the `CreateToolWindow2` method has executed, you can convert the object variable to the type of your `UserControl`. The first step in that process is to define a field to hold a reference to the `UserControl`:

```
MyUserControl muc;
```

Now you can cast the `obj` parameter that will hold a reference to your `UserControl` and store it in the field. You have one other thing to do—the window will open invisibly so you need to set the window's `Visible` property to make it visible:

```
muc = (MyUserControl) obj;
win.Visible = true;
```

Any code-generation code you put in the `ToolWindow` will need access to the `_applicationObject`. To enable that, add a write-only property to your `UserControl` and use it to pass the `_applicationObject` to the control. This property accepts the `_applicationObject` and moves it to a field in the `UserControl`:

```
DTE2 _applicationObject;

public DTE2 ApplicationObject
{
  set
  {
    _applicationObject = value;
  }
}
```

The code for opening the `ToolWindow` from your add-in would now look like this:

```
win = win2.CreateToolWindow2(_addInInstance, AssemblyLocation,
                    typeof(MyUserControl).FullName,
                    "Window Caption", WinGUID, ref obj);
muc = (MyUserControl) obj;
muc.ApplicationObject = _applicationObject;
win.Visible = true;
```

Saving Input Values

You can store the values entered in the `ToolWindow` wherever it makes sense to you. An obvious choice is a configuration file that you can design. You can also store the values in Visual Studio's `Globals` object.

To save a value in the `Globals` object, just pass a key name to the `Globals` object's indexer and set a value. When you add a new key to the `Globals` object, you must also call its `set_VariablePersists` method—this isn't necessary when updating a value.

BEST PRACTICE   There's no appreciable performance penalty in calling the `set_VariablePersists` method, so you might as well call the method each time you change a value.

To retrieve a value, just pass the key it was saved with to the `Globals` object's indexer. You can check to see if a key exists by calling the `Globals` object's `get_VariableExists` method, passing the name of the key.

You can save values in the `Globals` object at three levels: Visual Studio (through the DTE object, which is held in the `_applicationObject` variable), solution, or project. The following two utility methods save and restore values to the Globals object at the Visual Studio level when passed a key name and a value:

```
public static string GetValue(string Name)
{
 if (_applicationObject.Globals.get_VariableExists(Name))
 {
  return _applicationObject.Globals[Name].ToString();
 }
}

public static void SaveValue(string Name, string Value)
{
   _applicationObject.Globals[Name] = Value;
   _applicationObject.Globals.set_VariablePersists(Name, true);
}
```

To save a value at the solution level, use the Globals property on the Solution object; to save a value at the project level, use the Globals property on the Project object. (The Globals object is discussed in more detail at the end of Chapter 3.)

Another choice is to save values in the Windows registry. The following two methods save and retrieve values to the registry as a string under the key for Visual Studio 2008 (version 9.0):

```
public static string GetValue(string Name)
{
 Microsoft.Win32.RegistryKey key;

 key = Microsoft.Win32.Registry.CurrentUser.OpenSubKey(
              @"SOFTWARE\Microsoft\VisualStudio\9.0", false);
 return key.GetValue(Name, "").ToString();
}

public static void SaveValue(string Name, string Value)
{
 Microsoft.Win32.RegistryKey key;

 key = Microsoft.Win32.Registry.CurrentUser.OpenSubKey(
              @"SOFTWARE\Microsoft\VisualStudio\9.0", true);
 key.SetValue(Name, Value,
         Microsoft.Win32.RegistryValueKind.String);
}
```

BEST PRACTICE Storing values in the Windows registry allows you to review, debug, and set those values outside of Visual Studio and your add-in's code.

These methods can be placed in the `UserControl` being used to create the `ToolWindow` or placed in a separate class with other utilities. With either version of these routines, you can save a value by passing the name you want to store your values under and the value to the `SaveValue` method:

```
OptionsPage.SaveValue("TempFileLocation", this.FileTextBox.Text);
```

To retrieve a value, you only need to pass the name used when saving the value:

```
this.FileTextBox.Text = OptionsPage.GetValue("TempFileLocation");
```

Adding an Options Tab

Like a `ToolWindow`, a tab in the Options dialog is a `UserControl`. However, the DLL that the `UserControl` is part of must be put in Visual Studio's Addins folder (typically, My Documents\Visual Studio *version*\Addins). Rather than play with the compile settings for your add-in, it's a better idea to add a second Class Library project to your add-in solution (see Figure 2-13). Then, on the Compile tab in the new project's properties page, set the Build output path to put the results of build in the Addins folder.

You'll also need to add up to three references to this project:

- `EnvDTE` (plus any of `EnvDTE80`, etc.)
- `System.Drawing`
- `System.Windows.Forms`

Once you've configured the project, you must add a `UserControl` to the project and have it implement the `EnvDTE.IDTToolsOptionsPage` interface (the container for the Options pages calls methods on this interface when the developer clicks the OK or Cancel button in the Options dialog):

```
public class OptionsPage : UserControl, EnvDTE.IDTToolsOptionsPage
```

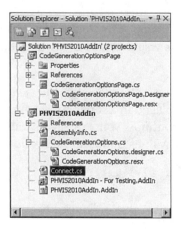

FIGURE 2-13   To support adding an Options tab, you should add a second project to hold your Options user control.

Once again, you can design the form as you would in any other application.

The last step in setting up your Options tab is to update the .addin file back in your add-in project to use the new user control you've created. The .addin file must reference your Options tab by adding the `ToolsOptionsPage` element, following the existing `</Addin>` element. Initially, you should put the element in the °– For Testing.Addin file in your project (this is the .addin file used when you are debugging). However, you must remember to transfer these settings to the "real" .addin file before releasing your add-in.

The `ToolsOptionsPage` element contains four mandatory elements:

- **Category**—The name that your Options page will appear under in the TreeView on the left side of the Options dialog.
- **SubCategory**—The second level within the Category in the TreeView.
- **Assembly**—The name of the DLL holding your Options user control.
- **FullClassName**—The full name of your Options user control (you *must* spell this name correctly, including matching any upper/lower-case characters).

A typical example would look like this:

```
<ToolsOptionsPage>
 <Category Name="Code Generation">
  <SubCategory Name="Temporary File Location">
```

```
<Assembly>GenerateAddIn.DLL</Assembly>
 <FullClassName>GenerateOptions.OptionsPage</FullClassName>
 </SubCategory>
 </Category>
</ToolsOptionsPage>
```

With these changes, when you go to Tools | Options you'll find the name you assigned in the Category tag listed in the TreeView. When you drill down through the TreeView, your UserControl will appear in the Options dialog. You'll need to add code to at least four methods in your UserControl:

- **OnAfterCreated**—Retrieve saved values and initialize the form. This method is passed a reference to Visual Studio.
- **OnOK**—Save the entries on the form and do any clean-up activities. (The developer has clicked the OK button on the Options dialog.)
- **OnCancel**—Do any clean-up activities (the developer has clicked the Cancel button on the Options dialog).
- **GetProperties**—Return values entered on the UserControl when requested by other code in the add-in.

The code in the first three methods will vary depending on what you're doing with your Options page. A default implementation for the GetProperties method is to set the PropertiesObject to null or Nothing:

```
public void EnvDTE.IDTToolsOptionsPage.GetProperties(
                                ref Object PropertiesObject)
{
 PropertiesObject = null;
}
```

As with a ToolWindow, it's still your responsibility to store and retrieve values entered in your Options tab.

Accessing and Saving Option Properties

In your add-in, you can access the values entered in the Tools | Options dialog using the get_Properties method in C# or through the Properties collection in Visual Basic (in Visual Basic, you'll need to put brackets around the word "Property" because it's a keyword) . You retrieve the values entered on any page by specifying the Category and SubCategory for the Options tab whose properties you want. This code, for instance, accesses the Properties collection for the General tab under Environment in the Options TreeView:

```
Properties props;
props = _applicationObject.get_Properties("Environment", "General");
```

Not all Category and SubCategory names are this obvious. Generally speaking, the names are the same as shown in the Options TreeView with any blanks removed (e.g., "Text Editor" becomes "TextEditor"). You find the list of the Categories and SubCategories in the Windows Registry. (Appendix B, "Case Study: Options Dialog Categories, SubCategories, and Properties," provides the key in the Windows Registry with the list along with code that will generate a list of all the Properties within the SubCategory.)

Once you've accessed the `Properties` collection you want, you can retrieve a specific property on the tab either by name or position. This code retrieves the `AnimationSpeed` property from the Environment | General page and then gets its value:

```
Property prop;
short Speed;

prop = props.Item("AnimationSpeed");
Speed = (short)prop.Value;
```

This code does the same thing but accesses the property by position:

```
Speed = (short)props.Item(0).Value;
```

If you've created a `ToolWindow`, you may want to access Visual Studio properties from it. However, for a `ToolWindow` to retrieve a property, it must have a reference to the `_applicationObject`. The easiest way to get that reference is to enhance the property on your `UserControl` that accepts the `_applicationObject`. As an example, this property extracts the predefined `AnimationSpeed` property and moves it to a text box on the `ToolWindow`:

```
public DTE2 ApplicationObject
{
   set
   {
     _applicationObject = value;
     Properties props;
     Property prop;
```

```
    props = _applicationObject.Properties("Environment", "General");
    prop = props.Item("AnimationSpeed");

    this.AniSpeedBox.Text = prop.Value.ToString();
  }
}
```

You can also use the Properties mechanism to retrieve values you've set through your Options tab UserControl. In order to do that, you must set up a class to define your properties. In this class, you must save and restore any values passed to your properties.

As an example, this class defines a property named TempFileLocation that stores its values in the Windows registry using the methods I showed earlier:

```
[System.Runtime.InteropServices.ComVisible(true)]
[System.Runtime.InteropServices.ClassInterface(
        System.Runtime.InteropServices.ClassInterfaceType.AutoDual)]
public class GenerationProperties
{
    public string TempFileLocation
    {
        get
        {
            return OptionsPage.GetValue("TempFileLocation");
        }
        set
        {
         OptionsPage.SaveValue("TempFileLocation", value);
        }
    }

}
```

All that's left is to have your Options tab UserControl return your properties class. An Options tab UserControl will have a GetProperties method (the method is required by the EnvDTE.IDTToolsOptionsPage interface that the UserControl must implement). In the GetProperties method, you must return your Property class (remember that code in your Property class handles the mechanics of saving and retrieving the values). A typical implementation would look like this, assuming that the Property class is named GenerationProperties:

```
public class OptionsPage : EnvDTE.IDTToolsOptionsPage
{
 GenerationProperties _opts = new GenerationProperties();

    public void EnvDTE.IDTToolsOptionsPage.GetProperties(
                                ref Object PropertiesObject)
    {
        PropertiesObject = _opts;
    }
}
```

Integrating with Visual Studio

In this chapter, you've seen the tools for creating a Visual Studio add-in. Still to be addressed is the content of your add-in: the code you will write to generate code. That includes manipulating the components of your project (discussed in Chapter 3, with special features for specific project types discussed in Chapter 5, "Supporting Project-Specific Features"), adding and removing code within a file (Chapter 4), generating language-neutral code (Chapter 6, "Generating Language-Neutral Code"), and some special tools (Chapter 8, "Other Tools: Templates, Attributes, and Custom Tools"). The case studies in Chapters 9 and 10 walk you through creating typical Visual Studio add-ins to show how some of the tools discussed in this chapter are used. Only the case study in Chapter 11, "Case Study: Generating Data-Conversion Code," which shows how to build a visual designer to let the developer generate T4 code, doesn't require creating an add-in.

CHAPTER 3

MANIPULATING PROJECT COMPONENTS

In this chapter:

- The Code Model
- Managing Projects and Solutions
- Generating Code
- Modifying and Analyzing Components
- Processing Components in a File
- Working with Retrieved Elements
- Working with the CodeType Objects
- Storing Information
- Working with Project Components

As part of any code-generation solution, you're going to need to generate new components for an application—everything from classes to variables to procedural code. In addition, to support regenerating code (and often as part of generating new code) you also need to find out what components already exist in the project. For instance, if you're generating code to be used with an existing class, you want to know what language the class is written in.

This chapter looks at one of the tools available to you when you're running your code from a Visual Studio add-in: the "code model" objects. These are a set of objects you can use for analyzing and generating code in an object-oriented and language-neutral fashion.

The first part of this chapter focuses on adding projects, files, and code using the code model objects. These objects (`CodeModel`, `FileCodeModel`, `CodeClass`, and more) give you the ability to add new components to a project, primarily in C#. The second part of this chapter looks at how to analyze the project to find out what components it contains in an object-oriented fashion.

This chapter (as with Chapters 4 through 8) is a "tools" chapter: I'm focusing on the objects, methods, and properties you'll use rather than on combining them to create a complete solution. Chapter 9, "Case Study: Generating a Connection String Manager," and Chapter 10, "Case Study: Generating Validation Code," describe two case studies where you can see how these tools are used together.

Although these objects work with all project types, a specific set of objects is available for working with the special features of C# and Visual Basic projects, and with projectless websites. While you can do many things with Visual Basic, C#, and projectless websites with the objects in this chapter, to access those special features you'll also need to use the tools described in Chapter 5, "Supporting Project-Specific Features."

The Code Model

What I'm referring to as the code model objects are a group of objects that share similar functions and interfaces. (They all implement, in part, the methods and properties defined by `CodeModel2` interface.) The primary difference between these objects is their scope. For instance, the `CodeModel` enables you to add new components to any file in a project; the `FileCodeModel` lets you add components but only to a specific file in the project; the `CodeClass` lets you add code to a specific class.

The components of an application that the code model objects let you manipulate might be classified as the structural parts of an application: namespaces, classes, functions, and so on, down to variable declarations. Procedural code, such as `Do...While` loops, `If...Then` structures, variable assignments, and so on, are omitted. These can be generated using the CodeDom described in Chapter 6, "Generating Language-Neutral Code," inserting strings into the file using the CodeEditor objects described in Chapter 4, "Modifying Code in the Editor," or by using the T4 language described in Chapter 7, "Generating Code from Templates with T4."

In this chapter, I'll first look at adding new projects to solutions and then adding folders and files to projects. Next, I look at adding code components to a file. This is a section that you should read sequentially. I start by retrieving the objects that let you manipulate high-level items in your project (a `Namespace`, for instance), and then work my way down through adding a class, methods, and so on. These `FileCodeModel` methods look very much alike, so while I go into detail for the options on these methods at the start of this section, by the time we get to the last methods I'm going to assume you've read the details earlier. This means that you won't have to plow through the same descriptions over and over again, but it also means if you skip straight to the method you want, you may find that my description doesn't give you all the information you need.

Code Model Caveats

The code model objects are language neutral and can be used, presumably, with many .NET language. (I've only tested with the two official languages: C# and Visual Basic.) This means you can't use the code model object to manipulate or analyze features that are specific to a language (technically speaking, features that aren't compliant with the Common Language Specification). If, for instance, you're using the code model objects to discover what members already exist in a class, you can determine the number of parameters, their names, and their data type. However, you can't determine if a parameter is optional or if it is an out parameter because these options are not part of the Common Language Specification. Similarly, when generating code with the `CodeModel`, you can't manage those language-specific features.

In addition, not all the implemented features of the code model objects are supported in all languages and project types. Although you can use the code model objects to analyze a code file in Visual Basic, many functions aren't implemented for Visual Basic projects. If you call a method on the code model objects and get the message, "This method or operation is not implemented," or "Value does not fall within the expected range," then one potential reason is that the method isn't supported for the project type and/or language you're using it in.

Don't panic! Even if the `FileCodeModel` doesn't support doing what you want, you do have alternatives as I noted before: You can add code by adding preconfigured files or templates (adding templates is described in this chapter; creating your own templates is described in Chapter 7), using the CodeDom (described in Chapter 6), or inserting strings using the CodeEditor (described in Chapter 4).

The good news is there's no reason why there can't be language-specific implementations of the `CodeModel2` interface. For instance, the .NET Framework includes the C++ `CodeModel`, which contains objects specific to C++. I ignore those extensions in this chapter to concentrate on the objects that you can use with C# and Visual Basic.

One last warning: When code is analyzed using the code model objects, the objects are designed to provide access to code that is compiled. Compiler directives, for example, are invisible to the code model objects (though comments are not). This also means that if you're using the DEBUG compiler directive to swap code in and out of the compile process, then the objects only see the set of code currently swapped in. In this example, if DEBUG is defined, then the code model objects will only see the declaration that sets the variable to True because it's in the True portion of the test:

```
#define DEBUG
#if (DEBUG)
    bool ByPassASPNETComponents = true;
#else
    bool ByPassASPNETComponents = false;
#endif
```

Managing Projects and Solutions

As part of generating code, you'll often need to add files to a project and folders. On occasion, you may even need to create a project to hold your generated code. This section discusses how to create new projects within a Visual Studio solution.

Creating Projects

Whereas most code-generation solutions happen inside existing projects, you can create new projects as part of your code-generation solution. The simplest (and most reliable) way to create a new project is to use the Solution2 object. You can get the Solution2 object from the _applicationObject's Solution property by casting the result to the Solution2 interface. The Solution2 object's AddFromTemplate method creates a project from a Visual Studio template when passed four parameters:

- The path to the template.
- The location to create the project.
- The name of the project.
- A Boolean indicating whether the project is to be added to the existing solution (True) or opened in a new solution (False). If you open a new solution, the current solution is closed without the developer being given the chance to save any changes.

The AddFromTemplate method returns a Project object.

Since Visual Studio 2005, templates have been kept in ZIP files. Rather than hard-code the path to the Visual Studio template that you pass to the AddFromTemplate method, use the Solution2 object's GetProjectTemplate method to retrieve the path to the template. The `GetProjectTemplate` method needs two parameters: the name of the ZIP file containing the template and the language type for the project (for example, CSharp or VisualBasic).

This code extracts the `Solution2` object and uses it to retrieve the path to the template for the Console application in C#:

```
Solution2 sln;
sln = (Solution2) _applicationObject.Solution;
string TemplatePath = sln.GetProjectTemplate(
                        "ConsoleApplication.zip", "CSharp");
```

This code uses the path to create a Console project:

```
string ProjectPath = @"C:\MyProjects\MyConsoleSolution";
Project prj = sln.AddFromTemplate(TemplatePath,
ProjectPath, "MyConsoleProject", true);
```

The result of executing this code is a folder in the MyProjects folder named MyConsoleSolution, holding all the components of the MyConsoleProject project (for example, the csproj file, the bin, and obj folders). The MyProjects folders would also hold the MyConsoleSolution SLN and SUO files.

The templates available to you will vary from one release of Visual Studio to another (and even from one service pack to another). In addition, you can download templates from Microsoft or create your own (refer to Chapter 8, "Other Tools: Templates, Attributes, and Custom Tools").

BEST PRACTICE To determine what templates are available on your computer, search the template folder (something like C:\Program Files\Visual Studio *version*\Common7\IDE\ItemTemplates for Visual Studio, C:\Program Files\Visual Studio *version*\Common7\IDE\VWDExpress\ItemTemplates for Web Developer Express, and so on). If you don't know the path to your template folder, then a search in Windows Explorer for ConsoleApplication.zip will turn it up.

To add further components to the project, you need a reference to the project's `ProjectItems` object. Once you've created a project, you can retrieve the `ProjectItems` from the `Project` object, as this code does:

```
ProjectItems pitms = prj.ProjectItems;
```

Referencing the Project Items Collection

You can retrieve a reference to an existing project in a solution through the `Solution2` object's `Projects` collection. This code retrieves a reference to the first project in the solution:

```
prj = sln.Projects.Item(1)
```

This code iterates through the projects in a solution, looking for a specific project by name. Once it finds the project, it sets a `Project` variable called `proj` to point to the project, breaks out of the loop, and uses the `prj` variable to extract the `Project's` `CodeModel`:

```
Project prj;
foreach (Project proj in _applicationObject.Solution)
{
  if (proj.Name == "CustomerBEL")
  {
    prj = proj;
    break;
  }
}
CodeModel cm = prj.CodeModel;
```

Once you have a reference to the `Project`, you can retrieve a reference to the `ProjectItems` object, as shown in the previous section. You can also retrieve the `ProjectItems` object from the `ContainingProject` property of the document currently open in the editor—the `ActiveDocument`—as this code does:

```
ProjectItems pjs = _applicationObject.ActiveDocument.ProjectItem.
                                ContainingProject.ProjectItems;
```

You can also retrieve the `ProjectItems` object from the `ContainingProject` property of the project item currently selected in Solution Explorer by using the `SelectedItems` collection, as this code does:

```
ProjectItems pjs =
        _applicationObject.SelectedItems.Item(1).ProjectItem.
                                ContainingProject.ProjectItems;
```

BEST PRACTICE When you're adding new project items using the `ProjectItems` object, the most reliable tool is the `ProjectItems` object retrieved from the `ContainingProject` object.

Adding Folders to a Project

Once you have a reference to the `ProjectItems` object, you can add new folders to your project using its `AddFolder` method. It's a good practice to keep the files holding code you generated in a separate folder. (I usually call the folder "GeneratedCode.") If the folder you want to use isn't present, then you need to add it—Visual Studio won't add it for you. The `AddFolder` method accepts two parameters and adds a new folder to the project: the name of the folder to add and a `vsProjectItemKind`* constant.

BEST PRACTICE The following code adds a folder and works with any type of application, including both projectless and project-based ASP.NET applications (assuming that you've retrieved a reference to the project you want to add the folder to). This example uses the `ActiveDocument` to retrieve the `Project` associated with the document currently being viewed in the editor:

```
Project prj;
prj = _applicationObject.ActiveDocument.ProjectItem.ContainingProject;
ProjectItem pi = prj.ProjectItems.AddFolder(
        "GeneratedCode",Constants.vsProjectItemKindPhysicalFolder);
```

Not all folders are created equal, though. The App_Code folder of a "projectless" ASP.NET application is a "special" folder and it doesn't appear in the list of constants. For these kinds of folders, you must pass the correct GUID for the folder type as the second parameter to the `AddFolder` method. This example creates a valid App_Data folder:

```
ProjectItem pi = prj.ProjectItems.AddFolder(
        "App_Data", "{6BB5F8EF-4483-11D3-8BCF-00C04F8EC28C}");
```

You can extract the GUID for any special folders from the folder's `Kind` property (as shown later in this chapter) and use those GUIDs in your code. Before using this sample code, however, read Chapter 5—often special items, like the App_Code folder, can be created using the objects described in that chapter.

Adding Files

You need to add files to your projects for two reasons:

- As a place to put your generated code that separates it from the code written by the developer
- As a way of generating code by adding files containing boilerplate text

Often, much of the code you want to add is boilerplate and doesn't change much from one generation to another. Using templates and the `CopyFromFile` method supports copying in boilerplate code. Even if your boilerplate code isn't a complete solution, you can use the `CodeElements` objects (discussed later in this chapter) to find components in your boilerplate and then modify those components to support a particular generation's requirements. The downside to copying in files is that it requires you to create an input file for each language you intend to support.

As with creating a new project, when adding new items to your project, you can use a Visual Studio template. (Later in this chapter you see how to add new files using the `CodeModel`.) The process is similar to creating a project:

- Retrieve the path to the template for the item you want to add by using the `Solution2` object's `GetProjectItemTemplate` method, specifying the template and the language.
- Use the `ProjectItems'` `AddFromTemplate` method to add the item, passing the path to the template and the name of the item.

This code would be used in an ASP.NET project to add a Visual Basic ASPX page with a code file named MyPage.aspx:

```
string ItemTemplatePath = sln.GetProjectItemTemplate("WebForm.zip",
                                              @"Web\VisualBasic");
ProjectItem pji = pjis.AddFromTemplate(ItemTemplatePath,
                                    "MyPage.aspx.vb");
```

You can add a component to a folder in your project by using the folder's `ProjectItems` collection. This code uses a `ProjectItems` collection retrieved earlier to retrieve a folder named GeneratedCode and uses the collection's `AddTemplate` method to add a class to the folder:

```
ProjectItem pji = pjis.Item("GeneratedCode").ProjectItems.
        AddFromTemplate(ItemTemplatePath,@"ConnectionManager.cs");
```

In most cases, if only a single item is added, the `AddFromTemplate` method returns a `ProjectItem` object (discussed in more detail later in this chapter). If no items are added because of some failure or if multiple items are added by the template, then the method returns Nothing/null. In addition, the `AddFromTemplate` method can be used to add a file using a Visual Studio wizard (a file with a .vsz extension). Because wizards do not return anything, the `AddFromTemplate` method also returns Nothing/null when a wizard is passed to the `AddFromTemplate` method. Finally, if you create your own custom template (discussed in Chapter 8), the method returns Nothing or null.

When adding a new file, you want to ensure that the name you use is unique. You can request a unique filename through the `GetUniqueFileName` method of the `VsLangProject.VsProject` object for Visual Basic, C#, and Visual J# projects. (The `VsLangProject` objects are discussed in Chapter 5).

BEST PRACTICE   The simplest solution for ensuring a unique name for a file is to delete any already existing version of the file with the name you want to use. (Deleting files is discussed later in this chapter.)

Be aware that having multiple versions of the development environment installed can create unexpected results. For instance, if you install Web Developer Express on the same computer as Visual Studio 9, you may pick up the Web Developer Express templates rather than the Visual Studio 9 version. The difference is significant. Adding the template for a WebForm from Web Developer Express creates a single file WebForm; adding the template from Visual Studio 9 creates a WebForm with a code file.

Copying Boilerplate Code

The `ProjectItems` collection also enables you to copy boilerplate code into a project with three other methods: `AddFromDirectory`, `AddFromFileCopy`, and `AddFromFile`. As with the `AddFromTemplate` method, these methods return a `ProjectItem` provided that only one item is added. `AddFromDirectory` allows you to add multiple files, whereas `AddFromFileCopy` and `AddFromFile` will add only one. `AddFromFileCopy` supports adding multiple copies of a single file to a project, whereas `AddFromFile` will ensure that you don't add a second copy of the file.

The `AddFromDirectory` method accepts a full path to a folder and adds all the contents of the file and any folders with their files to the project. The `AddFromFile` method adds the file to the project but, if the file isn't already in the project's folder, the method just adds a link to the file. The `AddFromFileCopy` method copies the file from its current location to the project's folder unless the file being copied is already in the project's folder, in which case it just adds the file to the project and doesn't copy it.

Although I've said that all these methods should have a full pathname, that isn't strictly true. All that's necessary is that you pass enough information to find the file.

BEST PRACTICE   Although you can pass relative pathnames to these methods, only a full pathname guarantees success.

You can also add files without copying from existing files by using the `FileCodeModel`, as described later in this chapter.

Generating Code

You have two separate related code models that you can use to work with the components of a project: `CodeModel` and `FileCodeModel`. This section describes the differences and similarities between the two models.

Introducing CodeModel and FileCodeModel

Once you've created any new projects and added any new files or folders, the next objects you need for generating or analyzing code are the `CodeModel` when working at the project level or the `FileCodeModel` when working with individual files. To put it another way, the `CodeModel` enables you to work with code in the project without having to retrieve the file first.

The `CodeModel` also lets you create new files to hold whatever component you're adding.

The `FileCodeModel` enables you to work only with the code within a specific, already existing file. Although the `FileCodeModel` and `CodeModel` have similar functionality, the `FileCodeModel` is slightly easier to use because, unlike the `CodeModel`, you don't have to specify the file to be changed.

BEST PRACTICE   In most cases, all your generated code is going into a single file so using the `FileCodeModel` is a better fit for most code-generation scenarios than the `CodeModel`.

In at least one case, you have no choice: If you're working with an ASP.NET project in projectless mode (for example, a website created through New Web Site in Visual Studio rather than New Project), then there's no `CodeModel` object associated with the website—the `CodeModel` property returns null.

Accessing the CodeModel for the Project

You can retrieve the `CodeModel` object for a project through the `Project` object's `CodeModel` property.

```
CodeModel cm;
cm = prj.CodeModel;
```

You can also retrieve the `CodeModel` for any item that makes up the project by using the item's `ContainingProject` property to access the `Project` that the item is part of. This code retrieves the `CodeModel` object associated with the project for the currently open document:

```
cm = _applicationObject.ActiveDocument.ProjectItem.
                        ContainingProject.CodeModel;
```

This code retrieves the `CodeModel` for the project of the item currently selected in Solution Explorer:

```
cm = _applicationObject.SelectedItems.Item(1).ProjectItem.
                        ContainingProject.CodeModel;
```

Accessing the FileCodeModel for a File

To retrieve the FileCodeModel for a specific file, you must first retrieve the ProjectItem object that represents the file. You can then retrieve the FileCodeModel object from the FileCodeModel property of the ProjectItem. This code retrieves the FileCodeModel object for the currently open document:

```
FileCodeModel fcm;
fcm = _applicationObject.ActiveDocument.ProjectItem.FileCodeModel;
```

This code retrieves the FileCodeModel for the currently selected item in Solution Explorer:

```
fcm = _applicationObject.SelectedItems.Item(1).
                              ProjectItem.FileCodeModel;
```

You can also use the Project object's Item method to retrieve a file's ProjectItem (which will give you the FileCodeModel), as this code does:

```
pi = prj.ProjectItems.Item("web.config");
```

If the item isn't found, an exception is raised.

Another option for finding specific files is to iterate through the collection of items in a project to find a ProjectItem with particular characteristics. This code iterates through all the ProjectItems in a project to find any subprojects:

```
foreach (ProjectItem projItem in prj.ProjectItems)
{
    if (projItem.SubProject != null)
    {
        pi = projItem;
        break;
    }
}
```

In a projectless ASP.NET site, not all ProjectItems have a FileCodeModel. The good news is that in a projectless ASP.NET application, any file loaded in the editor has a FileCodeModel associated with it, even if you don't access that file through the ActiveDocument object. As a result, all the previous methods for accessing the FileCodeModel work, provided that the ProjectItem you want is open in the editor.

However, if the item isn't loaded in the editor, the `FileCodeModel` property may return null. The solution is to load the `ProjectItem` into an invisible document window. The following code does the trick. (You may need to add a reference to `VsWebsite.Interop` to your code-generation project to use this code—there's more on the `VsWebsite` objects in Chapter 5.)

```
fcm = _applicationObject.SelectedItems.Item(1).
                            ProjectItem.FileCodeModel;
if (fcm == null)
 {
    VsWebSite.VSWebProjectItem tmpWPI;
    tmpWPI = (VsWebSite.VSWebProjectItem)_applicationObject.
                        SelectedItems.Item(1).ProjectItem.Object;
    tmpWPI.Load();
    fcm = tmpWPI.ProjectItem.FileCodeModel;
}
```

Generating Code

Once you've acquired a reference to either the `CodeModel` for the project or the `FileCodeModel` for a particular file, you can start adding code to your project.

Adding Namespaces

To add a namespace to your project, you call the `AddNamespace` method of either the `CodeModel` or the `FileCodeModel`. The `CodeModel's` version takes three parameters:

- The string that is to be the name of the namespace
- The file to add the namespace to
- The position in the file for the namespace

When you call the `AddNamespace` method, if the specified file doesn't exist, it will be added to the project. This example writes a `Namespace` called PHVIS to the start of a file called Customer.cs:

```
cm.AddNamespace("PHVIS", "Customer.cs", 0);
```

Assuming that the file didn't exist when the method was called, the resulting file would look like this:

```
namespace PHVIS
{
}
```

The `AddNamespace` method of the `FileCodeModel` omits the filename parameter. The method adds the `Namespace` to whatever file the `FileCodeModel` was retrieved from. This code adds the `Namespace` to the currently selected file in Solution Explorer:

```
FileCodeModel fcm;
fcm = _applicationObject.SelectedItems.Item(1).
                        ProjectItem.FileCodeModel;
fcm.AddNamespace("PHVIS",  0);
```

If the file does already exist, the `Namespace` is added to the file but does not wrap any existing classes or namespaces in the file. For instance, assume an already existing file with this class declaration:

```
class FirstClass
{
}
```

After the `AddNamespace` method is called to add a `Namespace` to this file with a position parameter of -1, the resulting code would look like this:

```
class FirstClass
{
}

namespace PHVIS
{
}
```

The `AddNamespace` method returns a `CodeNamespace` object, as in this example:

```
CodeNamespace cn;
cn =  fcm.AddNamespace("PHVIS", 0);
```

The `CodeNamespace` object can be used to add components to the `Namespace` or to make modifications to the `CodeNamespace` object itself (e.g., changing the Namespace's name or adding a comment to the Namespace, as described later in this chapter).

Using the Position Parameter

The position parameter is used in many of the code object methods, so you should be aware of the parameter's conventions:

- For most methods, passing -1 indicates that the component is to be added after all the other components in the file.
- Passing 0 indicates that the component is to be added before any other component in the file.

For most implementations of the methods discussed here, setting the position to a number greater than the number of components is equivalent to setting the position to -1. However, for some methods, setting the position to a number greater than the number of components will raise a "Value does not fall within the expected range" error.

Later in this chapter you'll be introduced to the CodeElement object, which represents a specific component in a code file (e.g., a Class). You can also use a CodeElement in the position parameter to add a new component following an existing component.

Working with Files and Folders

The filename passed to many methods can either be a relative or absolute file path, depending on the project type (most project types accept relative file paths). With a relative file path, to put the file in the main folder with the rest of the project's file, just use the name of the file as the examples in this chapter do; to put a file called Customer.cs in a subfolder named GeneratedCode, you'd use "GeneratedCode\Customer.cs."

Some project types require absolute addresses (for instance, "project-less" ASP.NET projects), forcing you to use the full path for the project. The following code retrieves the full pathname from the project and then appends a subfolder and filename to it. In this example, the project is retrieved through the document currently open in the editor:

```
Project prj;
string FilePath;

prj = _applicationObject.ActiveDocument.ProjectItem.ContainingProject;
```

```
FilePath = System.IO.Path.Combine(
                          System.IO.Path.GetDirectoryName(prj.FileName),
                          "GeneratedCode\\Customer.cs");
cm.AddNamespace("PHVIS", "FilePath", 0);
```

Ensuring Valid Names

When adding a Namespace (or any other component), you must use a valid name for the project type. Although the rules for what counts as a valid name vary from one language to another, you can determine if the name you want to use is valid for the project by using the CodeModel's IsValidID method. The IsValidID method accepts a single string parameter and returns True if the string is a valid identifier for the project type.

This example checks a string variable (called UsersNamespace) to determine if it's valid before creating a Namespace using that name:

```
if (cm.IsValidID(UsersNamespace))
{
  cm.AddNamespace(UsersNamespace, "Customer.cs", 0);
}
```

BEST PRACTICE In theory, the CreateUniqueId method (available from the CodeElements collection discussed later in this chapter) will return an automatically generated ID, guaranteed to be unique. However, the method so frequently raises a "not implemented" message that I haven't found it useful. You're welcome to try it, but you shouldn't count on it.

Adding Classes and Interfaces

To add a new class or an interface to your project, you can use one of three versions of the AddClass or AddInterface method, depending on what you want to accomplish:

- To create a new file containing the class or interface, use the CodeModel object.
- With an existing file, to add a class or interface, use either the CodeModel object or the FileCodeModel object.
- With an existing namespace in an existing file, to add a class or an interface, use the CodeNamespace object.

The `CodeModel`'s `AddClass` method expects to be passed six parameters:

- The name of the class.
- The name of the file.
- The position of the class in the file.
- An array of names of objects that the class will inherit from.
- An array of names of interfaces that the class is to implement. (It's your responsibility to add the members required by the interfaces.)
- An enumerated value indicating the class' scope (whether it is public, private, or the default for the project type).

The `AddInterface` method accepts the same parameters except that it omits the array of interface names. The `FileCodeModel` and `CodeNamespace`'s versions of the `AddClass` and `AddInterface` methods are almost identical to the `AddClass` method except that they omit the filename parameter.

Regardless of which object you use, `AddClass` returns a `CodeClass` object whereas the `AddInterface` method returns a `CodeInterface` object. These objects, like the `CodeNamespace` object, implement many of the methods of the `CodeModel2` interface. In the same way that the `FileCodeModel` is limited to manipulating components in a single file, the `CodeClass` is limited to manipulating components within a single class within a file; the `CodeInterface` is limited to manipulating components within a single interface within a file.

A minimal call to the `CodeModel`'s `AddClass` method would consist of the following:

- The name of the class
- The name of the file
- -1 as the file's position (to add the class to the end of the file)
- Two arrays with nothing in them (to specify no base classes or interfaces)
- The default setting for the class's scope

This example creates a class called `Customer` in a file called Customer.cs, using the default setting for the class's scope:

```
CodeClass cc;
object[] bases = { };
object[] interfaces = {   };
cc = cm.AddClass("Customer", "Customer.cs", -1, bases, interfaces,
                 vsCMAccess.vsCMAccessDefault);
```

If the Customer.cs file doesn't exist, it will be created; if the file does exist, the new class will be added after all other classes in the file.

The call to the `AddInterface` method is almost identical, except that you don't pass the interfaces parameter:

```
CodeInterface ci;
object[] bases = { };
ci = cm.AddInterface("ICustomer", "Customer.cs", -1, bases,
                     vsCMAccess.vsCMAccessDefault);
```

Using the `AddClass` or `AddInterface` method of the `FileClassModel` and the `CodeNamespace` objects is almost identical—you just omit the file-name parameter. The following code uses the `FileCodeModel`. The call specifies that the new `Class` is to inherit from a class called `PHVIS.Base` and is to implement two interfaces: `PHVIS.Transaction` and `PHVIS.Logging`. The call also passes 0 in the position parameter to make this class the first class in the file and explicitly sets the class's scope to `Public`:

```
object[] bases = {"PHVIS.Base"};
object[] interfaces = { "PHVIS.Transaction", "PHVIS.Logging" };
cc = fcm.AddClass("Customer", -1, bases, interfaces,
                     vsCMAccess.vsCMAccessPublic);
```

This code adds a public interface:

```
ci = fcm.AddInterface("ICustomer", -1, bases,
                     vsCMAccess.vsCMAccessPublic);
```

The result of calling the `AddClass` or `AddInterface` method on the `CodeNamespace` object is to nest the class or interface's code within the code represented by the `CodeNamespace` object. This code, for instance, creates a `Namespace` and then, using the returned `CodeNamespace`, adds a `Class` to the `Namespace`:

```
CodeNamespace cn;
cn =  fcm.AddNamespace("PHVIS", 0);
cc = cn.AddClass("Customer", -1, bases, interfaces,
                     vsCMAccess.vsCMAccessPublic);
```

The result would look something like this:

```
namespace PHVIS
{
 public class Customer : PHVIS.Base, PHVIS.Transaction, PHVIS.Logging
 {
 }
}
```

Very little error checking is done by any version of the `AddClass` or `AddInterface` method. If a class or interface with the same name already exists or you use an invalid name (e.g. `Customer$`), an error will be thrown. If the classes you're inheriting from don't exist, the `AddClass` method will still add the class or interface (though the resulting code won't compile, of course). As with namespaces, you can use the `IsValidID` method to check names before using them as class names.

You can use the `CodeClass` returned by the `AddClass` method to examine or further define the class. Most of the members of the `CodeClass` object support analyzing or modifying an existing class and will be covered later in this chapter. The same is true of the `CodeInterface` object.

Having said that, some members are useful when generating code. For instance, the only way to create a partial class is to set the `CodeClass`'s `ClassKind` property to the `vsCMClassKindPartialClass` enumerated value. Because the `ClassKind` property is only available on the `CodeModel2` interface, you must first cast your object to that interface, as this code does:

```
CodeClass2 cc2;
cc2 = (CodeClass2) cc;
cc2.ClassKind = EnvDTE80.vsCMClassKind.vsCMClassKindPartialClass;
```

If a class is a partial class, you can use its `PartialClasses` collection to iterate through all of the related partial classes:

```
if (cc2.ClassKind == EnvDTE80.vsCMClassKind.vsCMClassKindPartialClass)
{
   foreach (CodeClass2 pc in cc2.PartialClasses)
   {
   ...process related partial classes...
   }
}
```

Setting the `CodeClass2`'s `IsAbstract` property to True will make the class abstract; setting its `IsShared` property will make the class shared/static. The `IsGeneric` property, however, is read-only.

You can also use the `CodeClass`'s `AddImplementedInterface` method to add an interface to the class. This method adds an interface called `PHVIS.Transaction` to a class:

```
cc.AddImplementedInterface("PHVIS.Transaction", 1);
```

You can have your class derive from another class by using the `CodeClass`'s `AddBase` method. You can pass the `AddBase` method either a `CodeClass` object or the fully qualified name for a class, along with the position parameter. This example adds the `PHVIS.Logging` class to a `CodeClass` object:

```
cc.AddBase("PHVIS.Logging", -1);
```

A couple of things to be aware of: Although the `AddBase` method doesn't check to see if the class exists, the `AddImplementedInterface` does check to see if the interface exists and won't add an interface that can't be found. Neither the `AddBase` nor `AddImplementedInterface` add the signatures for the members of the base class or the interface—that is your responsibility.

When you add a class using templates, you may find that a class added through a template is derived from a class you don't want. You can use the `RemoveBase` method of the `CodeClass` object to remove a base class, just by passing the fully qualified name for the class:

```
cc.RemoveBase("PHVIS.Logging");
```

Similarly, if you find that a template contains a property or method that you don't want, you can remove it with the `RemoveMember` method. This example removes a member named `Delete`:

```
cc.RemoveMember("Delete");
```

BEST PRACTICE The `Remove*` methods are also useful when you're regenerating code because they let you selectively remove items that are either no longer required or need to be replaced.

Adding Delegates

If you're reading this chapter sequentially, you can probably predict how to use the code model objects to add a delegate to your code. The key difference between the AddDelegate method (available on the CodeModel, FileCodeModel, and CodeClass objects) and the previous methods is that you're more likely to use the CodeDelegate object returned by the AddDelegate method because it provides you with a way to add parameters to your delegate.

The AddDelegate method on the CodeModel object accepts five parameters:

- The name of the delegate
- The file to add the delegate to (omitted in the FileCodeModel and CodeClass versions)
- The data type returned from the delegate (must be one of the predefined types in the vsCMTypeRef enumeration)
- The delegate's position in the list of components in the file
- An enumerated value specifying the delegate's scope

The method returns a CodeDelegate object.

This example creates a delegate called InvalidCustomerIdEventHandler in the file Customer.cs that returns a value of type String. The delegate is to be added to the top of the file and is to have the default scope for the project type:

```
CodeDelegate cd;
cd = cm.AddDelegate("InvalidCustomerIdEventHandler", "Customer.cs",
      vsCMTypeRef.vsCMTypeRefString, 0, vsCMAccess.vsCMAccessDefault);
```

The result would look like this:

```
delegate string InvalidCustomerIdEventHandler ();
```

Adding Parameters

Most delegates will include parameters in their definition. For instance, if the delegate is being used to define an event, the .NET convention is as follows:

- The first parameter is named sender and is of type Object.
- The second parameter is named e and is some object that inherits from System.Eventarg.

You can add parameters to a delegate using the AddParameter method of the CodeDelegate object returned by the AddDelegate method. This method is passed:

- The name of the parameter
- The data type of the parameter (again, using the `vsCMTypeRef` enumeration)
- The position of the parameter in the list of parameters for the delegate

This example creates a public delegate called `InvalidCustomerId EventHandler` and then adds two parameters to it that almost meet the requirements for an event handler (the `e` parameter in this example is the wrong type). The delegate in this example doesn't return a value, so I pass `vsCMTypeRefVoid` in the third parameter. This example passes -1 for the position parameter to have each parameter added to the end of the list:

```
cd = cm.AddDelegate("MyDelegate", "Customer.cs",
        vsCMTypeRef.vsCMTypeRefVoid, 0, vsCMAccess.vsCMAccessPublic);
cd.AddParameter("sender", vsCMTypeRef.vsCMTypeRefObject, -1);
cd.AddParameter("e", vsCMTypeRef.vsCMTypeRefObject, -1);
```

The result would look like this:

```
public delegate void MyDelegate(object sender, object e);
```

Using Custom Data Types

If you want your delegate to return a value, to define a parameter using a data type not available in `vsCMTypeRef`, or to create a generic, you have two choices:

- Specify the fully qualified name of the data type instead of passing a `vsCMTypeRef` object.
- Create a custom `CodeTypeRef` object that describes the data type.

BEST PRACTICE   The simplest solution is to pass the fully qualified name.

The following example corrects the problem in my earlier example that didn't specify the right data type for the `e` parameter of an event delegate. This code sets the data type of the parameter to an object that, presumably, inherits from `System.EventArg`:

```
cd.AddParameter("e", "PHVIS.InvalidCustomerIDEventArg", -1);
```

Updating the earlier example with this new code generates the correct definition for an event delegate:

```
public delegate void MyDelegate(object sender,
                        PHVIS.InvalidCustomerIDEventArg e);
```

Using CodeTypeRef Objects

The problem with passing a string to specify the data type is that you get no error-checking on the data type until runtime and no design-time support when writing your code. A partial solution is to use the `CodeModel`'s `CreateCodeTypeRef` method, passing the fully qualified name of the data type you want to use. The best practice is to create a method that returns a `CodeTypeRef` object that can be used in the `AddParameter` method. Wrapping the `CreateCodeTypeRef` method in a function centralizes the creation of the `CodeTypeRef` and, at least, limits the extent of the problem.

As an example, this function—when passed the `CodeModel` object for a project—returns a `CodeTypeRef` object that represents a generic `List` object containing `PHVIS.Customer` objects (i.e., `System.Collections.Generic.List<PHVIS.Customer>`):

```
public CodeTypeRef ListOfCustomersCodeType(CodeModel cm)
{
  CodeTypeRef ctr;
  ctr = cm.CreateCodeTypeRef(
          "System.Collections.Generic.List<PHVIS.Customer>");
  return ctr;
}
```

This function can now be used when creating a parameter. The following code retrieves the `CodeModel` for the item currently selected in Solution Explorer and creates a delegate. The code then passes the `CodeModel` to my `ListOfCustomerCode` function. The `CodeTypeRef` returned by the function is then used with the `AddParameter` method to add a parameter called `Customers` to the delegate:

```
cm = _applicationObject.SelectedItems.Item(1).ProjectItem.
                ContainingProject.CodeModel;
cd = cm.AddDelegate("MyDelegate", "Customer.cs",
      vsCMTypeRef.vsCMTypeRefVoid, 0, vsCMAccess.vsCMAccessPublic);
```

```
CodeTypeRef ctr;
ctr = ListOfCustomersCodeType(cm);
cd.AddParameter("Customers",ctr, -1);
```

The result would look like this:

```
public delegate void MyDelegate(
        System.Collections.Generic.List<PHVIS.Customer> Customers);
```

There are still two problems with this strategy. The first is that, because the string passed to the `CreateCodeTypeRef` method uses C# syntax to specify the generic, this code assumes that the generated code is going to be used in a C# project—the generated code won't compile in a Visual Basic project (although, because you can't use the code model objects to add components in a Visual Basic project, the point is moot). The same would be true if the parameter accepted an array or any other construct that uses language-specific syntax. Creating a fully functional version of this function would require you to check the language being used and adjust the syntax used in the string passed to the `CreateCodeTypeRef` method. Later in this chapter, in the section on analyzing code using `CodeElements`, you'll see how to check the language that the code is written in.

BEST PRACTICE   If you don't want to tie your solution to a single language, consider using the CodeDom (as described in Chapter 6) rather than hard-coding support for different languages.

The second problem is that this strategy will only work if you have access to the `CodeModel` object for the project—something that isn't available in projectless ASP.NET applications.

Adding Enumerations

You can add enumerated values to your code using the `AddEnum` method of the `CodeModel` and `CodeClass` objects. On the `CodeModel`, the method expects to be passed the following:

- The name of the enumerated value
- The name of the file to put the enumeration in
- The position within the file

- An array of class names that the enumeration can inherit from
- The scope of the enumeration

The `CodeModel` version omits the filename.

The method returns a `CodeEnum` object. Using the `CodeEnum`'s `AddMember` method, you can add members to the enumeration. The `AddEnum` method must be passed three parameters:

- The name of the enumerated value.
- The value to be assigned to the enumerated value. (If you pass a zero-length string, no value is assigned.)
- The position of the value within the enumeration.

This example creates an enumeration called `CustomerCreditType` with three values: Deadbeat, Standard, and Prime. The Prime value is set to the value 99:

```
object[] bases = {  };

ce = cm.AddEnum("CustomerCreditType", "Customer.cs", 0, bases,
                                vsCMAccess.vsCMAccessDefault);
ce.AddMember("Deadbeat", "", 0);
ce.AddMember("Standard", "", -1);
ce.AddMember("Prime", "99", 0);
```

The resulting code looks like this:

```
enum MyEnum
{
 Deadbeat,
 Standard,
 Prime = 99,
}
```

Adding Structures

The `AddStruct` method of the `CodeModel`, `CodeNamespace`, and `CodeClass` objects lets you add structures to your code. The `CodeModel` version of this method requires six parameters:

- The structure's name
- The filename
- The position
- An array of base object names
- An array of interface names
- The scope of the structure

The method returns a CodeStruct object. The CodeNamespace and CodeClass versions of this method omit the filename. You add members to the structure using the CodeStruct's AddVariable method. (I describe the AddVariable method in more detail after the section on adding functions).

The following code creates a structure called CustomerData in the file Customer.cs. It then adds two variables to the structure: a string named CustomerID and one called CustomerType that uses a custom enumeration. Because the position of both variables is 0 (indicating they should appear at the start of the list) the second variable added will appear first in the structure:

```
cs = cm.AddStruct("CustomerData", "Customer.cs", 0, bases, interfaces,
                  vsCMAccess.vsCMAccessDefault);
cs.AddVariable("CustomerID", "System.String", 0,
                    vsCMAccess.vsCMAccessPublic, null);
cs.AddVariable("CustomerType", " CustomerCreditType", 0,
                    vsCMAccess.vsCMAccessPublic, null);
```

The resulting code looks like this, assuming that the arrays of bases and interfaces contain nothing:

```
struct CustomerData
{
 public CustomerCreditType CustomerType;
 public string CustomerID;
}
```

After you create the structure, you can set the CodeStruct's IsShared property to True to make the structure Shared/Static.

Adding Functions

You can add a function to a class by calling the CodeClass's AddFunction method, passing six parameters:

- The name of the function.
- The function's type (an enumerated value in the vsCMFunction enumeration).
- The data type returned by the function.
- The position of the function in the class.
- The function's scope.
- The file to place the function in. (This parameter is ignored.)

The method returns a CodeFunction object.

This example creates a function named MyFunction:

```
CodeFunction cf;
cf = cc.AddFunction("MyFunction", vsCMFunction.vsCMFunctionFunction,
              "System.String",0, vsCMAccess.vsCMAccessDefault,
              "Customers.cs");
```

The resulting code would look like this:

```
string MyFunction()
{
 return default(string);
}
```

Some notes on the function type parameter:

- The function type parameter lets you specify the type of function. To create a constructor, for instance, you would pass vsCMFunction.vsCMFunctionConstructor as the function type.
- The function type overrides other parameters. For instance, if you pass vsCMFunction.vsCMFunctionConstructor as the function type, the function name and return type are ignored.
- Not all function types are implemented for all project types. For instance, using the vsCMFunction.vsCMFunctionPropertyGet type in a C# project will raise a "not implemented" error in some versions of Visual Studio.
- Although the vsCMFunction enumeration contains a type of vsCMFunctionVirtual, it doesn't seem to work with C# projects. Setting the CodeFunction's CanOverride property does, however, create a virtual function.

- Function types can be OR'd together to create a function with multiple characteristics, assuming that the resulting type is supported by the project type.

Once the function has been created you can set the `CodeFunction`'s `IsShared` property to make the function Shared/Static or the `MustImplement` and `CanOverride` property to create virtual or abstract functions. As with the `CodeDelegate` object, the `IsGeneric` property is read-only, though.

Also, once the function has been created, you can add parameters using the `AddParameter` method of the `CodeFunction` object. (I described the `AddParameter` method earlier.)

This example creates a class called `Customer` and then adds a constructor to it with two string parameters named `CompanyID` and `CustomerName`:

```
cc = cm.AddClass("Customer", "Customer.cs", -1, bases, interfaces,
                    vsCMAccess.vsCMAccessDefault);
cf = cc.AddFunction("", vsCMFunction.vsCMFunctionConstructor,
                    "", 0, vsCMAccess.vsCMAccessPublic, "");
cf.AddParameter("CompanyID","System.String",0);
cf.AddParameter("CustomerName", "System.String", -1);
```

The resulting code looks like this:

```
public Customer(string CompanyID, string CustomerName)
{
}
```

AddProperty

The `AddProperty` method of the `CodeClass` object lets you add properties to your class. This method accepts five parameters:

- The name of the property setter.
- The name of the property getter. (In C#, the name of the property setter and getter must be identical.)
- The data type of the property.
- The property's scope.
- The file to place the property in. (This parameter is ignored.)

The method returns a CodeProperty object.

This example creates a public string property called `CompanyID` and puts it before any other components in the class:

```
CodeProperty cp = cc.AddProperty("CompanyID","CompanyID",
                     vsCMTypeRef.vsCMTypeRefString, 0,
                     vsCMAccess.vsCMAccessPublic, null);
```

The resulting property would look like this:

```
public string CompanyID
{
  get
  {
    return default(string);
  }
  set
  {
  }
}
```

To create a read-only property set the getter parameter to null or Nothing.

Because the keyword `this` can't be used in adding a property, you can't use `AddProperty` to add either an indexer or extension method. Because the `IsGeneric` property is read-only, you also cannot create a generic property.

Once the property has been created, you can set the `CodeProperty`'s `IsShared` property to make the function Shared/Static (provided you are working with a `CodeProperty2` object). However, depending on the language, you may not be able to cast a `CodeProperty` object to `CodeProperty2`. In that scenario, your alternative is to access the property's getter and setter routines through the `CodeProperty` object's `Getter` and `Setter` properties. The `IsShared` property on the `Getter` and `Setter` objects can be changed even for `CodeProperty` objects:

```
CodeProperty cp = cc.AddProperty("CompanyID","CompanyID",
                     vsCMTypeRef.vsCMTypeRefString, 0,
                     vsCMAccess.vsCMAccessPublic, null);
cp.Getter.IsShared = true;
cp.Setter.IsShared = true;
```

The `MustImplement` and `CanOverride` properties for the `CodeProperty` object are simpler: You must always set those properties on the `Getter` and `Setter`.

Adding Variables

The `AddVariable` method of the `CodeClass` object lets you add class-level variables/fields to a class. (There's no equivalent method on the `CodeFunction` object, unfortunately, so you can't create local variables using the code model objects.) The method takes five parameters:

- Variable name.
- Variable type.
- Position for the variable.
- Variable scope.
- File for the variable. (This is ignored.)

The method returns a `CodeVariable` object.

This code adds a private string variable named `CustomerId` to the class, putting it before any other components in the class:

```
cv = cc.AddVariable("CustomerId", vsCMTypeRef.vsCMTypeRefString, 0,
                vsCMAccess.vsCMAccessPrivate,"Customer.cs");
```

Once you've created the variable, you can set its `IsShared` property to make the variable Shared/Static.

After you've created the variable, you can also set its initial value using the `CodeVariable`'s `InitExpression` property. It's your responsibility to set any required delimiters. This example initializes the variable to a string value of 3:

```
cv.InitExpression = "\"3\"";
```

The results of these two sets of code would look like this:

```
private string CustomerId = "3";
```

However, to create a variable tied to a delegate or a structure, you'll have to use the `CodeModel`'s `CreateTypeCodeRef` or insert the fully qualified name of the object you want to use. This example creates a variable tied to an enumeration, for instance:

```
cv = cc.AddVariable("CustomerData", " PHVIS.CustomerCreditType", 0,
                vsCMAccess.vsCMAccessPrivate, "Customer.cs");
```

Similarly, initializing an object variable to a new instance of an object requires passing language-specific code to the InitExpression property.

BEST PRACTICE Using the CodeDom (as described in Chapter 6) would allow you to initialize the object without using language-specific code.

Although you can't create a generic or an array using the code model objects, you can create a constant by setting the CodeVariable2's ConstKind property to a member of the vsCMConstKind enumerated value. This example creates a string variable called BadRating and initializes it to a string value of "Bad". The code then casts the resulting CodeVariable to a CodeVariable2 and sets the ConstKind property to turn this variable into a constant:

```
cv = cc.AddVariable("BadRating", vsCMTypeRef.vsCMTypeRefString, 0,
                    vsCMAccess.vsCMAccessPrivate,null);
cv.InitExpression = "\"Bad\"";

CodeVariable2 cv2;
cv2 = (CodeVariable2) cv;
cv2.ConstKind = vsCMConstKind.vsCMConstKindConst;
```

The resulting code looks like this:

```
private const string BadRating = "Bad";
```

To create a read-only variable (a variable whose value can only be set in a constructor), set the ConstKind property to vsCMConstKind.vsCMConstKindReadOnly.

Adding Attributes to Components

Once you've added a component to your project, you may want to decorate it with an attribute. The AddAttribute method of the component you want to add the attribute to allows you to specify the name of the attribute and the parameters to be passed to the attribute's constructor.

To call the AddAttribute method from the most objects, you only need to provide three parameters:

- The name of the attribute.
- The values to pass to the attribute's constructor. This can be a comma-delimited list of values if the attribute's constructor requires multiple parameters. It's your responsibility to provide any delimiters required by the values. If the attribute requires no parameters, you can pass null as this parameter.
- The position of the attribute among any other attributes already decorating the class. Position can't be set to -1.

The following code uses the AddClass method to add a class to a file and retrieve the resulting CodeClass object. Using the CodeClass object's AddAddtribute method, the code then adds an attribute called MyAttribute to the class, passing a comma-delimited parameter list consisting of the values 2 and 5:

```
CodeClass cc;
cc = fcm.AddClass("Customer",  0, bases, interfaces,
vsCMAccess.vsCMAccessDefault);
cc.AddAttribute("MyAttribute", "2, 5", -1);
```

The result would look like this:

```
[MyAttribute(2, 5)]
    class Customer : PHVIS.Base, PHVIS.Transaction, PHVIS.Logging
```

The AddAttribute method of the CodeModel object and the FileCodeModel lets you add assembly attributes to a file. The CodeModel's version of the AddAttribute method requires that you pass four parameters:

- The name of the attribute
- The name of the file
- The values to pass to the attribute's constructor
- The position to place the attribute

The method also returns a CodeAttribute object.

This example adds an attribute called MyAttribute to the Customer.cs file with a parameter of 14:

```
cm.AddAttribute("MyAttribute", "Customer.cs", "14", 0);
```

The result would look like this:

```
[assembly: MyAttribute(14)]
```

The `AddAttribute` method on the `FileCodeModel` object omits the file parameter. This code uses the `FileCodeModel` to create an attribute, passing two literal string parameters ("Peter" and "Consultant") to the attribute's constructor. Because it is passing string parameters, this example escapes the double quotes around the string literals:

```
fcm.AddAttribute("MyAttribute", "\"Peter\",\"Consultant\"", 0);
```

The result would look like this:

```
[assembly: MyAttribute("Peter", "Consultant")]
```

Once the attribute is added, you can add code to set properties on the attribute through the `AddArgument` method of the `CodeAttribute2` object. The first step, then, is to cast the result returned by the `AddAttribute` method to a `CodeAttribute2` object:

```
CodeAttribute ca;
ca = cm.AddAttribute("MyAttribute", "Customer.cs", "14", 0);
CodeAttribute2 ca2;
ca2 = (CodeAttribute2) ca;
```

The `AddArgument` method accepts three parameters:

- The value that the property is to be set to
- The name of the property
- The position

This example sets the property called Company to the literal string "PH&V IS", following any existing entries:

```
ca2.AddArgument("\"PH&V IS\"","Company",-1);
```

The result, based on the earlier example, would look like this:

```
[assembly: MyAttribute(14, Company = "PH&V IS")]
```

Because property settings must follow the values being passed to the attribute's constructor, don't pass 0 in the `AddAttribute`'s position parameter when adding a property setting unless the attribute has a constructor that accepts no values.

Again, very little error-checking is done. If, for instance, you specify the name of an attribute that doesn't exist, the `AddAttribute` method will still run to completion.

Modifying and Analyzing Components

Now that you're familiar with adding code components to your application, it's time to look at analyzing the code in your application. Analyzing code may seem like a topic that's out of place in a book on generating new code. However, analyzing existing code is essential to support two key criteria for a successful code-generation solution:

- The developer must be able to regenerate the solution. To support regenerating code, you need to be able to find the components of the previous generation and remove them.
- Code-generation solutions build upon and integrate with existing code. To be able to integrate with the developer's already existing code, you need a tool for finding out what code already exists.

Even ignoring those two considerations, once you've added a component to your code, you can modify it using the properties on the component itself. As you've seen, not all the options you might want to set on a component can be specified in the method that adds the component, so modifying components you've just added is a critical part of generating code.

Finding Projects and Project Items

A solution consists of multiple projects, and projects consist of multiple files. You can process all the projects in a solution by using the `Solution` object's `Projects` collection. You can identify a project by its `Name`, `FullName` (the solution name + project name), or `UniqueName` (the full physical path name for the project's folder) properties. This code finds a `Project` in the "c:\Projects\MyProject" folder:

```
foreach (Project prj in _applicationObject.Solution.Projects)
{
  if (System.IO.Path.GetDirectoryName(prj.FullName) ==
              @"c:\\Projects\\MyProject ")
  {
```

```
    }
}
```

This code drills down through the first project in a solution to find a `ProjectItem` named Default.aspx.cs and then extracts the `FileCodeModel` for the item:

```
Project prj;
prj = _applicationObject.Solution.Projects.Item(1);
foreach (ProjectItem pji in prj.ProjectItems)
  {
    if (pji.Name == "Default.aspx.cs")
    {
      FileCodeModel2 cm = (FileCodeModel2) pji.FileCodeModel;
    }
  }
```

However, this also reveals another difference between Visual Basic and C# project websites. In a C# website, the Default.aspx.cs file is part of the `ProjectItems` collection accessible from the `Projects` object. In a Visual Basic project, however, Default.aspx.vb is part of the `ProjectItems` collection of the Default.aspx `ProjectItem`. Therefore, the following code would be necessary to drill down to the Default.aspx.vb file:

```
Project prj;
prj = _applicationObject.Solution.Projects.Item(1);
foreach (ProjectItem pji in prj.ProjectItems)
{
  if (pji.Name == "Default.aspx")
  {
    foreach (ProjectItem pjiDefault in pji.ProjectItems)
    {
      if (pjiDefault.Name == "Default.aspx.vb")
      {

      }
    }
  }
}
```

Because of these differences, it may be easier to find components by using the `Solution` object's `FindProjectItem`. Passed the name of a project item (e.g., the name of the file holding a class), the method returns the corresponding `ProjectItem`. This code finds the file Default.aspx.cs:

```
ProjectItem pji = _applicationObject.Solution.
                        FindProjectItem("Default.aspx.vb");
```

If there is no matching item, the method returns Nothing or null.

Unfortunately, there is no free lunch. If there are multiple items with the same name (though in different projects), `FindProjectItem` returns the first matching item. Because the `FindProjectItem` is part of the `Solution` object, this means you can't be sure which project the item is found in. If, for instance, the solution had two ASP.NET Visual Basic websites loaded, the previous code would return the Default.aspx.vb file from the first project. To improve the odds that you get the component you want, you can include more information in the search string.

For instance, by including the project name in the search string, I can ensure that I get the Default.aspx.vb file in that project for many project types. This code accesses the second project in the solution by using its name as part of the string passed to `FindProjectItem`:

```
Project prj;
prj = _applicationObject.Solution.Projects.Item(2);
ProjectItem pji = _applicationObject.Solution.FindProjectItem(
                        prj.Name + @"\Default.aspx.vb");
```

Unfortunately, for most project types, prefixing the filename with just the project name isn't enough—the `FindProjectItem` will return null unless you provide the full physical pathname (or just the filename—but that may not find the right file). The `FullName` of the project does provide the full physical path to the project file but also includes the name of the project file itself. Fortunately, you can pull the physical path from the `FullName` property, as this code does, and add that to the name of the file you want:

```
ProjectItem pji = _applicationObject.Solution.FindProjectItem(
    System.Io.Path.GetDirectory(prj.FullName) + @"\Default.aspx.vb");
```

Reading Project Properties

Once you have retrieved a `Project` object, you can read its properties (you cannot add new properties, however). The `Project` object's `Properties` collection allows you to access each individual `Property` object, retrieving the `Property` object's `Value` property. This code in an ASP.NET application checks each `Property`'s `Name` property and sets the `Value` property for the `StartPage` property:

```
foreach(Property prop in prj.Properties)
{
 if (prop.Name == "StartPage")
 {
  prop.Value = "NewDefault.aspx";
 }
}
```

Rather than iterate through the `Properties` collection, you can use its `Item` method to retrieve the `Property` object you want. This code does the same thing as the previous example but without the loop:

```
Property prop2;
prop2 = prj.Properties.Item("StartPage");
prop2.Value = "NewDefault.aspx";
```

If a `Property` object's `NumIndices` property is greater than 0, it indicates that the `Property` has indexed values. However, I haven't needed to use those as part of a code-generation project.

Removing Items

As part of regenerating code, you may want to remove a file containing code from a previous generation. The `Remove` method of the `ProjectItem` will remove the item from the project. If the item is a folder, the `Remove` method will remove the folder and everything in it. This code would remove the `ProjectItem` item found in the previous code:

```
pji.Remove();
```

Although the `Remove` method eliminates the item from the project, the item remains on the disk in the folder. For most code-regeneration scenarios, you'll also want to remove the item from the disk. For that you should use the `Delete` method:

```
pji.Delete();
```

Checking for Changes

The `Project` object's `IsDirty` property will be set to True if there have been changes made at the project level (e.g., adding new `class` files) that haven't been saved. You may want to check this property and give the developer a chance to save changes before generating new code.

Processing Components in a File

Once you've retrieved a specific file, you'll want to process the components of a file. This section discusses how to retrieve a component in a file and how to work with the retrieved component.

Processing All the Components in a File

All the components recognized by the `FileCodeModel` share the `CodeElement2` type. Each code element has a collection holding all of its child elements. A code file, for instance, has a collection of all the "top-level" elements in the file: `using`/`import` statements, namespaces (or classes), and the like. A namespace, in turn, has a collection of children that includes classes, fields, and so on.

To process all the elements in a file, you can take advantage of those collections to loop through `CodeElements` in the file. This is the technique you'll need to use if you want to determine what's in a file you haven't generated. (I'm assuming that if you have generated the code in the file, you'll know the names of the components and can retrieve them by name using the techniques in the next section.)

To demonstrate this technique, I'll process this sample code from a Windows Forms application:

```
using System;
using System.Collections.Generic;

namespace SampleCodeModel
{
```

```
    // A class level comment
    /// <summary>Code generated using the FileCodeModel</summary>
    public partial class Form1 : Form
    {
        public Form1()
        {
            InitializeComponent();
        }
    }
    // A trailing class level comment

}
```

This code retrieves the `FileCodeModel` for the file currently open in the editor window and retrieves the top-level elements in the file from the `FileCodeModel`'s `CodeElements` collection:

```
FileCodeModel2 fcm = (FileCodeModel2)
        _applicationObject.ActiveDocument.ProjectItem.FileCodeModel;
```

The next step is to loop through all the `CodeElements` in the collection. In this code I'm using the `CodeElement2` interface available in Visual Studio 2008 (in Visual Studio 2005, use the `CodeElement` interface). This code would find the `using` statements and the namespace in the Windows Form code:

```
foreach (CodeElement2 elmFileChild in fcm.CodeElements)
{
```

Although the `FileCodeModel` has a `CodeElements` collection, to retrieve the components under a `CodeElement` object you must use the `CodeElement`'s `Children` property.

BEST PRACTICES   Not all elements have children; therefore, before attempting to access the children of any `CodeElement`, check the `Kind` property on the `CodeElement`—this property tells you what kind of element you've just retrieved.

The `Kind` property returns a value from the `vsCMElement` enumeration: An `Import` or `using` statement, for instance, will return the value `vsCMElementImportStmt`, whereas a `Namespace` will return `vsCMElementNamespace`.

This code checks to see if the retrieved element represents a Namespace and, if it does, starts a block that will process the Namespace's children:

```
if (elmFileChild.Kind == vsCMElement.vsCMElementNamespace)
{
```

Within the Namespace, I want to find any classes it may contain. The following code checks to see if one of the children of the Namespace is a class and then processes all the components in the class. For the Windows Form class, this code will find the constructor (Form1) and the event handler (button1_Click):

```
foreach (CodeElement2 elmNamespaceChild in elmFileChild.Children)
{
 if (elmNamespaceChild.Kind == vsCMElement.vsCMElementClass)
 {
   foreach (CodeElement2 elmClassChild in elmNamespaceChild.Children)
   {
     ...processing Form1 and button1_Click ...
   }
 }
}
```

Because CodeElements processes the text in the file, you'll need to treat Visual Basic and C# files differently. Although Visual Basic projects always have a namespace, it's not standard practice to include the Namespace in the text of the project files (unlike C#). Instead, in Visual Basic, the Namespace is set in the project's properties. As a result, in Visual Basic files, the top-level components accessed through the FileCodeModel's CodeElements collection will normally be classes; in C# files, the top-level components will normally be a namespace.

Once you've retrieved a CodeElement, you can use its properties to retrieve information about the component. Some components can also be cast to a CodeType object (discussed later), which gives you more options both when finding and modifying code.

Retrieving Components by Name

You can retrieve components from the collection they are part of using the Item method of CodeElements collection (for the FileCodeModel object) or the Children collection (for the CodeElement object). This code retrieves the

CodeElement representing the Namespace from the sample Windows Forms code shown earlier. After retrieving the Namespace, the code uses the CodeNamespace's Item method to retrieve the Form1 element:

```
CodeElement ceNs = fileCM.CodeElements.Item("MyNamespace");
CodeElement ceCl = ceNs.Children.Item("Form1");
```

Requesting an element that doesn't exist will raise an ArgumentException error.

Although working with CodeElements restricts you to searching for components in a specific file, you can search for some components (those that are represented by CodeType objects) across all the files in a project. I'll show you how to do that in the section on working with the CodeType object.

Retrieving Components by Location

Four members of the CodeElement object are useful when working with the CodeEditor objects to manipulate text in the file and will be discussed in detail in Chapter 4: StartPoint, EndPoint, GetStartPoint, and GetEndPoint. Start and end points describe where a component's code begins and ends in the file.

However, the FileCodeModel's CodeElementFromPoint provides you with another way to retrieve elements. When passed a StartPoint and the vcCMElement enumeration that represents the CodeElement that the point is inside of, CodeElementFromPoint returns the CodeElement containing the StartPoint. This code passes a StartPoint from within a class and the vsCMElementNamespace value. As a result, the CodeElement representing the Namespace that the StartPoint is inside of is returned:

```
CodeElement ceNs = fcm.CodeElementFromPoint(cls.StartPoint,
                              vsCMElement.vsCMElementFunction);
```

The same code, using the same StartPoint but with vsCMElementClass passed in the second parameter, returns the enclosing Class:

```
CodeElement ceCl = fcm.CodeElementFromPoint(cls.StartPoint,
                              vsCMElement.vsCMElementClass);
```

Working with Retrieved Elements

Typically, once you've retrieved an element, you'll want to modify it. This section covers how to modify elements that you've retrieved.

Determining If an Element Can Be Modified

The `InfoLocation` property will tell you whether you can retrieve information about the `CodeElement` and whether it can be modified. Here are the three values the property returns:

- **vsCMInfoLocationProject**—You can retrieve information about the `CodeElement` and modify it.
- **vsCMInfoLocationExternal**—You can retrieve information about the `CodeElement` but it may require using Reflection to pull information from the DLL (or pulling information from some other location). You won't be able to modify the `CodeElement`.
- **vsCMInfoLocationNone**—No information is available about the `CodeElement` and it can't be modified.

The `Name` property on the `CodeElement` returns the name of the current code element, whereas the `FullName` property returns the fully qualified name. Using the sample Windows Form code from earlier in this chapter, the `Class` file's `Name` property would return "Form1" whereas `FullName` (namespace + class name) would return "SampleCodeModel.Form1."

Be aware that changing some properties on a `CodeElement` can invalidate that object. For instance, if you set a variable to point to a `CodeElement` and use the `Name` property to change the `CodeElement`'s name, the variable may no longer be valid and using it may raise an error. After this code executes, for instance, using the `ceFunction` variable may result in an error:

```
CodeElement ceFunction;
ceFunction = ceForm.Children.Item("MyFunction");
ceFunction.Name = "YourFunction"
```

BEST PRACTICE   When a `CodeElement` is invalidated, reset the variable to point to the `CodeElement` under its new name:

```
ceFunction = ceForm.Children.Item("YourFunction");
```

Writing Language-Specific Code

The CodeElement's Language property returns the GUID for the language that the code is written in. Fortunately, these GUIDs are held in the CodeModelLanguageConstants so you can test for the enumerated value rather than hard-coding the GUIDs (constants exist for C#, Visual Basic, Visual C++, and IDL).

Earlier in this chapter, I provided a function that returns a CodeTypeRef object for data types not supported by the code model (e.g., a generic List object). Using the Language property, I can rewrite that function to generate the correct code for the current language. The first step is to extend the function to accept a second parameter, the CodeElement being processed. The second step is to use the CodeElement's Language property to check for the language the code is written in and generate a CodeTypeRef using the appropriate language:

```
public CodeTypeRef ListOfCustomersCodeType(CodeModel cm,
                                           CodeElement ce)
{
  if (ce.Language ==
        EnvDTE.CodeModelLanguageConstants.vsCMLanguageCSharp
  {
   CodeTypeRef ctr;
   ctr = cm.CreateCodeTypeRef(
           "System.Collections.Generic.List<PHVIS.Customer>");
   return ctr;
  }
  if (ce.Language ==
        EnvDTE.CodeModelLanguageConstants.vsCMLanguageVB
  {
   CodeTypeRef ctr;
   ctr = cm.CreateCodeTypeRef(
           "System.Collections.Generic.List(of PHVIS.Customer)");
   return ctr;
  }
}
```

Using CodeElement with the Position Parameter

As mentioned earlier, any of the Add* methods (AddClass, AddParameter) will accept a CodeElement in the position parameter. This allows you to insert new code following specific items already in a file. The following code finds a file named Default.aspx.cs, extracts its `FileCodeModel`, and then searches the file for the first class in the file. Once the code finds that class, it adds a new class following it:

```
Project prj;
ProjectItem pji = _applicationObject.Solution.
                    FindProjectItem(prj.Name + @"\Default.aspx.cs");
if (pji != null)
{
 FileCodeModel fcm = pji.FileCodeModel;
 foreach (CodeElement ce in fcm.CodeElements)
 {
  if (ce.Kind == vsCMElement.vsCMElementClass)
  {
   object[] bases = { };
   object[] interfaces = { };
   fcm.AddClass("NewClass", ce, bases, interfaces,
              vsCMAccess.vsCMAccessPublic);
  }
 }
}
```

Choosing Interfaces

Once you've retrieved a `CodeElement`, you have three choices when modifying it. First, you can cast the `CodeElement` to the correct `Code*` object type (e.g., `CodeClass`, `CodeNamespace`). You can then use the members of the `Code*` object to modify the `CodeElement`.

This code, after determining that a `CodeElement` object is a `Namespace`, casts the code element to a `CodeNamespace` object:

```
if (elmFileChild.Kind == vsCMElement.vsCMElementNamespace)
{
 CodeNamespace ns = (CodeNamespace) elmFileChild;
```

Second, to write general-purpose code that will work with any code component, you can manipulate the component through the members on the `CodeElement` object. The `CodeElement` object, however, provides a more limited range of options for manipulating code than the `Code*` object.

Your third choice is to cast the CodeElement to a CodeType object, which provides more options for working with code than CodeElement (although not as many as the specific Code* object). The restriction on CodeType is that only a limited number of CodeElement objects (classes, interfaces, delegates, structures, and enumerations) can be cast to a CodeType object. The IsCodeType property tells you if a CodeElement can be cast as a CodeType object. In the next few sections, I discuss using the CodeType. Because some members are repeated between the CodeType and CodeElement object (e.g., FullName), much of what I say here also applies to the CodeElement object.

The CodeEvent Object

Although the CodeModel does support a CodeEvent object for working with Visual Basic event declarations, it's not much use. To begin with, there is no AddEvent method to create a CodeEvent object as part of code generation. Using the CodeElement collection, it is possible to find and process event declarations in Visual Basic code. However, there's no way to process the parameters on an event declaration.

Working with the CodeType Objects

The CodeType object provides you with additional functionality over and above what's available with the Code* or CodeElement objects. For instance, using the CodeType objects allows you to find a component in your project no matter what file it's in. You could use this feature, for instance, to retrieve code you've generated without having to keep track of what file you put it in. Often, the CodeType object provides an easier way to navigate the components of a class.

Finding Components with CodeType

Using the project's CodeModel object (not available in "projectless" ASP.NET applications), you can retrieve the CodeType object for any component in the project by providing the full name of the component, regardless of what file is currently open. This code, for instance, gets the CodeModel for the project through the ActiveDocument but then retrieves the CodeType object for the class Form1 in the namespace SampleCodeModel, regardless of what file the class is in:

```
cm = _applicationObject.ActiveDocument.ProjectItem.
                        ContainingProject.CodeModel;
CodeType ct = cm.CodeTypeFromFullName("SampleCodeModel.Form1");
```

If `CodeTypeFromFullName` doesn't find a matching component, the method returns Nothing or null.

This feature allows you to search for a particular class across several files and, once you find it, retrieve the `CodeElements` inside the component through the `CodeType`'s `Children` property. Having found `Form1` in the previous code, for instance, you can process the members of the `Class` with this code:

```
foreach (CodeElement elmClassChild in ct.Children)
{
    ...processing class members...
}
```

The `CodeType` object also has a `Members` property that lets you retrieve the members of the component by name. For instance, this code retrieves the `button1_Click` method in the `Class` retrieved previously and casts it to a `CodeFunction`:

```
CodeFunction cf = (CodeFunction) ct2.Members.Item("button1_Click");
```

If the `Item` method doesn't find a matching member, an `ArgumentException` error is raised.

You can also access other components at the same "level" as a `CodeElement` through the `CodeElement`'s `Collection` property. (To continue the parent/child metaphor, you can think of these as the member's "siblings": its brothers and sisters.) For instance, having retrieved a `CodeElement` that represents the `button1_Click` event handler in my Windows Form sample code, you can use the `Collection` property to access all the other members of the same class, like this:

```
if (ce.Name == "button1_Click")
{
  foreach(CodeElement ceClass in ce.Collection)
  {
    ...processing all members in the Class with button1_Click...
  }
}
```

In addition to working with a component's children and siblings, the `CodeType` object also lets you work "up" the family tree through the

CodeType's Parent property. If the ct variable in this code is referencing the Form1 class, this code would return the Namespace that the Form1 class is inside of:

```
CodeElement ce = (CodeElement) ct.Parent;
```

This is a good time to reinforce a point I've mentioned before: The CodeModel objects analyze the *text* of your application. Because it's not common practice in a Visual Basic project to include a Namespace declaration inside a Class file, the Visual Basic equivalent of my sample Windows Form would, typically, look like this:

```
Public Class Form1

    Private Sub Button1_Click(ByVal sender As System.Object, _
                        ByVal e As System.EventArgs)

    End Sub

End Class
```

Although the Form1 class does have a Namespace, it's not present in the text of the file. Because the CodeModel analyzes the text in the file, asking for either the Parent or Namespace property of Form1's CodeType object won't return a useable result when analyzing this Visual Basic code.

On the other hand, Visual Basic code can have an explicit Namespace declaration, as this example does (which also introduces a new level in the Class's full name):

```
Namespace MyForm
    Public Class Form1

        Private Sub Button1_Click(ByVal sender As System.Object, _
                            ByVal e As System.EventArgs)

        End Sub

    End Class

End Namespace
```

With this text in the file, reading either the Parent property or the Namespace property of the Form object does return a CodeNamespace object.

Simple CodeType Options

The `CodeType`'s `Access` property returns or sets whether the `CodeElement` is Private, Protected, and so on, using the `vsCMAccess` enumeration. This code checks to see if a `CodeElement` supports the `CodeType` interface, casts the `CodeElement` to a `CodeType`, and changes its `Access` property to Protected:

```
if (ce.IsCodeType == true)
{
  CodeType ct;
  ct = (CodeType) ce;
  ct.Access = vsCMAccess.vsCMAccessProtected;
}
```

The `Namespace` property returns the `CodeNamespace` object for the `CodeElement`:

```
EnvDTE.CodeNamespac
e ns;
ns = ct.Namespace;
```

Working with Comments and Documentation Comments

The `CodeType`'s `Comment` property returns any comments preceding the `CodeElement` in the file and following any other `CodeElement`. All comment markers are stripped out but some formatting codes are embedded. In the sample Windows Form code, the comment that appears before the class declaration ("// A class level comment") will be returned from the `Comment` property as "A class level comment\r\n". The comment following the class won't be returned.

To change or add a comment, set the `Comment` property to any string value—the necessary comment delimiters will be added. In C#, the single-line comment format ("//") will be added. This code adds a two-line comment with a line break:

```
ct.Comment = "Autogenerated code \r\nAdded by PH&VIS";
```

Added to C# code, the result would look like this:

```
//Autogenerated code
//Added by PH&VIS
```

Be aware: Setting the `Comment` property replaces *all* the existing comments preceding the `CodeElement` object.

The `CodeType`'s `DocComment` property returns or sets the XML documentation preceding the `CodeElement` (assuming that the language supports XML documentation). The property returns the XML content of the documentation with the comment markers removed. For the sample Windows Form code, the `DocComment` property would return the following:

```
<doc><summary>Code generated using the FileCodeModel</summary></doc>
```

The value returned by the `DocComment` property varies between C# and Visual Basic: The value returned from a Visual Basic project doesn't include the `<doc>` element's tag. Similarly, when setting the `DocComment` property in a Visual Basic application, don't include the `<doc>` elements tags. If no `DocComment` is present in C# code, the value "<doc>\r\n</doc>" is returned; Visual Basic returns a zero-length string.

In a C# application, this code would set the `DocComment`'s summary element:

```
ct.DocComment = "<doc><summary> Written by PH&VIS </summary></doc>";
```

The result would look like this:

```
/// <summary> Written by PH&VIS </summary>
```

For a Visual Basic application, this code would set the `DocComment`'s summary element:

```
ct.DocComment = "<summary> Written by PH&VIS </summary>";
```

The result would look like this:

```
''' <summary> Written by PH&VIS </summary>
```

Working with Related Classes

When working with classes, you can use the `CodeType`'s `Bases` collection to retrieve any classes associated with a class (e.g., classes that the `CodeType` inherits from or interfaces that the `CodeType` implements). The `Bases`' `Item` method returns an object, so you must cast the result to a `CodeClass` if you want to use it as a class:

```
CodeClass cc = (CodeClass) ct.Bases.Item(1);
```

You don't have to iterate through the `Bases` collection to determine if a class is derived from another class: The `get_IsDerivedFrom` method, when passed the fully qualified name of a class, returns True if the current class is derived from another class. This example checks to see if the class is derived from `PHVIS.Logging` before removing it:

```
if (ct.get_IsDerivedFrom("PHVIS.Logging"))
{
  cc.RemoveBase("PHVIS.Logging");
}
```

In Visual Basic, you can also use the `DerivedTypes` collection to get a collection of objects that derive from the current `CodeType` object. (This collection is also available on the `CodeClass` object.)

BEST PRACTICE If you're making multiple changes to a project, call the `FileCodeModel`'s `BeginBatch` method before making changes—this reduces the overhead associated with the changes. When you've completed any changes made through the `FileCodeModel`, you call its `EndBatch` method to have Visual Studio update the user interface with your changes. The `FileCodeModel`'s `IsInBatch` method returns True if you're currently in a batch.

Storing Information

As discussed in Chapter 2, "Integrating with Visual Studio," you will sometimes need to store input from the developer that you will use as part of the code-generation process. In addition, to support regeneration, you may need to store information about a generation to be used to find and delete code created in a previous generation. The `CodeModel` provides you with the `Globals` object to store strings for a `Project`.

Storing Strings in the Globals Object

The Project's Globals object provides a simple mechanism for storing strings: Just specify the name you want to save the item under and assign a value. By default, any value you place in the Globals object will be discarded when the project is closed. If you want to save the value until the next time that the Project is opened, you have to flag the value as persistent.

This code retrieves the first project in the solution and saves the current date and time under the name LastGeneration. After setting the value, the code then uses the Globals object's set_VariablePersists method, passing the name of the variable and the value True to cause the value to survive until the project is next opened:

```
prj = _applicationObject.Solution.Projects.Item(1);
prj.Globals["LastGeneration"] = DateTime.Now;
prj.Globals.set_VariablePersists("LastGeneration", true);
```

To retrieve the value, you can just ask for it by name:

```
LastGeneration = (DateTime) prj.Globals["LastGeneration"];
```

If you do want to save the value of the variable, you only need to set the persistence value once—the first time that you set the value. You can check to see if you're setting the value for the first time by checking to see if the variable already exists using the Globals object's get_VariableExists method, passing the name of the variable:

```
prj.Globals["LastGeneration"] = DateTime.Now;
if (prj.Globals.get_VariableExists("LastGeneration") == false)
{
 prj.Globals.set_VariablePersists("LastGeneration", true);
}
```

Alternatively, you can use the Globals get_VariablePersists method to determine whether the variable has been made persistent. If the variable isn't persistent, you can make it persistent:

```
prj.Globals["LastGeneration"] = DateTime.Now;
if (prj.Globals.get_VariablePersists("LastGeneration") == false)
{
 prj.Globals.set_VariablePersists("LastGeneration", true);
}
```

Working with Project Components

This chapter has provided you with the tools to add or analyze the components of a project. Using the `FileCodeModel`, you can add files to your project and retrieve existing files. You can also add many code structures, such as classes and namespaces, to your application in C# (and, in many cases, to Visual Basic also). What the `FileCodeModel` won't do for you is to give you the code that goes inside of those structures or a means of inserting that code. You can generate that code using any toolset you want or use the CodeDom to support generating code in a language-neutral fashion (described in Chapter 6). To insert code into your file or to copy in boilerplate code, you'll want to use the Code Editor objects (Chapter 4).

The `FileCodeModel` also does not support features that are specific to some of the project types. For instance, Visual Basic supports project-level `Imports` statements, which the `FileCodeModel` does not. Those features can be accessed through the objects in the `VsLangProj` and `VsWebsite` object models (Chapter 5).

Creating your own custom templates to use with the `AddFromTemplate` method is covered in Chapter 7, as is creating your own attributes.

As I noted at the start of the chapter, I've focused on the individual tools rather than how to use them together. The case studies in Chapters 9 and 10 provide end-to-end examples of how to create code-generation solutions that use the `FileCodeModel`.

CHAPTER 4

MODIFYING CODE IN THE EDITOR

In this chapter:

- Opening and Closing Documents and TextDocuments
- Backing Out Changes
- Creating EditPoints to Access Text
- Retrieving Information
- Accessing Text with an EditPoint
- Working with Bookmarks
- Inserting, Replacing, and Formatting Text
- Inserting and Reading Text

The `Document` and `TextDocument` objects, described in this chapter, are the primary tools you will use to add, read, and modify code in the files in your project. Whereas the `FileCodeModel` (Chapter 3, "Manipulating Project Components") and `VsLangProject/VsWebsite` objects (Chapter 5, "Supporting Project-Specific Features") will allow you to insert some code into your code files (class declarations and other structures), they don't support all the code required for a complete solution. The CodeDom (Chapter 6, "Generating Language-Neutral Code"), on the other hand, supports generating code but doesn't support getting the code into the file. The two scenarios where you won't need the tools in this chapter are if you are using a custom tool (Chapter 8, "Other Tools: Templates, Attributes, and Custom Tools") or if you are using a visual designer (Chapter 11, "Case Study: Generating Data-Conversion Code"), where the process of creating and adding a file is handled for you by Visual Studio,.

The objects discussed in this chapter fulfill an essential requirement for any code generation project: getting code into the right place in the file. In addition, if you're allowing the developer to enter his or her inputs to the code-generation process into files in your project (and you're not using

XML), this chapter covers the tools that allow you to retrieve the text the user has entered. For instance, in the case study in Chapter 9, "Case Study: Generating a Connection String Manager," I use a TextDocument to determine if the developer has used a specific server-side control in an .aspx file and retrieve the values set in the control's attributes.

At the start of this chapter, I'll discuss how to retrieve a document and access parts of the document. These sections also show you how to access the various objects associated with a document (TextDocument, Document, and EditPoints). The rest of the chapter, however, isn't organized around the objects. Instead, I'll cover the typical tasks you may need to perform in adding or modifying code, and many of these tasks require a combination of methods and properties from different objects.

One caveat: This is not a full discussion of the functionality of these objects. Because I'm focusing on code generation, I assume, for instance, that you'll be working with lines of code rather than individual words or characters and will ignore the related methods. For the same reason, I haven't discussed dealing with the text that the developer has currently selected in the editor window.

Opening and Closing Documents and TextDocuments

This section describes how to access the Document and TextDocument objects for a file. Those objects will then let you manipulate the text in the files. However, in many cases, the objects that are made available through the TextDocument and TextDocument objects can also be accessed through the FileCodeModel objects, as you'll also see in this chapter.

Accessing the Document/TextDocument

You can access the Document and TextDocument objects only for a file open in an editor window. However, Visual Studio gives you several ways to access those Document and TextDocument objects. First, for the file that the developer is currently editing, you can retrieve the corresponding:

- Document object from the _applicationObject's ActiveDocument property.
- TextDocument object through the ActiveDocument's Object property (in Visual Studio 2008, you must pass the string "TextDocument" as a parameter in order to retrieve the TextDocument object). You must cast the output from the Object property into a TextDocument.

In addition, if you've just created a file using the `FileCodeModel`, it's automatically opened in an editor window and will be the file pointed to by the `_applicationObject`'s `ActiveDocument` property.

For files other than the one in the current editor window, you'll need to open the file in a document window using the `Open` method of the file's related `ProjectItem` (for more information on retrieving a file in a project, see Chapter 3, "Manipulating Project Components," on working with the `FileCodeModel`). The `Open` method must be passed an enumerated parameter to indicate the kind of editor to be used—for code, you would pass `Constants.vsViewKindTextView` to open most code files. You don't need to check whether the file is already open: If the file is already open in a window, it will remain open; if the file was not yet open, it will be opened in a hidden window.

The `Open` method returns the `Window` object for the document, which has both `Document` and `Object` properties that will let you access the `Document` and `TextDocument` objects for the file. The document also becomes the `ActiveDocument`, so you can use the `ActiveDocument` property to retrieve the `Document` object for the file.

This example retrieves the item currently selected in Solution Explorer and opens it in a hidden text `Window`. Once the `Window` is open, the code first retrieves the `Document` object from the `Window`'s `Document` property and then retrieves the corresponding `TextDocument` object through the `ActiveDocument`'s `Object` property:

```
ProjectItem pji = _applicationObject.SelectedItems.Item(1).ProjectItem;
Window win = pji.Open(Constants.vsViewKindTextView);
Document doc = win.Document;
TextDocument td = (TextDocument)
        _applicationObject.ActiveDocument.Object("TextDocument");
```

Making the Document Available to the Developer

After the file is open, you may want to make the file available to the developer. To do that, you must set the corresponding `Window` object's `Visible` property to True. Because a `Document` can be open in multiple `Window`s, you access the current `Window` by reading one of the items in the `Document` object's `Windows` collection. Because every open document will have at least one `Window`, you're guaranteed to get a `Window` if you retrieve the first item in the `Document`'s `Windows` collection.

This example makes the Document visible (the Window will also become the topmost window in the editor):

```
doc.Windows.Item(1).Visible = true;
```

Alternatively, you can make the file visible and make it the "topmost" window by calling the Activate method on the Document object itself:

```
doc.Activate();
```

In addition to making a file visible to the developer, after making changes to the code you may also make the portion of the file you changed visible by using the TryToShow method discussed later in this chapter.

BEST PRACTICE Effective code-generation solutions are invisible to the developer. Only consider making a file visible to the developer if you've generated a class of "stubs" that the developer needs to complete.

Closing the Document

If you decide not to make the file available to the developer, when you're finished modifying the contents of the file you should close it (to conserve memory). To close the document, call the Document object's Close method, passing vsSaveChanges.vsSaveChangesYes to save changes without prompting the developer. Because it's possible that the save might fail, you should check the Document object's Saved property afterward and notify the developer if you were unable to save the file.

This example attempts to save the file; if the save fails, Visual Studio's status bar is updated with a message indicating that the file isn't saved:

```
doc.Close(vsSaveChanges.vsSaveChangesYes);
if (!doc.Saved)
{
    _applicationObject.StatusBar.Text = "oops";
}
```

You cannot, however, call the Document object's Close method from an event handler. If you want to close an open document in an event handler, use the `Close` method of the `Window` associated with the document (you can still pass the `vsSaveChangesYes` option). This code closes the item displayed in the first `Window`:

```
doc.Windows.Item(1).Close(vsSaveChanges.vsSaveChangesYes);
```

Backing Out Changes

If you are modifying the developer's custom code, you can give the developer an opportunity to undo your changes. The `DTE` object's `UndoContext` allows you to wrap all your changes in a single package that crosses multiple files so that the developer can back all your changes out with a single click on Visual Studio's Undo menu item. You can also use the `UndoContext` as a kind of transaction manager so that, if something goes wrong during code generation, you can back out all your changes.

BEST PRACTICE Use an `UndoContext`, especially if your code is mixed in with the developer's code in the same file. The developer should always have the option to throw away your changes—and you will always want the ability to back out your changes if something goes wrong.

Creating and Finishing a Context

The first step in managing Undo is to retrieve Visual Studio's `UndoContext` object from the `DTE` object's `UndoContext` property (the `DTE2` object is normally passed to your add-in in the `_applicationObject` parameter). Once you've accessed the `UndoContext`, you must open it, assigning it a name (any string), and specifying a Boolean for the second parameter.

The following code first retrieves and opens the `UndoContext`. After all changes have been made (and if the `UndoContext` is still open), the code closes the `UndoContext`. As a result of this code, if the developer wants to get rid of your changes, only a single Undo is required:

```
bool CreatedUndo = false;
UndoContext undo = _applicationObject.UndoContext;
```

```
if (!undo.IsOpen)
{
 undo.Open("Fixing Name", true);
 CreatedUndo = true;
}
//...changes to code
if (undo.IsOpen && CreatedUndo)
{
 undo.Close();
}
```

BEST PRACTICES Only a single UndoContext is available: Attempting to open the UndoContext if it is already open will raise an error. So, at the start of your code, first check that the UndoContext isn't already open. Second, closing an UndoContext that isn't open raises an error. It would also be a bad practice to close an UndoContext that you didn't open. For instance, the previous example's code only closes the UndoContext if it was opened within the code snippet and the UndoContext is still open.

In addition, failing to close an open UndoContext has dire consequences. If you don't close an UndoContext you've opened, you effectively disable Undo for the developer. Always close your contexts!

The first parameter passed to the Open method is an arbitrary string you can set to any value you want. The second parameter specifies whether you're opening the context in strict mode. In strict mode, all changes are part of one context: In other words, if you make changes to two documents and the developer uses Visual Studio's Undo function, changes in both documents will be backed out. If you don't use strict mode, if the developer uses Undo in one document, then only the changes in that document will be backed out.

The SetAborted method backs out all the changes made in the context and closes the UndoContext. Calling SetAborted on an UndoContext that isn't open raises an error, so typical code for backing out your changes should look like this:

```
if (undo.IsOpen)
{
 undo.SetAborted();
}
```

BEST PRACTICE   If, while generating code, you run into an error condition, your best option is to back out all your changes by calling the SetAborted method on your UndoContext object.

Getting Information on the Context

The UndoContext object has three properties that allow you to check its status:

- **IsAborted**—True if the SetAborted method has been called since the Open method on the UndoContext object was called.
- **IsOpen**—True if neither the Close nor the SetAborted method has been called since the UndoContext was opened.
- **IsStrict**—True if the UndoContext was opened in Strict mode. This property can only be checked if the UndoContext is still open.

Creating EditPoints to Access Text

Now that you've retrieved a document and can open and close it (and have set both yourself and the developer up to back out any changes if anything goes wrong), you're ready to start making changes. The most common code-generation activity you'll perform with the TextDocument object is inserting new code into a file. To insert code, however, you may need to locate the code where you want to insert your new code (this is especially likely if your design requires you to change custom code generated by the developer or if your generated code is intermixed with developer code). The key tool for inserting (or retrieving) code is the EditPoint object, which specifies a point in the text from where you can make changes.

An EditPoint object marks a position in the file where you can make changes. EditPoints are created from TextPoint objects, which also mark a point in the text but do not support changing the file's content. You create an EditPoint from any TextPoint by calling the TextPoint's CreateEditPoint method. Rather than discuss the TextPoint object separately, I'll just cover the EditPoint object—where the TextPoint object has the same method or property, you can assume it has the same functionality.

Retrieving EditPoints with the TextDocument

The TextDocument object returns TextPoint objects from its StartPoint and EndPoint properties. As you might expect, the StartPoint property returns a TextPoint positioned at the start of the document, whereas the EndPoint property returns a TextPoint from the end of the document. Once you've accessed a TextPoint, you can create an EditPoint positioned at that point in the document.

This code, for instance, retrieves the TextPoints at the start and end of the document and creates EditPoints from them:

```
EditPoint edStart;
EditPoint edEnd;

edStart = td.StartPoint.CreateEditPoint();
edEnd = td.EndPoint.CreateEditPoint();
```

Retrieving EditPoints with the FileCodeModel

You can also retrieve EditPoints from the FileCodeModel objects you use when generating code: The GetStartPoint method on the FileCodeModel objects returns an EditPoint positioned at the start of the code element. Similarly, the GetEndPoint method on FileCodeModel objects returns an EditPoint at the end of the code element.

For instance, if you've added a CodeProperty object to a class, you can call the GetStartPoint method on the CodeProperty's Getter property and retrieve the EditPoint for the property's Get routine. This would allow you, for instance, to insert the code you want in the Get portion of the property.

This example creates a property, returning a CodeProperty object. The code then retrieves an EditPoint based on the Get portion of the property:

```
CodeProperty cp = cc.AddProperty("MyProperty", "MyProperty",
                vsCMTypeRef.vsCMTypeRefString, -1,
                vsCMAccess.vsCMAccessPublic,null);
EditPoint epGetter = cp.Getter.GetStartPoint(
                vsCMPart.vsCMPartBody).CreateEditPoint();
```

Where the EditPoint is positioned is controlled by the parameter passed to the GetStartPoint method. Passing vsCMPart.vsCMPartBody positions the EditPoint at the start of the content inside the property's get method (the part highlighted in bold):

```
public string MyProperty
{
  get
  {
   return default(string);
  }
  set
  {
  }
}
```

The parameters listed next can be used to control the position of the EditPoint, but be warned: You shouldn't count on all the options being implemented in all language/project types or even that what's returned matches the documentation. The position specified by each parameter will vary from one code element to another.

In addition to setting the position of the EditPoint, the parameter also sets the EditPoint's LineLength, which controls how much text will be retrieved if you use the EditPoint's GetText method (discussed later in this chapter).

BEST PRACTICE   Often, when modifying existing text, you want to replace a specific set of text (e.g., all the text within a property or a method's name and declaration). Use the parameters discussed here with the GetStartPoint of a FileCodeModel object to set the LineLength to give the text you want. (And trust nothing: While you're testing your solution, check that the parameter actually gets the text you expect.)

The following descriptions specify how much text will be retrieved with the default LineLength using examples based on getting the EditPoint for the Getter of a CodeProperty. As you can see, the text not only includes code but also whitespace, carriage returns, and linefeeds (I've omitted some trailing spaces in these examples):

- **vsCMPart.vsCMPartAttributes**—Before the attributes that decorate the code section. Includes all the attribute text but not the delimiters.
- **vsCMPart.vsCMPartHeader**—The header portion (e.g., for a property Getter in Visual Basic, just before the Get keyword).
- **vsCMPart.vsCMPartHeaderWithAttributes**—Before the first attribute but with a LineLength that includes the header for the component.
- **vsCMPart.vsCMPartBody**—The contents of the code block.

- **vsCMPart.vsCMPartBodyWithDelimiter**—Same as before, but with a `LineLength` that includes any closing delimiters.
- **vsCMPart.vsCMPartName**—Before the text that sets the code element's name (e.g., after any keywords in the header like `public`). For instance, for a Visual Basic property's Get section, this returns `MyProperty() As String\r\n Get\r\`.
- **vsCMPart.vsCMPartNavigate**—Before the content of the code object with a `LineLength` that includes any closing text. For a Visual Basic `Get` routine, this would be `Return (\"x\")\r\n End`.
- **vsCMPart.vsCMPartWhole**—In theory, the content of the code object without its body. For a Visual Basic Getter, this would be `Get\r\n`.
- **vsCMPart.vsCMPartWholeWithAttributes**—As with `vsCM PartWhole`, but with a `LineLength` that includes any attributes.

BEST PRACTICE   Attempting to retrieve the `EditPoint` for a section that doesn't have the corresponding content can raise an exception. To avoid problems, you should always use the `GetStartPoint` method inside a `try...catch` block, as in this example:

```
EditPoint ept = null;
try
{
  ept = cp.Getter.GetStartPoint(vsCMPart.vsCMPartAttributes).
                        CreateEditPoint();
}
catch{}
```

Retrieving CodeElements from Text

Working with text is a key part of inserting and modifying code, but the `FileCodeModel` objects also allow you to modify code and to do it in an object-oriented and language-neutral way. As a result, for some operations, you may want to switch between using text manipulation with `EditPoint` objects to working with the properties and using the methods of the `FileCodeModel` objects. The `get_CodeElement` method of the `EditPoint` lets you retrieve any of the `CodeElement` objects that the `EditPoint` is positioned inside. Because an EndPoint is typically nested inside of several CodeElements (e.g., an EndPoint inside a property is also nested inside the class that the property is part of), you must pass a vsCMElement enumerated value to specify which code element you want.

For instance, for an EditPoint positioned inside of the Get routine of a property, either of the following lines of code would work. The first line would retrieve the CodeElement representing the class that the EditPoint is positioned inside of, whereas the second line would retrieve the CodeElement representing the property:

```
CodeElement ce = ept.get_CodeElement(vsCMElement.vsCMElementClass);
CodeElement ce = ept.get_CodeElement(vsCMElement.vsCMElementProperty);
```

Requesting a CodeElement that the EditPoint is not inside of raises an error. For instance, for an EditPoint inside a property, this line of code would raise an exception because it's requesting the text for a function:

```
CodeElement cpx = ept.get_CodeElement(vsCMElement.vsCMElementFunction);
```

Rather than using the generic CodeElement, you can declare the receiving variable more specifically as long as you do the appropriate casting. This code, for instance, retrieves a CodeElement representing a property into a CodeProperty object:

```
CodeProperty cp = (CodeProperty)
            ept.get_CodeElement(vsCMElement.vsCMElementProperty);
```

Retrieving Information

The EditPoint, TextDocument, and Document objects have several properties that provide information about the EditPoint's location. The Document object offers a few more options than the TextDocument, so I'll separate the members of these two objects out.

Document and TextDocument Objects

- **Language**—A string representing the language (e.g., "CSharp")
- **TabSize**—The number of characters in a tab stop (e.g., 4)

Document Object Only

- **FullName**—The full name (including the path) of the file (e.g., "C:\\Course\\512\\WebSiteCS\\App_Code\\ConnectionManager. Generation.cs")
- **Name**—The name of the file without the path (e.g., "ConnectionManager.Generation.cs")
- **Path**—The path to the file with the trailing slash (e.g., "C:\\Course\\512\\WebSiteCS\\App_Code\\")
- **Kind**—The kind of file, often a GUID (e.g., "{8E7B96A8-E33D-11D0-A6D5-00C04FB67F6A}")
- **ReadOnly**—True if the file can't be changed

EditPoint

- **AtStartOfDocument**—True if on the first line of the document; False otherwise.
- **AtEndOfDocument**—True if on the last line of the document; False otherwise.
- **Line**—Line number (1 based).
- **LineLength**—Number of characters in the line.
- **GreaterThan**—When passed a TextPoint or an EditPoint, returns True if the EditPoint is closer to the end of the file than the position represented by the TextPoint or EditPoint.
- **LessThan**—When passed a TextPoint or an EditPoint, returns True if the EditPoint is closer to the start of the file than the position represented by the TextPoint or EditPoint.
- **ReadOnly**—Returns True if the text at the EditPoint can't be changed.

Accessing Text with an EditPoint

Before beginning this section, I just want to remind you of the difference between some of the objects I've discussed so far in this book: The FileCodeModel and CodeElement objects allow you to retrieve *objects* that represent many of these components of your code; the EditPoint gives you access to the *text* in the file. Whereas the FileCodeModel provides a language-neutral method for adding some of the code components you require, the EditPoint object, because it's accessing the text in the file, requires you to work with a specific language. If any of these methods seem awkward to you, remember that you can use the EditPoint object's get_CodeElement method to switch back to working with the FileCodeModel objects.

Retrieving Text

Once you've retrieved an EditPoint, if you want to process the text at that point then you can use the EditPoint's GetText method, which will return the amount of text specified in the EditPoint's LineLength property (as noted earlier, depending on how you retrieved the EditPoint, the LineLength will already have a default value set that may reflect the text that you want to retrieve). The GetText method also accepts a parameter to specify the amount of text to return. You can either pass a number to get that number of characters returned or another point object.

This code, for instance, retrieves the two EditPoints at the start and end of the document. Once the EditPoints are retrieved, the code uses the GetText method to retrieve 1,000 characters of text (in the case of the EndPoint's EditPoint, the code uses a negative number to retrieve the text before the EditPoint):

```
EditPoint ed;
ed = td.StartPoint.CreateEditPoint();
string tx = ed.GetText(1000);
ed = td.EndPoint.CreateEditPoint();
string tx = ed.GetText(-1000);
```

If you ask for a specific number of characters and there aren't that many characters in the section, you'll get all the text from the start of the section up to the end of the file. No exception will be raised.

BEST PRACTICE If you're not sure how much text you want, ask for too much and use standard string-handling functions to locate where you want to stop. You can then reposition your EditPoint and pass the correct LineLength.

Instead of passing the number of characters you want, you can also pass the GetText method an EditPoint or TextPoint to retrieve all the text up to that `EditPoint` or `TextPoint`. As an example, this code retrieves all the text between the start of the document and the end of the document by passing the `TextPoint` from the `TextDocument`'s `EndPoint` property:

```
EditPoint ed;
ed = td.StartPoint.CreateEditPoint();
string tx = ed.GetText(td.EndPoint);
```

If the `EditPoint`'s `LineLength` hasn't been set through a parameter passed to the `GetStartPoint` method (described earlier) then the `EditPoint`'s `LineLength` property will return the length of the line that the `EditPoint` is currently on. This lets you use the `LineLength` to retrieve all of the line that the `EditPoint` is positioned on. This code, for instance, returns the full line at the top of the document:

```
EditPoint ed;
ed = td.StartPoint.CreateEditPoint();
string tx = ed.GetText(ed.LineLength);
```

However, the `LineLength` normally refers to a line in the editor and not to a statement in the programming language. Both of the following examples represent one line in the editor but the first line contains two C# statements whereas the second line is a partial Visual Basic statement:

```
using System; using System.Data;
For Each(cust As Customer _
```

As described earlier, if you used the `GetStartPoint` method of a `FileCodeModel` object to create your `EditPoint`, the `LineLength` property will be set to a length that includes all of the text specified by the parameter passed to the method—you're more likely to get complete statements in whatever programming language the code in the file is written in. For instance, passing `vsCMPart.vsCMPartBody` to `GetStartPoint` will set the `LineLength` on the resulting `EditPoint` object to include all the statements in the body of the `CodeElement` (including newlines and tabs). As a result, passing an `EditPoint`'s `LineLength` to the `GetText` method can retrieve a single statement that covers multiple lines.

If you do want to retrieve the line (rather than the statement) that the `EditPoint` is positioned on, it may be simpler to use the object's `GetLines` method. This method requires two parameters: the number of lines to start with (the first line in the file is at position 1) and the number of the last line to be retrieved plus 1. Because `GetLines` uses the line number in the file, the actual position of the `EditPoint` in the file is irrelevant. Control characters will appear between the lines retrieved but not following the last line: This code retrieves the second and third lines of the file:

```
ed = td.StartPoint.CreateEditPoint();
string tx = ed.GetLines(2, 4);
```

Let's assume that the start of the file looks like this:

```
using System;
using System.Data;
using System.Collections.Generic;
using System.Linq;
using System.Web;
```

In this case, the result of calling `GetLines` would be `"using System.Data;\r\nusing System.Collections.Generic;"`.

BEST PRACTICE If what you want to retrieve are lines, then rather than using `GetText` and `LineLength` to retrieve the current line, you should use `GetLines`, passing the current line number as the start and the end as the current line number plus 1. The current line for the `EditPoint` is available through the `EditPoint`'s `Line` property. Here's an example of the technique:

```
string tx = ed.GetLines(ed.Line, ed.Line + 1);
```

Relocating the EditPoint

Once you've retrieved an `EditPoint`, rather than create a new `EditPoint` you can move the `EditPoint` to somewhere else in the document. The `EditPoint`'s `LineUp` and `LineDown` methods, for instance, move the `EditPoint` to the next (or previous) line in the document.

This example uses `LineDown` to process all the lines in a document. It first retrieves the `EditPoint` positioned at the start of the document. The code then moves through the document, line by line, using the `EditPoint`'s `LineDown` method (passing 1 to the method to move down a single line at a time). The loop ends when the `EditPoint`'s `AtEndOfDocument` method returns True:

```
ed = td.StartPoint.CreateEditPoint();
while (!ed.AtEndOfDocument)
{
```

```
txt = ed.GetText(ed.LineLength);
ed.LineDown(1);
}
```

Other methods: for relocating an `EditPoint` include the following:

- **LineUp**—Moves toward the top of the file. No error is raised if the `EditPoint` is already at the first line of the file.
- **StartOfDocument**—Moves to the start of the first line of the file.
- **EndOfDocument**—Moves to the end of the last line of the file.
- **MoveToPoint**—Moves to the `TextPoint` or `EditPoint` passed to the method.
- **StartOfLine**—Moves to the start of the current line. Useful when positioned at the end of a line (e.g., after using `EndOfDocument`) or inside a line (after using one of the find methods discussed in the next section).
- **EndOfLine**—Moves to the end of the current line. Useful when you want to insert new code after the existing line.
- **MoveToLineAndOffset**—Accepts a line number and a character offset (to move to the start of a line, pass 1 as the second parameter). No error is raised if the line is past the end of the document.

Finding Text

You can also move an `EditPoint` by finding specific text within the file using the `EditPoint`'s `FindPattern` method. The `FindPattern` method is especially useful when finding code that was generated in a previous execution that isn't represented by a `FileCodeModel` object. Alternatively, even if you want to work with a `FileCodeModel` object, if you know some of the text you're looking for, it may be easier to use `FindPattern` to locate the text and then use `get_CodeElement` to retrieve the corresponding `CodeElement` than to try and drill down through the `FileCodeModel` objects.

If you're willing to keep track of the previous and current versions of the developer's input, `FindPattern` can let you support changes to the inputs without having to delete and regenerate all of the code. If, for instance, the developer changes the name of a generated method and you've kept track of the original method name, you could use `FindPattern` to update just the name of the function (although it might be easier to use the `ReplacePattern` method discussed later in this chapter).

If you're supporting a design where the developer can customize the code in a separate partial class, then when you regenerate your code you can invalidate the developer's custom code. Changing the name of a generated method, for instance, will cause any code that calls that method to fail. With FindPattern you can search the partial class containing the developer's code and replace any references to old method or property names with their new names (but, again, only if you're willing to keep track of the original name).

The FindPattern method accepts four parameters:

- The string or regular pattern to search for
- One or more vsFindOptions
- An optional EditPoint object, passed by reference
- An optional TextRanges object, passed by reference

The method returns True if the pattern is found. If the string or regular expression is found, the EditPoint is moved to that point in the file; if the string or regular expression is not found, the EditPoint is left in its original position.

If you do pass an EditPoint in the third parameter and the string is found, that EditPoint is set to the point immediately after the end of the found string. Passing that EditPoint to the GetText method of the relocated EditPoint allows you to retrieve just the found text.

As an example, this code looks for the string in the variable OriginalName, passing an EditPoint in the third parameter. If the text is found, the string variable Name is set to that text by calling the GetText method on the original EditPoint and passing the EditPoint passed in the third parameter:

```
EditPoint edFound = null;
TextRanges txts = null;
if (ed.FindPattern(OriginalName, (int)
     vsFindOptions.vsFindOptionsFromStart, ref edFound, ref txts))
{
   string Name = ed.GetText(edFound);
}
```

The vsFindOptions support most of the options you find in the Visual Studio Find dialog (searching multiple files is missing). As with the Find dialog, you can pick multiple options by adding options together. This example, for instance, reduces the chances of false matches by requiring the case to match and restricting matches to whole words (the word being searched for is assumed to still be in the variable OriginalName):

```
ed.FindPattern(OrginalName,
     (int)  vsFindOptions.vsFindOptionsMatchWholeWord +
     (int)  vsFindOptions.vsFindOptionsMatchCase, ref edFound, ref txts))
```

BEST PRACTICE Unless you know that you're searching for text embedded in a word, always use the Whole Word option to avoid false matches (e.g., searching for "For" and falsely matching on "ForeignEntry" because you didn't use the Whole Word option).

Finding Text with Regular Expressions

If you use a regular expression in the first parameter, you must include the `vsFindOptions.vsFindOptionsRegularExpression` in the second parameter.

If you are using regular expressions, the fourth parameter passed to the `FindPattern` method becomes useful: It returns a `TextRanges` collection containing a `TextRange` object for the found text. Normally, the `TextRanges` object just duplicates the functionality of the `EditPoint` passed in the third parameter. However, if your regular expression uses tagged subexpressions, the `TextRanges` collection will hold one `TextRange` object for each matching text item. Each `TextRange` object has a `StartPoint` and `EndPoint` property that returns the `TextPoints` at the beginning and the end of the matching text.

The following example assumes that the first parameter is a regular expression using a tagged subexpression. As a result, the `TextRanges` collection in the fourth parameter will be populated with a `TextRange` for each match in the file. If the `FindPattern` method returns True (indicating that at least one match was found), the code loops through each matching `TextRange` creating an `EditPoint` for the `StartPoint` of each `TextRange`. The code then uses the starting `EditPoint`'s `GetText` method, passing the `TextPoint` from the end of the `TextRange` to retrieve all the matching text:

```
EditPoint edFound = null;
TextRanges txts = null;
ed = td.StartPoint.CreateEditPoint();

if (ed.FindPattern(RegularSubExpression, (int)
  vsFindOptions.vsFindOptionsRegularExpression, ref edFound, ref txts))
{
  foreach (TextRange txt in txts)
```

```
{
  EditPoint ed;
  ed = txt.StartPoint.CreateEditPoint();
  string t = ed.GetText(txt.EndPoint);
  //...processing for the matching text...
  }
}
```

Working with Bookmarks

Bookmarks can be used in the code-generation process for at least two purposes: to mark a line (or lines) that you need to move an EditPoint to later in the process and to mark lines that the developer will need to process after code generation is complete. The major limitation with bookmarks is that there is no way to distinguish between any bookmarks that the developer has added to the file and the bookmarks that you add as part of generating code.

Creating Bookmarks

The EditPoint's SetBookMark property allows you to set a bookmark at the EditPoint. This example, for instance, sets a bookmark on each line found using a regular expression:

```
foreach (TextRange txt in txts)
  {
    EditPoint ed;
    ed = txt.StartPoint.CreateEditPoint();
    ed.SetBookmark();
  }
```

You can set multiple bookmarks in a document with one statement by using the MarkText method on either the Document or TextDocument object. On both objects, the MarkText method works much like the EditObject's FindPattern method, even accepting vsFindOptions enumerated values in the second parameter. Unlike the FindPattern method, however, no EditPoint is moved—instead a bookmark is created at each line. Unlike my previous example (using FindPattern and SetBookmark), MarkText does not allow you to check the text before setting the bookmark.

This example adds bookmarks to all the lines containing the value in `OriginalName`. To reduce the chances that a "bad" match is made, the `MatchCase` and `WholeWord` options are used:

```
doc.MarkText(OriginalName,(int) vsFindOptions.vsFindOptionsMatchCase
            + (int) vsFindOptions.vsFindOptionsMatchWholeWord);
```

Once bookmarks have been created, you can move an `EditPoint` to the next (or previous bookmark) by calling the `EditPoint`'s `NextBookmark` (or `PreviousBookmark`) method. Both methods return False if there is no next (or previous) bookmark. You can remove any bookmark by calling the `EditPoint`'s `ClearBookmark` method once the `EditPoint` has been moved to the bookmark.

BEST PRACTICE   Always clear a bookmark. If you don't clear the bookmark, `NextBookmark` can just take you to the current bookmark over and over again.

This example processes all the bookmarks in a file by using `NextBookmark` to move to each bookmark, clearing each bookmark as it processes the text at that line (there's no need to move to the start or end of the file before calling `NextBookmark` or `PreviousBookmark`):

```
while (ed.NextBookmark())
{
 string tx2 = ed.GetText(ed.LineLength);
 //...process text
 ed.ClearBookmark();
}
```

If you don't need to examine the text you are replacing, you can accomplish the same goal with one command by using the `ReplacePattern` method discussed later in this chapter.

You can remove all the bookmarks in a document by calling either `Document` or the `TextDocument` object's `ClearBookmarks` method (although this will also remove any bookmarks added by the developer—use it sparingly).

Inserting, Replacing, and Formatting Text

Once you've retrieved an `EditPoint`, you can use it to modify text. If you think that developers will be looking at your code, you can also use the commands in this section to format the text you insert.

Inserting and Deleting Text

The primary tool for adding text to your file is the `EditPoint`'s `Insert` method, which accepts a single parameter: the text to be inserted. You can also include the following control characters to format your text:

- **\r**—Adds a new line.
- **\n**—Adds a new line if the current line has text on it.
- **\t**—Inserts a tab (the number of spaces moved can be determined from the `TabSize` property on the `Document` or `TextDocument` objects). Before using `\t`, consider the `EditPoint`'s `Indent` and `SmartFormat` methods, discussed later in this chapter.

After an `Insert`, the `EditPoint` is positioned after the last character inserted.

Often, there will already be text where you want to insert your text. Because the `Insert` method adds text at the `EditPoint`, if your `EditPoint` is positioned at the start of a line, your text will be added in front of the existing content—which will probably generate a compile-time error.

BEST PRACTICE To prevent conflicts with exiting content, end your new text with either \t or \r so that the original text will be separated from your new text (you'll also improve the readability of your code).

For instance, assume that you want to add a comment to a property `Get` routine that looks like this:

```
get
{
    return null;
}
```

If the `EditPoint` is positioned at the start of the "return null;" line, then this code would insert the comment, tab the comment in, and add a new-line character at the end of the line:

```
ed.Insert("\t //No return value required in version 2.3 \r");
```

The result would look like this:

```
get
{
    //No return value required in version 2.3
    return null;
}
```

Most of the time, you'll simply want to delete any existing text. The `Delete` method, when passed an end point or number of characters to delete, will remove the corresponding text from the file. Assuming that the variable cp is a `CodeElement` referencing a property's `Get` routine, this code would remove all the existing content in the body of the `Get` routine before inserting the new text:

```
epGetter.Delete(cp.Getter.GetEndPoint(vsCMPart.vsCMPartBody));
ed.Insert("\t //No return value required in version 2.3 \r");
```

Replace Selected Text

Rather than delete and insert text in two separate commands, you can perform the same operation in one step by using the `EditPoint`'s `ReplaceText` method. Like the `Delete` method, this method accepts as its first parameter one of a `TextPoint`, `EditPoint`, or number of characters—this controls which text is deleted. The second parameter to the method is the code to insert.

The third parameter accepts a set of options (the `vsEP ReplaceTextOptions` enumeration) controlling what is kept or discarded with the text and how the new text is formatted. Here are your choices:

- **vsEPReplaceTextKeepMarkers**—No bookmarks/shortcuts and the like are discarded.
- **vsEPReplaceTextAutoformat**—Text is automatically formatted based on the editor's default settings. Avoid this option if you're using control characters to set indenting.
- **vsEPReplaceTextNormalizeNewlines**—Ensures that the default for newlines is maintained.

- **vsEPReplaceTextTabsSpaces**—Ensures that the Keep Tabs setting in the editor's options is honored.

This example replaces the text in the getter and maintains any existing text markers that the developer may have put in place:

```
epGetter.Delete(cp.Getter.GetEndPoint(vsCMPart.vsCMPartBody),
        "\t //No return value required in version 2.3 \r",
        (int) vsEPReplaceTextOptions.vsEPReplaceTextKeepMarkers);
```

BEST PRACTICE   To maintain consistency with existing text, omit tabs from your inserted text and use the options listed in this section.

Bulk Insertions

Often code generation consists of inserting "boilerplate" text: large sections of code that are identical from one implementation to another. Rather than embed that code in your add-in and add it with multiple calls to the Insert method, you can put the code in a file and add all of it with a single call to the EditPoint's InsertFromFile method. The method accepts a single parameter, which is the path to the file.

BEST PRACTICE   After the text from the file is inserted, the EditPoint is positioned after the last character inserted from the file. As a result, the text on the line with the EditPoint is pushed to the right to make room for the inserted text but stays on the same line with the last line in the file. To prevent errors, end your code file with a blank line.

Cleaning Up after Insertions

Generally speaking, if you're adding code to existing code and worried about the appearance of your code, it's a good idea to finish any insert operations by calling the EditPoint's DeleteWhitespace method. Effectively, this method deletes any whitespace (blanks and tabs or line feeds) on either side of the EditPoint up to the next character. The DeleteWhitespace method accepts a value from the vsWhitespaceOptions enumeration that controls what's removed: blanks and tabs (vsWhitespaceOptionsHorizontal) or blanks and newlines (vsWhitespaceOptionsVertical). Using vsWhitespaceOptionsVertical will eliminate any stray blank lines that result from your insert operations.

Bulk Replacements

You can also insert text into multiple locations by using the TextDocument or EditPoint's ReplacePattern methods. Effectively, these methods are extensions of the EditPoint's FindPattern method with the added ability of changing the matching text. Unlike using the FindPattern or MarkText methods shown earlier, the ReplacePattern methods do not allow you to check the text before it is updated.

The EditPoint's version of the ReplacePattern accepts, as its first parameter, a TextPoint that marks the end of the range to be searched for the text (the EditPoint marks the beginning of the range). The method's second and third parameters are the string (or regular expression) to search for and the text to replace any matching code. The fourth parameter is the same vsFindOptions enumeration that the FindPattern method uses (remember to include the vsFindOptionsRegularExpression option if you're searching with regular expressions). The final parameter, as with the FindPattern method, is a TextRanges object that will return a collection of TextRanges for matching locations when tagged subexpressions are used.

This example uses ReplacePattern to update a name in the file from the EditPoint to the end of the file:

```
ed.ReplacePattern(td.EndPoint, OriginalName, NewName,
        (int) vsFindOptions.vsFindOptionsMatchCase, ref txts);
```

The TextDocument and Document objects' version of the ReplacePattern method replaces all the matching text in the whole file. Because these versions operate on the file as a whole, they don't accept an end point. Other than that, the parameters to the methods are the same:

```
td.ReplacePattern(OriginalName, NewName,
        (int) vsFindOptions.vsFindOptionsMatchCase, ref txts);
```

The TextDocument method is similar to the object's ReplacePattern but does a simple text search and doesn't support regular expressions:

```
td.ReplaceText(OldName, NewName,
          (int) vsFindOptions.vsFindOptionsMatchCase);
```

Controlling the Text Being Displayed

After modifying code, one of the things that you may want to do is to display the new text to the developer, either because it contains code that the developer will need to customize or because you've run into a problem in the code-generation process. The `EditPoint`'s `TryToShow` method causes the line containing the `EditPoint` to be moved into the editor window.

The second parameter passed to the `TryToShow` method controls how the `EditPoint`'s line is displayed. You have three choices:

- **vsPaneShowTop**—The line is moved to the top of the editor window.
- **vsPaneShowAsIs**—The line is not moved unless it's outside the window. If the line is outside the window, the line is scrolled to display in the center of the window.
- **vsPaneShowCentered**—The line is displayed in the center of the window.

The second parameter to the `TryToShow` method is an optional `TextPoint` or `EditPoint` that marks the end of the text to be displayed. Providing this parameter allows you to ensure that all of a block (or as much of it that will display in the window) is shown. Passing a `TextPoint` along with the `vsPaneShowCentered` parameter causes the whole block to be centered in the editor rather than centering the line with the `EditPoint`.

This example displays a block beginning at an `EndPoint` and extending to the position marked by the `EndPoint` property of a `TextPoint` with the first line of the block at the top of the window:

```
ed.TryToShow(vsPaneShowHow.vsPaneShowTop,txt.EndPoint)
```

BEST PRACTICE As with making a file containing generated code visible, unless the developer needs to complete the code you've generated, your best practice is not to display generated code to the developer.

Formatting Code

In most cases, the only formatting you will want to perform on your inserted code is to indent the code based on how the code is nested within other code structures. The most useful formatting method—and the most dangerous—is SmartFormat. A more taxing, but safer method is Indent.

Although you can indent code you're inserting by using \t control characters, if the file's TabSize is different from the IndentSize (both properties can be found on the Document and TextDocument objects), the results of using tab characters can look "wrong." However code is inserted, the EditPoint is positioned after the inserted text, forcing you to reposition the EditPoint to the start of the text before using either SmartFormat or Indent. Using \t eliminates the need to reposition because the formatting is performed as the code is inserted.

Smart Formatting

The EditPoint's SmartFormat method automatically indents lines based on the formatting options for the current language. All you need is to pass the end point for the text you want to format to the method. For an EditPoint positioned at the start of a property's Get routine, this code should apply the appropriate formatting to the contents of the Get routine:

```
ed.SmartFormat(cp.Getter.GetEndPoint(vsCMPart.vsCMPartBody));
```

As you can probably expect from your own experience with Visual Studio, SmartFormat may not always give you the formatting you would prefer.

BEST PRACTICE If your code isn't going to be displayed to the developer (and most generated code isn't), then don't use any formatting at all—let the settings in Visual Studio decide how to display your code.

Controlled Indenting

An alternative to SmartFormat is to specify how many levels you want your code indented by using the EditPoint's Indent method. Like with the SmartFormat method, you must pass an end point. However, with the Indent method, you must also specify the number of levels to indent. If you are confident of how many levels deep you're inserting code, Indent gives you more control over how your code is formatted.

This example indents the line between the EditPoint and the end of the property by three levels:

```
ed.Indent(cp.Getter.GetEndPoint(vsCMPart.vsCMPartBody), 3);
```

Inserting and Reading Text

This chapter has covered the tools you need to both read and insert text in the files that make up your project. Where you need to process text that isn't represented by a FileCodeModel object, the TextDocument find methods and edit/text points let you read in the text you want (the case study in Chapter 10 demonstrates using these techniques to find a set of server-side tags, for instance). You can generate your code using any technique you want (concatenating strings, XSLT transforms, or the CodeDom). But it's the objects in this chapter that will let you get your code into a file so that it can be compiled and used by the developer creating an application.

CHAPTER 5

SUPPORTING PROJECT-SPECIFIC FEATURES

In this chapter:

- Introducing the VSLangProj Libraries
- Managing a "Projectless" Website
- Project-Specific Features

In Chapter 3, "Manipulating Project Components," I discussed the `FileCodeModel`, which provides a set of objects for adding components to your project. However, the `FileCodeModel` is designed to work with all project types and, as a result, doesn't support features that are restricted to specific project types. If you limit yourself to working with the `FileCodeModel`, you'll eventually discover something you want to change in a project that is either impossible or—at least—very difficult to do. Often these activities are specific to certain project types (in an ASP.NET project, adding a WebForm page with a separate code file that uses a MasterPage, for instance), so it doesn't make sense for the cross-language, general-purpose `FileCodeModel` to support them. When you run into those deficiencies in the `FileCodeModel`, you should look at the objects covered in this chapter: the `VSLangProj` and `VSWebsite` libraries. The `VSLangProj` and `VSWebsite` objects extend the `FileCodeModel` objects for three .NET languages: Visual Basic, Visual C#, and Visual J#. The `VSLangProj` objects support activities that are specific to each language (project-wide imports in Visual Basic, for instance) and to project types (e.g., ASP.NET). The `VsWebsite` objects extend the `FileCodeModel` to work with "projectless" websites.

Introducing the VSLangProj Libraries

Like the DTE objects, working with the VSLangProj objects is made more awkward by the number of class libraries involved. The original version of the objects can be found in the VSLangProj library. When Microsoft extended some of those objects, they put the new versions in the VSLangProjLang libraries. The next set of extensions went in a library called VSLangProj80. The library released with Visual Studio 2008 was VSLangProj90 (whose namespace is VslangProj90, with a lowercase *s* and *l*). Visual Studio 2010 added the VSLangProj100 library (with the namespace VslangProj100; lowercase *s* and *l*).

Some objects have only one version. The VSLangProjWebReferencesEvents object, for instance, is a relatively new addition and exists only in the VSLangProj80 library. The References object has been present from the first release and has never been replaced. However, because it has never been updated, it appears only in the original VSLangProj library. On the other hand, the ProjectConfigurationProperties object is updated every time a new option is added to project configurations, so it appears in three libraries, under a different name each time: VSProjLang (ProjectConfigurationProperties), the VSLangProj2 library (ProjectConfigurationProperties2), and the VSLangProj80 library (ProjectConfigurationProperties3). There are two versions of the CSharpProjectProperties object and they both appear in VSLangProj90: CSharpProjectProperties4 and CSharpProjectProperties5. As the names of the objects in these examples demonstrate, each new version of an object has a name that ends with a version number (although not with the same version number that the library uses).

BEST PRACTICE   From the developer's point of view, your simplest solution is to add references to all the libraries installed with your version of Visual Studio (VSLangProj, VSLangProj2, VSLangProj80, VslangProj90, VslangProj100) and then add Imports/using statements to your code file for the libraries you've added (that's the approach that I'll take in this chapter):

```
using VSLangProj;
using VSLangProj2;
using VSLangProj80;
using VslangProj90;
using VslangProj100;
```

You can then use the latest version you have available.

In this chapter, I'll always use the latest version of any object. If you're using Visual Studio 2005, this means you won't be able to use the version of those objects drawn from the VSLangProj90 and VSLangProj100 libraries.

The VSLangProj objects can be considered an extension of the FileCodeModel objects discussed in Chapter 3. Often you retrieve a VSLangProj object by casting from an existing FileCodeModel object. For instance, to retrieve the VSProject2 object, you retrieve a FileCodeModel project object and then cast from its Object property to the VSProject2 object. This example retrieves the VSProject2 object for the first project in the solution:

```
VSLangProj80.VSProject2 vsp2 = (VSLangProj80.VSProject2)
    _applicationObject.Solution.Projects.Item(1).Object;
```

The arrangement is reciprocal: Often the VSLangProj objects have a property that returns the FileCodeModel object they are derived from. The VSProject object, for instance, has a Project property that returns a FileCodeModel Project object.

I'm not going to cover all aspects of VSLangProj in this chapter (see the Visual Studio Help files for a complete reference). I'll ignore methods and properties that don't support code generation and members whose purpose is obvious (e.g., the Count property on a collection).

The VSLangProj objects can be organized into four categories, and I will handle each differently:

- **Primary objects**—These are objects derived from FileCodeModel objects. I'll cover the functionality they provide that's relevant to code generation and goes beyond what's provided by the FileCodeModel.
- **Collections**—These objects manage collections of other objects. I'll cover these objects where they differ from a standard collection.
- **Event collections**—These objects allow you to wire up event handlers that will fire when changes are made to a project. I'll discuss the ReferencesEvents in detail to show how these events are used and discuss the other event objects only where they are different from ReferencesEvents.
- **Reference objects**—These are objects that aren't used in your code but provide lists of names that you use to retrieve property values from other objects. They are described at the end of this section.

Working with Projects

The `VSProject` object of `VSLangProj` allows you to work with references to class libraries and Web Services. With a Visual Basic project, the `VSProject` object also allows you, in Visual Basic, to work with project-level imports. Some utility functions associated with the `VSProject` are covered at the end of this section.

Working with References

As part of generating code, you may need to add references to .NET or custom libraries to support your code. This section will show you how to add references and check for existing references.

Adding and Removing References
The `VSProject` object's `References` collection lets you add, remove, and examine a project's `References` to other class libraries. The `References` collection's `Add` method allows you to add new references by passing the name of the assembly (the `Add` method returns the resulting `Reference` object). This example adds a reference to `System.Data`:

```
Reference rf = vsp2.References.Add("System.Data");
```

To add a reference to a DLL of your own, just pass the full pathname to the DLL, as in this example:

```
vsp2.References.Add("C:\MyDLLs\MyDll.dll");
```

The `References` collection's `AddProject` method, when passed a `FileCodeModel Project` object, adds a project reference. This code adds a reference to the second project in the solution:

```
rf = vsp2.References.AddProject(
            _applicationObject.Solution.Projects.Item(2));
```

Adding a reference that already exists does not raise an error.

BEST PRACTICE Even though no error is raised with adding a reference that already exists, there's no benefit, either: Check for an existing reference before adding it. It's probably faster to check for an existing reference than to add one that's already present.

To check for an existing reference, you can use either the References collection's Find or Item method. Passed the value of the Identity property of an assembly (for .NET components, the Identity property holds the assembly's name), both methods return the matching Reference object if the assembly already exists in the collection and null/Nothing if it does not. This example uses the Find method to check whether the project contains a reference to System.Data and adds a reference if it does not:

```
if (vsp2.References.Find("System.Data") == null)
{
 vsp2.References.Add("System.Data");
}
```

Retrieving Information About References   The References collection holds one or more Reference objects. Each Reference object has multiple properties, including the following:

- **Identity**—The assembly's identifier. Used by the Find and Item methods. For project references, the project name; for COM objects, the object's GUID.
- **Name**—Usually the same value as found in the Identity property, except for COM objects where the Name property is the library's filename with the extension removed.
- **Description**—A description of the DLL, often the filename.
- **Version, MajorVersion, MinorVersion, RevisionNumber, BuildNumber**—Version information.
- **Path**—Path to the DLL.
- **SourceProject**—For project references, returns a FileCodeModel Project object; otherwise null/Nothing.
- **CopyLocal**—True if a copy of the DLL is placed in the project.
- **StrongName**—True if the assembly has been assigned a strong name.

Typical results (using a reference to System.Data) look like this:

- **Identity**—System.Data
- **Name**—System.Data
- **Description**—System.Data.dll
- **Version**—2.0.0.0
- **Major version**—2
- **Minor version**—0

- **Revision number**—0
- **Build number**—0
- **Path**—C:\WINDOWS\Microsoft.NET\Framework\v2.0.50727\ System.Data.dll
- **CopyLocal**—False
- **StrongName**—True

The following code iterates through the References collection, checking to see if any project references exist:

```
int ProjectCount = 0;
foreach (Reference rf in vsp2.References)
{
  if (rf.Project != null)
  {
   ProjectCount++;
  }
}
```

To remove a reference from a project, retrieve the Reference and call its Remove method.

Using Events to Monitor Changes to References   Events in the VSLangProj namespace follow the same model as in FileCodeModel. There is an *Events object that returns references to a specific event and an event handler delegate. (The delegate's name is in the format _dispVSLangProj *NameOfTheEventObject*.) The process for setting the *Events object is not the same for all *Events objects, however.

BEST PRACTICE   Monitoring references allows you to generate code (or remove code) as references are added and deleted. If, for instance, you distribute a DLL to other developers, monitoring the references events would let you generate support code (or just a sample class file) to a project when developers add your DLL to their projects. Similarly, when a reference is deleted from a project, you can delete code that will no longer compile without your DLL.

The ReferencesEvents provides an example of one way that an *Events object is handled. Before adding the event routine, you'll need to initialize the event variable. First, use the FileCodeModel to find the Project object representing the project you want. Then cast the Project object's Object property to a `VSProject2` class. Finally, retrieve the event object from the appropriate property on the `VSProject2` object.

This example sets the event to the `ReferenceEvents` for the first project in the solution, which was retrieved from the `Projects` collection of the `Solution` object:

```
Dim vsp2 As VSProject2
vsp2 = CType(_applicationObject.Solution.Projects.Item(1).Object,
                                     VSLangProj80.VSProject2)

re = vsp2.Events2.ReferencesEvents
```

The `ReferencesEvents` object supports three events: `ReferenceAdded`, `ReferenceRemoved`, and `ReferenceChanged`. The following code wires up the `ReferenceAdded` event in C#. Assuming that the `ReferencesEvents` variable is set, the code uses the += operator to add the related event handler:

```
re.ReferenceAdded += new
  _dispReferencesEvents_ReferenceAddedEventHandler(re_ReferenceAdded);
```

With the reference added, you can write the event-handling routine. All three `ReferenceEvents` routines have the same signature: They all accept the `Reference` object being added, changed, or removed. Here is the skeleton for the `ReferenceAdded` event that corresponds to the code in the previous example:

```
void re_ReferenceAdded(Reference pReference)
{

}
```

Wiring up events in Visual Basic is simpler. First, you need to declare a `ReferencesEvents` object at the class level, using the `WithEvents` keyword:

```
Dim WithEvents re As ReferencesEvents
```

Once you've set your `ReferencesEvents` variable, you can select the variable and the event from Visual Studio's editor's window as you would in any Visual Basic project in order to have Visual Studio generate the event-handling routine for you. Here is a sample of the skeleton for the `ReferenceAdded` routine that would be generated:

```
Private Sub re_ReferenceAdded(ByVal pReference As VSLangProj.Reference)
                                        Handles re.ReferenceAdded

End Sub
```

For C#, you'll typically want to put your event wire-up code in the Solution object's Open event so that, as Solutions are opened, you can search the Solution's projects to see if any have References you want to monitor (wiring up the Solution object's events is discussed in Chapter 3).

The ReferencesEvents objects have a unique feature that the other event packages don't have: You can initialize the ReferenceEvents object to pick up changes to References for any project in a solution. The only change is in the way that the ReferenceEvents variable is initialized: Use the GetObject method of the _applicationObject's Events property to retrieve the correct event package page. Having said that, in Visual Studio 2008, I was only able to get the package for Visual Basic ("VBReferencesEvents") to work.

This example catches events for all the Visual Basic projects in a solution:

```
ReferencesEvents reVB;
reVB = (ReferencesEvents) _applicationObject.Events.Events.
                        GetObject("VBReferencesEvents");
```

Web Services

In the same way that you may need to add references to .NET or custom libraries, in today's world of service-oriented architectures, you may need to add references to Web Services to support the code that you generate.

Adding and Removing References   You can add a reference to a Web Service with the VSProject's AddWebReference method by passing the URL for a Web Service. If the project doesn't contain a Web References folder, the folder will be added. You can also add the Web References folder without adding a reference by calling the VSProject's Create WebReferencesFolder method; you can check to see if the folder already exists by reading the VSProject object's WebReferencesFolder property. (The property returns null/Nothing if the folder doesn't exist.)

This example adds a Web References folder to the first project in a solution if it doesn't already exist. With the folder added, the code then adds a Web Reference:

```
VSLangProj80.VSProject2 vsp2 = (VSLangProj80.VSProject2)
              _applicationObject.Solution.Projects.Item(1).Object;
if (vsp2.WebReferencesFolder == null)
{
  vsp2.CreateWebReferencesFolder();
}
vsp2.AddWebReference(
        @"http://MyServer/ApplicationServices/Licensing.asmx");
```

Web References are added with a name based on the server name (e.g., the previous example would add a reference named "MyServer"). Adding a reference to a Web Service that's already present deletes the existing version and adds a new version with the same name.

You can use the `ProjectItems` collection of `WebReferencesFolder` to manage the collection of Web References. This example iterates through the collection to determine whether a Web Reference already exists in the folder before adding it:

```
bool FileFound = false;


if (vsp2.WebReferencesFolder != null &&
    vsp2.WebReferencesFolder.FileCount > 0)
{
  foreach (ProjectItem pji in vsp2.WebReferencesFolder.ProjectItems)
  {
    if (pji.Name == "MyServer")
    {
      FileFound = true;
    }
  }
}

if (!FileFound)
{
vsp2.AddWebReference(
        @"http://MyServer/ApplicationServices/Licensing.asmx");
}
```

You might be tempted, before adding any Web Reference, to check to see whether a reference to the service already exists and remove the Web Reference if it's already present. However, the result is that your new reference is added with an enumerated name (e.g., "MyServer" is replaced with "MyServer1"). Because this will cause any existing code that uses the reference to fail, you should just replace any Web Service references you want to update.

BEST PRACTICE   In Visual Studio, after a Web Reference is added, the convention is to expand the folder in Solution Explorer to show the new reference. You can expand the Web Reference folder's view by calling its `ExpandView` method:

```
vsp2.WebReferencesFolder.ExpandView();
```

Monitoring Web Reference Changes   The `VSLangProjWebReferencesEvents` object works in the same way as the `ReferencesEvents` object. It even supports the same three events, although with slightly different names: `OnAfterWebReferenceAdded`, `OnBeforeWebReferenceRemoved`, and `OnAfterWebReferenceRenamed`.

Working with Project Level Imports in Visual Basic

In addition to `Imports` statements in individual code files, Visual Basic supports global `Imports` that apply to all the files in a `Project`. You can find the list of `Imports` in Project Properties at the bottom of the References tab (see Figure 5-1). If, in your generated code, you don't want to use the fully qualified name for objects, adding a project-level `Imports` statement can simplify your code.

Adding, Removing, and Processing Imports   The entries in the project `Imports` are simple strings you can read, add, and remove using the `VSProject`'s `Imports` collection. This code retrieves the `Imports` collection for a `Project` (the `Imports` property returns null for C#). The code then iterates through the collection to see if a particular `Imports` exists and adds it if it's not present (an error is raised if a duplicate `Imports` is added):

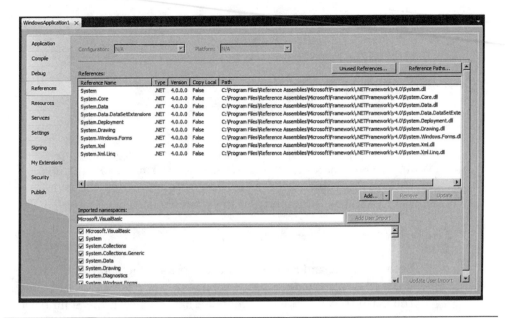

FIGURE 5-1 Visual Basic projects support project-wide Imports declarations, which are shown at the bottom of the References tab in Project Properties.

```
Imports imps = vsp2.Imports;
bool ImportFound = false;
for (int i = 1;i < imps.Count;i++)
{
   string impName = imps.Item(i);
   if (impName == "System.Linq")
   {
      ImportFound = true;
   }
}
if (!ImportFound)
{
  imps.Add("System.Linq");
}
```

No checking is done to ensure that the appropriate reference has been added to support the Imports statement.

To remove an Imports statement, call the Remove method on the Imports collection, passing the string for the Imports that you want to remove. Because an error is raised if the item doesn't exist, you should check that the Imports exists before deleting it or call the Remove method inside a try...catch block, as this example does:

```
try
{
  imps.Remove("System.Linq");
}
catch (Exception ex)
{}
```

Monitoring Import Events   The VBImportsEvents object supports two events: ImportAdded and ImportRemoved. You can retrieve the VBImportsEvents object for a specific project from the VSProject's Events2.ImportsEvents property, as this example does:

```
ie = vsp2.Events2.ImportsEvents;
```

Both the Added and Removed events are passed the name of the Imports being added or removed.

You can also catch Imports events for any project in the Solution. For this, you must retrieve the VBImportEvents object from _applicationObject by using the GetObject method on the Events property, as in this example:

```
ImportsEvents ie = (ImportsEvents)
        _applicationObject.Events.GetObject("VBImportsEvents");
```

Unfortunately, there is no way to determine which project the Imports is being added to.

Other Useful VSProject Functions

You can generate a unique name with the VSProject2's GetUniqueFileName method. This is useful if you have a code-generation project that meets either of these conditions:

- It adds files to the developer's application and it's possible for a developer to have multiple copies of your file (e.g., GeneratedCodeFile1, GeneratedCodeFile2).
- Your filename could conflict with an existing file that the developer has added (e.g., if you intend to add a file called ConnectionManager and the project may already contain a file called ConnectionManager).

The method takes three parameters: A `Project` object (not a `VSProject` object), the filename, and the file extension. The easiest way to retrieve the related `Project` object is to use the `VSProject` object's `Project` property.

This example generates a unique filename using "MyName" for the name and "cs" for the extension:

```
string filename = vsp2.GetUniqueFilename(vsp2.Project,"MyName","cs");
```

If there is no "MyName.cs" file in the project referenced by the variable `vsp2`, then the method will return "MyName.cs"; if there is a file with that name already, the method will return "MyName1.cs".

If you intend to support developers working on ASP.NET projects who are developing against remote servers, you may not want to generate code if the project is offline (unable to communicate with the remote server). The `VSProject`'s `WorkOffLine` property returns True unless the project is an ASP.NET project in offline mode, so it's always safe to check the property, as this example does:

```
if (!prj.WorkOffLine)
{
    ...generate code...
```

BEST PRACTICE As this example suggests, if the project is offline you probably shouldn't generate new code.

If you've added new files or folders to the project, you may want to refresh the view of the project in Solution Explorer to ensure that the developer can see the results of your work by calling the `VSProject`'s `Refresh` method.

If you're working with custom tools, the `BuildManager` object available from the `VSProject`'s `BuildManager` property is useful for monitoring custom tools, retrieving the compiled version of any generated code, and forcing a custom tool to regenerate its code. The `BuildManager` is discussed in Chapter 8, "Other Tools: Templates, Attributes, and Custom Tools," as part of describing how to build custom tools.

Reference Objects

As in the `FileCodeModel`, when retrieving `Property` objects using a `Properties` collection (e.g., from the `VSProject2.Properties` collection), you must pass the name of a property. Several objects included in the `VsLangProj` namespace have properties whose names duplicate the strings you can pass to the various `Properties` collections. These objects are not used in your code; they are purely a reference tool:

- **`ProjectProperties3`**—Property names that can be used with the project's `Properties` property for Visual C# and Visual J# projects.
- **`VBProjPropId100`**—The language version for a Visual Basic project.
- **`VBProjectProperties`**—Property names that can be used with the project's `Properties` property for Visual Basic projects. Same names as on the `ProjectProperties3` object but also includes the properties that occur only on Visual Basic projects: `MyApplication` and `MyType`.
- **`FileProperties2`, `FolderProperties2`**—Property names that can be used on `ProjectItem` objects that represent files and folders in the project.

Managing a "Projectless" Website

Like the `VSLangProj` objects, the `VsWebSite` objects extend the `FileCodeModel` for specific project types—in this case, "projectless" websites. The `VsWebSite` objects support sites written in any of three languages: Visual Basic, Visual C#, or Visual J#.

BEST PRACTICE As with the `VsLangProj` objects, the simplest way to use the objects is to add references to all the `VsWebSite` libraries installed on your computer (`VsWebSite.Interop`, `VsWebSite.Interop90`, `VsWebSite.Interop100`) and add `Imports`/`using` statements for all of them.

One note: In this section about the `VsWebSite` objects, I'll be referring to "the website" as shorthand for saying "the 'projectless' website in

Solution Explorer." For the rest of this chapter, when I say "website," I don't mean the deployed website on some web server—I mean what the developer would refer to as the "project in Solution Explorer." The problem is that, when talking about "projectless" websites, I shouldn't be referring to a "project" at all because these sites aren't, in the sense that Visual Studio uses the term, "projects." In Visual Studio, a "website" consists of all the files in a particular folder and its subfolders—there is no corresponding project file holding references to the components of the project. So, for the rest of this chapter, you're not working with a "project," you're working with a "website."

Working with the Website

Samples of code using the vsWebSite objects can be confusing because the Namespace is called "VsWebSite" and the object that represents the website is called "VSWebSite"—the only difference between the two is the case of the second letter in the name (s vs. S). I won't expect you to spot that difference. For all of this code, I've assumed that there is a using/Imports statement for the VsWebsite namespace at the top of the code file. Because of that, where you see VSWebsite in this chapter, I'm talking about the object that represents the website and not the namespace.

Managing the Website

The first step in working with the website is to retrieve a reference to the site by casting the FileCodeModel Project object's Object property. This example assumes that the first project in the Solution is a website and retrieves a reference to it:

```
VSWebSite vsw;
Project prj = _applicationObject.Solution.Projects.Item(1);
vsw = (VSWebSite) prj.Object;
```

You can retrieve the URL for the development web server associated with the site (and start the server running) by calling the VSWebSite object's EnsureServerRunning, which returns the URL for the server:

```
string serverURL = vsw.EnsureServerRunning();
```

If the server is already running, just the URL is returned.

You can retrieve the file path to your site using the URL property:

```
string sitePath = vsw.URL;
```

As an example of the difference, the EnsureServerRunning method would return a string such as http://localhost:1681/LicenseSite whereas the URL property would return C:\\512\\LicenseSite\\.

BEST PRACTICE   Although calling most methods will pause your add-in's code until the method completes, some methods do not wait long enough (e.g., methods that add a Web Reference). You should pause your code until any background processes complete by calling the VSWebSite's WaitUntilReady method:

```
vsw.WaitUntilReady();
```

This is a "no harm, no foul" method call: If no wait is necessary, the method does nothing. This method is also available on the **VsWebProjectItem** class.

Adding New Components

The first step in adding a new file to a website is to generate a unique filename. Unlike, for instance, a Windows Forms project, websites' filenames only need to be unique within a folder (rather than within the project as a whole). The VsWebSite object has a specialized GetUniqueFileName method that accepts a relative path to a folder, the base name for the file, and file extension, and it returns a unique filename.

This example generates a unique name within the HelpPages folder (if the folder specified doesn't exist, a "ProjectItem was unavailable" error is raised):

```
string fn = vsw.GetUniqueFilename("HelpPages", "Help", "vb");
```

If a file named Help.vb already exists in the folder, the name Help1.vb is returned from this method.

To add a new item, you need to use the VsWebSite object's AddFromTemplate method. The method accepts seven parameters:

- A relative path to the folder to put the files in. (To put the folder in the root folder, pass a zero-length string in this parameter.)
- The name of the template file for the item type you're adding.
- The language that the item is written in ("C#", "VB", "J#").

- The name of the file to be created.
- A Boolean value indicating whether a separate code file should be created (pass True for a separate code file).
- The name of a MasterPage to use with this page (pass a zero-length string to not use a MasterPage).
- A final, unused string value.

If an item with the name already exists, the developer will be prompted to replace the object. No error is returned. The method returns a `ProjectItem`.

After adding a new item, the developer may have to wait for IntelliSense to update its lists to represent the class. You should pause your code while IntelliSense updates by calling the `VSWebProjectItem`'s `WaitUntilReady` method.

You can retrieve the `VSProjectItem` for the item you added from the `ProjectItem` returned from the `AddFromTemplate` method by casting the `ProjectItem`'s `Object` property.

The following example generates a unique filename and then uses it to add a new `WebForm` using the `AddFromTemplate` method. The example creates a C# `WebForm` called MainHelp.aspx in the HelpPages folder. The .aspx file will have a separate code file (which will be called MainHelp.aspx.cs) and will be based on the MyMaster.Master MasterPage. After the item is added, the code retrieves the `VSWebProjectItem` for the new `ProjectItem` and calls its `WaitUntilReady` method to pause processing until Visual Studio catches up:

```
string fn = vsw.GetUniqueFilename("HelpPages", "Help", "vb");
ProjectItem pjiNew = vsw.AddFromTemplate("HelpPages",
      "WebForm.vstemplate", "C#", "MainHelp.aspx", true,
      "MyMaster.Master", "");
VSWebProjectItem = (VSWebProjectItem) pjiNew.Object;
pjiNew.WaitUntilReady();
```

The `WebSiteProperties3` and `WebSiteProperties4` objects provide a list of property names that can be used with a `Properties` collection on the `Project` object that represents the website. You do not use these objects directly: They're purely there for reference (think of them as documentation stored in code).

BEST PRACTICE Because there is no project file, a website just consists of all the items in the site's folder. However, if you make changes outside of the object models described in this book (e.g., by copying existing files into the site's folder), you should call the `VSWebSite` object's `Refresh` method to update Solution Explorer with the results of your changes.

Adding, Removing, and Processing References

You can add and remove references to other class libraries using the VSWebSite object's References property. This property returns a collection of AssemblyReference objects, each of which represents a reference. To add new references you can use the References object's AddFromGAC, AddFromFile, or AddFromProject method. Each takes a different kind of parameter, depending on what you want to add:

- **AddFromFile**—To add a custom DLL. Provide the full pathname to the DLL.
- **AddFromGAC**—To add a DLL installed with .NET or installed into the GAC. Provide the namespace for the DLL
- **AddFromProject**—To add a project in the same solution. Provide a Project object.

This example adds three references: one to a custom DLL, one to the .NET System.DLL library, and one to the second project in the solution:

```
vsw.References.AddFromFile(\MyD@:CLLs\MyDLL.dll");
vsw.References.AddFromGAC("System.DLL");
Project prj = _applicationObject.Solution.Projects.Item(2);
vsw.References.AddFromProject(prj);
```

Adding a reference to an item already in the collection doesn't raise an error.

You can process the collection using a For...Each loop to determine what AssemblyReferences exist before adding new references. The AssemblyReference object has a number of properties that return information about the AssemblyReference:

- **ReferencedKind**—A value from the AssemblyReferenceType enumeration indicating the kind of reference (AssemblyReferenceBin for custom DLLs or any DLL held in the Bin folder, AssemblyReferenceConfig for references from the GAC or any DLL specified in the web.config file, AssemblyReferenceClientProject for project references).
- **FullPath**—For a project reference, returns the path to the Project; for a DLL, the path to the DLL.
- **Name**—The name of the DLL.
- **ReferencedProject**—A Project object if the reference is to a project; Nothing or null otherwise.
- **StrongName**—The full name of the DLL.

As an example, this is the information returned from a reference to
.NET's `System.WorkflowServices`:

- **ReferencedKind**—AssemblyReferenceConfig
- **FullPath**—C:\\Program Files\\Reference Assemblies\\Microsoft\\
  Framework\\v3.5\\System.WorkflowServices.dll
- **Name**—System.WorkflowServices
- **ReferencedProject**—null
- **StrongName**—System.WorkflowServices, Version=3.5.0.0, Culture=
  neutral, PublicKeyToken=31BF3856AD364E35

You can remove an existing `AssemblyReference` by calling its `Remove`
method.

Adding, Removing, and Processing Web References and Web Services

The `VsWebSite` provides the `WebReferences` collection for processing references
to Web Services. The `WebReferences` collection's `Add` method allows you to add
new references to Web Services. The `Add` method accepts the URL to the service's description and the namespace to add the reference under. You should
always call the `VsWebSite`'s `WaitUntilReady` method after adding a `WebReference`.

This example adds a reference to a Licensing service, using the namespace "`License`." After adding the service, the code pauses until Visual
Studio catches up:

```
vsw.WebReferences.Add(
    "http://www.phvis.com/LicensingService/Licenser.asmx", "License");
vsw.WaitUntilReady();
```

To create an instance of the `LicenseManager` object in this service, you
would use the License namespace applied when the reference was added,
as in this example:

```
License.LicenseManager lm = new License.LicenseManager();
```

You can process the list of `WebReferences` to determine what
`WebReferences` already exist before adding a new one. The `WebReferences`
collection contains `WebReference` objects that have several useful properties:

- **Namespace**—The namespace for the Web Service

- **ServiceName**—The names of the service (e.g., the .asmx file without its extension)
- **DynamicPropName**—Namespace and ServiceName (actually, the name of the entry in `appsettings` that holds the Web Service's URL)
- **ServiceDefinitionUrl**—The URL used to retrieve the information used to create the reference
- **ServiceLocationUrl**—The URL that the service is called at
- **WsdlAppRelativeUrl**—The path to the WSDL file describing the service held in the website

The `DynamicUrl` property returns the value of the `appsettings` element in the web.config file, which controls the URL that the Web Service will call when invoked by code (the `DynamicPropName` property returns the name of the `appsettings` element). The `DynamicUrl` property is updateable, which allows you to point an existing `WebReference` to another URL.

Typical values for `WebReference` properties look like this (based on the `WebReference` added in the earlier example):

- **Namespace**—License
- **ServiceName**—Licenser
- **ServiceDefinitionUrl**—
  http://www.phvis.com/LicensingService/Licenser.asmx?disco
- **ServiceLocationUrl**—
  http://www.phvis.com/LicensingService/Licenser.asmx
- **WsdlAppRelativeUrl**—
  ~/App_WebReferences/fred/Service1.wsdl
- **DynamicUrl**—
  http://www.phvis.com/LicensingService/Licenser.asmx
- **DynamicPropName**—License.Licenser

You can remove an existing reference by calling the `WebReference` object's `Remove` method (this removes the .disco file under the service entry in the App_WebReferences folder). You can also have the reference refetch its reference and update itself for any changes in the service by calling the `WebReference`'s `Update` method.

This example searches the `WebReferences` collection for a `WebReference` object with the namespace "License" and updates the reference's `DynamicURL` property in the `appsettings` portion of the web.config file:

```
foreach (VsWebSite.WebReference wr in vsw.WebReferences)
{
```

```
if(wr.Namespace == "License")
{
  wr.DynamicUrl = "www.phvis.com/NewLicensingService/License.asmx";
  }
}
```

You can also retrieve a `WebReference` using the collection's `Item` method by passing either the position of the `WebReference` in the collection or the service's `ServiceLocationUrl`. This example retrieves the reference at a specific URL and then removes it:

```
WebReference wr = vsw.WebReferences.Item(
                "www.phvis.com/LicensingService/License.asmx");
wr.Remove();
```

Managing CodeFolders

Websites have an App_Code folder that can be accessed through the `VsWebSite`'s `CodeFolders` property. Whereas a website can have only one App_Code folder, it can have multiple subfolders in the App_Code folder.

BEST PRACTICE Websites allow you to generate code in a language different from the one that the developer is using (i.e., you can generate C# code into a class file in the App_Code folder even if the rest of the code in the project is written in Visual Basic). You should, however, put any files holding code in a language different from what the developer is using in a subfolder of the App_Code folder. You should also be separating your generated code files from the developer's code files—subfolders are an excellent way to do that in websites.

All code folders (including the App_Code folder) can be retrieved through the `VsWebSite`'s `CodeFolders` collection, which holds `CodeFolder` objects. This example returns the `VsWebSite`'s App_Folder, which is always the first item in the `CodeFolders` collection:

```
CodeFolder cf = vsw.CodeFolders.Item(1);
```

Each `CodeFolder` object has a `FolderPath` property that returns the relative path to the folder from the website's root (with a trailing slash) and the Language for code in the folder. Typical values look like this for the App_Code folder in a website for a Visual Basic site:

- **FolderPath**—App_Code/
- **Language**—VBCodeProvider

You can add an App_Code folder with the VsWebSite objects with this code:

```
vsw.CodeFolders.Add("App_Code");
```

You add subfolders using the CodeFolders collection's Add method, passing a relative path for the folder. The Add method returns a CodeFolder object that represents the new folder. After adding a folder, you should call the WaitUntilReady method to allow Visual Studio to catch up.

In addition to retrieving a CodeFolder from the CodeFolders collection's by passing an integer to the Item method, you can also retrieve a CodeFolder by passing a folder path (if a matching folder doesn't exist, an error is raised). This example checks to see if a subfolder called GeneratedCode exists; if it doesn't exist, the folder is added:

```
try
{
 CodeFolder cf = vsw.CodeFolders.Item("App_Code\\GeneratedCode");
 vsw.WaitUntilReady();
}
catch
{
 vsw.CodeFolders.Add("App_Code\\GeneratedCode");
}
```

You can remove any CodeFolder subfolder except the App_Code folder itself by calling the CodeFolder object's Remove method. This example processes all of the CodeFolders, removing all folders except the App_Code folder:

```
foreach (CodeFolder cf in vsw.CodeFolders)
{
 if(cf.FolderPath != "App_Code/")
 {
  cf.Remove();
 }
}
```

The `WebFolderProperties` object provides a list of property names that can be used with the `ProjectItem`'s `Properties` collection for the `ProjectItem` that represents the folder.

Working with Website Items

A website consists of multiple types of files. Most can be handled through the `FileCodeModel`'s `ProjectItem` class. The `ProjectItem` is extended by the `VSWebProjectItem` object, which provides additional functionality. In addition, a special collection and object exist for handling any Web Services exposed by the project.

Project Items

You can retrieve a `VSWebProjectItem` from a `ProjectItem` by casting the `ProjectItem`'s `Object` property. The `VSWebProjectItem` has additional properties for working with items that make up a website. The `VSWebProjectItem`, for instance, has a `RelatedFiles` property that returns a collection that holds references to the code file (and/or resource files) that are associated with an .aspx file.

This example adds an .aspx file to the website and then casts the resulting `ProjectItem` to a `VSWebProjectItem`. The code then uses the `Item` method on the `RelatedFiles` collection to retrieve the associated code file:

```
ProjectItem pjiNew = vsw.AddFromTemplate("HelpPages",
                "WebForm.vstemplate", "C#", "MainHelp.aspx", true,
                "MyMaster.Master", "");

VSWebProjectItem vspji = (VSWebProjectItem)pjiNew.Object;
vspji.WaitUntilReady();
ProjectItem pjiCode = vspji.RelatedFiles.Item(1);
```

Processing Web Services

The `VsWebSite` object's `WebServices` collection provides access to all the Web Services in the site. The collection contains one `WebService` object for each .asmx file in the site. The `WebService` object has three properties you may find useful when generating code:

- **AppRelativeUrl**—The relative path from the site's root to the .asmx file

- **ClassName**—The name of the class defined in the code file
- **URL**—The URL for the service in the development server

Typical values for a file called License.asmx would look like this:

- **AppRelativeUrl**—~/License.asmx
- **ClassName**—License
- **URL**—http://localhost:2321/Licenser/License.asmx

```
bool FileFound = false;
foreach (WebService ws in vsw.WebServices)
{
  if (ws.ClassName == "License")
  {
    FileFound = true;
  }
}
```

Unloading Files from the Editor

If a `VSWebProjectItem` has been loaded into the editor using the `Load` method so that it can be manipulated using the Code Editor (see Chapter 4, "Modifying Code in the Editor"), you can unload it by calling the `VSWebProjectItem` object's `Unload` method.

BEST PRACTICE   When working with remote websites, you should make sure that the local copy is up to date before making changes to it by calling its `UpdateLocalCopy` method (you can put your changed version of the file back on the remote server by calling the `UpdateRemoteCopy` method—but you should probably leave that to the developer).

Project-Specific Features

Although the `FileCodeModel` objects let you work with any Visual Studio project, they don't give you access to features supported only by specific languages or "projectless" websites. This chapter covered the two sets of objects that give you access to those features for applications created in Visual Basic, C#, and ASP.NET.

CHAPTER 6

GENERATING LANGUAGE-NEUTRAL CODE

In this chapter:

- A Comprehensive Example
- Declarations
- Defining Classes
- Class Members
- Statements and Expressions
- Code Structures
- When All Else Fails: Code Snippets
- Other Code Features
- Code Providers
- Generating Code

If you need to produce code in multiple languages, the CodeDom is the tool you need. The CodeDom lets you build a description of procedural code (a `CodeCompileUnit`) using a set of objects and then attach that set of objects to a code provider that will convert those objects into procedural code in a specific language. In theory, you can produce code in any language that a CodeDom provider exists for. The code provider also includes support for compiling the resulting source code, although there is also a CodeDom provider that will convert your `CodeCompileUnit` directly into Microsoft Intermediate Language.

Although the `FileCodeModel` objects discussed in Chapter 3, "Manipulating Project Components," are also language neutral, the CodeDom can generate most kinds of procedural code whereas the `FileCodeModel` is limited to code structures (e.g., classes and methods) and declarations. In addition, whereas the `FileCodeModel` potentially supports multiple languages, in practice only C# is fully supported. The CodeDom supports any language that a provider exists for and a new provider can, of course, be added by developers who want to support a new language.

In practice, the CodeDom has three significant limitations. The first is that the CodeDom supports only those features that are common to all .NET languages—and not even all of those. (For instance, the Select...Case/switch construct isn't supported, nor is ElseIf.) Second, the CodeDom essentially targets .NET 2.0—the absence of direct support for LINQ is especially disappointing. Finally, writing CodeDom code is time consuming: it takes a lot of CodeDom to generate a little generated code. As a result, unless you have a driving need to support multiple languages, you may be better off generating procedural code just by inserting strings of code, copying code from a text file, or using a T4 template.

The first part of this chapter introduces the CodeDom with an example that generates six lines of simple code (and requires about 50 lines of CodeDom-related code) in order to show the structure of a CodeDom solution. In the following sections, I discuss the individual objects that make up the CodeDom in terms of the language constructs you would want to generate. If there is no CodeDom object that will do what you want, you can insert "literal" code—strings of text in some language— using code snippets, also discussed in this chapter. If you want to support features specific to your language, you may need to look at the support provided through the UserData object, also discussed in this chapter.

In the final section of this chapter, I cover the language providers and how to use them to generate your code. In addition to generating complete CodeCompileUnits, code providers support generating individual sections of your code, which can be helpful when debugging CodeDom solutions. I also show you how to use the code providers to create compiled code from your source code and to provide valid variable names.

A Comprehensive Example

The best way to introduce the CodeDom is to walk through an example that generates a simple piece of code. The typical process for writing CodeDom code is to first create the code you want to generate in the language of your choice and then to work through that code, translating it into CodeDom constructs, one line at a time. As you'll see in the section "Generating Partial Code" near the end of this chapter, you can also test your solution one piece at a time to see if your CodeDom code is generating the final code you want.

For this example, I translate a simple class (called MathFunctions) that has a single method (called AddTwoIntegers). The AddTwoIntegers method accepts two integers, adds them together, puts the result in a holding variable, and then returns the value that was stored returns the holding variable.

The Code to Be Generated

The code generated as the end result of this example will look like this in C# (I've removed some blank lines and reformatted the comments to fit in the page):

```
//---------------------------------------------------------------
// <auto-generated>
//     This code was generated by a tool.
//     Runtime Version:2.0.50727.3053
//
//     Changes to this file may cause incorrect behavior
//     and will be lost if the code is regenerated.
// </auto-generated>
//---------------------------------------------------------------
namespace CodeDomGenerator {
    public class MathFunctions {

    public virtual int AddTwoIntegers(int Number1, int Number2) {
            int Holding = 0;
            Holding = (Number1 + Number2);
            return Holding;
    }
  }
}
```

In Visual Basic, the equivalent generated code would look like this (I've deleted the comments and taken some liberty with indenting to fit the code on the page):

```
Option Strict Off
Option Explicit On

Imports System

Namespace CodeDomGenerator

Public Class MathFunctions

    Public Overridable Function AddTwoIntegers( _
            ByVal Number1 As Integer, _
```

```
            ByVal Number2 As Integer) As Integer
    Dim Holding As Integer = 0
    Holding = (Number1 + Number2)
    Return Holding
  End Function
 End Class
End Namespace
```

In general, when generating code, you want to avoid using CodeSnippets to insert "literal" code: Every time you use literal code, you take the chance that you won't be able to generate valid code for a target language. So, in this example, I've avoided using CodeSnippets completely. In addition, because a single variable name often has to be used in multiple places in CodeDom code, I've stored all my identifiers (e.g., variable names) in strings and then used those strings throughout my code. Storing identifiers in strings makes my CodeDom code easier to maintain should I want to change any variable's name (and supports letting the developer specify the identifiers to be used).

For this example, I've assumed two Imports/using statements to support this code:

```
using System.CodeDom;
using System.CodeDom.Compiler;
```

Using Variables, Data Types, and Literals

First, I set up the CodeDom objects that I'll need to work with the variables and parameters in my code. To refer to a variable in code, you create a CodeVariableReferenceExpression object, passing the variable name; to refer to a parameter passed to a method, you create a CodeArgumentReferenceExpression object, passing the name of the parameter. The following code sets the name for the variable used in the generated code (Holding) and the two parameters passed to the method (Number1, Number2). The code then creates CodeVariableReferenceExpression and CodeArgumentReferenceExpression objects for the variable and the two arguments. The code also defines a string to hold the name of the method (AddTwoIntegers):

```
string add2IntsName = "AddTwoIntegers";
string holdingName = "Holding";
string number1Name = "Number1";
string number2Name = "Number2";
```

```
CodeVariableReferenceExpression cvreHolding =
     new CodeVariableReferenceExpression(holdingName);
CodeArgumentReferenceExpression careNum1 =
     new CodeVariableReferenceExpression(number1Name);
CodeArgumentReferenceExpression careNum2 =
     new CodeVariableReferenceExpression(number2Name);
```

To specify data types, you use `CodeTypeReference` objects. The following code creates a `CodeTypeReference` object that specifies an integer data type. To represent literals in your code, you use `CodePrimitiveExpression` objects. The following code creates a `CodeTypeReference` for the int data type and `CodePrimitiveExpression` for the number zero:

```
CodeTypeReference ctrInt = new CodeTypeReference(typeof(int));
CodePrimitiveExpression cpeZero = new CodePrimitiveExpression(0);
```

Creating Namespaces and Classes

With those useful objects created, it's time to start assembling the code projects. The code objects (or graph) form a series of nested objects. The outermost object is the `CodeCompileUnit`. In this example, the first object I want to nest within the `CodeCompileUnit` is a namespace. To specify a namespace, I must create a `CodeNamespace` object, passing the name to be used for the namespace. I then add the `CodeNamespace` to the `CodeCompileUnit`'s Namespaces collection.

This example creates a `CodeCompileUnit` and then extracts the namespace for the first project in the solution and uses that to create the `CodeNamespace` object. Finally, the code adds the `CodeNamespace` to the `CodeCompileUnit`:

```
CodeCompileUnit ccu = new CodeCompileUnit();
Project prj = _applicationObject.Solution.Project.Item(1);
string namespcName =
     prj.Properties.Item("DefaultNamespace").Value.ToString();
CodeNamespace cn = new CodeNamespace(namespcName);
ccu.Namespaces.Add(cn);
```

Within the Namespace, you can have Imports/using statements (represented by `CodeNamespaceImport` objects). To create a `CodeNamespaceImport` object, you pass the name of the namespace you're adding and then add the `CodeNamespaceImport` to the `CodeNamespace`'s Imports collection. This example adds an Imports/using statement for the System namespace:

```
CodeNamespaceImport cni = new CodeNamespaceImport("System");
cn.Imports.Add(cni);
```

Within the namespace, I add my `MathFunctions` class, represented by a `CodeTypeDeclaration`. To create a `CodeTypeDeclaration`, you pass the name of your class and then add the `CodeTypeDeclaration` to the `CodeNamespace` object's `Types` collection. This example creates a class called `MathFunctions` and adds it to the `CodeNamespace`:

```
CodeTypeDeclaration ctd = new CodeTypeDeclaration("MathFunctions");
cn.Types.Add(ctd);
```

Adding Methods with Parameters

Within a `Class`, you can add methods, represented by `CodeMemberMethod` objects. Unlike the previous objects, you can't specify the name of the method when you create the `CodeMemberMethod`—you must set the `CodeMemberMethod` object's `Name` property after creating it. In addition, methods are private by default (unlike `CodeTypeDeclarations`, which are public by default), so you must set the `CodeMemberMethod` object's `Attributes` property to a member of the `MemberAttributes` enumeration (these values can be OR'd together to assign multiple attributes to the same method). The `CodeMemberMethod` has a `ReturnType` property that allows you to specify the type of the value returned by the method (if the method doesn't return a value, you should set its `ReturnType` to `typeof(void)`).

This code creates a public method called `AddTwoIntegers` and sets the `ReturnType` to the `CodeTypeReference` for int I created earlier:

```
CodeMemberMethod cmm = new CodeMemberMethod();
cmm.Attributes = MemberAttributes.Public;
cmm.Name = add2IntsName;
cmm.ReturnType = ctrInt;
ctd.Members.Add(cmm);
```

Most methods are passed parameters, which are represented by `CodeParameterDeclarationExpression` objects. To create a `Code ParameterDeclarationExpression`, you pass the parameter's data type (using a `CodeTypeReferenceExpression` object) and the name of the parameter. Once a parameter is created, you can add it to the `CodeMemberMethod`'s `Parameters` collection. This code creates two parameters using the strings holding the names of the parameters and the `CodeTypeReferenceExpression` I created earlier. After each parameter is created, the code adds it to the `CodeMemberMethod`'s `Parameters` collection:

```
CodeParameterDeclarationExpression cpde1 =
   new CodeParameterDeclarationExpression(ctreInt, number1Name);
cmm.Parameters.Add(cpde1);

CodeParameterDeclarationExpression cpde2 =
   new CodeParameterDeclarationExpression(ctrInt, number2Name);
cmm.Parameters.Add(cpde2);
```

Adding Statements to Methods

Within a `CodeMemberMethod`, you can add complete code statements to its `Statements` collection.

The first statement in my sample method is a declaration that defines an integer variable called `Holding` that is initialized to zero. Declarations are represented by `CodeVariableDeclarationStatements`, which are passed a `CodeTypeReferenceExpression` object that specifies the variable's data type, the variable's name, and the variable's initialization value. This example creates a variable using the `CodeTypeReferenceExpression` for an int, the variable name in a string, and a `CodePrimitiveExpression` for a literal 0. Once created, the code adds the `CodeVariableDeclaration` to the `CodeMemberMethod`'s `Statements` collection:

```
CodeVariableDeclarationStatement cvds =
    new CodeVariableDeclarationStatement(ctreInt, holdingName, cpeZero);
cmm.Statements.Add(cvds);
```

To create the code inside the `AddTwoIntegers` method, the next line of code adds two variables and puts the result in a third variable. This single line of code requires two objects: a `CodeBinaryOperatorExpression` object that represents any operation involving two inputs (in this case, the two numbers to be added) and a `CodeAssignStatement` object that represents a statement that assigns an expression to a variable.

To create a `CodeBinaryOperatorExpression`, you pass references to the two inputs (`CodeVariableReferenceExpression` objects for variables, `CodePrimitiveExpression` objects for values) and a value from the `CodeBinaryOperatorType` enumeration specifying the operation to perform.

When creating a `CodeAssignStatement`, you pass two parameters: a `CodeVariableReferenceExpression` for the variable being set and the expression holding the variable.

This example first creates the `CodeBinaryOperatorExpression` object, passing references to the `Number1` and `Number2` parameters (created earlier) along with the Add value from the CodeBinaryOperatorType enumeration. The code then creates a CodeAssignStatement, passing the CodeBinaryOperatorExpression and a reference to the Holding variable (also created earlier). Once the CodeAssignStatement is created, the code adds it to the CodeMemberMethod's Statements collection:

```
CodeBinaryOperatorExpression cboe =
    new CodeBinaryOperatorExpression(careNum1,
            CodeBinaryOperatorType.Add, careNum2);
CodeAssignStatement cas = new CodeAssignStatement(cvreHolding, cboe);
cmm.Statements.Add(cas);
```

The final statement in the generated method returns the Holding variable. A return statement is represented by a Code MethodReturnStatement, which must be passed a CodeVariable ReferenceExpression that points to the variable to return. This example creates a CodeMethodReturnStatement by passing a CodeTypeReference Expression for the Holding variable. The code then adds the return statement to the Statements collection for the CodeMemberMethod:

```
CodeMethodReturnStatement crs = new
                CodeMethodReturnStatement(cvreHolding);
cmm.Statements.Add(crs);
```

Generating Code

To generate code from the graph, you need to provide something to hold the generated text. The code-generation process writes to a stream object so you can send output, if you wish, directly to a file on your hard disk. Typically, however, I prefer to hold code in a string variable so that I can insert it into a file using the CodeEditor objects (discussed in Chapter 4, "Modifying Code in the Editor"). The first step, therefore, in generating code is to create a StringBuilder to hold the code and a StringWriter to pass the generated code to the StringBuilder:

```
StringBuilder generatedCode;
System.IO.StringWriter codeWriter;

generatedCode = new StringBuilder();
codeWriter = new System.IO.StringWriter(generatedCode);
```

To actually generate your code, you need to create a code provider object specific to the language you want to generate. Once you've created a code provider object, you call its `GenerateCodeFromCompileUnit` method, passing your graph of CodeDom objects (the `CodeCompileUnit`), the `StringWriter`, and a third option specifying any generation options (discussed later in this chapter).

This code creates the generator for Visual Basic and writes the code to the `StringWriter` created in the previous example without specifying any generation options:

```
Microsoft.VisualBasic.VBCodeProvider vbProv =
        new Microsoft.VisualBasic.VBCodeProvider();
vbProv.GenerateCodeFromCompileUnit(ccu, codeWriter, null);
```

This example does the same thing for C#:

```
Microsoft.CSharp.CSharpCodeProvider csProv =
        new Microsoft.CSharp.CSharpCodeProvider();
csProv.GenerateCodeFromCompileUnit(ccu, codeWriter, null);
```

The result would be the code shown at the start of this section.

The rest of this chapter describes the CodeDom objects in detail. One note: I've made the assumption that, when creating a CodeDom object, you'll pass as many parameters as possible to the object's constructor. However, most of the CodeDom objects will also let you create the object without passing any values to the constructor. After creating the object, you can then configure it by setting the object's properties.

Declarations

In the CodeDom, generating variable declarations has two components: declaring the variable and using the variable in code.

BEST PRACTICE   Because you must use the name of the variable both when declaring it and when creating a reference to it, declare your variable names as string values that you can use in both places. It's considerably easier to change the values of fields declared at the start of the class rather than track down the first place in your code where you use the name.

Local Scalar Variables

To generate the declaration for a scalar variable, you create a `CodeVariableDeclarationStatement` object, passing the data type of the object, its name, and the value it is to be initialized to. To specify the data type, you should use a `CodeTypeReference` object, passing it the Type of the data type you want to use in the declaration. For your initialization value, you can use a `CodePrimitiveExpression` object, which can represent most literals (e.g., strings, null/Nothing, and numbers but not dates).

The following code first initializes a variable with the name `cust` that will be used in the generated code. The code then creates a `CodeTypeReference` object of type Customer and a `CodePrimitiveExpression` set to null (this will be converted to Nothing if Visual Basic code is generated). Finally, the example creates a `CodeVariableDeclarationObject`, passing the Customer data type, the name to be used for the variable, and the reference to Nothing/null:

```
string customerName = "cust";
CodeTypeReference ctrCust = new CodeTypeReference(typeof(Customer));
CodePrimitiveExpression cpeNull = new CodePrimitiveExpression(null);
CodeVariableDeclarationStatement cvdsCust =
  new CodeVariableDeclarationStatement(ctrCust, customerName, cpeNull);
```

The resulting code would look like this in C# (notice that the type declaration includes the namespace):

```
NorthwindObjects.Customer cust = null;
```

The code would look like this in Visual Basic:

```
Dim cust As NorthwindObjects.Customer = Nothing
```

If the type you want to use in the declaration doesn't exist (e.g., if the type is also going to be generated), you can pass a string to the `CodeTypeReference` object when creating it:

```
CodeTypeReference ctrCust = new CodeTypeReference("Customer");
```

To initialize a variable to the default value for its data type, you can create a `CodeDefaultValueExpression`, passing a `CodeTypeReference`. You can then use the `CodeDefaultValueExpression` as the third parameter passed when creating the `CodeVariableDeclarationStatement`. This example creates an integer variable called `counter` and initializes it to the default value for an integer:

```
CodeTypeReference ctr = new CodeTypeReference(typeof(int));
CodeDefaultValueExpression cdve = new CodeDefaultValueExpression(ctr);
CodeVariableDeclarationStatement cvds;
CodeVariableDeclarationStatement =
    cvds = new CodeVariableDeclarationStatement(ctr, "counter", cdve)
```

The result would look like this in C# (which uses C#'s `default` keyword):

```
int x = default(int);
```

In Visual Basic, the code is less obvious:

```
Dim x As [Integer] = CType(Nothing, [Integer])
```

To use the local variable whose declaration you've generated in your code, you create a `CodeVariableReferenceExpression`. For instance, to use the `cust` variable declared in the previous section, you would create a `CodeVariableReferenceExpression` object that refers to the `cust` variable. To create a `CodeVariableReferenceExpression`, you pass the name of the variable used to create the declaration. This example creates a `CodeVariableReferenceExpression` using the `cust` variable and then uses it to create a return statement:

```
CodeVariableReferenceExpression cvreCust =
        new CodeVariableReferenceExpression(customerName);
CodeMethodReturnStatement crsCust =
        new CodeMethodReturnStatement(cvreCust);
```

Alternatively, you can use the `Name` property of the `CodeVariable DeclarationStatement` when creating your `CodeVariableReferenceExpression`, as this example does:

```
CodeVariableReferenceExpression cvreCust =
        new CodeVariableReferenceExpression(cvdsCust.Name);
CodeMethodReturnStatement crsCust =
        new CodeMethodReturnStatement(cvreCust);
```

The result would look like this in C#:

```
return cust;
```

The resulting code would look like this in Visual Basic:

```
Return cust
```

To declare a variable as a generic type, just pass the name of the parameter type. This example creates a generic declaration of type T:

```
string ParmType = "T";
string holdingName = "Holding";
CodeVariableDeclarationStatement cvdsGeneric =
 new CodeVariableDeclarationStatement(ParmType, holdingName);
```

The result in C# would be the following:

```
T Holding;
```

And here's the result in Visual Basic:

```
Dim Holding As T
```

If you're creating a `CodeTypeReference` for a Generic data type, you'll need to add an argument for the generic's type parameter. The type parameter is also created as a `CodeTypeReference` object, but you should set the `CodeTypeReference`'s `Options` property to the `CodeTypeReference Options.GenericTypeParameter` enumerated value.

This example first creates a `CodeTypeReference` for a `List`. It then creates a second `CodeTypeReference` for the `T` argument to be used with the `List`. The code sets the `Options` property on the `CodeTypeReference` object for the `T` argument and adds it to the `TypeArguments` collection for the original `List`. Finally, the code creates a `CodeVariableDeclaration` using the `CodeTypeReference` for the `List`:

```
CodeTypeReference ctrList = new
        CodeTypeReference(typeof(System.Collections.Generic.List));
CodeTypeReference ctrParm = new CodeTypeReference("T");
ctrParm.Options = CodeTypeReferenceOptions.GenericTypeParameter;
ctrList.TypeArguments.Add(ctrParm);
CodeVariableDeclarationStatement cvds =
    new CodeVariableDeclarationStatement(ctrList, "MyList", Nothing);
```

The resulting C# code would look like this:

```
System.Collections.Generic.List<T> myLists;
```

The VB code, like this:

```
Dim myList As System.Collections.Generic.List(Of T)
```

Arrays

Working with arrays involves three activities: declaring the array, initializing it, and accessing positions in the array (discussed in the section "Accessing Arrays" later in this chapter).

To generate the declaration for an array, you create a `CodeVariableDeclarationExpression` as you would for a scalar variable, but pass a `CodeArrayCreateExpression` for the array's initialization value. When creating the `CodeArrayCreateExpression`, you specify the type of the array and set its size in one of two ways:

- By specifying the size
- By providing the values for the array

To create a `CodeArrayCreateExpression` specifying the array's size, you first create a `CodeTypeReference` that specifies the data type of the array and a `CodePrimitiveExpression` holding the size of the array. You then pass those parameters to the `CodeArrayCreateExpression`. You next create the `CodeVariableDeclarationStatement`, passing the array's data type, the name of the array, and the just-created `CodeArrayCreate Expression`. This example creates an array of strings that has five positions:

```
CodeTypeReference ctrString = new CodeTypeReference(typeof(string));
CodePrimitiveExpression cpeArraySize = new CodePrimitiveExpression(5);
CodeArrayCreateExpression cace =
 new CodeArrayCreateExpression(ctrString, cpeArraySize);

string arrayName = "Employees";
CodeTypeReference ctrStringArray =
 new CodeTypeReference(typeof(string[]));
CodeVariableDeclarationStatement cvdsArray =
 new CodeVariableDeclarationStatement(ctrStringArray, arrayName, cace);
```

The resulting code would look like this in C#:

```
string[] Employees = new string[5];
```

The generated code looks less obvious in Visual Basic:

```
Dim Employees((5) - 1) As String
```

To initialize the array by providing a set of values, ensure that the second parameter you provide when creating a `CodeArrayCreateExpression` is not an integer or provides more than two parameters. In either of those cases, the `CodeArrayCreateExpression` assumes that you are providing a set of values to initialize the array (to put it another way, you can't initialize an array with a single integer variable—the `CodeArrayCreateExpression` will assume that the integer is the array's size, not a value).

This example first creates `CodePrimitiveExpressions` for each of the values to be used in initializing the array ("Pat" and "Sam"). These values are then passed as the second and subsequent parameters to the `CodeArrayCreateExpression` object when it is created. Finally, the resulting `CodeArrayCreateExpression` is passed to a `CodeVariableDeclaration Statement` object:

```
CodeTypeReference ctrString = new CodeTypeReference(typeof(string));
CodePrimitiveExpression cpeArraySize = new CodePrimitiveExpression(5);

CodePrimitiveExpression cpePat = new CodePrimitiveExpression("Pat");
CodePrimitiveExpression cpeSam = new CodePrimitiveExpression("Sam");
CodeArrayCreateExpression cace =
    new CodeArrayCreateExpression(ctrString, cpeArraySize,
                                              cpePat, cpeSam);

string arrayName = "Employees";
CodeTypeReference ctrStringArray =
 new CodeTypeReference(typeof(string[]));
CodeVariableDeclarationStatement cvdsArray =
   new CodeVariableDeclarationStatement(ctrStringArray, arrayName,cace);
```

The resulting code would look like this in C#:

```
string[] Employees = new string[] {"Pat", "Sam"};
```

In Visual Basic, the code would look like this:

```
Dim Employees() As String = New String() {"Pat", "Sam"}
```

The CodeDom doesn't directly support arrays with multiple dimensions. You can create arrays with multiple dimensions by using nested

`CodeArrayCreateExpressions,` but you're at the mercy of your code provider as to how that will be interpreted (and, if the language doesn't support arrays with multiple dimensions, your code won't generate at all).

BEST PRACTICE   Avoid using arrays with multiple dimensions—create multiple arrays instead.

To access your array by position, create a `CodeVariableReference Expression` as you would for any other variable.

Delegates

Generating code for a delegate can require up to three separate steps. First, you need to define the delegate itself. Second, before you can use a delegate, you must declare a variable to hold a reference to the delegate. Finally, you can invoke the delegate, passing any parameter values that the underlying method requires. (Invoking a delegate is discussed in the section "Invoking Delegates" later in this chapter.)

Defining a Delegate

The first step in generating a delegate is to create a `CodeTypeDelegate` object, passing the name of the delegate. If the delegate returns a value, you can set the `CodeTypeDelegate` object's `ReturnType` property to the data type of the value returned, using a `CodeTypeReference` object. If the delegate accepts parameters, you must create `CodeParameterDeclarationExpression` objects for each parameter, passing a `CodeTypeReference` specifying the data type of the parameter and its name. As you create each `CodeParameterDeclarationExpression`, you can add it to the `CodeParameterDeclarationExpression` object's `Parameters` collection using its `Add` method.

This example begins by storing the delegate's name in a string variable and then using that to create the `CodeTypeDelegate` object. Because the delegate returns a string value, the next step sets the `CodeTypeDelegate` object's `ReturnType` property to a `CodeTypeReference` for a string. The code then creates a parameter using a `CodeParameterDeclarationExpression`, passing a string and the name of the parameter (`AddressType`). Once the `CodeParameterDeclarationExpression` is created, the code adds the parameter to the `CodeTypeDelegate` object's `Parameters` collection. In the final line, the `CodeTypeDelegate` is added to the `CodeNamespace` object:

```
string delegateName = "AddressDelegate";
CodeTypeDelegate ctd = new CodeTypeDelegate(delegateName);
```

```
ctd.ReturnType = ctrString;

string addressTypeName = "AddressType";
CodeParameterDeclarationExpression cpde =
   new CodeParameterDeclarationExpression(ctrString, addressTypeName);
ctd.Parameters.Add(cpde);

cn.Types.Add(ctd);
```

The resulting code would look like this in C#:

```
public delegate string AddressDelegate(string AddressType);
```

In Visual Basic:

```
Public Delegate Function AddressDelegate( _
                        ByVal AddressType As String) As String
```

Instantiating the Delegate

The declaration for the variable that holds a reference to the delegate and also instantiates the delegate is created using two objects: a `CodeDelegateCreateExpression` object, which specifies the delegate and is passed to the `CodeVariableDeclarationStatement`. To create a `CodeDelegateCreateExpression`, you pass a reference to the delegate to be created, a reference to the class holding the method to be called, and the name of the method to call.

This example creates an instance of the `AddressDelegate` delegate, pointing to the `Address` method of the object referenced by the `cust` variable. The first two lines of code create a `CodeVariableReferenceExpression` that points to the object variable holding the method to be called. The next two lines store the name of the method in a string and create a `CodeTypeReference` object for the delegate's type. The fifth line creates a `CodeDelegateCreateExpression` using the return type, the object variable, and the name of the method. The final two lines of code create the `CodeVariableDeclarationStatement` object using the delegate type again, the name to be used for the variable holding the reference to the delegate, and the just-created `CodeDelegateCreateExpression`:

```
string customerName = "cust";
CodeVariableReferenceExpression cvreCust =
        new CodeVariableReferenceExpression(customerName);
```

```
string getAddressName = "getAddress";
CodeTypeReference ctrDelegate =
            new CodeTypeReference(typeof(AddressDelegate));

CodeDelegateCreateExpression cdce = new
    CodeDelegateCreateExpression(ctrDelegate, cvreCust, getAddressName);

string addressName = "address";
CodeVariableDeclarationStatement cvdsDelegate = new
    CodeVariableDeclarationStatement(ctrDelegate, addressName, cdce);
```

The resulting code would look like this in C#:

```
CodeDomGenerator.AddressDelegate address =
                new NorthwindObjects.AddressDelegate(cust.Address);
```

And like this in Visual Basic:

```
Dim address As CodeDomGenerator.AddressDelegate =
                AddressOf cust.Address
```

As with creating a reference to a class, if the delegate doesn't exist at the time you generate this code, you can pass a string to the CodeTypeReference object instead of the delegate's Type object:

```
CodeTypeReference ctrDelegate = new CodeTypeReference("MyAddress");
```

Defining Classes

The following was shown in the original example at the start of this chapter:

- To create a namespace you create a CodeNamespace object, passing the name of the namespace.
- To create an Imports or using statement, you create a CodeNamespaceImport object, passing the name of the namespace and then add it to the namespace's Imports collection. (You must still add any references required by the namespaces using the FileCodeModel described in Chapter 3.)

■ To create a class, you create a `CodeTypeDeclaration` object, passing the name of the class, and add the `CodeTypeDeclaration` to the `CodeNamespace` object's `Types` collection. You can set the `CodeTypeDeclaration`'s `Attributes` property to make the class public, private, shared, and so on.

In this section, I look at what you can do with a class once you've created it. You can have your class inherit from another class, implement interfaces, or define the class as a generic. Adding custom attributes (e.g., `<Serialization>`), inserting comments, and using directives are discussed in the section "Other Code Features" later in this chapter.

Inheritance and Interfaces

To have your generated class inherit from some other class, you must first create a `CodeTypeReference` to the base class. You can then add that `CodeTypeReference` to the `CodeTypeDelaration` object's `BaseTypes` collection.

This example creates a `CodeCompileUnit`, a `CodeNamespace`, and a `CodeTypeDeclaration` representing a derived class. The code then creates a `CodeTypeReference` representing a base class and adds it to the `CodeTypeDeclaration` object's `BaseTypes` collection:

```
string namespaceName = "MyNamespace";
string className = "MyClass";

CodeCompileUnit ccu = new CodeCompileUnit();
CodeNamespace cn = new CodeNamespace(namespaceName);
ccu.Namespace.Add(cn);

CodeTypeDeclaration ctd = new CodeTypeDeclaration(MyClass);
cn.Types.Add(ctd);

CodeTypeReference ctrCust = new CodeTypeReference(typeof(Customer));
ctd.BaseTypes.Add(ctrCust);
```

The result would look like this in C# (assuming that the `Customer` object is in a namespace called `NorthwindObjects`):

```
Namespace MyNamespace{
    public class MyClass : NorthwindObjects.Customer {
```

And like this in Visual Basic:

```
Namespace MyNamespace

Public Class MyClass
        Inherits NorthwindObjects.Customer
```

Adding a `CodeTypeReference` that references an interface is identical to the code for adding a base object. The resulting code is different only in Visual Basic:

```
Namespace MyNamespace

Public Class MyClass
        Implements NorthwindObjects.ICustomer
```

Adding an interface does not implement the interface. It's your responsibility to add the members that the interface requires and to tie those members back to the interface (discussed later in this chapter in the section "Class Members" in the subsection "Methods").

Generics and Partial Classes

To create a generic class, you only add a parameter to represent the class's data type to the `CodeTypeDeclaration` object's `TypeParameters` collection. To create a partial class, you only need to set the `CodeTypeDeclaration` object's `IsPartial` property to True. This example does both, adding a parameter called `T` to the `TypeParameters` collection and setting the `IsPartial` property to True. Because it's critical to coordinate the name used for type parameters, the name of the type parameter is stored in a string:

```
CodeTypeDeclaration ctd = new CodeTypeDeclaration("MathFunctions");
string classTypeParmName = "T";
ctd.TypeParameters.Add(classTypeParmName);
ctd.IsPartial = true;
```

The result would look like this in C#:

```
public partial class MathFunctions<T> {
```

And like this in Visual Basic:

```
Partial Public Class MathFunctions(Of T)
```

Class Members

Once you've created a class, you'll want to add methods, properties, events, and fields to it. Your methods will typically require parameters, and you'll need to reference those parameters (and fields) from code in your methods. In addition, for both your methods and properties you may want to create a `Generic` parameter or create parameters that are passed by reference instead of being passed by value. In addition to the standard members of a class, you'll also need to create the special members of a class: constructors, indexers, and entry points (`Sub Main` and `Main`).

Fields

In the CodeDom, you create fields in a way similar to local variables: You create a reference to the data type and then a `CodeMemberField` object from the type reference (which you add to the class rather than to a member).

BEST PRACTICE   For any field that you'll be using in your code (and why else would you define a field?), create a `CodeFieldReferenceExpression` object that points to the field. Use this object when creating expressions and statements that reference the field.

Here's what you need for creating a field and a reference to it:

- A string variable to hold the name of the field. (This allows you to centralize control of your field names into a section of your code that declares all of the names you use in your code.)
- A `CodeTypeReference` for the data type for the field.
- A `CodeMemberField` that declares the field.
- An expression to initialize the field through the `Init` property on the `CodeMemberField`.
- A `CodeFieldReferenceExpression` that references the field and allows you to use the field in code generated later in the project.

Once the `CodeMemberField` is created, you can use its `InitExpression` property to set the field's initialization value (you can't create a read-only field because that option is language-specific and not supported by the CodeDom). The `CodeTypeReference` is added to the `Members` collection of a `CodeTypeDeclaration` object.

This example creates an integer field called `Holding` and initializes it to zero using a `CodePrimitiveExpression`. After initializing the field, the code adds it to the Members collection of the CodeTypeDeclaration object that represents the class:

```
string holdingName = "Holding";
CodeTypeReference ctrInt = new CodeTypeReference(typeof(int));
CodeMemberField cmfHolding = new CodeMemberField(ctrInt, holdingName);

CodePrimitiveExpression cpeZero = new CodePrimitiveExpression(0);
cmfHolding.InitExpression = cpeZero;

ctd.Members.Add(cmfHolding);
```

The result looks like this in C#:

```
private int Holding = 0;
```

And like this in Visual Basic:

```
Private Holding As Integer = 0
```

When creating a CodeFieldReferenceExpression to use later in your code-generation process, you must pass a reference to the object that contains the field and the name of the field. For the reference to the containing object just pass null or Nothing as the first parameter to the CodeFieldReferenceExpression object. You can use null/Nothing for the containing object because you usually can't access fields in other objects (most fields are declared as private)—typically you will be accessing fields in the same object as your code. This example creates a reference to be used whenever the Holding field created in the previous example is needed and uses the Name property of that CodeMemberField object to pass the name of the field:

```
CodeFieldReferenceExpression cfre =
    new CodeFieldReferenceExpression(null, cmfHolding.Name);
```

Methods

A method is created using the CodeMemberMethod object. Unlike most of the objects in the CodeDom, you can't pass any parameters to the object when it is created: All customization is done by setting properties on the CodeMemberMethod after it is created.

This example stores the name of the method in a string and then creates a CodeMemberMethod and uses the string to set the object's name. Like a field, a `CodeMemberMethod` is added to the `Members` collection of the `CodeTypeDeclaration` object that represents the class:

```
string add2IntsName = "AddTwoIntegers";
CodeMemberMethod cmm = new CodeMemberMethod();
cmm.Name = add2IntsName;
ctd.Members.Add(cmm);
```

The result would look like this in C#:

```
private void AddTwoIntegers() {
```

And like this in Visual Basic:

```
Private Sub AddTwoIntegers()
```

Other properties on the `CodeMemberMethod` include the following:

- **ReturnType**—Set this property to a `CodeTypeReference` object to specify the data type of the values returned by this method.
- **Attributes**—Control attributes on the method (e.g. `public`, `static`) by setting this property to members of the `MemberAttributes` collection (these members can be OR'd together to set multiple values).
- **ImplementationTypes**—If the method is implementing part of an interface, the `CodeTypeReference` for that interface should be added to the `ImplementationTypes` collection. When generating C# code, the method must have the same name as the member in the interface. In Visual Basic, the method can have any name.
- **PrivateImplementationType**—For a method that implements a member of an interface, set this property to the `CodeTypeReference` that points to the interface.
- **Statements**—The code that makes up the method is to be added to this collection.

The settings of these properties are interrelated. For instance, setting the `PrivateImplemenationType` property will make the member private even if you set the `Attributes` property to `MemberAttributes.Public`. Setting the `Attributes` property solely to `MemberAttributes.Public` will also make the member `virtual`/`Overridable`.

The following code creates a method that implements the `Delete` method of the `ICustomer` interface that returns a Boolean value. The code first creates a variable to hold the method name and then initializes `CodeTypeReference` objects for a Boolean data type and the `ICustomer` interface. The `CodeMemberMethod` object is then created and its properties set using those variables. Finally, the configured `CodeMemberMethod` is added to the `Members` collection of the `CodeTypeDeclaration` object that represents the `Class`:

```
string deleteName = "Delete";
CodeTypeReference ctrBool = new CodeTypeReference(typeof(bool));
CodeTypeReference ctrICust = new CodeTypeReference(typeof(ICustomer));

CodeMemberMethod cmm = new CodeMemberMethod();
cmm.Name = deleteName;
cmm.Attributes = MemberAttributes.Public | MemberAttributes.Final;
cmm.ReturnType = ctrBool;
cmm.ImplementationTypes.Add(ctrICust);

ctd.Members.Add(cmm);
```

In C#, the resulting code would look like this (you can see that adding the `ICustomer` interface has no effect on C# code—the method name just needs to match the name of the corresponding method in the interface to tie the method to the interface):

```
public bool Delete() {
```

In Visual Basic, the result would look like this (in Visual Basic, adding the interface generates code that explicitly connects the member to the corresponding method in the `ICustomer` interface):

```
Public Function Delete() As Boolean _
    Implements NorthwindObjects.ICustomer.Delete
```

BEST PRACTICE If you intend to call your method from elsewhere in your code, create a `CodeMethodReferenceExpression` object for each method you generate.

When creating a `CodeMethodReferenceExpression` object, you must pass a reference to the class holding the object and the name of the method. (Calling the method is discussed in the section "Invoking Methods.") This example creates a reference to the method in the base class that this class inherits from:

```
CodeMethodReferenceExpression cmre =
        new CodeMethodReferenceExpression(
                new CodeBaseReferenceExpression(), cmm.Name);
```

You can also create a `CodeMethodReferenceExpression` by passing a reference to an object variable and the name of the method. Optionally, you can pass any necessary parameters. This example creates a reference to a method called `Delete` in the current class without passing any parameters:

```
string deleteName = "Delete";
CodeMethodReferenceExpression cmre =
    new CodeMethodReferenceExpression(new CodeThisReferenceExpression(),
                deleteName);
```

Generic Methods

To create a generic method, you must add a `CodeTypeParameter` to the `CodeMemberMethod` object's `CodeTypeParameters` collection. To create a `CodeTypeParameter`, you just pass the string name to be used for the parameter. You'll want to use the same string that was used to define the type parameter you used when defining the class (see the earlier section "Generics and Partial Classes"). This example uses a string value to specify the type parameter:

```
string methodTypeParmName = "T";
CodeTypeParameter ctp = new CodeTypeParameter(methodTypeParmName);
cmmCreateCustomer.TypeParameters.Add(ctp);
```

The resulting code in C# looks like this:

```
private void CreateCustomer<T>()    {}
```

And like this in Visual Basic:

```
Private Sub CreateCustomer(Of T)()
End Sub
```

A `CodeTypeParameter` can have constraints added to it that restrict the data types that are permitted to be used with the generic. This example sets the `Generic` parameter for the `Customer` class and classes that derive from it before adding the `CodeTypeParameter` to the method's `TypeParameters` collection:

```
Dim ccm As New CodeMemberMethod
ccm.Name = "DeleteCustomer"
Dim ctp As New CodeTypeParameter("T")
Dim ctr As New CodeTypeReference("Customer")
ctp.Constraints.Add(ctr)
ccm.TypeParameters.Add(ctp)
```

The resulting code would look like this in C#:

```
private void DeleteCustomer<T>()
    where T : Customer {
}
```

In Visual Basic:

```
Private Sub DeleteCustomer(Of T As Customer)()
End Sub
```

You can also specify that the class passed into the Generic parameter must have a default constructor by setting the CodeTypeParameter's HasConstructorConstraint property to True.

Parameters

To add a parameter to your method, you create a CodeParameterDeclarationExpression object, passing the data type and the name of the parameter. Once the CodeParameterDeclaration Expression object is created, you add it to the CodeMemberMethod object that represents the method. Parameters must be added in the order you want them to appear in when your code is generated.

This example creates a method named AddTwoIntegers and then creates two integer parameters and adds them to the method:

```
string add2IntsName = "AddTwoIntegers";
string number1Name = "Number1";
string number2Name = "Number2";
CodeMemberMethod cmm = new CodeMemberMethod();
cmm.Name = add2IntsName;

CodeParameterDeclarationExpression cpde1 =
   new CodeParameterDeclarationExpression(ctrInt, number1Name);
CodeParameterDeclarationExpression cpde2 =
```

```
    new CodeParameterDeclarationExpression(ctrInt, number2Name);
cmm.Parameters.Add(cpde1);
cmm.Parameters.Add(cpde2);
```

In C#, the result would look like this:

```
private void AddTwoIntegers(int Number1, int Number2) {
```

In Visual Basic, the result would look like this:

```
Private Sub AddTwoIntegers(ByVal Number1 As Integer, _
        ByVal Number2 As Integer)
```

To create an `out` (or reference) parameter, set the `Direction` property of the `CodeParameterDeclarationExpression` to a member of the `FieldDirection` enumeration, which includes `in` (the default), `out`, and `ref`. For Visual Basic, the `ref` and `out` settings generate the same code. This example creates a reference parameter:

```
cpde2.Direction = FieldDirection.Ref;
```

Events

Defining an event, raising it, and creating a handler for the event requires generating code for the following:

- The delegate that defines the event
- The event declaration
- The code that raises the event
- The method that will handle the event
- The code that wires up the event to the handler

BEST PRACTICE   Because these components often share a common "root" name (e.g., if the event is named `CustomerNotFound`, the delegate is named `CustomerNotFoundEventHandler`), it's a good practice to first define a string variable to hold that root name:

```
string notFoundName = "CustomerNotFound";
```

Defining the Delegate

The first step in generating an event is to define the delegate. (Delegates are described in detail in the earlier section, "Delegates.") This example generates the code to create a delegate called CustomerNotFoundHandler that follows the standard pattern for an event: two parameters, with the first called sender (of type object) and the second called e (of type EventArgs). Once the delegate's code is generated, the code adds it to the CodeNamespace object's Types collection and creates a CodeTypeReference to the delegate:

```
string delegateNotFound = notFoundName + "EventHandler";
CodeTypeDelegate ctdNotFound = new CodeTypeDelegate(delegateNotFound);

string senderName = "sender";
CodeTypeReference ctrObject =
      new CodeTypeReference(typeof(object));
CodeParameterDeclarationExpression cpdeSender =
      new CodeParameterDeclarationExpression(ctrObject, senderName);
ctdNotFound.Parameters.Add(cpdeSender);

string eName = "e";
CodeTypeReference ctrEventArgs =
      new CodeTypeReference(typeof(EventArgs));
         CodeParameterDeclarationExpression cpdeE = new
            CodeParameterDeclarationExpression(ctrEventArgs, eName);
ctdNotFound.Parameters.Add(cpdeE);

cn.Types.Add(ctdNotFound);
CodeTypeReference ctrNotFound =
      new CodeTypeReference(delegateNotFound);
```

The resulting code would look like this in C#:

```
public delegate void CustomerNotFoundEventHandler(
            object sender, System.EventArgs e);
```

And like this in Visual Basic:

```
Public Delegate Sub CustomerNotFoundEventHandler(
         ByVal sender As Object, ByVal e As System.EventArgs)
```

Defining the Event

Once the code for generating the delegate is created, you can define the event by creating a CodeMemberEvent object and setting its Name, Attributes, and Type properties. The Type property must be set to the CodeTypeReference for the delegate. You then add the CodeMemberEvent to the Members collection of the CodeTypeDeclaration object that represents a Class. This example defines a public event named CustomerNotFound that uses the CustomerNotFound delegate created in the previous example and adds it to the Class:

```
CodeMemberEvent cme = new CodeMemberEvent();
cme.Name = notFoundName;
cme.Attributes = MemberAttributes.Public;
CodeTypeReference ctrNotFound =
        new CodeTypeReference(delegateNotFound);

ctd.Members.Add(cme);
```

In C#, the resulting code would look like this:

```
public event CustomerNotFoundEventHandler CustomerNotFound;
```

In Visual Basic, the code looks like this:

```
Public Event CustomerNotFound As CustomerNotFoundEventHandler
```

Raising an Event

With the code that generates the event created, you can generate the code to raise the event. You first need a CodeEventReferenceExpression to reference the event. The CodeEventReferenceExpression requires a reference to the class holding the event (if the event is in the same class as the method, you can use the CodeThisReferenceExpression object) and the name of the event. This example creates a CodeEventReferenceExpression for the event defined in the previous examples:

```
CodeEventReferenceExpression cereNotFound =
    new CodeEventReferenceExpression(
        new CodeThisReferenceExpression(), cme.Name);
```

You can now use the CodeEventReferenceExpression to generate the code that raises the event by passing it to a CodeDelegateInvokeExpression.

(The `CodeDelegateInvokeExpression` is described in detail in the section "Invoking Delegates.") In this example, rather than passing the two parameters (`sender` and `e`) to the `CodeDelegateInvokeExpression` object when the object is created, this code adds them to the object's `Parameters` collection. Once the `CodeDelegateInvokeExpression` is created, the code adds it to a method called `OnCustomerNotFound` and then adds that method to the class:

```
CodeDelegateInvokeExpression cdieNotFound =
        new CodeDelegateInvokeExpression(cereNotFound);
cdieNotFound.Parameters.Add(new CodeThisReferenceExpression());
CodeVariableReferenceExpression cvreEName =
        new CodeVariableReferenceExpression(eName);
cdieNotFound.Parameters.Add(cvreEName);

CodeMemberMethod cmmOnNotFound = new CodeMemberMethod();
cmmOnNotFound.Name = "On" + notFoundName;

cmmOnNotFound.Statements.Add(cdieNotFound);
ctd.Members.Add(cmmOnNotFound);
```

In C#, the generated code would look like this:

```
private void OnCustomerNotFound() {
   this.CustomerNotFound(this, e);
}
```

And like this in Visual Basic:

```
Private Sub OnCustomerNotFound()
 RaiseEvent CustomerNotFound(Me, e)
End Sub
```

Creating an Event Handler

You can also generate a method that will handle the event.

BEST PRACTICE Although an event handler is just another method, you can reuse the `CodeParameterDeclarationExpression` object created when defining the delegate to ensure that you define a method that accepts the correct parameters.

This example creates a method by recycling the event's `CodeParameterDeclarationExpression`. Once the method is created, the code adds it to the `CodeTypeDeclaration` that represents the `Class`:

```
CodeMemberMethod cmmNotFound = new CodeMemberMethod();
cmmNotFound.Name = "Handle" + notFoundName;
cmmNotFound.Parameters.Add(cpdeSender);
cmmNotFound.Parameters.Add(cpdeE);
ctd.Members.Add(cmmNotFound);
```

In C#, the resulting method would look like this:

```
private void HandleCustomerNotFound(object sender, System.EventArgs e){
}
```

And like this in Visual Basic:

```
Private Sub HandleCustomerNotFound(ByVal sender As Object,
                            ByVal e As System.EventArgs)
End Sub
```

Wiring Up an Event

With the method and its handler defined, you can generate the code to wire up the event to the handler method. This is a two-step process. First, you must generate the part of the statement that instantiates the delegate by creating a `CodeDelegateCreateExpression`. When you create the `CodeDelegateCreateExpression`, you pass a `CodeTypeReference` object for the delegate, a reference to the class holding the delegate, and the name of the method that will handle the event. For the second step, you create a `CodeAttachEventStatement` by passing a reference to the class holding the handler method, the name of the event, and the `CodeDelegateCreate Expression` you just created.

This example generates the code to wire the `CustomerNotFound` event to the `HandleCustomerNotFound` method, both of which are in the current class:

```
CodeDelegateCreateExpression cdce =
    new CodeDelegateCreateExpression(ctrNotFound,
        new CodeThisReferenceExpression(), cmmNotFound.Name);
CodeAttachEventStatement caes =
    new CodeAttachEventStatement(new CodeThisReferenceExpression(),
```

```
                                    notFoundName, cdce);
cmm.Statements.Add(cvdsDelegate);
```

The resulting code would look like this in C#:

```
this.CustomerNotFound += new CustomerNotFoundEventHandler(
                                this.HandleCustomerNotFound);
```

And like this in Visual Basic:

```
AddHandler CustomerNotFound, AddressOf Me.HandleCustomerNotFound
```

To generate the code to remove a method from an event, you create a `CodeRemoveEventStatement`, passing a reference to a `CodeEventReferenceExpression` and a reference to the method that handles the event:

```
CodeRemoveEventStatement cres =
        new CodeRemoveEventStatement(cereNotFound, cmre);
```

The resulting code would look like this in C#:

```
this.CustomerNotFound -= this.AddTwoIntegers;
```

And like this in Visual Basic:

```
RemoveHandler CustomerNotFound, Me.AddTwoIntegers
```

Constructors

To create a constructor for a class, just create a `CodeConstructor` object and add it to the `CodeTypeDeclaration` that represents the class, as this example does:

```
CodeConstructor cc = new CodeConstructor();
ctd.Members.Add(cc);
```

The resulting code looks like this in C# (the name of the constructor is set by the class that the constructor belongs to):

```
private MathFunctions() {}
```

In Visual Basic, the code includes a call to the constructor for the base class (the name of the constructor is always New):

```
Private Sub New()
   MyBase.New
End Sub
```

You can add parameters to your constructor as you would any other method.

In a constructor in a derived class, you must call the constructor for the base object. You can control the parameters that are passed to the call to the base object's constructor by adding values to the CodeConstructor object's BaseConstructorArgs collection. This example passes the number zero to the base object's constructor:

```
CodeConstructor cc = new CodeConstructor();
CodePrimitiveExpression cpeZero = new CodePrimitiveExpression(0);

cc.BaseConstructorArgs.Add(cpeZero);
ctd.Members.Add(cc);
```

The result in C# would look like this:

```
private MathFunctions() :
    base(0)   {
}
```

And like this in Visual Basic:

```
Private Sub New()
    MyBase.New(0)
End Sub
```

On occasion, in a constructor for a Class you want to call a different version of the constructor for the Class. You can generate the code for this by adding values to the CodeConstructor object's ChainedConstructorArgs collection. This example adds a null/Nothing value to the collection to trigger generating a call to another version of the current Class's constructor:

```
cc.ChainedConstructorArgs.Add(cpeNull);
```

In C#, the result looks like this:

```
private MathFunctions()
    this(null) {
}
```

And like this in Visual Basic:

```
Private Sub New()
    Me.New(Nothing)
End Sub
```

In C#, you can call both the base object's constructor and another constructor for the same class. In Visual Basic, adding a value to the ChainedConstructorArgs collection suppresses any calls to the base object's constructor.

Entry Points

Both C# and Visual Basic support special methods that form the entry point for a class. In C#, this is the Main method:

```
public static void Main() {
}
```

In Visual Basic, it's the Main subroutine:

```
Public Shared Sub Main()
End Sub
```

Both of these constructs can be generated by adding a CodeEntryPointMethod object to the CodeTypeDeclaration object that represents the class, as this example does:

```
CodeEntryPointMethod cepm = new CodeEntryPointMethod();
ctd.Members.Add(cepm);
```

A CodeEntryPointMethod is similar to any other method—it has, for instance, a Statements collection that you can add statement objects to. (Statement objects are discussed later in this chapter in the section "Statements.") However, to support all language types, the CodeEntryPointMethod can't return a value or be passed parameters, so you'll have to create workarounds to implement equivalent functionality (e.g., updating global variables to hold return values and using the Environment object's GetCommandLineArgs method to retrieve parameter values).

Properties

To define a property, you create a CodeMemberProperty object and then configure it by setting its properties. Here are the essential properties you'll want to set:

- **Name**—The property's name.
- **Type**—The return type for the property.
- **Parameters**—This collection allows you to specify the parameter to be passed to the property. For a typical property, you'll create a parameter named value.
- **HasGet, HasSet**—By default, the property you create won't have a getter or setter. Setting the HasGet or HasSet property to True will add those routines to your property.
- **GetStatements, SetStatements**—These collections allow you to add statements to the property's getter or setter.
- **ImplementationTypes, PrivateImplementationType**— As with methods, your properties can be tied to an interface. (See the section "Inheritance and Interfaces" for how to have your property implement an interface.)

In addition, a special object exists for specifying the pseudovariable used to hold the value passed into the setter: CodePropertySetValueReferenceExpression.

This example creates a property named CustomerId with a getter and a setter. The getter returns a field held in the CodeFieldReferenceExpression cvreCust (declaring and referencing fields was discussed earlier). The return statement is held in a CodeMethodReturnStatement (discussed later in this chapter in the section "Return Statements") that is added to the GetStatements collection of the CodeMemberProperty. The setter assigns the value passed into the setter to the field using a CodeAssignStatement (also discussed later in the section "Assignment Statements") that is added to the SetStatements collection for the CodeMemberProperty. Finally, the code adds the completed CodeMemberProperty to the CodeTypeDeclaration that represents the class:

```
CodeMemberProperty cmp = new CodeMemberProperty();
cmp.Name = "CustomerId";
```

```
cmp.HasGet = true;
cmp.HasSet = true;

cmp.Type = new CodeTypeReference(typeof(string));

CodeMethodReturnStatement cmrsGet =
         new CodeMethodReturnStatement(cfreCust);
cmp.GetStatements.Add(cmrsGet);

CodeAssignStatement cas =
         new CodeAssignStatement(cvreCust,
                  CodeFieldReferenceExpression);
cmp.SetStatements.Add(cas);
ctd.Members.Add(cmp);
```

The resulting generated property would look like this in C#, assuming that the field being referenced was called _customerId:

```
private string CustomerId {
    get {
        return _customerId;
    }
    set {
        _customerId = value;
    }
}
```

And like this in Visual Basic:

```
Private Property CustomerId(ByVal value As String) As String
    Get
        Return _customerId
    End Get
    Set
        _customerId = value
    End Set
End Property
```

To use your property later in generating code, you need to create a CodePropertyReferenceExpression as the following example does. The CodePropertyReferenceExpression must be passed a reference to the class holding the property and the name of the property. This example generates a reference to a property in the same class using the CodeMemberProperty just created:

```
CodePropertyReferenceExpression cpre = new
    CodePropertyReferenceExpression(new CodeThisReferenceExpression(),
                                                       cmp.Name);
```

Creating an Indexer

To add an indexer to your class, you must define a property with the name Item. This example creates an indexer that accepts a string variable called CustomerId and returns a Customer object:

```
CodeMemberProperty indexer = new CodeMemberProperty();
indexer.Name = "Item";
indexer.Type = new CodeTypeReference(typeof(Customer));
indexer.HasGet = true;
string indexerName = "CustomerId";

CodeParameterDeclarationExpression cpdeIndexer =
      new CodeParameterDeclarationExpression(ctrString, indexerName);
indexer.Parameters.Add(cpdeIndexer);
ctd.Members.Add(indexer);
```

The resulting code looks like this in C#:

```
private Customer this[string CustomerId] {
    get {
    }
}
```

And like this in Visual Basic:

```
Private Default Property Item(ByVal CustomerId As String) As Customer
    Get
    End Get
End Property
```

Statements and Expressions

The various CodeDom statement objects represent complete code statements that can be added to the Statements collection of various CodeDom objects (e.g., CodeMemberMethod, CodeConstructor, and a CodeMemberProperty object's SetStatements or CodeStatements collection). The CodeDom supports several specific statement types (e.g., variable declarations and return statements), some of which must be passed expression objects as part of creating the statement. As a result, this section begins by discussing the types of expressions you can create before showing you how to create statements using those expression objects.

Expressions

Expressions are the components you assemble to create a complete statement. For instance, a code-assignment statement consists of a variable reference on the left side of the equals sign and an expression on the right side. That expression might be instantiating an object, calling a method, or just another variable reference.

Expressions include references to other elements (literals, variables, parameters, etc.). Beyond simple references, expressions include a general-purpose object for creating operations involving two references (e.g., tests, logical operations, math operations). In addition to that general-purpose object, however, the expression objects also include objects to handle specific kinds of expressions (e.g., invoking methods, instantiating objects).

Referring to Code Elements

To refer to the other elements in your code, you must create one of the several reference expression objects. The code components and the expression objects they use are listed here:

- **The current class**—CodeThisReferenceExpression.
- **Base objects**—CodeBaseReferenceExpression.
- **Type objects**—CodeTypeReferenceExpression.
- **Variables**—CodeVariableReferenceExpression.
- **Fields (class-level variables)**—CodeFieldReferenceExpression.
- **Methods**—CodeMethodReferenceExpression.
- **Property**—CodePropertyReferenceExpression.
- **Parameters**—CodeArgumentReferenceExpression objects are used in statements that refer to parameters passed to a method.
- **Events**—CodeEventReferenceExpression.

The following code creates the examples just listed:

```
CodeThisReference self = new CodeThisReference();
CodeBaseReferenceExpression cbreBase = new
```

```
        CodeBaseReferenceExpression();
CodeTypeReferenceExpression ctreString = new
        CodeTypeReferenceExpression(typeof(string));
CodeVariableReferenceExpression cvreCust = new
        CodeVariableReferenceExpression(customerName);
CodeFieldReferenceExpression cfre = new
        CodeFieldReferenceExpression(null, fieldName);
CodeMethodReferenceExpression cmre =
        new CodeMethodReferenceExpression(
              new CodeThisReferenceExpression(), cmm.Name);
CodePropertyReferenceExpression cpre =
        new CodePropertyReferenceExpression(
             new CodeThisReferenceExpression(), cmp.Name);
CodeArgumentReferenceExpression careNum1 = new
        CodeArgumentReferenceExpression(number1Name);
CodeEventReferenceExpression cereNotFound = new
        CodeEventReferenceExpression(
              new CodeThisReferenceExpression(), eventName);
```

Most of the reference objects are discussed in detail in the earlier sections on creating the code elements they refer to. For instance, `CodeEventReferenceExpression`s are discussed in the section on creating events. This section covers those expression objects not discussed elsewhere.

Literals, Self, and Base

The `CodePrimitiveExpression` object creates an expression that refers to a literal item in the language. This example creates a reference to the number 0:

```
CodePrimitiveExpression cpeZero = new CodePrimitiveExpression(0);
```

The `CodeThisReferenceExpression` object generates a reference to the current class: either `this` (in C#) or `Me` (in Visual Basic). Similarly, `CodeBaseReferenceExpression` generates a reference to the base class: either `base` (in C#) or `MyBase` (in Visual Basic).

Binary Operations

The most flexible expression object is the `CodeBinaryOperatorExpression`. This object represents any expression that consists of two items (variables, literals, or reference expression objects) with an operator. The operators supported by the object are listed in the CodeBinaryOperatorType enumeration and support creating math operations, tests, and logical operations.

The following example generates an expression that adds two numbers by combining two CodePrimitiveReferenceExpressions. The resulting statement is then added to the Statements collection of a CodeMemberMethod:

```
CodePrimitiveExpression cpeZero = new CodePrimitiveExpression(0);
CodePrimitiveExpression cpeOne = new CodePrimitiveExpression(1);

CodeBinaryOperatorExpression cboe =
    new CodeBinaryOperatorExpression(cpreNum1,
            CodeBinaryOperatorType.Add, cpreNum2);
CodeAssignStatement cas = new CodeAssignStatement(cvreHolding, cboe);
cmm.Statements.Add(cas);
```

Assignment Statements

To assign a value (or expression) to a variable or property, you must create a CodeAssignStatement, passing the item to be set and the value to assign. Assuming that cpreOrderValid is a CodePropertyReferenceExpression that refers to a property called isValid on an Order object, this code assigns a CodePrimitiveExpression to the property:

```
CodeAssignStatement setIsValidFalse;
setIsValidFalse = new CodeAssignStatement(cpreOrderValid, cpeFalse);
```

In C#, the resulting code might look like this:

```
order.IsValid = false;
```

Here's what it looks like in Visual Basic:

```
order.IsValid = False
```

Accessing Enumerated Values

To access a value in an enumeration, you must first create a CodeTypeReferenceExpression object, passing a reference to the type of the enumeration. You can then create a CodeFieldReferenceExpression for the enumerated value you want, passing a reference to the

CodeTypeReferenceExpression you just created and the name of the value you want. This code retrieves the Int value in the SqlDbType enumerated value:

```
CodeTypeReferenceExpression ctreEnumeration;
CodeFieldReferenceExpression cfreValue;
ctreEnumeration = new CodeTypeReferenceExpression(typeof(SqlDbType));
cfreValue =  new CodeFieldReferenceExpression(ctreEnumeration,"Int");
```

Accessing Arrays

To access a position in an array, you must first create a CodeArrayIndexerExpression, passing the reference to your array and a position in that array.

This example creates a CodeVariableReferenceExpression for an array and a CodePrimitiveExpression holding the position in the array. Those two items are then used to create a CodeArrayIndexerExpression. Finally, the CodeArrayIndexerExpression is used to create a return statement:

```
CodeVariableReferenceExpression cvreArray =
            new CodeVariableReferenceExpression(arrayName);
CodePrimitiveExpression cpePosition = new CodePrimitiveExpression(0);
CodeArrayIndexerExpression caie =
            new CodeArrayIndexerExpression(cvreArray, cpePosition);

CodeMethodReturnStatement crsArray =
            new CodeMethodReturnStatement(caie);
```

The result would look like this in C#:

```
return Employees[0];
```

In Visual Basic, the code would look like this:

```
Return Employees(0)
```

To assign a value to a position in the array, you would use the CodeArrayIndexerExpression in creating a CodeAssignStatement.

Accessing an Indexer

To access an indexer on an object, you must create a `CodeIndexerExpression` object, passing a reference to the object being indexed and an array of `CodeExpressions` holding the parameters to be passed to the index. This example creates a `CodeIndexerExpression`, passing a `CodeVariableReferenceExpression` and an array with a single parameter containing a string value. The result is then used in an assignment statement:

```
CodeIndexerExpression cie;
CodeExpression[] parms1 = new CodeExpression[1];
parms1[0] = cvreCustomerName;
cie = new CodeIndexerExpression(cvreCustomers, parms1);
CodeAssignStatement cas = new CodeAssignStatement(cvre, cie);
```

The resulting code would look like this in C#:

```
cust = Customers["Vogel"];
```

And like this in Visual Basic:

```
cust = Customers("Vogel")
```

Instantiating Objects

To generate the code to create a new instance of an object, you must create a `CodeObjectCreateExpression` object, passing a `CodeTypeReference` to the object. Once the `CodeObjectCreateExpression` is created, you can use the expression to create a statement. This example creates a `CodeObjectCreateExpression` object that creates an instance of a `Customer` object and then uses it to create an assignment statement:

```
CodeTypeReference ctrCust = new CodeTypeReference(typeof(Customer));
CodeObjectCreateExpression coce =
            new CodeObjectCreateExpression(ctrCust);
CodeAssignStatement casCust = new CodeAssignStatement(cvreCust, coce);
```

This is what the result would look like in C#:

```
cust = new NorthwindObjects.Customer();
```

And here's the result in Visual Basic:

```
cust = New NorthwindObjects.Customer
```

If the object's constructor requires parameters to be passed to it, you pass those parameters to the `CodeObjectCreateExpression` following the reference to the class. This example passes two `CodePrimitiveExpression` objects (false and 1) as parameters to the `CodeObjectCreateExpression`:

```
CodeObjectCreateExpression coce2 =
        new CodeObjectCreateExpression(ctrCust, cpeFalse, cpeOne);
```

The result looks like this in C#:

```
cust = new NorthwindObjects.Customer(false, 1);
```

In Visual Basic, it looks like this:

```
cust = New NorthwindObjects.Customer(False, 1)
```

Casting and Returning Types

To reference an object type, you must create a `CodeTypeOfExpression` object, passing a `CodeTypeReference` that points to the class whose type you want to return. This example creates a `typeof` function (in C#) or a `GetType` function (in Visual Basic) for the `Customer` class:

```
CodeTypeOfExpression ctoe = new CodeTypeOfExpression(ctrCust);
```

To cast an object to another type, you must create a `CodeCastExpression`. To create a `CodeCastExpression` object, you must pass a `CodeTypeReference` for the class you are casting to and a reference expression object pointing to the object you want to cast. This example creates a `CodeCastExpression` that converts a variable named c to a Customer data type and then uses the expression in an assignment statement:

```
CodeTypeReference ctrCust = new CodeTypeReference(typeof(Customer));
CodeVariableReferenceExpression cvreEName =
        new CodeVariableReferenceExpression("c");
```

```
CodeCastExpression cce = new CodeCastExpression(ctrCust, cvreEName);
CodeAssignStatement casCast = new CodeAssignStatement(cvreCust, cce);
```

In C#, the resulting code would look like this:

```
cust = ((NorthwindObjects.Customer)(c));
```

In Visual Basic, it looks like this:

```
cust = CType(c,NorthwindObjects.Customer)
```

You can also create a `CodeTypeReferenceExpression` that points to a type by name. This example creates a `CodeTypeReferenceExpression` to the string type:

```
CodeTypeReferenceExpression ctreString =
    new CodeTypeReferenceExpression("string");
```

Invoking Delegates

Generating code that invokes a delegate requires two steps: First, you create a `CodeVariableReferenceExpression` that references the variable holding the delegate; second, you pass that reference to a `CodeDelegateInvokeExpression` object along with any parameters the method pointed to by the delegate requires (you can pass as many parameters as necessary).

This example creates a `CodeVariableReferenceExpression` to a variable that holds a reference to a delegate. (Creating and instantiating delegates is discussed earlier in this chapter in the section "Delegates.") The code then creates a `CodePrimitiveExpression` object to hold the value passed to the delegate's method (the string `"Business"`). The third line creates the code that invokes the delegate passing the `CodePrimitiveExpression` as the parameter. The last two lines create an assignment statement that assigns the results of calling the delegate to a variable called `businessAddress`:

```
CodeVariableReferenceExpression cvreDelegate =
        new CodeVariableReferenceExpression(addressName);
CodePrimitiveExpression cpeBusiness =
        new CodePrimitiveExpression("Business");
CodeDelegateInvokeExpression cdie =
```

```
       new CodeDelegateInvokeExpression(cvreDelegate, cpeBusiness);

string busAddressName = "businessAddress";
CodeVariableReferenceExpression cvreBusAddress =
        new CodeVariableReferenceExpression(busAddressName);
CodeAssignStatement cas =
        new CodeAssignStatement(cvreBusAddress, cdie);
```

The generated code would look like this in C#:

```
businessAddress = Address("Business");
```

And, in Visual Basic, like this:

```
businessAddress = Address("Business")
```

Statements

Statements are assembled out of expressions, primitives, and reference
expressions. In addition, some expressions can be used as statements without additional changes (e.g., calling a method on an object): The
CodeExpressionStatement object provides a way for expression objects to be
converted to statement objects. Once a statement object is created, it can
be added either to a method or a property.

The CodeDom objects you need to declare and reference variables are
discussed in the section "Declarations" earlier in this chapter. This section
discusses the "executable" statement types.

Creating Assignment Statements

To create a statement that assigns an expression to a variable, you must create a CodeAssignStatement object, passing a CodeVariableReference
Expression that points to the variable accepting the value and an expression
object representing the value being assigned. This example assigns the
value 0 to the variable i:

```
string iName = "i";
CodeVariableReferenceExpression cvreI =
    new CodeVariableReferenceExpression(iName);
CodePrimitiveExpression cpeOne = new CodePrimitiveExpression(1);

CodeAssignStatement casIncI = new CodeAssignStatement(cvreI, cpeOne);
```

The resulting code would look like this in C#:

```
i = 0;
```

And like this in Visual Basic:

```
i = 0
```

The section "Arrays" earlier in this chapter shows how to assign a value to a position in an array.

Invoking Methods

To invoke a method, you use a `CodeMethodInvokeExpression`, passing parameters. Before creating the `CodeMethodInvokeExpression`, you must create a `CodeMethodReferenceExpression` that references the method. This example adds a `CodeMethodReferenceExpression` to a method called `AddCustomer` on a `CodeVariableReferenceExpression` that references an object variable:

```
CodeMethodReferenceExpression cmdCusAdd;
string customerAddMethod = "AddCustomer";
cmdCustAdd = new CodeMethodReferenceExpression(cvre, "AddCustomer");
```

You can now create a `CodeMethodInvokeExpression`, passing the `CodeMethodReferenceExpression` and an array of `CodeExpression` objects holding the parameters. This example invokes the `AddCustomer` method, passing two parameters:

```
CodeMethodInvokeExpression cmdCustAddInvoke;
CodeExpression[] parms2 = new CodeExpression[2];
parms2[0] = cvreCustomerId;
parms2[1] = cvreAddStatus;
cmdCustAddInvoke = new CodeMethodInvokeExpression(
                          cmdCustAdd, parms2);
```

The resulting code would look like this in C#:

```
cust.AddCustomer(custId, addStat);
```

And like this in Visual Basic:

```
cust.AddCustomer(ByVal custId, addStat)
```

When passing a parameter that is a `ref` or `out` parameter, you must create a `CodeDirectionExpression` object, passing an option from the `FieldDirection` enumeration and a reference to the variable being passed to the method. This example converts the second parameter from the previous code sample into an `out` parameter before placing it in the array that's passed to the method:

```
CodeDirectionExpression outDeleteStatus;
outResultRef = new CodeDirectionExpression(
                        FieldDirection.Ref, cvreDeleteStatus);
parms2[1] = cvreAddStatus;
cmdCustAddInvoke = new CodeMethodInvokeExpression(
                        cmdCustAdd, parms2);
```

The resulting code would look like this in C#:

```
cust.AddStatus(custId, ref delStat);
```

And like this in Visual Basic:

```
cust.AddStatus(ByVal custId, ByRef delStat)
```

Converting Expressions to Statements

The `CodeExpressionStatement` object converts an expression object into a `CodeStatement` object so that you can add it to a `Statements` collection. For instance, if you're invoking a method that returns a value, you would use a `CodeMethodInvokeExpression` object as part of creating a `CodeAssignStatement`. However, if the method doesn't return a value, the invoke expression forms a standalone statement all by itself. So, to call a method, although you must create a `CodeMethodInvokeExpression` object, in order to add that `CodeMethodInvokeExpression` to a `CodeMemberMethod` object's `Statements` collection, you must convert it to a `CodeExpressionStatement` object. This example creates a statement that calls the `Delete` method on a `Customer` object and then converts it to a `CodeExpressionStatement` object before adding it to the `Statements` collection of a `CodeMemberMethod`:

```
CodeTypeReferenceExpression ctre =
    new CodeTypeReferenceExpression(typeof(Customer));
string methodName = "Delete";
CodeMethodInvokeExpression cmie =
    new CodeMethodInvokeExpression(ctreCust, methodName);

CodeExpressionStatement ces = new CodeExpressionStatement(cmie);
cmm.Statements.Add(ces);
```

Return Statements

To create a return statement, just pass an expression object representing the item that is to be returned to the CodeMethodReturnStatement object. This example returns a CodeVariableReferenceExpression representing a variable called customerName:

```
string CustomerName = "Vogel";
CodeVariableReferenceExpression cvreCust =
    new CodeVariableReferenceExpression(customerName);
CodeMethodReturnStatement cmrs =
new CodeMethodReturnStatement(cvreCust);
```

The resulting code would look like this in C#:

```
return CustomerName;
```

And like this in Visual Basic:

```
Return CustomerName
```

Throwing Exceptions

To throw an exception, you create a CodeThrowExceptionStatement, passing an expression object that represents the message to be returned. This example creates a CodePrimitiveExpression to hold the message and uses that to create the throw statement:

```
CodePrimitiveExpression cpeMessage =
    new CodePrimitiveExpression("Customer does not exist");
CodeThrowExceptionStatement ctes =
    new CodeThrowExceptionStatement(cpeMessage);
```

The result would look like this in C#:

```
throw new Exception("Customer does not exist");
```

And here's the result In Visual Basic:

```
Throw New Exception("Customer does not exist")
```

GoTo and Labeled Statements

You can also create a labeled statement (if your target language supports it) using the CodeLabeledStatement object and a GoTo statement that transfers control to a labeled statement (again, if your target language supports it) using the CodeGotoStatement object.

BEST PRACTICE   Even in generated code, it's wise to avoid the GoTo construct. Structured code that avoids GoTos is easier to debug and understand so that, when you're diagnosing a problem with your code-generation solution, you'll find it easier to work with structured than unstructured code.

Code Structures

The CodeDom supports three programming structures: If...Then...Else, a For/Do Until loop, and the Try...Catch block. The Select...Case and ElseIf constructs aren't supported (you must just nest If statements within each other), nor is the Do While loop. The For loop construct does not support a local variable to act as the counter in the loop.

If...Then

The CodeDom generates an If block as a binary operation (the test) plus up to two arrays of statements: one set to execute if the test is true and an optional set to execute if the test is false. If blocks generated by the CodeDom look like this in C#:

```
if ((Number1 == Number2)) {
 Holding = (Number1 + Number2);
}
```

```
else {
 Holding = 0;
}
```

And like this in Visual Basic:

```
If (Number1 = Number2) Then
 Holding = (Number1 + Number2)
Else
 Holding = 0
End If
```

The first step in creating an If block is to create the arrays of statements to be executed after the test is evaluated. This example creates two arrays, each holding one statement:

```
CodeStatement[] csTrue = new CodeStatement[1];
csTrue[0] = casAdd;
CodeStatement[] csFalse = new CodeStatement[1];
csFalse[0] = casZeroed;
```

The next step is to create the test by creating a CodeBinaryOperatorExpression using one of the test values from the CodeBinaryOperatorType enumeration. This example uses the ValueEquality value, which generates "==" in C# and "=" in Visual Basic (other values include GreaterThanOrEqual and IdentityEquality).

```
CodeBinaryOperatorExpression cboeIf = new CodeBinaryOperatorExpression(
    careNum1, CodeBinaryOperatorType.ValueEquality, careNum2);
```

The final step is to create the If block by creating a CaseConditionStatement object, passing the CodeBinaryOperatorExpression and the two arrays of statements, as this example does:

```
CodeConditionStatement ccs =
    new CodeConditionStatement(cboeIf, csTrue, csFalse);
```

For Loops

Generating a For loop is made complicated because of the number of components involved. You must create the following:

- The variable used to count inside the loop.
- The statement that initializes the counter.
- The test that determines when the loop is complete. (The loop terminates when the test evaluates to false.)
- The statement that increments the counter.
- The statements that go inside the loop.

Each of these components can also have multiple constituent components. Only after assembling all these components do you create your loop by creating a CodeIterationStatement.

This example shows the kind of code generated by the CodeIterationStatement. The most important thing to note about this code is that the counter for the loop is *not* local to the loop. You must declare a variable that's local to the method. In C#, a generated loop would look like this:

C#:
```
int i = 0;
for (i = 0; (Number1 <= Number2); i = (i + 1)) {
    Number1 = (Number1 + i);
}
```

The same loop in Visual Basic would look like this:

```
Dim i As Integer = 0
i = 0
Do While (Number1 <= Number2)
  Number1 = (Number1 + i)
  i = (i + 1)
Loop
```

The first step in creating your loop is to assemble an array of statements to be put inside the loop:

```
CodeStatement[] csLoop = new CodeStatement[1];
csLoop[0] = casLoop;
```

The second step is to declare the variable that will be used as the counter inside the loop. This code generates a declaration for an integer variable named i (initialized to 0) and adds it to the statements collection of a CodeMemberMethod:

```
string iName = "i";
CodeVariableDeclarationStatement cdsI = new
    CodeVariableDeclarationStatement(ctrInt, iName, cpeZero);
cmm.Statements.Add(cdsI);
```

The third step is to create the statement that increments the counter. This code creates a CodeVariableReferenceExpression that points to the i variable just declared and a CodePrimitiveExpression holding the number 1. It then uses them to create a CodeBinaryOperatorExpression that adds the 1 to the i variable. Finally, this code creates a CodeAssignStatement that sets the variable i to the result of the addition:

```
CodeVariableReferenceExpression cvreI =
    new CodeVariableReferenceExpression(iName);

CodePrimitiveExpression cpeOne = new CodePrimitiveExpression(1);
CodeBinaryOperatorExpression cboeIncI =
    new CodeBinaryOperatorExpression(careNum1,
                            CodeBinaryOperatorType.Add, cpeOne);

CodeAssignStatement casIncI = new CodeAssignStatement(cvreI, cboeIncI);
```

The fourth step is to create the test that terminates the loop and the statement that initializes the counter. These are the simplest of the components to assemble. The test is simply a CodeBinaryOperatorExpression using one of the comparison values out of the CodeBinaryOperatorType (the following example uses LessThanOrEqual). The initialization statement can be equally simple. The following example creates a CodeAssignStatement that sets the i variable to a CodePrimitiveExpression representing 0:

```
CodeBinaryOperatorExpression cboeItTest =
    new CodeBinaryOperatorExpression(careNum1,
                CodeBinaryOperatorType.LessThanOrEqual, careNum2);
CodePrimitiveExpression cpeZero = new CodePrimitiveExpression(0);
CodeAssignStatement casInitI = new CodeAssignStatement(cvreI, cpeZero);
```

With all the components created, creating the loop-generation code is straightforward—create a CodeIterationStatement, passing the initialization statement, the test expression, the increment statement, and the array of statements to put inside the loop:

```
CodeIterationStatement cis =
    new CodeIterationStatement(casInitI, cboeItTest, casIncI, csLoop);
cmm.Statements.Add(cis);
```

For Each, Do Until, and Do While loops are not directly supported for C#. Although the Do Until loop is supported for Visual Basic, it's just a thinly disguised For...Next loop. For instance, to create a Do While loop that checks for an end-of-file condition, you must still declare, initialize, and increment a counter variable. However, your test doesn't need to refer to the counter variable, as in this example which checks the EOF property on an object after each trip through the loop:

```
int i = 0;
for (i = 0; (rs.EOF != true); i = (i + 0)) {
    //...other processing
    rs.MoveNext;
}
```

However, you can often use the components of the CodeIterationStatement to manipulate the objects used inside the loop. This example uses the initialization component to create an object and the increment component to handle part of the loop's processing:

```
RecordSet rs = null;
for (rs=new RecordSet(); (rs.EOF != true); rs.MoveNext()) {
    //...other processing
}
```

The equivalent Visual Basic code would look like this:

```
Dim rs As RecordSet = Nothing
rs = New Recordset
Do While (rs.EOF <> true)
  rs.MoveNext
Loop
```

Try...Catch

A Try...Catch block is generated by using a CodeTryCatchFinallyStatement object to which you can add multiple CodeCatchClause objects. Both the CodeTryCatchFinallyStatement and the CodeCatchClause objects can be passed arrays of CodeStatement objects that make up the body of the Try, Catch, and

Finally blocks. As with creating a loop, creating a Try...Catch block requires assembling multiple components before using them to generate a block.

Here is a sample of the code that would be generated by a CodeTryCatchFinallyStatement in C#:

```
try {
    Holding = (Number1 + Number2);
}
catch (System.Exception ex) {
    Holding = 0;
}
finally {
    return Holding;
}
```

The same block in Visual Basic looks like this:

```
Try
    Holding = (Number1 + Number2)
Catch ex As System.Exception
    Holding = 0
Finally
    Return Holding
End Try
```

The first step in creating a Try...Catch block is to create at least one array of code statements to hold the statements that go in the Try block. You can also create a second array of CodeStatement objects to hold any code you want to put in the Finally block. This example creates two arrays (one for the Try block, one for the Finally block), each with one position, and puts a single code statement in each array:

```
CodeStatement[] csTry = new CodeStatement[1];
csTry[0] = cas;
CodeStatement[] csFinally = new CodeStatement[1];
csFinally[0] = crs;
```

The next step is to create the CodeCatchClause object that specifies the Catch block. Again, you'll need an array of CodeStatements to hold the code you want to put in the Catch block. You'll also need to create a CodeTypeReference for the exception type you're using and specify the name for the variable that will hold the exception object. You can't, however, simply use the CodeCatchClause when you create the

CodeTryCatchFinallyStatement object. In order to support Try...Catch blocks with multiple Catch blocks, the CodeTryCatchFinallyStatement must be passed an array of CodeCatchClause objects.

This example creates an array with a single position and puts a CodeStatement in the array. The code then stores the exception object's name (Ex) in a string and creates a CodeTypeReference for the System.Exception type. With all the components assembled, the code creates a CodeCatchClause, passing the name of the exception variable, the CodeTypeReference, and the array of CodeStatements to be used in the Catch block. Finally, the code creates an array of CodeCatchClauses and puts the newly created CodeCatchClause in the array:

```
CodeStatement[] csExcept = new CodeStatement[1];
csExcept[0] = casZeroed;

string nameExcept = "ex";
CodeTypeReference ctrExcept =
        new CodeTypeReference(typeof(System.Exception));
CodeCatchClause ccc =
        new CodeCatchClause(nameExcept, ctrExcept, csExcept);

CodeCatchClause[] cccs = new CodeCatchClause[1];
cccs[0] = ccc;
```

If the exception object you want to use doesn't exist at the time you're writing this code, instead of passing a Type object to the CodeTypeReference object, you can pass the name of your exception class:

```
CodeTypeReference ctrExcept =
    new CodeTypeReference("NorthwindObjects.CustomerNotExistException");
```

At this point, all the pieces have been assembled to create a CodeTryCatchFinallyStatement. All that's left is to pass the object to the constructor the array of CodeStatement objects to be used in the Try block, the array of CodeCatchClause objects, and the array of CodeStatements to go into the Finally block, as this example does:

```
CodeTryCatchFinallyStatement ctcfs =
    new CodeTryCatchFinallyStatement(csTry, cccs, csFinally);
```

If you want to create a `Try...Catch` block without a `Finally` block, just omit the third parameter when creating your `CodeTryCatchFinallyStatement`:

```
CodeTryCatchFinallyStatement ctcfs =
    new CodeTryCatchFinallyStatement(csTry, cccs);
```

To create an empty `Catch` block, create the `CodeCatchClause` object without passing any parameters:

```
CodeCatchClause ccc = new CodeCatchClause();
```

The result is an empty `Catch` block that catches the default `System.Exception` object. The resulting code will look something like this in C#:

```
try {
    Holding = (Number1 + Number2);
}
catch (System.Exception ) {
}
```

In Visual Basic, a default name for the exception object is still generated:

```
Try
    Holding = (Number1 + Number2)
Catch _exception As System.Exception
End Try
```

You can get the same result by passing a zero-length string or null/Nothing as the first parameter when creating your `CodeCatchClause`, like this:

```
CodeCatchClause ccc = new CodeCatchClause("", ctrExcept);
```

When All Else Fails: Code Snippets

If you can't generate the code you want with the CodeDom (or if it just seems like too much trouble), you can always insert a code snippet—a string of text written in a specific language.

BEST PRACTICE Using code snippets doesn't mean that your code is no longer language neutral. However, if you do want to support multiple languages, you'll need to check to see which language the project is written in (as described in Chapter 3) and insert a version of the code appropriate for the project's language.

Code snippets come in three varieties, and you can insert snippets into any part of the code-generation process:

- **Expressions**—Portions of a complete statement that can be used when creating any statement object that accepts expression objects (e.g., `CodeAssignStatement`).
- **Statements**—A complete statement in the programming language. These can be added to any `Statements` collection (e.g., `CodeMemberMethod`, `CodeMemberProperty`).
- **Type member**—A member of a class (e.g., a method). You can add these snippets to the `Members` collection of a `CodeTypeDeclaration`.

In addition, you can create a complete class as a code snippet that you can then compile as a single object.

Snippet Expressions and Statements

To create a `CodeSnippetExpression`, you only need to pass some text that forms a part of a complete statement to the `CodeSnippetExpression`. This example creates a `CodeSnippetExpression` containing a simple addition expression. The code then uses the expression to create an assignment statement by combining the expression with a reference to a variable expression. The final line adds the statement to the `Statements` collection of a `CodeMemberMethod`:

```
CodeSnippetExpression cse = new CodeSnippetExpression("2 + 2");
string answerName = "answer";
CodeVariableReferenceExpression cvreAnswer =
        new CodeVariableReferenceExpression(answerName);
CodeBinaryOperatorExpression cboeAdd =
        new CodeBinaryOperatorExpression(
                cvreAnswer, CodeBinaryOperatorType.Assign, cse);

cmm.Statements.Add cboeAdd;
```

The resulting code would look like this in C#:

```
answer = 2 + 2;
```

And like this in Visual Basic:

```
answer = 2 + 2
```

To create a `CodeSnippetStatement`, you just pass a complete statement (in some .NET language) to the object's constructor. This example creates a return statement and adds it to the `Statements` collection of a `CodeMemberMethod`:

```
CodeSnippetStatement css = new CodeSnippetStatement("return answer");
cmm.Statements.Add(css);
```

Compile Units

A `CodeSnippetCompileUnit` represents a complete class (or group of classes) that can be compiled as a complete unit. This example creates a string and then loads that string with the code for a class that accepts a parameter and returns that parameter concantenated with "Hello":

```
string cs = "using System; namespace Manners " +
            "{ public class Greetings {" +
            " public SayHello(string name)" +
            " {return \"Hello, \" & name}; } }";
CodeSnippetCompileUnit csnu = new CodeSnippetCompileUnit(cs);
```

You can generate code using the `CodeSnippetCompileUnit` as you would for a `CodeCompileUnit`. This example wires the `CodeSnippetCompileUnit` up to the Visual Basic code generator and writes the result to a `StringBuilder`:

```
StringBuilder generatedCode;
System.IO.StringWriter codeWriter;

generatedCode = new StringBuilder();
codeWriter = new System.IO.StringWriter(generatedCode);
Microsoft.VisualBasic.VBCodeProvider vbProv =
        new Microsoft.VisualBasic.VBCodeProvider();
vbProv.GenerateCodeFromCompileUnit(csnu, codeWriter, null);
```

Other Code Features

This section covers features that are either available from code providers (the ability to generate valid identifiers) or are available on many CodeDom objects (the ability to add attributes, comments, and other decorations to your code). In addition, this section shows how the UserData property supports language-specific features and how you can insert regions into your code.

Generating Valid Names

You can use either of two methods on the code provider to create valid names to use in your generated code. Both methods accept a single string containing your proposed identifier and return a string containing the identifier modified, if necessary, to avoid conflicts with keywords in the provider's language. The difference is in how the methods modify your identifier if it conflicts with a keyword in the language:

- **CreateEscapedIdentifier**—Your identifier is escaped. For example, in Visual Basic, the text will be enclosed in square brackets. This ensures that identifiers that are also keywords in the language won't generate compile time errors.
- **CreateValidIdentifier**—Modifies your identifier by adding characters (e.g., adding a leading underscore).

As an example of the difference between the two methods, if the Visual Basic keyword Dim is used as an identifier, CreateValidIdentifier returns _Dim whereas CreateEscapedIdentifier returns [Dim].

You can check to see if an identifier is valid by calling the code provider's IsValidIdentifier method and passing an identifier. The method returns True if the identifier is valid within the language and False if the identifier isn't.

BEST PRACTICE It makes sense to store valid identifiers in the fields holding your variable names early in the code generation process. To support this, you'll need to have the developer specify the language that code is to be generated in at the start of the process so that you pick the correct provider.

This example accepts a string from a user interface (TextBox), tests it using the `IsValidIdentifier` method, and, if the identifier fails the test, passes the string to the `CreateValidIdentifier` method to get a valid result. The code then uses the valid result as the name for a `CodeTypeDeclaration` object:

```
Microsoft.VisualBasic.VBCodeProvider vbProv =
        new Microsoft.VisualBasic.VBCodeProvider();

string className = this.ClassNameTextBox.Text;
if (!vbProv.IsValidIdentifer(className))
{
  className = vbProv.CreateValidIdentifier(className);
}
CodeTypeDeclaration ctd = new CodeTypeDeclaration(className);
```

Adding Comments

Many of the CodeDom objects have a `Comments` property that allows you to add `CodeCommentStatement` objects to code elements (e.g., namespaces, methods, and properties). In addition, `CodeCommentStatement`s can be added to the `Statements` collection that many objects have (e.g., a `CodeMemberMethod`), allowing you to insert comments in between lines of code.

BEST PRACTICES Use comments either to document your code for yourself or to provide helpful information to developers working with your generated code.

To create a `CodeCommentStatement`, just pass your comment to the object when creating it. This example adds a comment to a `CodeMemberMethod`:

```
CodeCommentStatement ccst = new CodeCommentStatement(
     "Called when requested customer does not exist to raise event ");
cmmOnNotFound.Comments.Add(ccst);
```

The resulting code would look like this in C#:

```
// Called when requested customer does not exist to raise event
private void OnCustomerNotFound()   {
```

And like this in Visual Basic:

```
' Called when requested customer does not exist to raise event
Private Sub OnCustomerNotFound()
```

If you pass True as the second parameter to the `CodeCommentStatement` when creating it, your comment will be marked as a document comment (e.g., in C#, your comment will begin with ///). It's your responsibility to pass a valid document comment as the string for the comment.

Each `CodeCommentStatement` appears on a separate line, so you can't use `CodeCommentStatement`s to add comments to the end of lines of code.

Adding Custom Attributes

To decorate your code with attributes, you'll need to use two CodeDom objects: a `CodeAttributeDeclaration` to specify the attribute and, optionally, one or more `CodeAttributeArgument`s to add values to be passed to the attribute's constructor (what are sometimes referred to as the "positional parameters" on an attribute). The CodeDom does not directly support setting properties on attributes (what are sometimes referred to as "named parameters" on an attribute)—you'll have to use a code snippet if you need to set those values.

To create a `CodeAttributeDeclaration` object, you must pass a `CodeTypeReference` for the type of the attribute you are adding (or the name of the type if the attribute isn't available when you're creating the `CodeAttributeDeclaration` object). Along with the attribute's type, you can also pass any `CodeAttributeArgument`s you need to set values through the attribute's constructor. To create a `CodeAttributeArgument`, you only need to pass the value that the argument represents.

This example creates a `CategoryAttribute` (a `CategoryAttribute` is added to a Property routine to control where in Visual Studio's Property List the property should appear). The `CategoryAttribute`'s constructor accepts a string value that is the category name. The code first creates the parameter to be passed to the `CodeTypeDeclaration`: a `CodeTypeReference` for the `CategoryAttribute`. The example then creates the parameter to be passed to the `CodeAttributeArgument`: a string for holding the name of the category (in this example, the category is being set to "Appearance"). The string is held in a `CodePrimitiveExpression`. With those building blocks in place, the code creates a `CodeAttributeArgument`, passing the name of the category in the

`CodePrimitiveExpression`. The code then creates the `CodeAttribute Declaration`, passing the `CodeTypeReference` and the `CodeAttribute Argument`. Finally, the resulting `CodeAttributeDeclaration` is added to the `CustomAttributes` collection of a `CodeMemberProperty`:

```
CodeTypeReference ctrAttribute =
    new CodeTypeReference(typeof(CategoryAttribute));
string AppearanceName = "Appearance";
CodePrimitiveExpression cpeAppearance =
    new CodePrimitiveExpression(AppearanceName);

CodeAttributeArgument caa = new CodeAttributeArgument(cpeAppearance);
CodeAttributeDeclaration cad =
    new CodeAttributeDeclaration(ctrAttribute, caa);
cmp.CustomAttributes.Add(cad);
```

The resulting code in C# would look like this:

```
[Category("Appearance")] public string...
```

And like this in Visual Basic:

```
<Category("Appearance")> Public Property...
```

Using Directives to Organize Code into Regions

Many of the CodeDom objects have a `StartDirectives` and an `EndDirectives` collection that you can use to add compiler and editor directives to your code (e.g., C#'s `#if` directive to control which parts of the code are to be processed). You can use these collections to add Visual Studio regions to your code to group related code elements together.

BEST PRACTICE   In order to use regions effectively, you'll need to ensure that your code elements are generated in the order that you add them to your `CodeCompileUnit` (by default, the code providers generate all the fields first, for instance). The section on setting code-generation options later in this chapter discusses how to override that default when you generate your code.

To define a region, you must generate two `CodeRegionDirective` objects: one to mark the start of the region and one to mark the end. You specify whether the directive you're creating is a start or end directive by passing a value from the `CodeRegionMode` enumeration as the first parameter when creating the `CodeRegionDirective` (either `CodeRegionMode.Start` or `CodeRegionMode.End`). You must pass the string that acts as the region's identifier as the second parameter to the start `CodeRegionDirective` (you must also pass a string to the end directive, but the value you pass to the end directive is ignored).

`CodeRegionDirective`s must be added to either the `StartDirectives` or `EndDirectives` collection of a CodeDom object. Typically, you'll add the start `CodeRegionDirective` to the `StartDirectives` collection of the first CodeDom object in the region and add the end `CodeRegionDirective` to the `EndDirectives` collection of the last CodeDom object.

This example encloses all the constructors for a class in a region called "Constructors." The code first creates a start `CodeRegionDirective` using the region name and adds the directive to the `StartDirectives` collection of the first `CodeConstructor`. The code then creates an end `CodeRegionDirective` and adds it to the `EndDirectives` collection of the last `CodeConstructor`:

```
string constructorRegion = "Constructors";
CodeRegionDirective crdStart =
    new CodeRegionDirective(CodeRegionMode.Start, constructorRegion);
cc1.StartDirectives.Add(crdStart);
CodeRegionDirective crdEnd =
    new CodeRegionDirective(CodeRegionMode.End, "");
cc2.StartDirectives.Add(crdEnd);
```

The result is the same in both Visual Basic and C# (regions are really a feature of Visual Studio rather than a particular language):

```
#region Constructors
...code...
#endregion
```

UserData (Option Strict and Option Compare)

Many objects in the CodeDom have a `UserData` property to which you can add name/value pairs in order to trigger language-specific constructs by your code provider. In Visual Basic, for instance, by setting the

UserData property on the CodeCompileUnit, you can generate the following statements:

- **Option Strict**—Add a key of "AllowLateBound" set either to True (for Option Strict Off) or False (for Option Strict On)
- **Option Explicit**—Add a key of "RequireVariableDeclaration" set either to True (for Option Explicit On) or False (for Option Explicit Off)

This example generates both the Option Strict and the Option Explicit statement set to Off:

```
unit.UserData.Add("AllowLateBound", true);
unit.UserData.Add("RequireVariableDeclaration", false);
```

The resulting code would look like this:

```
Option Strict Off
Option Explicit Off
```

Code Providers

The final step in generating code is to create a code provider, pass your CodeCompileUnit to it, and get back your generated code. The base implementation for code providers also supports additional functionality that is implemented in both the C# and Visual Basic providers (including the ability to generate valid identifiers for the generated language, as discussed in this chapter's "Other Code Features" section). For instance, in addition to generating source code, you can also compile your code. However, not all methods in the code provider are implemented even in the Visual Basic and C# implementations (the Parse method, which is intended to convert source code back into a CodeCompileUnit, isn't implemented for either the Visual Basic or C# code providers, for instance).

Generating Code

To generate code from your CodeCompileUnit you must create a code provider and then pass it your CodeCompileUnit, a TextWriter object, and (optionally) a

`CodeGeneratorOptions` object specifying how you want your generated code to be formatted. The various code providers aren't held in the same namespace but are, instead, members of their language's namespace (e.g., the Visual Basic code provider is in the `Microsoft.VisualBasic` namespace).

In the comprehensive example that began this chapter, I showed how to generate code and store it in a string using either the Visual Basic or the C# code provider. This example shows how to generate the code into a file using the Visual Basic code provider. The example uses the code provider's `FileExtension` property to retrieve the conventional extension for the file:

```
string filPath = @"C:\Code\MyCode." + vbProv.FileExtension;
if (System.IO.File.Exists(filPath))
{
 System.IO.File.Delete(filPath);
}

System.IO.StreamWriter fileWriter =
        new System.IO.StreamWriter(filPath);
vbProv.GenerateCodeFromCompileUnit(caes, fileWriter, null);
FileWriter.Close();
```

Although the available options are not well documented, you can customize the code provider when you create it by creating a `Dictionary` object containing name/value pairs and passing it to the code provider's constructor. This example invokes the compiler for Visual Basic version 3.5:

```
Dictionary<string, string> dict = new Dictionary<string,string>();
dict.Add("CompilerVersion","v3.5");
Microsoft.VisualBasic.VBCodeProvider vbProv =
        new Microsoft.VisualBasic.VBCodeProvider(dict);
```

The `CodeGeneratorOptions` object provides a set of properties you can set to control how your generated code is formatted. Here are the properties you can set on the `CodeGeneratorOptions` object:

- **BlankLinesBetweenMembers**—When set to False, this property eliminates the blank line automatically added between methods and properties.
- **ElseOnClosing**—When set to True, this property automatically adds an `Else`, `Catch`, or `Finally` block to the closing line of any `If` or `Try` block.

- **BracingStyle**—In C# (and, presumably, all C-type languages), this property controls whether the initial brace in a block appears on the same line as the block's definition. The default is "Block" and gives the results shown in this chapter's examples. Setting this property to "C" causes the initial brace to appear on the following line.
- **IndentString**—The string the provider will use when indenting code (the default is four spaces).
- **VerbatimOrder**—By default, the code provider doesn't generate class members in the order you add them. Instead, all fields are generated, then all constructors, and then all properties, and so on. Setting VerbatimOrder to True causes members to be generated in the order you add them. This can be especially useful if you intend to use regions to group related members or want to place field declarations immediately before the members that use them.

This example creates a CodeGeneratorOptions object, overrides all the default settings, and passes it to the GenerateCodeFromCompileUnit method:

```
CodeGeneratorOptions cgo = new CodeGeneratorOptions();
cgo.BracingStyle = "C";
cgo.BlankLinesBetweenMembers = false;
cgo.IndentString = " ";
cgo.VerbatimOrder = true;
vbProv.GenerateCodeFromCompileUnit(ccu, codeWriter, cgo);
```

You can also check to see if a particular code provider supports some option that may not be available in all languages by passing a value from the GeneratorSupport enumeration to the code provider's Supports method. This example checks to see if the current provider supports creating multidimensional arrays before attempting to nest one array inside another:

```
if (vbProv.Supports(
        CodeDom.Compiler.GeneratorSupport.MultidimensionalArrays))
{
```

Generating Partial Code

Rather than generating code for the complete `CodeCompileUnit`, you can pass CodeDom objects to methods on the provider to generate portions of your code. These methods are useful in two scenarios: When most of your code is created through some other tool (e.g., through the `FileCodeModel`, described in Chapter 3) and when debugging, so that you can see what you are generating without having to generate the complete code file. The methods, with the exception of their first parameter, accept the same parameters as the `GenerateCodeFromCompileUnit`. Here are the methods and the objects they accept as their first parameter:

- **GenerateCodeFromNamespace**—`CodeNamespace`
- **GenerateCodeFromType**—`CodeTypeDeclaration`
- **GenerateCodeFromMember**—`CodeMemberMethod` or `CodeMemberProperty`
- **GenerateCodeFromStatement**—Any statement object
- **GenerateCodeFromExpression**—Any expression object

The following example generates code from a `CodeAttachEventStatement`:

```
CodeAttachEventStatement caes = new CodeAttachEventStatement(
        new CodeThisReferenceExpression(),notFoundName,cdce);

vbProv.GenerateCodeFromStatement(caes, codeWriter, null);
string statementText = generatedCode.ToString();
```

Compiling Code

Although it's beyond the scope of this book, in addition to generating source code, you can also compile your generated code into an assembly. The simplest method is to call the code provider's `CompileAssemblyFromDom` method, passing a `CompilerParameters` object and one or more `CodeCompileUnits`.

The `CompilerParameters` object allows you to specify the following:

- A list of names of assemblies that are referenced by your code
- The name of the output file to generate (optional)
- A Boolean value indicating whether debug information is to be included in the assembly (optional)

In addition to creating your EXE or DLL file, the CompileAssemblyFromDom method returns a CompilerResults object. Using the CompilerResults object's properties, you can retrieve information about the assembly and its files. In addition, by using the CompilerResults' CreateInstance method, you can load an instance of any class defined in your assembly.

The following example creates a CompilerParameters object, adds two assembly references to it, and sets the GenerateInMemory property to True. The code then calls the CompileAssemblyFromDom method, passing the CompilerParameters object and a CodeCompileUnit, and catches the CompilerResults object returned by the method. Finally, the code uses the CreateInstance method to return a Customer object from the resulting assembly:

```
CompilerParameters cp = new CompilerParameters();
cp.ReferencedAssemblies.Add("System.IO");
cp.ReferencedAssemblies.Add("System.Data.SqlClient");
cp.GenerateInMemory = true;
CompilerResults cr = csProv.CompileAssemblyFromDom(cp, ccu);
Customer cust =
    (Customer) cr.CompiledAssembly.CreateInstance("Customer");
```

In addition to compiling from the CodeCompileUnit, you can also compile from your source code either by passing a string containing your code to the provider's CompileAssemblyFromSource or by saving your code to a file and using the CompileAssemblyFromFile method.

Generating Code

The primary criticism leveled against the CodeDom is that it's wordy. (In the case study in Chapter 10, "Case Study: Generating Validation Code," it takes approximately 300 lines of CodeDom-related code to generate the two dozen or so lines of code required by the solution.) However, even if you need to support multiple languages, you'll probably be creating solutions containing boilerplate code for every language you intend to support—code that can be loaded from text files or included in a template. Alternatively, much of the code that you need could be generated by other tools described in this book. In those scenarios, using the CodeDOM isn't an unreasonable solution because the amount of code that must be generated by the CodeDOM may be small. For instance, the first case study in this book generates most of the required code using the `FileCodeModel` objects—only a single additional line of code is required, which could be generated using only a few lines of CodeDom code.

You also shouldn't assume that just because you can write code in a particular language that you can generate that code using the CodeDom. The CodeDom, for instance, has very limited support for creating conditional loop structures (e.g., `Do Whiles`). Also, any feature that is specific to a language is probably not going to be available through the CodeDom (e.g., the unsafe operator in C#), although it may be available through a special extension implemented using the `UserData` property (as is the case with Visual Basic's `Option Strict` directive). You shouldn't even assume that unusual but supported activities (such as nesting namespaces) are supported.

The key issue in CodeDom generation is assembling the components of a CodeDom solution into a complete application. In the second case study in this book I've highlighted portions of a typical CodeDom solution to show how you can use the components together to create a complete application.

CHAPTER 7

GENERATING CODE FROM TEMPLATES WITH T4

In this chapter:

- T4 in Visual Studio
- T4 Code-Generation Strategies
- Creating a T4 Template
- Extending T4
- Invoking Templates from Code
- Leveraging Templates

If you've looked at the two case studies in this book, you may well be concerned about the complexity of a typical code-generation solution (especially if you've looked at the CodeDom solution in Chapter 10, "Case Study: Generating Validation Code"). The main thing that you should be worried about is maintenance: Most shops spend 75 percent of their time extending, modifying, and (occasionally) fixing existing code. As a result, developers prefer solutions that are easy to maintain. You may be concerned that, because of the complexity of the case study solutions, extending or modifying them is just an "accident waiting to happen."

Of course, there is no substitute for good program design. You'll want to organize and structure the code in your code-generation solutions to reduce the chance of an error when it comes time to modify your code-generation solution. However, there is a code-generation technology that reduces some of the complexity in code generation solutions: templates.

Rather than "having code that writes code," a template reduces complexity by allowing you to just type in the code you want to generate into a file. When the template is processed, that text is simply transferred into the output file in your project. By itself, a template isn't a very useful solution unless you want to generate exactly the same code every time. However, templated solutions only require you to incorporate your own code into those parts of the template that generate customized output. Inside a template in those sections where the generated code is the same in every generation, the code is simple: It's just the text that you want to output. Where you need customization, the template is more complex because it incorporates "code that writes code." Effectively the complexity of your solution is limited to those places where you need complexity. Many code-generation packages (e.g., CodeSmith from CodeSmithTools) use templates for this reason.

One of the main benefits of using templates is that it empowers developers using your solution. If the developer isn't happy with the code your solution is generating, the developer can just modify the template (assuming you distribute your templates as part of your solution rather than, for instance, embedding the templates in a resource file). If the developer wants to make a simple change in the code you're generating, that change will, generally speaking, only require a simple change to your template. It's more likely, therefore, that developers will be able to get the code they want without having to modify your generated code—they'll be able to modify your templates instead.

As part of developing its support for domain-specific languages (DSLs), Microsoft developed the Text Templating Transformation Toolkit (T4 for short). However, T4 isn't restricted to generating code for DSLs—the ASP.NET MVC team uses them also, for instance.

The simplest way to see T4 in action is to perform the following steps:

1. Open Visual Studio.
2. Open a VB or C# project.
3. From the Add New Item dialog, select Text File (in Visual Studio 2010, you can use select Text Template and skip the next step).
4. Change the extension of the text file to ".tt". You'll get a dialog that this file might potentially harm your computer—click the OK button.
5. Add the file to your project.
6. In the file, add the following line (in Visual Studio 2010, add this line after the default text already in the file):

```
Hello, World
```

7. Save the file.

You should get the result in Solution Explorer shown in Figure 7-1. If you open the file nested underneath your TT file, it should contain the text "Hello, World."

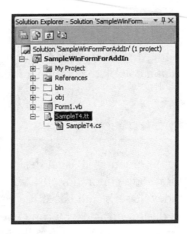

FIGURE 7-1 Visual Studio shows the file holding the code generated by the templates in the CS file underneath the TT file.

To create a code-generation solution using templates, you need two components: a template and a Visual Studio add-in that will invoke the template and pass parameters to it. The code in your template will use those parameters to customize the code generated by the template. You can also create custom classes that will work with T4 to extend it and provide new functionality that you can use within your template.

In this chapter, I first discuss some strategies for using T4 and then show you how to create a template. In the last part of the chapter, I show you how to call a template from your Visual Studio add-in and cover the techniques that can only be used in that environment, including passing parameters to your template. You'll also see how to create a custom host for T4 code generation that allows you to include processing features not available through the host supplied by Visual Studio.

T4 in Visual Studio

If you're using Visual Studio 2008 or 2010, you can start using T4 immediately. If you're using Visual Studio 2005, you'll need to download the toolkit. (Search MSDN using the following: Domain Specific Languages "Visual Studio 2005" Download.) To keep up to date with the toolkit, visit http://code.msdn.microsoft.com/DslTools.

With Visual Studio 2008 and later, you can use T4 without downloading the rest of the DSL toolkit. (They really are two separate technologies—DSL is just one of several technologies that makes extensive use of T4.)

However, as the case study in Chapter 11, "Case Study: Generating Data-Conversion Code," demonstrates, the DSL toolkit gives you the ability to create a visual designer for developers to use to create their input files—a very useful feature in a complete code-generation solution.

T4 Code-Generation Strategies

If you are planning on creating a visual designer for developers to use to supply the inputs for code generation, T4 templates are an excellent tool for recording the developer's inputs. As the developer drags and drops components on the design surface, you can generate a T4 file that will then be automatically processed by Visual Studio to generate code. A related option is to create a custom tool (as described in Chapter 8, "Other Tools: Templates, Attributes, and Custom Tools") that can be associated with any file of input specifications and call your template from code in your custom tool. Creating a visual designer to generate a T4 template is discussed as part of the case study in Chapter 11, as is associating a custom tool with the resulting template so that code is generated automatically.

However, you can use T4 templates in other ways to generate code dynamically as part of the developer's code-development process. If you are invoking your template from a Visual Studio add-in, you can use the same process described in earlier chapters: Analyze the developer's inputs and use that information to generate code. In that scenario, T4 is best used in those solutions where either most of the code is identical from one generation to another or where only a few values provided by the developer control the code-generation process.

A T4 template is, essentially, a string. As a result, you can store it in a file or a database. By building a library of partial templates, you can create code-generation solutions by concatenating those partial templates together with some additional text pulled from the developer's input. Alternatively, you can embed format specifications (e.g., {1}) in your template and, at code generation time, use the `Format` method of the `String` object to substitute in values based on the developer's input.

BEST PRACTICE   Use T4 from a Visual Studio add-in where most of the generated code never varies or where a few parameters from the developer control generation.

You can extend the T4 environment with custom code so another strategy would be to have the developer supply code for your extensions. You would then invoke the developer's code when running your template by calling those methods. This is similar to the way that Personalization works in ASP.NET: the developer writes a class that the Personalization class inherits from.

Options for Extending T4

T4 offers several ways to extend its processing environment. For instance, all T4 templates must execute inside a "host environment": a program that provides support for T4 processing. Visual Studio provides a default host environment you can use, but you can also create your own host environment. With your own host environment, you can add methods to your host environment to extend T4 code generation. You match the host to the template at runtime, so you have a great deal of flexibility in deciding what functionality needs to be embedded in your template and what you can provide through the host.

You can also define custom directives, consisting of name/value pairs, which you can use in your template. In the processor for your custom directive, you can examine those name/value pairs and use them to control the code you generate.

You can also extend the T4 framework by providing a new base class for the processing engine. When it comes time to generate code, your template can use methods from your custom base class to gather information to use when generating code.

There are limitations to T4, the most obvious of which is that it's not language neutral: If you want to support multiple languages, you'll have to create a template for each language.

The T4 Process

The process for generating T4 code consists of two steps. First, your template is used to generate a custom program. That program is then executed, and it is that program that writes out the code you want. Most of the time, you can ignore this process and just consider that your code is generated directly from your template. However, there is the odd feature that only makes sense when you consider the whole process, as you'll see.

Officially, the program created from your template is called the "generated transformation class." However, the word "generated" appears often enough in this book that introducing another term containing it would only be confusing. In this chapter, I refer to the program created from your template as "the intermediate program."

Creating a T4 Template

There is no editor for creating templates in Visual Studio 2005/2008 or, as of this writing, in Visual Studio 2010. There are, however, several editors you download from the Internet. (I'm not going to recommend one.) In this chapter, I've assumed that you're creating your templates in Visual Studio's text editor, which means that you're working without IntelliSense.

The simplest template is just code, containing text, in a file with the .tt extension. When that file is processed, the text in the file will be automatically dropped into a file with the .cs extension (.txt in Visual Studio 2010), created beneath the template file. So, this is a perfectly acceptable template that will create a code file that will compile (at least in a C# project):

```
namespace T4
{
  public class T4Class
  {
    public void DoSomething()
    {
    }
  }
}
```

In Visual Studio 2010, to get the code to compile, change the value in the extension attribute on the output directive at the top of the file from ".txt" to ".cs".

I refer to the code that is copied to the output file without modification as "text."

Of course, this example isn't much good as a code-generation solution: The output text is whatever is in the template file. To support customizing the output text, you can include code within your template to control what is placed in the output file. This allows you to customize the text, add multiple copies of text, or omit text that isn't required. Although the following examples all use C# as the code language, you can use Visual Basic to manipulate your text (see the section "Directives" later in this chapter for how to specify your code language).

To include code in your template, you must enclose it inside `<# #>` delimiters. This example causes the DoSomething method to be added to the output file twice:

```
namespace T4
{
  public class T4Class
  {
<#
    for (int i=0;i < 2;i++)
    {
#>
        public void DoSomething()
        {
        }
<#
    }
#>
  }
}
```

You can use expressions in your code to embed code that returns values directly in the text. Expressions are delimited by `<#=` and `#>`. This example extends the previous example by using an expression to generate a unique name for each instance of the DoSomething method:

```
<#
  for (int i=0;i < 2;i++)
  {
#>
  public void DoSomething<#= i.ToString()#>()
  {

  }
<#
  }
#>
```

When you use C# as your programming language, expressions do not include the semicolon at the end of the line. If you're writing your code in Visual Basic, you can't use the line continuation character in expressions.

Be aware: Any space not inside the `<# #>` delimiters will end up in your generated code. For instance, the code in the previous example generates the following output (note the blank line inside the methods that is copied from the text outside of the `<# #>` delimiters in the template):

```
public void DoSomething0()
{
```

```
        }
        public void DoSomething1()
        {

        }
```

Leaving whitespace around the `<#= #>` delimiters can create problems. For instance, this example has whitespace between "`DoSomething`" and the `<#=` delimiter:

```
public void DoSomething <#= i.ToString()#>()
```

The result is code generated with an embedded space in the method name:

```
public void DoSomething 0()
{
}
public void DoSomething 1()
{
}
```

T4 BEST PRACTICE   Minimize white space around code blocks to prevent unintended blanks and empty lines appearing in your generated code.

An alternative to manipulating the text in your template with code is to use the `Write` or `WriteLine` method to insert text into the output file. Both methods accept a string and insert it into the output file—the `WriteLine` method adds a carriage return to the end of the string. This example modifies the previous example to change the name of the method each time the loop is executed:

```
<#
  for (int i=0;i < 4;i++)
  {
  WriteLine("public void DoSomething" + i.ToString() + "()");
#>
    {
    }
<#
  }
#>
```

To do the same thing with the `Write` method, I would have written this code:

```
for (int i=0;i < 4;i++)
{
#>
public void <#Write("DoSomething" + i.ToString());#>()
{
```

The `Write` and `WriteLine` methods also accept a string containing format specifications and an array of items to be inserted at the formatting specifications. This example creates a method with the name DoSomething1 and DoSomething2 by supplying an array named `texts` (containing two strings) to another string that contains format specifications:

```
<#
for (int i=0;i < 4;i++)
{
  string[] texts = new string[2];
  texts[0] = "Something";
  texts[1] = i.ToString();
  WriteLine("public void Do{0}{1}()",texts);
#>
```

I find using `Write` and `WriteLine` makes it easier to work with variables (e.g., when you pass parameters to your template from your add-in using the `CallContext` class, as discussed in the section "Passing Parameters to a Template") than embedding variables into a template. However, using `Write`/`WriteLine` makes it harder for developers to read (and, therefore, modify) your template, thus defeating one of the primary reasons for using templates.

Escape Characters

To include special characters in your code, you use the standard escape character (\). Similarly, you can use the escape character to include the delimiters in your generated code file (i.e., you can use "\<#" to add "<#" to your output file).

Directives

You can customize the code-generation process by adding directives to your template. There are six built-in directives you can use to customize the code-generation process:

- **template**—Specify the code language used in your template and specify how you will be extending T4's functionality (either through a custom host or a custom base class).
- **assembly**—Add references to DLLs that you can then use in the code in your template.
- **imports**—Specify namespaces for the objects used in the intermediate program.
- **output**—Specify the file extension and encoding for the output file.
- **include**—Add text from files to your template at code-generation time (the text can include control code).
- **parameter**—Can be used to support passing parameters to your template but is only available in Visual Studio 2010. In earlier versions of Visual Studio you can use the CallContext, as described in the section "Passing Parameters to a Template."

The template Directive

The template directive has five attributes: language, debug, hostspecific, inherits, and culture.

The language attribute allows you to specify the language used for the code in the template. You can set the language attribute to either "C#" (the default) or "VB". In Visual Studio 2008, you can also add "v3.5" (e.g., VBv3.5) to enable the language features of .NET 3.5. (Visual Studio 2010 always uses the 4.0 syntax so no version number is required.)

The debug attribute, when set to True, is intended to let you step through your template's code when you invoke your template from code (as described in the section "Invoking Templates from Code").

The hostspecific attribute, when set to True, allows you to call methods on the template engine's Host object. With hostspecific set to True, for instance, you can access a host's CurrentDateTime property and use it in your template code:

```
<#= Host.CurrentDateTime #>
```

This feature can be useful if you run your template from code with your own host because it allows you to extend T4 with your own code.

The `inherits` attribute lets you specify a class that the intermediate program will inherit from. Adding a base class provides another way to extend T4 host (as described in the section "Creating a New Base Class"). In order for T4 to find your class, you must either install it in the Global Assembly Cache (GAC) or use the `assembly` directive described in the next section.

This example sets the coding language for the code in the template to VB 3.5, turns on debugging, makes it possible to call methods in the host, and makes `PHVT4Utils.PhvBase` the base class for the intermediate program. (Because no assembly statement is used, this example assumes that the class has been installed in the GAC.)

```
<#@ template language="VBv3.5" debug="true"
        hostspecific="true" inherits="PhvT4Utils.PhvBase" #>
```

T4 BEST PRACTICE Don't install base classes in the GAC—use the `assembly` directive.

The assembly Directive

The `assembly` directive has one attribute: `name`.

The `name` attribute allows you to specify an assembly that will be added to the references for the intermediate program. Using the attribute allows you to use the classes and methods from that assembly in the code in your template file (e.g., by adding a reference to the ADO.NET libraries, you could use ADO.NET in your template code to extract data to insert into your generated code).

For the .NET assemblies you only need to give the name of the assembly's DLL, as in this example:

```
<#@ assembly name="System" #>
```

For other assemblies, you'll need to provide the full path to the DLL. To support a class used in the `inherits` attribute of the template directive, for instance, I would provide the full pathname to the DLL, as in this example:

```
<#@ template language="VBv3.5" debug="true"
        hostspecific="true" inherits="PhvT4Utils.PhvBase" #>
<#@ assembly name="C:\T4Utilities\PhvT4Utils.dll" #>
```

You can have multiple assembly directives in a template.

The import Directive

The import directive has a single attribute: namespace.

The import directive's namespace attribute allows you to specify a namespace to be added to the intermediate program (i.e., this allows you to add a using or imports statement to the intermediate program). This example adds the namespace for System.Data:

```
<#@ import namespace="System.Data" #>
```

If you are using the inherits attribute in the template directive, you can shorten your class name down to just the name of the class by including the namespace with the import directive, as in this example:

```
<#@ template language="VBv3.5" debug="true"
             hostspecific="true" inherits="PhvBase" #>
<#@ import namespace="PhvT4Utils" #>
```

You can have multiple import directives in a template.

The include Directive

The include directive's name attribute allows you to copy text or code (or a combination of both) into your template. If you include template code into your file, it will be executed and used to generate code:

```
<#@ include name="C:\T4Utils\StandardText.txt" #>
```

You can have multiple include directives in your template and can put them anywhere in the template except inside the <# #> delimiters.

The output Directive

The output directive has two attributes: extension and encoding.

The extension attribute allows you to control the extension put on the file generated by the template. This example specifies that the file extension for the output file should be ".xml":

```
<#@ output extension=".xml" #>
```

The default extension is ".cs".

You can use the encoding attribute on the output directive to specify how the output text is to be encoded (the default is the current ANSI code page). However, this directive is only relevant when your template is being invoked from Visual Studio rather than from your own code. When you invoke a template from your code in a Visual Studio add-in, the results of the processing are returned to you as a string. You could then use the objects in the FileCodeModel (discussed in Chapter 3, "Manipulating Project Components") to add that code to a file in your project.

The parameter Directive

The parameter directive supports passing parameters from an external program to the template. Although you can pass parameters to your template in all versions of Visual Studio and .NET, the parameter directive is only available in Visual Studio 2010/.NET 4. In all versions of Visual Studio, you can pass parameters by adding values to the CallContext class (discussed in the section "Passing Parameters to a Template"). In Visual Studio 2010, using the parameter directive, you can simply use the variable defined in the directive; in Visual Studio 2005/2008, you will need to use remoting code to retrieve the value (also discussed later in this chapter along with the CallContext class).

The parameter directive has two attributes: type and string.

The type attribute allows you to specify the data type of the data that's being passed in the parameter (provide the fully qualified name of the type: system.integer rather than just integer). The name attribute provides the name of the parameter that will be passed.

This example defines a string parameter called ClassName:

```
<#@ parameter type="System.string" name="ClassName"#>
```

Adding Helper Methods

As noted earlier, T4 code generation is a two-step process: First, a program is generated from your template and then that intermediate program is executed to generate your output file. The <#+ #> delimiters allow you to add helper methods (called "class features") to the intermediate program generated in the first step. You can then call those helper methods from the code in your template file.

This example calls a helper method named CreateFunctionName to generate method names and then adds that method:

```
<#
  for (int i=0;i < 2;i++)
  {
#>
    public void <#= CreateFunctionName(i)#>()
    {
```

```
    }
<#
    }
#>
   }
}

<#+
public string CreateFunctionName(int counter)
{
 switch (counter)
 {
  case 0:
   return "DoSomethingOne";
   break;
  case 1:
   return "DoSomethingTwo";
   break;
 }
 return string.Empty;
}
#>
```

As this example demonstrates, your class features must be the last items in your template file. You can have multiple class features in a template and define multiple helper methods in each class feature.

A class feature block can contain expressions and code blocks just like the template itself. Rather than use the return statement, CreateFunctionName in the previous example could have been written like this:

```
<#+
public void CreateFunctionName(int counter)
{
 switch (counter)
 {
  case 0:
#>
    "DoSomethingOne"
<#+
   break;
  case 1:
#>
    "DoSomethingTwo"
<#+
   break;
```

```
    }
  }
#>
```

This feature allows you to use parameters passed to your template to control the creation of your helper functions.

You can also use class function blocks to add structures, constants, or most other language features to the intermediate program.

Generating Errors and Warnings

The text templating engine will generate any errors that prevent it from producing an output file. However, you may have additional criteria that you want to check for and report on. Use the Error and Warning methods to report any errors you discover. You can customize what these methods do. For instance, if you create a custom host, you can use code in your custom host to decide what to do with each message. (The case study in Chapter 11 discusses how to extend the validation of T4 templates generated using a visual designer—you would also use the Error and Warning methods to report problems that code in your visual designer discovers.)

This example uses the simplest form of the Error method:

```
<#+
public string CreateFunctionName(int counter)
{
  switch (counter)
  {
    case 0:
     return "DoSomethingOne";
     break;
    case 1:
     return "DoSomethingTwo";
     break;
  }
  Error("Too large an index passed to CreateFunctionName");
  return string.Empty;
}
#>
```

Calling the Error method doesn't stop the text templating engine from continuing to process your template. To stop processing, you should throw an exception. (The exception's message will also be written to the Output window.)

Review

Before going on, this is a good time for a quick review of the code-generation process in T4: Your T4 template is used to generate an intermediate program that is then executed and writes out your code. That intermediate program inherits from either the TextTransformation class or a class that inherits from it. The TextTransformation class includes, among other methods, the Warning and Error methods mentioned in the last section. In a later section ("Creating a New Base Class"), you'll see how to create your own base class derived from TextTransformation and extend that base class with your own code by supplying additional methods that can be used in your template as the Warning and Error methods are.

Accessing the Generated Code

As the intermediate program generates code, the generated code is placed in a StringBuilder, which you can access through the GenerationEnvironment method. (Warning, Error, and GenerationEnvrionment are methods of the TextTransformation class that your intermediate program inherits from.) Any changes that you make through GenerationEnvironment will be reflected in the text written to the output file. This example, for instance, removes all the code generated to this point in the template file:

```
<# CodeGeneration.Remove(0, CodeGeneration.Length); #>
```

Controlling Code Indentation

You can control the indentation of the generation code in your output file by using the TextTransformation class's PushIndent method to insert characters to be used in front of any generated line of code. As the name implies, each time you call the PushIndent method, the string that you pass to the method is added to whatever indentation characters are already present. The PopIndent method removes the last indent item added and the ClearIndent method removes them all.

This example adds a tab to the indentation characters and follows that with a second tab (in Visual Basic you could use the vbTab constant). The code then removes the second tab added and finally removes all the indentation characters:

```
PushIndent("\t");
WriteLine("first");
PushIndent("\t");
WriteLine("second");
PopIndent();
WriteLine("third");
ClearIndent();
WriteLine("fourth");
```

The resulting output file would look like this:

```
first
      second
   third
fourth
```

T4 BEST PRACTICE   Use indenting sparingly. Developers have probably con-figured Visual Studio to display their code the way they want. Although, ideally, developers won't want to modify your generated code, they may want to review it. Using indents can conflict with the developer's code display settings, making it harder for developers to review your code.

Extending T4

You have three primary ways of extending T4 processing: defining a new base class for the class generated from your T4 template, defining new directives, or using a custom host. This section discusses creating a new base class and creating custom directives. Using a custom host is discussed later in this chapter in the section "Invoking Templates from Code."

Creating a New Base Class

The first step in defining a new base class is to create an abstract class that itself inherits from `Microsoft.VisualStudio.TextTemplating`, as this example does:

```
using Microsoft.VisualStudio.TextTemplating;
namespace PhvT4Utils
```

```
{
    public abstract class PhvBase: TextTransformation
    {
    }
}
```

Within the base class you can add public (or protected) functions that you can call from your template. There are two approaches you can take:

- Create methods that return string values that can be used in expressions in your template code.
- Create methods that write directly to the output file using either Write or WriteLine.

These two methods both generate a copyright notice as a C# comment, but one method returns the copyright text while the other writes it to the output file:

```
public string ReturnCopyright()
{
   return "//Copyright PH&V Information Services, 2010";
}

public void WriteCopyright()
{
   WriteLine( "//Copyright PH&V Information Services, 2010");
}
```

The two methods could be used like this in your template code:

```
<#= ReturnCopyright()#>
<# WriteCopyright(); #>
```

In order for T4 to find your class, you can install it into the GAC or reference it from an assembly directive. To create a project that will automatically install into the GAC when it is built, see the steps in the section "Installing to the GAC" in Chapter 8, where I discuss creating a custom tool. However, it's probably easier to use T4's assembly directive, as shown here, to reference your class:

```
<#@ template language="C#v3.5" debug="true" hostspecific="true"
        inherits="PhvT4Utils.PhvBase"#>
<#@ assembly name="C:\T4Utils\PhvT4Utils.dll" #>
```

T4 BEST PRACTICE   Use class features for common methods used only in a single template. Use include files for code and text that you want to share across multiple templates (especially if you may be updating the contents of the include file). Use base classes to extend functionality in T4 across multiple templates. You can also place especially useful class features in include files so that they can be shared across templates.

In Visual Studio 2010, you can also access environment variables and Visual Studio macro variables. For instance, this example uses the $(ProjectDir) and %programFile% variables to reference the folder that the project is in and the Program Files folder:

```
<#@ assembly name="$(ProjectDir)MyCustom.dll" #>
<#@ assembly name="%programfiles%MyT4Utils.dll" #>
```

Defining Custom Directives

Directives provide a way to embed information into the template using name/value pairs. The T4 engine allows you to create your own custom directives to support common activities. Your custom directive can have whatever attributes you want but must include an attribute called processor that you use to specify the class that will process your directive. In this section, I show you how to extend your host to support a custom directive and how to create a very simple class for processing your custom directive.

For this example, I use custom copyright directive:

```
<#@ copyright name="PH&V Information Services" year = "2010"
        processor="copyright" #>
```

The code that I want generated from this directive would look like this:

```
//Copyright by PH&V Information Services, 2010
```

If you're using the Visual Studio host (rather than a custom host), you must register your directive in the Windows registry. You'll want to add your key under the entry:

```
HKEY_LOCAL_MACHINE\SOFTWARE\Microsoft\VisualStudio\
    VisualStudioVersion\TextTemplating\DirectiveProcessors
```

The name of your key is the name of your class. Assuming that you're not putting the DLL with your class in the GAC, here are the subkeys that you must add to the key:

- **(Default)**—A description of your processor
- **Class**—*Namespacename.Languagename.Classname*
- **CodeBase**—Full path to your DLL in the format *file:///c:/foldername/.../filename.*DLL

If you're creating a Visual Studio package (not an option for Visual Studio 2005), you can also register your class by adding the `ProvideDirectiveProcessor` attribute to your package.

The class that processes your directive must inherit from the `Microsoft.VisualStudio.TextTemplating.DirectiveProcessor` class. For this example, I need a `StringBuilder` that will be used from two different methods, so I declare that at the top of the class:

```
class CopyrightDirective :
    Microsoft.VisualStudio.TextTemplating.DirectiveProcessor
{
 private StringBuilder copyrightField = new StringBuilder();
```

My sample directive process class generates the code for a property that returns a value (the property is then added to the intermediate program and used to add code to the output file). The simplest possible directive processor creates a read-only property that returns a string literal. For my copyright directive shown earlier, I want to write the code for a property that looks like this:

```
public string copyRightNotice
{
 get{return "//Copyright by Peter Vogel, 2010";}
}
```

You build the property's code in the processor's `ProcessDirective` method. The method is passed the name of the directive and a dictionary object containing one KeyValuePair for each attribute on the directive. This version of the ProcessDirective generates the property for the copyright directive and stores it in a StringBuilder:

```
public override void ProcessDirective(
        string directiveName, IDictionary<string, string> arguments)
{
 string copyrightNotice = string.Empty;

 copyrightNotice = "\"//Copyright by " + arguments["name"] +
                ", " + arguments["year"] + "\"";
 copyrightProperty.Append("public string copyrightNotice ");
 copyrightProperty.Append("{");
 copyrightProperty.Append("get {return " + copyrightNotice + ";}");
 copyrightProperty.Append("}");
}
```

You need to return the code for your property from the GetClassCodeForProcessingRun method. This example returns the code from the StringBuilder used in the ProcessDirective method:

```
public override string GetClassCodeForProcessingRun()
{
 return copyrightProperty.ToString();
}
```

You also need to add code to the IsDirectiveSupported method. The template engine calls the processor's IsDirectiveSupported method, passing the name of the directive, to give you a chance to indicate whether you will let the directive execute. Because I'm confident that this class will never be used inappropriately, I just return True:

```
public override bool IsDirectiveSupported(string directiveName)
{
 return true;
}
```

For the simple processor that I'm creating here, the other methods in the class just need to return nulls:

```
public override string[] GetImportsForProcessingRun()
{
 return null;
}
```

```
public override string GetPostInitializationCodeForProcessingRun()
{
 return null;
}

public override string GetPreInitializationCodeForProcessingRun()
{
 return null;
}

public override string[] GetReferencesForProcessingRun()
{
 return null;
}
```

This is the simplest possible directive processor. If I thought that my directive was going to be called multiple times, for instance, I would need to increment a counter that I would add to the end of the property name to ensure that I generate a unique property name for each directive. I can also add fields, import statements, and other code to the intermediate class by using the other methods in the processor class.

Directive processors also allow you to support language-neutral coding in T4. The `StartProcessingRun` method of the class is called before any other method on the class and is passed a `CodeDomProvider` set to the language of the output file generated by the template. You can use that provider to generate your property using language-neutral code (as discussed in Chapter 6, "Generating Language-Neutral Code") instead of hard-coding for a particular language, as I've done here.

Invoking Templates from Code

Once you've created a template, you can invoke it from code. Invoking your template from code allows you to control the code-generation process and provides you with additional opportunities for extending T4.

To invoke your template from code, you must either generate it at run-time from the developer's input or store a previously created template in a separate file or database. In your Visual Studio add-in, when it comes time to generate code (either because the developer has selected a menu item or triggered an event in Visual Studio), you pass the template to the T4 engine and receive back a string containing your generated code. You can then use the `FileCodeModel` objects (discussed in Chapter 3) to add the code to a file in your project.

This section covers how to invoke your template from code and how you can extend T4 in that environment.

Configuring the Project

To invoke a template from code (and integrate into the development process), you'll need to begin by creating a Visual Studio add-in as described in Chapter 2, "Integrating with Visual Studio." From the add-in, you'll gather the inputs for your code-generation process, retrieve your template, generate your code, and insert the code into a file in the project.

To invoke a template from code, you'll need to download and install the Visual Studio Software Development Kit and, for Visual Studio 2005, the domain-specific language (DSL) package. For Visual Studio 2005/2008, you'll need to add references to the following:

- Microsoft.VisualStudio.TextTemplating.dll
- VisualStudio.TextTemplating.VSHost.dll

Both can be found in the SDK's VisualStudioIntegration\Common\ Assemblies folder. You'll also need to add a reference to `Microsoft.VisualStudio.OLE.Interop` from the .NET tab in the Add Reference dialog. For Visual Studio 2010, you'll need to add references to the following:

- Microsoft.VisualStudio.TextTemplating 10.0.dll
- VisualStudio.TextTemplating.VSHost 10.0.dll

Both are in the SDK folders. For all versions of Visual Studio, you'll need to add a reference to the `Microsoft.VisualStudio.Shell.Interop` library from the .NET tab in the Add Reference dialog. Similarly, anyone using your templates is going to need these DLLs, so you'll need to make sure they're installed on the computers of the developers you're distributing your solution to. These DLLs should be installed on any computer with Visual Studio installed, except for developers using Visual Studio 2005—those computers will need the DSL redistributable package.

Invoking the Template Using the Visual Studio Host

When you process your template, you'll need to retrieve a reference to the engine that performs the transformation and a host for the process. You can use the host that comes with Visual Studio (which helps ensure that your template is processed consistently in any environment) or you can create a custom host. In this section, I look at using the Visual Studio host, which is also your simplest solution when creating an add-in. The next section looks at how you could invoke the template with a custom host (a good solution for standalone converters operating outside of Visual Studio) and, following that, how to create a custom host.

To use the Visual Studio host, you'll need to add references to these libraries (or as many of them as you have):

- `Microsoft.VisualStudio.Shell.Interop`
- `Microsoft.VisualStudio.Shell.Interop.8.0`
- `Microsoft.VisualStudio.Shell.Interop.9.0`

In your add-in, you can save yourself some typing by adding this namespace directive:

```
using Microsoft.VisualStudio.TextTemplating.VSHost;
```

The next step in processing your template is to retrieve a reference to the text templating engine. In an add-in you retrieve the templating engine by casting the DTE object to the IServerProvider interface and then calling its GetService method, passing the type STextTemplating. Cast the return value as an ITextTemplating class.

Once you've retrieved a reference to the engine, you can call its ProcessTemplate method. For a minimal call to ProcessTemplate, you can just pass the text of your template as the second parameter. The ProcessTemplate method returns the generated code as a string.

This example retrieves a reference to the engine and calls the ProcessTemplate method, passing a literal string containing a T4 template. The resulting code is returned to a variable called, in this case, code:

```
IServiceProvider isp = (IServiceProvider) _applicationObject;
ITextTemplating tt =
    (ITextTemplating)isp.GetService(typeof(STextTemplating));
string code = tt.ProcessTemplate("", T4Template,null,null);
```

For the first parameter you can pass the filename of a template to use in error reporting.

Invoking the Template with a Custom Host

If you're not generating code from a Visual Studio add-in, you can create an instance of the engine. However, outside of Visual Studio, you'll have to provide your own host. This section shows the code to create the engine and then goes on to show how to create a custom host.

This is the code to create an instance of the Text Templating Engine and a custom host object. In this code, I've assumed that the host is called PHVT4Host:

```
Microsoft.VisualStudio.TextTemplating.Engine eng;
eng = new Microsoft.VisualStudio.TextTemplating.Engine();
PHVT4Host tth = new PHVT4Host();
```

You'll also need to retrieve the path to the file containing your template. For this example, I've assumed that the template file is being kept in the same folder as my add-in. This code determines the path to the add-in's folder and then combines that with the name of the template (I've hard-coded in a filename of "ClassFile.TT") to create the complete path. The code then reads the contents of the template file into a string:

```
string templatePath =
    System.IO.Path.GetDirectoryName(tth.GetType().Assembly.Location);
if (templatePath.LastIndexOf("\\bin") > 0)
{
   templatePath =
      templatePath.Remove(templatePath.LastIndexOf("\\bin"));
}
string TemplateText =
      System.IO.File.ReadAllText(System.IO.Path.Combine(
                                 templatePath, "ClassFile.TT"));
```

Now you can pass the string containing the template and the host to the `ProcessTemplate` method of the `TextTemplatingEngine` created earlier:

```
string Contents = eng.ProcessTemplate(TemplateText, tth);
```

If you use the host described in the next section, you can determine if there were problems in processing the template by checking the `HasErrors` property on the `CompilerErrorCollection` collection returned by my host's `Errors` property. If there are errors, you should loop through the collection retrieving each of the `CompilerError` objects and display the properties on the `CompilerError` object that will help you debug your template. Not all errors are fatal: The `CompilerError` objects have an `IsWarning` that indicates the level of the error. (If `IsWarning` is False, no code will have been generated.)

This sample code concatenates all the properties on the `CompilerError` object (except for `IsWarning`) to create a message. The code uses a utility developed in the case study in Chapter 9, "Case Study: Generating a Connection String Manager," to display the messages in Visual Studio:

```
if (tth.Errors.HasErrors)
{
 string message;
 Utilities util = new Utilities(applicationObject, "T4Generator");
 foreach (System.CodeDom.Compiler.CompilerError err
                                    in tth.Errors)
 {
  message = err.ErrorText + " in " + err.FileName +
            " at line/column " + err.Line + "/" + err.Column +
            " (" + err.ErrorNumber + ") ";
  if (err.IsWarning != true)
  {
   util.WriteOutput(message,GenerationLevel.Severe);
  }
  else
  {
   util.WriteOutput(message,GenerationLevel.Warning);
  }
 }
}
```

Any messages that you write with the `Error` or `Warning` methods are added to the `CompilerErrorCollection`.

Defining a Custom Host

To support invoking a template from outside of Visual Studio, you need to create a text templating host class that implements the `ITextTemplatingEngineHost` interface. During text generation, the template engine will call members of the host during processing. You can also call members of the host class to extend T4 with your own custom code.

To create a host like the sample in this section, you'll need these namespace directives in your host's class file:

```
using System;
using System.Collections.Generic;
```

```
using System.Text;
using System.Data;
using System.CodeDom.Compiler;
```

At the top of the class I add the following fields:

- A List to hold the names of any assemblies I want to make available to my template code
- The name of the folder holding any .NET assemblies that I use to resolve the path to those assembles
- A variable that can hold the CompilerErrorCollection object

That code looks like this:

```
class PHVT4Host : ITextTemplatingEngineHost
{
 public List<string> assemblies = new List<string>();
 const string netversion = "v2.0.50727";
 CompilerErrorCollection errors;
```

A number of the members on the host are intended to be used to convert tokens in the template into their "real" values. (The names of these methods begin with "Resolve.") This example demonstrates one implementation for the ResolvePath members that converts paths in the template into real file pathnames. In my simple host, I just check that the file path passed from the template is valid and return it if it is. (I return nothing if the file path isn't valid.) This effectively forces the template to contain the exact file path required for any file:

```
string ITextTemplatingEngineHost.ResolvePath(string path)
{
 if (System.IO.File.Exists(path))
 {
  return path;
 }
 else
 {
  return string.Empty;
 }
}
```

Two routines are involved with handling assemblies. You use the StandardAssemblyReferences member to preload a List with the names of any assemblies that the intermediate program will need and return that List to the engine. Effectively, this method performs the same function as the assembly directive in a template. In my host I add references to System and System.Runtime.Remoting to support using the CallContext class. (I use CallContext to pass parameters to the template, as discussed in the section "Passing Parameters to a Template.")

You use the ResolveAssemblyReference member to convert any assembly names into full references. In this sample code, I first check to see if the assembly name passed in is a full file path pointing to an existing file. If that test fails, I check to see if the assembly exists in the same folder as the host. If that also fails, I check to see if the assembly exists in the .NET folder:

```
IList<string> ITextTemplatingEngineHost.StandardAssemblyReferences
{
 get
 {
  assemblies.Add("System");
  assemblies.Add("System.Runtime.Remoting");
  return assemblies;
 }
}

string ITextTemplatingEngineHost.ResolveAssemblyReference(
            string assemblyReference)
{
 string assemblyPath = CheckFile(assemblyReference);

 if (assemblyPath == string.Empty)
 {
  string dllPath = System.IO.Path.GetDirectoryName(
    this.GetType().Assembly.Location);
  assemblyPath = CheckFile(System.IO.Path.Combine(
    dllPath, assemblyReference));
 }

 if (assemblyPath == string.Empty)
 { string gac = (Environment.GetEnvironmentVariables()
            ["windir"] as string) +
            System.IO.Path.DirectorySeparatorChar +
            "Microsoft.NET" + System.IO.Path.DirectorySeparatorChar +
            "Framework" + System.IO.Path.DirectorySeparatorChar +
            netversion;
```

```
assemblyPath = CheckFile(System.IO.Path.Combine(gac,
                                    assemblyReference));
    }
    return assemblyPath;
}
```

You use the `LoadIncludeText` member to retrieve the contents of any file specified in `include` directives. This version assumes that all the file paths in the template are complete and correct. When passed a file path, this code checks to see if the file exists and, if it does, reads all the text from the file and returns it through the method's content parameter:

```
bool ITextTemplatingEngineHost.LoadIncludeText(
    string requestFileName, out string content, out string location)
{
  location = string.Empty;
  if (System.IO.File.Exists(requestFileName))
  {
    content = System.IO.File.ReadAllText(requestFileName);
    return true;
  }
  else
  {
    content = string.Empty;
    return false;
  }
}
```

The engine calls the host's `LogErrors` method at the end of processing and passes a collection of `CompilerError` objects representing any errors or warning found while processing your template. You can use the `LogErrors` method to write any errors out to a log file. In my simple host I add a second property and a field to make the collection of errors available to the add-in. In the `LogErrors` method, I pass the collection to my own `Errors` property. My `Errors` property has a private set part that updates a `List` with the collection passed to it. Code in the add-in calls the public `get` part of the property to retrieve the collection after processing is done:

```
void ITextTemplatingEngineHost.LogErrors(
    System.CodeDom.Compiler.CompilerErrorCollection errors)
{
  processErrors = errors;
```

```
        }

        public CompilerErrorCollection processErrors
        {
          get
          {
          return _processErrors;
          }
          private set
          {
           _processErrors = value;
          }
        }
```

You can use the host's GetHostOption method to return different values or objects depending on a parameter passed to the method (or you can just always return Nothing/null from this method). This example takes the optionName parameter passed to the method and uses it to initialize a Customer object that is returned to the template:

```
object ITextTemplatingEngineHost.GetHostOption(string optionName)
{
 return new Customer(optionName);
}
```

In this simple host, there are several members of the interface that I don't put much code in. For instance, I don't expect the host to specify the file extension that my add-in will use, so I don't put any code in the FileExtension method.

The following code also assumes that no custom directives are being used so I return nothing from the ResolveDirectiveProcessor method. (As described in the section "Defining Custom Directives" earlier in this chapter, you need to put code in this method if you are using custom directives.) The CurrentDateTime member in this simple host returns the current time in a specific format. I've also included the CheckFile helper method that appeared in earlier code in this section:

```
Type ITextTemplatingEngineHost.ResolveDirectiveProcessor(
                string processorName)
{
   return null;
}
```

```
string ITextTemplatingEngineHost.ResolveParameterValue(
    string directiveId, string processorName, string parameterName)
{
 return string.Empty;
}

public string CurrentDateTime()
{
 return DateTime.Now.ToLongTimeString();
}

AppDomain ITextTemplatingEngineHost.ProvideTemplatingAppDomain(
            string content)
{
    return AppDomain.CurrentDomain;
}

string ITextTemplatingEngineHost.TemplateFile
{
 get
 {
  return string.empty;
 }
}

void ITextTemplatingEngineHost.SetFileExtension(string extension)
{

}

void ITextTemplatingEngineHost.SetOutputEncoding(
      Encoding encoding, bool fromOutputDirective)
{

}

IList<string> ITextTemplatingEngineHost.StandardImports
{
 get
 {
  return null;
 }
}
```

```
string CheckFile(string TestPath)
{
 if (System.IO.File.Exists(TestPath))
 {
  return TestPath;
 }
 else
 {
  return string.Empty;
  }
}
```

As noted before, you can call members of the host from your template, provided you set the `hostspecific` attribute on the template directive to True (the template directive was discussed earlier in this chapter) and use the `Host` keyword. Calling the sample `GetHostOption` method that I showed earlier would look like this, for instance:

```
<#Customer cust = (Customer) Host.GetHostOption("phv"); #>
```

Adding Custom Methods to the Host

In addition to providing code for the members of the `ITextTemplatingHostEngine` interface, you can also add new members to the host. This example adds a method that returns a copyright notice:

```
public string GetCopyRight ()
{
 return "//Copyright PH&V Information Services, 2010";
}
```

To call the method you must add an `assembly` directive that points to the DLL containing the host (which might be the DLL for the add-in). You can then cast the `Host` variable to the type of your host and call its methods. This example calls the `GetCopyRight` method shown before:

```
<#@ assembly name=""C:\T4Utilities\PhvT4Utils.dll"" #>
<#
    T4TestGeneration.PHVTextTemplateHost phvtt =
                (T4TestGeneration.PHVTextTemplateHost)Host;
    WriteLine(phvtt.GetCopyRight());
```

To call methods that you've added to the host, you'll also need to make your host class a public class. (This isn't necessary if you're just using it to host the template engine process.)

Once you start casting the host, you need to get Visual Studio to stop invoking your template. (Attempting to cast the Host when Visual Studio invokes your template will generate an error and prevent your add-in from compiling.) The easiest way to do that is, in the Properties window, to clear the Custom Tool property on your template file. (The property defaults to TextTemplatingFileGenerator.)

BEST PRACTICE When choosing between adding functionality by creating either a custom host or a custom base class, consider this: Use custom hosts to extend T4 with functionality that you want to use with many but not all templates. Use a custom base class for functionality you want to make available to all templates.

Passing Parameters to a Template

Although you could generate a custom template in your add-in's code or assemble one from partial templates in text files, it's more likely that you will pass parameters to your template and use those parameters in your template to control what code is generated. Prior to Visual Studio 2010, the easiest way to pass parameters is, in your add-in, to write data to the current thread using the CallContext class's SetLogicalData method. This method allows you to add named variables to threads that can then be retrieved, by name, from within the template using the CallContext class's GetLogicalData method.

This example adds a named item called FunctionName to the thread, with the value "Something":

```
System.Runtime.Remoting.Messaging.CallContext.LogicalSetData(
                              "FunctionName", "Something");
```

In your template you can retrieve the value with code like this:

```
FunctionName = (string) System.Runtime.Remoting.Messaging.
            CallContext.LogicalGetData("FunctionName");
```

In order to use `CallContext` in the template, you must add a reference to `System.Runtime.Remoting` to the intermediate program. You can do that with the assembly directive; however, I use this feature often enough that I include it in my host's `StandardAssemblies` method (as shown earlier in this chapter).

Supporting Custom Directives

To have your custom host support custom directives, you must enhance your host to return the class that will handle the directive. You do that by adding code to the host's `ResolveDirectiveProcessor` method. The `ResolveDirectiveProcessor` method is passed the value in the custom directive's processor attribute and must return the type of the class that will handle the directive. This sample code can be extended to handle multiple directive processors and will throw an error when passed the name of a processor it doesn't handle:

```
Type ITextTemplatingEngineHost.ResolveDirectiveProcessor(
                string processorName)
{
  switch(processorName)
  {
   case "copyright" :
     return typeof(CopyrightDirective);
     break;
  }
   throw new Exception(
        processorName + "is not a known directive processor.");
}
```

As with casting the `Host` variable, adding a custom directive will prevent your add-in from compiling when using a custom host. You'll need to clear the Custom Tool property for the file to prevent errors when building your add-in. Unlike using the Visual Studio host, you don't need to register a custom directive.

Leveraging Templates

Templates provide a way to manage the complexity of code generating by separating generated code that is identical from one scenario to another (often the largest part of the generated code) from the code that does change. In this chapter you've not only seen how to incorporate T4 into your projects, you've also seen how to invoke T4 templates from code in a Visual Studio add-in. In addition to allowing you to integrate generating code from templates with Visual Studio, calling T4 templates from code lets you extend the T4 framework in a variety of ways.

In this chapter, I've concentrated on using T4 templates from your own code (probably in a Visual Studio add-in). The case study in Chapter 11 uses a different approach: It shows how to create a visual designer that you can distribute to other developers. Once developers install your visual designer, they will create a T4 template by dragging and dropping components, setting properties on those components, and connecting those components to each other. Visual Studio will then automatically generate code from the resulting T4 template.

OTHER TOOLS: TEMPLATES, ATTRIBUTES, AND CUSTOM TOOLS

In this chapter:

- Item Templates
- Attributes
- Generating Code from Custom File Formats
- Reviewing the Tools

The tools covered so far have been dedicated to supporting Visual Studio or generating/modifying code. However, three more tools, more general purpose in nature, should also be part of your code-generation toolkit: templates, attributes, and custom tools.

Templates are useful because on many occasions the code you add to a solution is boilerplate: The code is virtually identical from one solution to another. Even when a solution's detailed code is different for every generation, the overall structure of the solution usually doesn't change. For instance, the code in the members of a generated class may change with every generation, but the structure of the class—its methods and properties—may remain constant. Rather than generate this boilerplate code using your code-generation code, your best practice is to create a template containing the boilerplate code and use that as the base for the code you generate. If your code-generation solution starts from an effective base, your actual code generation may just consist of finding and replacing text markers in the template. And, of course, the fewer changes you have to make when generating code, the less testing you'll have to do.

Attributes perform two different functions as part of supporting code generation: providing input and storing key information. Attributes offer a structured way for developers to provide input to your code-generation process and allow developers to provide that information as part of writing their own code. If your solution extends a developer's own code, attributes are the most convenient way for developers to annotate their code to mark what parts should be extended and how the code should extended. You can also use attributes as part of the code-generation process: As you generate code, you can add your own attributes to your generated code to record information to be used during subsequent generations. (XML comments provide another place to store information but aren't supported in all languages—and, unlike attributes, they can't be extended.)

The third tool discussed in this chapter, custom tools, lets developers enter their input into a separate file rather than add their input to existing code or configuration files. You can specify any format for these files (although an XML format will make processing the input easier for you). A developer then associates your custom tool with the file by setting a property on the file; then, whenever the developer saves or switches away from the file, your tool will generate new code based on the file's content. The case study in Chapter 11, "Case Study: Generating Data-Conversion Code," shows how to create a visual designer to help developers enter their inputs for the code-generation process into the file.

One warning: Using the tools discussed in this chapter does make distributing your code-generation solution more complicated. For instance, if you use templates, you must ensure that your template is compatible with the developer's version of Visual Studio (this can mean creating multiple distribution packages: one for each version of Visual Studio you intend to support) and that the template is installed in the correct location on the developer's computer. Using attributes or custom tools requires that your installation package copy the supporting DLL to the developer's computer. For attributes, the developer will have to add a reference to your attribute's DLL; custom tools must be registered with Windows as part of being installed on the developer's computer. With all of these tools, source control becomes important because you must make sure that the version of the template used by the developer is the same version that your code-generation solution expects.

Item Templates

Item templates are ZIP files that can be used with the `ProjectItems` collection's `AddFromTemplate` method (described in Chapter 3, "Manipulating Project Components") to add files to your solution with preset content. Each ZIP file contains the file (or files) to be added, an icon file, and an XML document (the .vstemplate file) that specifies how the template is to be used by

Visual Studio. Item templates allow you to incorporate information from the project into your code (e.g., the project's namespace) by using replaceable parameters and to conditionally include or exclude text in your files.

If you're working with Visual Studio 2008 or 2010, the easiest way to create an item template is to use the Visual Studio Export Template Wizard. If you're working with Visual Studio 2005, you'll have to build the components of your template from scratch using a text editor (i.e., Notepad). However, even if you intend to use the wizard to generate your template, you'll need to understand the format of the code file and the .vstemplate file so that you can modify the ones generated by the Visual Studio 2008/2010 editor.

Using the Wizard

To convert any file in your application into a template using the wizard, all you need to do is select File | Export Template. The initial form in the wizard (see Figure 8-1) allows you to create either a project template (which will bundle up all the items in a project) or an item template (which only includes a single file or a set of related files).

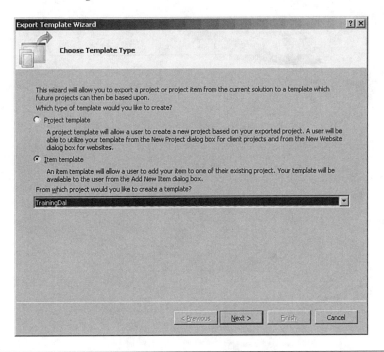

FIGURE 8-1 The first form in the Export Template Wizard allows you to select between creating a project or item template and to select which project in the solution you want to work with.

BEST PRACTICE   For most code-generation projects, you'll be creating a base
for a new class, so you should select the Item Template option.

In addition to selecting the type of template, if the current solution
contains more than one project then, from the bottom of the form, you'll
also need to select which project contains the file you want to convert into
a template.

Assuming that you selected Item Template, the second page in the
wizard allows you to select which file (or files) you want to use in your template (see Figure 8-2). Even if you're including multiple files, you may only
need to select one file because the wizard will automatically pick up related files (e.g., in an ASP.NET application, if you select the .aspx file, the
associated language and resource files will automatically be included).

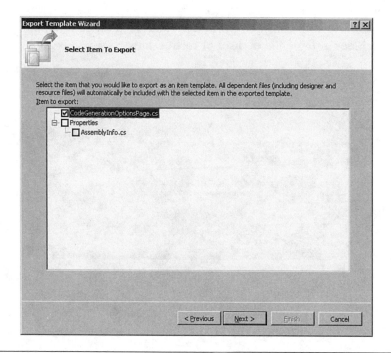

FIGURE 8-2   On the second form in the wizard, you select the file you want to include in
your template.

The third page in the wizard allows you to select which references
should be added to a project as part of adding the files that make up your

template (see Figure 8-3). This form lists all the references in the project you're pulling your template from. There's no need to select references that are normally part of a project (e.g., System) but there's no penalty, either.

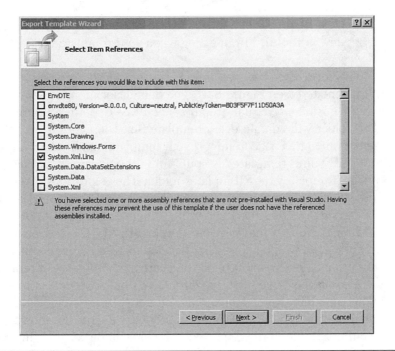

FIGURE 8-3 On the third form in the wizard, you can choose which references you want to add with the template.

BEST PRACTICE Selecting all references you think your generated code will need means never having to say that you're sorry—the AddFromTemplate method won't generate duplicate references.

You can get a warning message at this stage if you add a reference to an assembly that's not distributed with .NET 2.0. (This includes assemblies that are part of .NET 3.0/3.5 such as System.Linq or your own assemblies.) You'll need to ensure that these assemblies are included in your deployment package (unless you're very sure that the DDLs will exist on the computer of all the developers using your code generation tool).

The fourth page of the wizard lets you add some documentation:

- **Icon**—The icon displayed in Visual Studio's Add Item dialog.
- **Name**—The short text displayed under the icon in the Add Item dialog. This is also the default name for the file when it's added to a project.
- **Description**—The longer text displayed at the bottom of the tree view in the Add Item dialog when your template is selected.

This form also shows you one of the two locations where the template will be created (see Figure 8-4). The default location for your template is in your *documents*\Visual Studio *version*\My Exported Templates folder. (This folder will contain every template that you ever create.) If you pick the option on this page to import your template into Visual Studio, another copy of your template is put into the *documents*\Visual Studio *version*\Templates\ItemTemplates folder. These locations can be changed in the Tools | Options menu in the Projects and Solutions | General tab. For instance, setting the User Item Templates Location option (normally the ItemTemplates folder in the developer's My Documents folder) to a network share would allow other developers to use any templates you create so that a development team can share a common set of templates.

Also on this page of the wizard you can pick an option to display the folder containing your template. If you select this option, when the wizard is finished, a Windows Explorer window will pop up showing you the resulting ZIP file in the Exported Templates folder (see Figure 8-5).

Template Components

If you're working in Visual Studio 2005, you'll need to create the ZIP file yourself. As with the ZIP file created by the wizard, this ZIP file must contain a minimum of three files (shown in Figure 8-6):

- The base code file (Connect.cs in the figure)
- An icon file
- The .vstemplate file

You can customize your template through the contents of the .vstemplate file and the base code file, as described later in this chapter. (Later in this chapter, I've included a base template for the vstemplate file if you need to create one from scratch.)

If you distribute your template to other developers, you can use a .vsi installation file to place your template in Visual Studio's templates in the

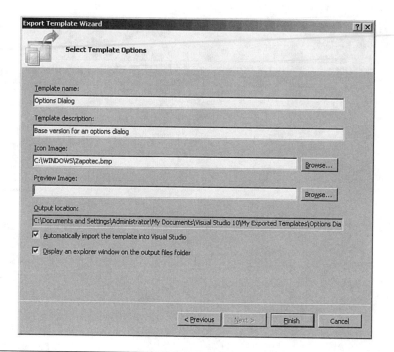

FIGURE 8-4 On the fourth form in the wizard, you can document your template (among other options).

Program Files folder. Creating .vsi installation files is described in Appendix D, "Distributing Code-Generation Solutions."

BEST PRACTICE Keeping your templates in the ItemTemplates folder in My Documents (and separate from the standard Visual Studio templates) makes it easier to find your templates.

Using Your Template from Code

You can add an item to your project using the `ProjectItems` collection's `AddFromTemplate` method, although, unlike the templates delivered with Visual Studio, no `ProjectItem` is returned by the method. To determine which file (or files) is added to the project, you can wire up the `ProjectItemsEvents ItemAdded` event. (The details of how to connect to Visual Studio events are described in Chapter 2, "Integrating with Visual Studio.")

As with the templates provided with Visual Studio, you should first use the `GetProjectItemTemplate` method to get the full path to your template's ZIP file and then pass that path to the `AddFromTemplate` method. Assuming

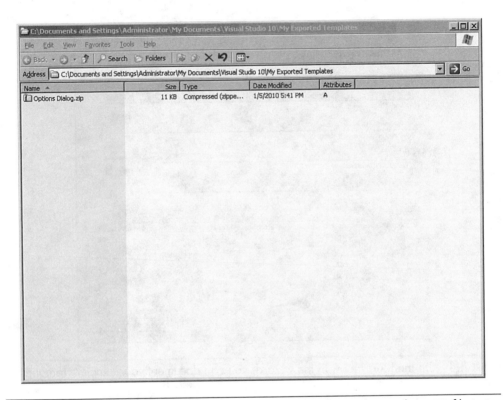

FIGURE 8-5 After your template is exported, Visual Studio shows the resulting ZIP file in its folder.

that you've put your ZIP file in the My Documents/Visual Studio *version*/Templates folder, all you need to provide as the second parameter to the `GetProjectItem` method is the language type.

This example creates a C# item from a template in a ZIP file called ConnectionClass.zip. The item is added to the project with the name MyConnection.cs (assuming that the template is set up to use the second parameter as the name of the file):

```
string ItemTemplatePath = ((Solution2) _applicationObject.Solution).
GetProjectItemTemplate("ConnectionClass.zip", "CSharp");
proj.ProjectItems.AddFromTemplate(ItemTemplatePath, "MyConnection.cs");
```

Testing Your Template

The easiest way to test your template is to open Visual Studio's Add New Item dialog—your template will appear at the bottom of the dialog in the My Templates section (see Figure 8-7). If your template doesn't appear in

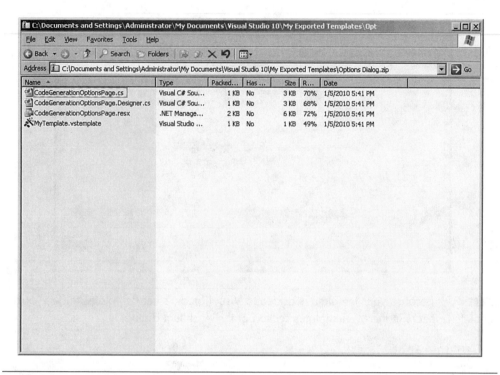

FIGURE 8-6 The ZIP file containing your template will have a minimum of three files: the template file, the icon displayed in Visual Studio, and the .vstemplate control file.

the Add New Item dialog, the most likely cause is an error in your .vstemplate file.

The copy of your template used by the Add New Item dialog is the one in Visual Studio's Templates\ItemTemplates folder, so it's that version of the file you must make your changes to when testing.

If you have a problem with your template, you'll often just get an uninformative "System Exception" message. However, some error messages are written to the Windows Event Log and can be seen using the Event Viewer (Control Panel | Administrative Tools) in the Application section.

Modifying/Creating a Template Control File

You can control how the item is added to your project by modifying the template's .vstemplate file. A typical .vstemplate file generated by the Export Template Wizard for a `class` file's item template will look like this:

```
<VSTemplate Version="2.0.0"
    xmlns="http://schemas.microsoft.com/developer/vstemplate/2005"
    Type="Item">
```

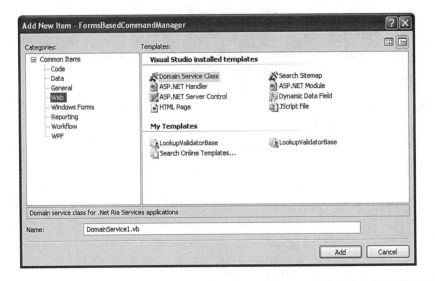

FIGURE 8-7 Because your template is added to Visual Studio's ItemTemplates folder, your template appears in the My Templates section of the Add Item dialog.

```
<TemplateData>
  <DefaultName>ConnectionClass.cs</DefaultName>
  <Name>ConnectionClass</Name>
  <Description>Flags methods for ConnectionManager</Description>
  <ProjectType>CSharp</ProjectType>
  <SortOrder>10</SortOrder>
  <Icon>__TemplateIcon.ico</Icon>
</TemplateData>
<TemplateContent>
  <ProjectItem SubType="Code"
               TargetFileName="$fileinputname$.cs"
               ReplaceParameters="true">Connect.cs</ProjectItem>
</TemplateContent>
</VSTemplate>
```

Controlling How Visual Studio Uses the Template

The `TemplateData` element holds the tags that control how your item template is treated by Visual Studio. A number of the tags you can use in `TemplateData` don't apply to user-created templates or apply only to project templates (rather than item templates). I'll ignore those.

Here is a list of the essential tags:

- **`Icon`**—The icon displayed in the dialog.

- **Name**—The name displayed below the template's icon.
- **Description**—The description displayed at the bottom of the tree view when the item is selected.
- **ProjectType**—Specifies the language type (CSharp, VisualBasic, etc.).
- **SortOrder**—Controls the order that templates are displayed in the Add New Item dialog (lower numbers are displayed first). Must be a multiple of ten.
- **DefaultName**—The name to be applied to the file created by the template if a name isn't provided.

You can add these tags to the TemplateData element to customize the way your template is used (or not used) in the Add New Item dialog:

- **Hidden**—When set to True, this tag prevents the template from appearing in the Add New Item dialog.
- **RequiredFrameworkVersion**—A version number (e.g., 3.5) specifying the minimum level of the .NET Framework that the project must be targeted at for the template to be visible in the Add New Item dialog. It has no effect when adding a template from code.
- **ProvideDefaultName**—When set to False, this tag prevents a default name from being provided when the template is selected.

Three options for controlling the Add New Item dialog are only relevant for ASP.NET projects:

- **SupportsCodeSeparation**—When this option is true, the Place Code in a Separate File check box is displayed in the Add New Item dialog.
- **SupportsLanguageDropDown**—When this option is true, the Language drop-down is displayed in the Add New Item dialog. Also indicates that the language template is different for different languages.
- **SupportsMasterPage**—When this option is true, the Select Master Page check box is displayed in the Add New Item dialog.

I'm including a final element for the sake of completeness—you should just leave it at its default value:

- **CreateInPlace**—When this item is set to true (the default), parameter replacement is done after the template is added to the project, which speeds processing. (When it's set to false, the template files are copied to a temporary folder, parameter replacement is performed, and then the template files are added to the project.)

Using Replaceable Parameters

In both your .vstemplate file and your code files, you can use replaceable parameters (marked by paired dollar signs) to replace file text. These parameters can be used both in the .vstemplate file and in your code file. When your item template is loaded, these parameters are replaced with values from the environment.

For instance, in your code file you can ensure that your code uses the namespace of the project that it's being loaded into by using the $rootnamespace$ parameter, as in this example:

```
namespace $rootnamespace$
```

You can retrieve the filename set in the AddFromTemplate command or set by the developer in the Add New Item dialog through the $safeitemname$ parameter. The $safeitemname$ parameter has all unacceptable characters removed or replaced with valid characters. This example from a .vstemplate file sets the name of the file being added to the project to the name passed to AddFromTemplate or entered by the developer:

```
<ProjectItem TargetFileName="$safeitemname$" ...
```

BEST PRACTICE   You should always use the $safeitemname$ parameter to set your file's name.

If you've used the Export Template Wizard to generate the initial version of your item template, you'll find that the wizard has replaced every occurrence of the namespace and filename that it found in your code with the appropriate parameter.

BEST PRACTICE   The Export Template Wizard's blind insertion of replaceable parameters may not give you the results you want; therefore, if you used the wizard, it's always a good idea to check your code file in the template for all instances of $ to make sure only valid changes have been made.

The replaceable parameters provided by Visual Studio can be broken up into five groups. First, you can retrieve information about the version of .NET targeted by the development environment:

- **targetframeworkversion**—The version of the .NET Framework that the IDE is targeted for. This parameter is useful in conjunction with conditional code inclusion, discussed in the next section.
- **clrversion**—The version of the Common Language Runtime that the IDE is targeted for.

Information about the filename provided when the item was added is also available:

- **itemname**—The name passed in the second parameter of the AddFromTemplate method (or the name provided by the developer in the Add New Item dialog).
- **safeitemname**—The itemname, modified to remove all unacceptable characters. Acceptable and unacceptable names are language dependent. (For instance, if the name provided for a CSharp class was "Connection Class", the safeitemname will be set to "Connection_Class.cs".)
- **fileinputname**—The inputname with the extension removed.
- **fileinputextension**—The extension from the inputname.
- **safeitemrootname**—The value from inputname with unacceptable characters removed and without the file extension.

You can also retrieve date information, but the format is fixed:

- **time**—The current time in the format DD/MM/YYYY 00:00:00.
- **year**—The year in the format YYYY.

Information about the current computer and user can be retrieved through these four parameters:

- **machinename**—The name of the computer.
- **registeredorganization**—The registry key value from HKLM\Software\Microsoft\WindowsNT\CurrentVersion\ RegisteredOrganization.
- **userdomain**—The name of the user's domain.
- **username**—The name of the user.

Two final parameters provide values that you may want to use in your
code files:

- **rootnamespace**—The root namespace of the current project.
- **guidn**—This parameter generates up to ten different GUIDs that
  you can insert into your templates (typically useful in assembly
  files): guid1, guid2, ... guid10. These GUIDs don't include the
  enclosing curly braces ({...}) so, depending on where you're using
  these parameters, you may need to supply the braces in the sur-
  rounding text.

All these parameters can be used both in your code files and the
.vstemplate file.

Here are some typical examples of the values available through the
parameters (the filename provided for this example is "Connection
Class"):

- **Framework version**—3.5
- **CLR version**—2.0.50727.3053
- **Item name**—Connection Class
- **Safe item name**—Connection_Class.cs
- **Filename**—Connection Class
- **File extension**—cs
- **Machine name**—PHVLaptop4
- **Organization**—PH&V Information Services
- **User domain**—PHVLaptop4
- **Username**—PHVogel
- **Time**—12/31/2008 8:58:42 PM
- **Year**—2008
- **Safe root name**—Connection_Class1
- **Namespace**—CodeEditorDev
- **guid1**—4e68b4e1-4ceb-46f0-b4a4-76e47bfc802e
- **guid2**—ce4250b6-9944-431c-8c48-7f6950c3d9e3

Defining Your Own Replaceable Parameters

In addition to the built-in parameters, you can specify your own replaceable parameters by using the CustomParameters tag. Within the
CustomParameters tag, you can add multiple CustomParameter tags. On each
tag, use the Name attribute to establish the name for your parameter

(including the enclosing dollar signs) and the `Value` attribute to set the value for your parameter.

This example established a parameter named `$developer$` with its value set to Peter_Vogel. It then uses that parameter to set the name of the file to be added to the project:

```
<CustomParameters>
    <CustomParameter Name="$developer$" Value="Peter_Vogel"/>
</CustomParameters>
<ProjectItem TargetFileName="$developer$.cs">Connect.cs</ProjectItem>
```

You can't use a replaceable parameter to build the value for a custom parameter.

If you're building your .vstemplate file in Visual Studio, you'll find that you'll have to change the schema name to "http://schemas.microsoft.com/developer/vstemplate/2006" (the default version provided by the wizard ends in "2005") to prevent schema errors. However, you must set the schema name back to "2005" before releasing it in order to have your template recognized by all versions of Visual Studio.

Specifying the Item to Be Added

Inside the `TemplateContent` element, you use the `ProjectItem` tag to specify which items in the template's ZIP file are to be added to the project. The simplest possible `ProjectItem` just contains the name of the file in the item template's ZIP file to add.

This example adds a file from the template called ConnectionUser.cs. The resulting file in the project will have the correct file extension, but the filename will be set to the name of the template (or the name in the `DefaultName` element if it is provided):

```
<ProjectItem>ConnectionUser.cs</ProjectItem>
```

By including multiple `ProjectItem` elements, you can add several files to the project. When adding multiple files you use the `TargetFileName` attribute on the `ProjectItem` to set the filename of each item. If you want, you can add the same item from the ZIP file multiple times with different names each time.

This example adds two files to the project: one called ConnectionUser.Generation.cs and one called ConnectionUser.Custom.cs.

Each file is renamed using the `TargetFileName` attribute and the `safeitemname` parameter:

```
<ProjectItem TargetFileName="$safeitemname$.Generation.cs">
ConnectionUser.Generation.cs</ProjectItem>

<ProjectItem TargetFileName="$safeitemname$.Custom.cs">
ConnectionUser.Custom.cs</ProjectItem>
```

In addition to the `TargetFileName`, the `ProjectItem` tag accepts up to six other attributes:

- **SubType**—This specifies the editor that Visual Studio will use to open the file. Typically, for code generation, you'll set this to Code. To invoke a different editor, the best solution is to open the corresponding template provided with Visual Studio and see what its `SubType` is set to. You can find these templates in C:\Program Files\Microsoft Visual Studio *version*\Common7\IDE\Item Templates\. Use that value in your .vstemplate file.
- **ReplaceParameters**—When set to True, this attribute lets you use replaceable parameters in your code file.
- **OpenInEditor**—When set to False, this attribute prevents the file from being displayed in an editor window in Visual Studio after the file is added (the default is True).
- **OpenOrder**—When you're adding multiple files that will be opened in editor windows, the `OpenOrder` attribute controls the order in which the files are opened. The file with the lowest value will be in the "topmost" window (i.e., visible to the developer) when all files are added.
- **OpenInWebBrowser**—When set to True, this attribute causes the file to be displayed in a browser window in Visual Studio after the file is added. This feature allows you to include documentation files in your template that will be added to the project and displayed to the developer when the template completes.
- **OpenInHelpBrowser**—When set to True, this attribute causes the file to be displayed in the Help browser in Visual Studio after the file is added. Like `OpenInWebBrowser`, this feature allows you to include documentation files in your template.

In the following example, the first `ProjectItem` specifies that the file UserConnect.cs is to be added from the Zip file, that the editor for the file is the one used for user controls, that replaceable parameters can be used in the code file, that the file will be renamed to a safe version of the name provided by the developer or calling program, and that the file is not to be opened in an editor window. The second `ProjectItem` adds a file called DeveloperNotes.HTML to the project with the name User Connection Help.htm and opens it in a browser window:

```
<ProjectItem
    SubType="Form/Component/CustomControl/UserControl"
    ReplaceParameters="true"
    TargetFileName="$safeitemname$"
    OpenInEditor="false">
        UserConnect.cs
</ProjectItem>

<ProjectItem OpenInWebBrowser="true"
            TargetFileName="User Connection Help.htm">
            DeveloperNotes.html</ProjectItem>
```

Adding References

Inside the `TemplateContent` element, you can use the `References` element to add references to the project as part of adding your files. The `References` element can contain one or more `Reference` elements, each of which contains a single `Assembly` element containing the name of the assembly to be added to the project.

When adding a reference for a .NET component, you enter the same text that you would use in a `using` or `Imports` statement. This example, for instance, adds a reference to the `System.Data` assembly:

```
<References>
  <Reference>
    <Assembly>System.Data</Assembly>
  </Reference>
</References>
```

To add references to your own assemblies, you'll need to provide the full name of the assembly. This example extends the previous example with a reference to a custom library:

```
<References>
  <Reference>
    <Assembly>System.Data</Assembly>
  </Reference>
<Reference>
    <Assembly>DBUtilities, Version=3.1.5401.0, Culture=neutral,
        PublicKeyToken=c41cff31ecd8991b, Custom = null</Assembly>
  </Reference>
</References>
```

If adding a reference to your own class library looks daunting, remember that if you create the initial version of your item template with the Export Template Wizard, you can select any references that are part of the project you are exporting from a list. The wizard will then write out your references section for you.

Sample Template

The following example defines an item template with the following features:

- It's named ConnectionClass, has a short description, and uses the icon _TemplateIcon.ico (`Name`, `Icon`, and `Description` elements).
- It's a C# project (`ProjectType` element).
- It prevents the template from appearing in the Add New Item dialog (`Hidden` element).
- It adds a reference to `System.Drawing` to the project (`References` and `Reference` elements).
- It defines a new replaceable parameter named `$developer$` and sets it to a value (`CustomParameters` and `CustomerParameter` elements).
- It adds a Code project item from the ZIP file called Connect.cs that supports replaceable parameters and renames it using the safe filename (first `ProjectItem` element).
- It adds a second Code project item named User.cs and renames it using the custom parameter. This file is not automatically opened in the editor (second `ProjectItem` element).

```
<VSTemplate Version="2.0.0"
    xmlns="http://schemas.microsoft.com/developer/vstemplate/2005"
    Type="Item">
  <TemplateData>
    <Name>ConnectionClass</Name>
    <Description> Flags methods for ConnectionManager</Description>
```

```
    <Icon>__TemplateIcon.ico</Icon>
    <ProjectType>CSharp</ProjectType>
    <SortOrder>500</SortOrder>
    <Hidden>true</Hidden>
  </TemplateData>
  <TemplateContent>
    <References>
      <Reference>
        <Assembly>System.Drawing</Assembly>
      </Reference>
    </References>
    <CustomParameters>
        <CustomParameter Name="$developer$" Value="Peter Vogel"/>
    </CustomParameters>
    <ProjectItem
        SubType="Code"
        ReplaceParameters="true"
        TargetFileName="$safeitemname$">Connect.cs</ProjectItem>
    <ProjectItem
        SubType="Code"
        OpenInEditor="false"
        ReplaceParameters="true"
        TargetFileName="$developer$.cs">User.cs</ProjectItem>
  </TemplateContent>
</VSTemplate>
```

Using Wizards

If the functionality described here doesn't provide you with all the features you need, you can create a wizard class that will be executed as part of executing your wizard. You specify the class to invoke with the WizardExtension tag. This, for instance, is the WizardExtension element to invoke the wizard used by Visual Studio when adding WebForms:

```
<WizardExtension>
    <Assembly>Microsoft.VisualStudio.Web, Version=9.0.0.0,
        Culture=neutral, PublicKeyToken=b03f5f7f11d50a3a</Assembly>
    <FullClassName>
Microsoft.VisualStudio.Web.Wizard.VsWebFormItemTemplateWizard
    </FullClassName>
</WizardExtension>
```

BEST PRACTICE   Using a wizard requires that your wizard class be distributed with your add-in. Rather than use a wizard, it may be simpler to modify the code inserted by the template from your add-in's code after any files are added to the project.

Conditional Inclusion

In your code file you can use an if...$else$...$endif$ construct to test for specific conditions (typically by checking replaceable parameters) and use those to include or exclude text. In order to use this feature, however, you must set the version attribute on your .vstemplate tag to 3.0.0:

```
<VSTemplate Version="3.0.0"
```

The if constructor only supports testing for equality (using the == operator) but does support an $elseif$ for handling false conditions. This example checks the version of the .NET Framework targeted by Visual Studio. If the version is 3.5, an Imports statement for System.Linq is included; for any other version, an Imports statement for System.Data is included:

```
$if$ ($targetframeworkversion$ == 3.5)
Imports System.Linq
$else$
Imports System.Data
$endif$
```

Be aware that any newlines included inside your text will be added to the file. For instance, the previous example includes some spurious newlines. The result, in a project targeted towards .NET 3.5, would look like this:

```
Imports System

Imports System.Linq

Imports System.Data
```

This would be the result in a project targeted to .NET 2.0:

```
Imports System

Imports System.Data
```

To eliminate any unnecessary linefeeds, place if and $endif$ on the same lines as your code, as in this example:

```
Imports System
$if$ ($targetframeworkversion$ == 3.5)Imports System.Linq$endif$
Imports System.Data
```

Getting the if...$else$...$endif$ structure wrong can generate a System Exception error when the file is added (the error will be reported in the Windows Event log). However, the error message ("There were errors parsing the XML content in the .vstemplate file.") is unhelpful because it points to errors in the .vstemplate file rather than to parsing errors in the code file.

Attributes

Perhaps the most obvious place for developers to put the inputs to the code-generation process is in code files related to the code that needs to be generated. There are a number of tools that you can use to let developers provide input. You can, for instance, analyze the developer's own code either as a set of objects by using the CodeElement objects (Chapter 3, "Manipulating Project Components") or as raw text using the Document/TextDocument objects (Chapter 4, "Modifying Code in the Editor"). Either of those two objects would let you, for instance, analyze the XML comments associated with a class or member.

The problem with all these mechanisms is determining—among all the stuff in a file—which stuff is intended by the developer to be inputs to the code-generation process. Even if you find the developer's input, determining the developer's intent can be difficult unless the input method is highly structured. And, of course, when developers are given a structured method for input, it's easier for developers to get the input right (and, for many forms of structured input, IntelliSense will provide support for the

developers as they enter their input). Providing developers with a way to
structure their inputs to the code-generation process makes life easier for
both of you.

Attributes provide a partial solution to this problem. Because attributes are specific types, it's easier to search the developer's code for them.
You can also specify which components of a class an attribute can be
assigned to, limiting the places where you have to look and clarifying the
developer's intent. Finally, attributes (like XML comments) provide a
structured way for developers to provide inputs to the code-generation
process through properties on the attribute.

The major limitation to attributes is that they must be processed as
part of the DLL or EXE, not as part of the source code. This means that a
developer can't use the results of a code-generation process that involves
attributes until the application's code compiles and a DLL or EXE holding
the attributes is available. Further, because "projectless" websites don't
have a DLL available until the site is published, attributes aren't a good
choice for code-generation solutions for that kind of ASP.NET site.

Introducing Attributes

Attributes are objects that developers can use to decorate components of
other objects (classes, events, methods, etc.). At runtime other programs
can process the resulting DLL or EXE to find those attributes. Like other
objects, attributes have properties and methods. When developers use an
attribute in their code, they are limited to passing values to the attribute's
constructors or setting properties. When you retrieve an attribute as part
of the code-generation process, in addition to accessing the attribute's
properties, you can call any of the methods on the attribute. Like other
kinds of objects, attributes can call other objects or Web Services.

In order for a developer to use an attribute, the developer must add a reference to the attribute to his or her application. In addition, you will need to
add a reference to the attribute to your code-generation package, not only to
use the attribute in your code but also to facilitate finding the attribute in the
developer's code. To support a developer adding references to your attributes,
it may make sense to install any Class libraries containing attributes into the
Global Assembly Cache (GAC). The steps for setting up a project to be added
to the GAC are discussed in the next section as part of creating a custom tool.

Using an Attribute

Once the developer has added a reference to the attribute's class library to
a project, the developer can use the attribute with virtually any component

of the application (e.g., class and variable declarations, properties, methods). This process is called "decorating" the code. When using an attribute to decorate part of their code, developers usually must pass some values to the attribute either as parameters to the attribute's constructor or as values to the attribute's properties. You may, however, discover that your attributes don't need any values passed to them: It's sufficient for your application that the developer simply mark part of the application by decorating it with your attribute.

A typical attribute, added to a class declaration, might look like this (by convention, attributes are written on a separate line from the item they are decorating):

```
[ConnectionUser("web.config",ConnectionName="Northwind")]
public class MyClass
{
```

The parameters passed to the attribute (the strings "web.config" and "Northwind" in the example) fall into two categories:

- **Values being passed to the `attribute`'s constructor**—These values are not part of a name/value pair and must precede any name/value pairs.
- **Values used to set the `attribute`'s properties**—These are the name/value pairs that follow any parameters passed to the constructor. The name portion of the name/value pair must be the name of a property on the constructor.

As part of designing an attribute, you'll need to decide which values you want passed to the attribute's constructor and which should be set through the attribute's properties. The benefit of having values set in the attribute's constructor is consistency and integrity: All the necessary values must be passed to the constructor (any missing values are caught at compile time) and error code for checking the values can be centralized in the attribute's constructor.

Using properties, however, makes the developer's code more readable: Providing descriptive names for your properties can make the attribute's settings self-documenting. However, because there are no "required" properties, it's possible for a developer using your attribute to omit setting a critical property. Missing property values won't be caught until the attribute is processed by your code-generation solution.

BEST PRACTICE Have all required values set in the constructor's parameters and all optional parameters set through properties. Ensure that all properties have default values that you can use if the developer skips setting the property. One warning: The CodeDom does not support setting properties on attributes, so any attribute you intend to have generated as part of a CodeDom solution should just use values passed to its constructor.

A Note on Naming

The convention used by the .NET development team when creating attributes is to append "Attribute" to the name of the class. Rather than, for instance, calling your attribute `ConnectionUser`, you could call it `ConnectionUserAttribute`. When developers use your attribute in their code, however, they can omit the appended "Attribute" suffix.

So, for instance, take an attribute class declared like this:

```
public class ConnectionUserAttribute
```

The attribute would be used by the developer as follows:

```
[ConnectionUser]
```

Creating a Custom Attribute

An attribute is simply a class that inherits from `System.Attribute`. This example defines an attribute named `ConnectionUser` with a single field:

```
namespace MyAttributes
{
 public class ConnectionUser : System.Attribute
 {
   string configFileName = string.Empty;
```

Within an attribute, you can choose to accept values as part of the attribute's constructor. If so, you should check for invalid values and throw an exception if one is found, as this example does:

```
public ConnectionUser(string ConfigFileName)
{
 if (ConfigFileName == string.Empty)
 {
   throw new ArgumentNullException(
      "Invalid value passed for ConnectionUser ConfigFileName");
 }
   configFileName = ConfigFileName;
}
```

A developer using an attribute with this constructor would pass a value to the constructor like this:

```
[MyAttributes.ConnectionUser("Web.config")]
```

If you accept all the values that the attribute requires as part of the attribute's constructor, you only need to provide read-only properties to allow your code to retrieve the values set in the constructor. However, if you want to help make the developer's code more self-documenting, you can provide read/write properties. Properties in an attribute look exactly like properties in any other class:

```
public string ConfigFileName
{
 get
 {
  return configFileName;
 }
 set
 {
  if (value == "")
  {
   throw new ArgumentNullException(ConfigFileName,
     "Invalid value passed to ConnectionManager");
  }
  configFileName = value;
 }
}
```

A developer using an attribute with this property would write code like this:

```
[MyAttributes.ConnectionUser(ConfigFileName="Web.config")]
```

You can also include methods in your attributes that can be called from your code-generation solution. This example, for instance, accesses a Web Service to check licensing:

```
public String AccessLicensing()
{
 MyHost.LicenseService ls = new MyHost.LicenseService();
 return ls.CheckLicense;
}
```

The ability to include methods in your attributes allows you to integrate attributes into your code-generation process. You could, for instance, have a method that, when passed a reference to the DTE object, actually generates the necessary code. All that your add-in would need to do is call the appropriate method on the attribute. The benefit of embedding code-generation code into an attribute is ease of upgrading: Instead of developers needing to replace your Visual Studio add-in when upgrading to a new version of your code-generation solution, they'd only need to upgrade the related attribute in the GAC.

Controlling Where Attributes Are Used

In most cases, there are a limited number of places where a developer can use any attribute you create. An attribute that draws on class information, for instance, should only decorate class declarations. You can prevent a developer from using an attribute to decorate an inappropriate component by decorating your attribute class with the AttributeUsage attribute.

The AttributeUsage's constructor accepts a value from the AttributeTargets enumeration, which allows you to specify which components your attribute can decorate. This example, for instance, limits the attribute to being used to decorate classes:

```
[AttributeUsage(AttributeTargets.Class)]
public class ConnectionUser : System.Attribute
{
```

If you create an attribute that can be used to decorate multiple kinds of components, you can combine AttributeTargets by using the Visual Basic Or operator or the C# | operator. This example specifies that the attribute is to be used only on methods and properties:

```
[AttributeUsage(AttributeTargets.Property | AttributeTargets.Method)]
public class ConnectionUser : System.Attribute
{
```

The AttributeUsage attribute has two properties: AllowMultiple and Inherited. The AllowMultiple property, when set to True, allows developers to put multiple copies of your attribute on a single component. This is useful when you want to allow the developer to provide multiple sets of inputs. Rather than create a complex attribute that accepts multiple values, you can create a simple attribute that accepts single values and lets the developer apply your attribute multiple times. The Inherited property, when set to False, prevents the options set by AttributeUsage from being passed on to any class that inherits from the class your attribute is decorating or applying to methods or properties that override any members that your attribute is decorating.

This example restricts the ConnectionUser attribute to decorating classes, permits the attribute to be used multiple times on a single class declaration, and prevents these options from being inherited by any class that inherits from ConnectionUser:

```
[AttributeUsage(AttributeTargets.Class,
                AllowMultiple=true,Inherited=false)]
public class ConnectionUser : System.Attribute
{
```

A class that uses this ConnectionUser attribute might look like this:

```
[ConnectionUser("web.config")]
[ConnectionUser("app.config")]
public class CustomerData
{
```

Processing Attributes with Reflection

The first step in processing attributes is finding the project's DLL or EXE. Assuming that you're processing the attribute as part of a Visual Studio add-in, you'll need to pull together three pieces of information:

- The full path to the project, available through the Project object's Properties collection under the name "FullPath"
- The current path to the compiled output for the current configuration, available through the Project object's ActiveConfiguration property's Properties collection under the name "OutputPath"
- The name of the output file, available through the Project object's Properties collection under the name "OutputFileName"

This code will retrieve the full path to the DLL or EXE related to the first project in the solution:

```
Project proj;
proj = _applicationObject.Solution.Projects.Item(1);

string assemblyPath =
   proj.Properties.Item("FullPath").Value.ToString() +
   proj.ConfigurationManager.ActiveConfiguration.Properties.
                            Item("OutputPath").Value.ToString() +
   proj.Properties.Item("OutputFileName").Value.ToString();
```

Once you've retrieved the assembly's path, you can load it using the LoadFrom method of the System.Reflection.Assembly object. This method returns an Assembly object that you can search for attributes:

```
asb = System.Reflection.Assembly.LoadFrom(assemblyPath);
```

A typical assembly will contain many classes (referred to as types when using Reflection). You can use the FileCodeModel to determine the current class that the developer is working on and use that as a basis for retrieving a specific class from the assembly using its GetType method. The GetType method only needs the namespace and name of the class you want and returns a Type object that represents that class. This example retrieves, from a loaded assembly, a class named Form1 in the namespace MyWindowsForm:

```
Type classForm = asb.GetType("MyWindowsForm.Form1");
```

BEST PRACTICE Retrieve all the classes in the assembly so that you can find and process all your attributes that the developer has used throughout the application.

To retrieve all the classes in an assembly, call the assembly's GetTypes method, which returns an array of Type objects (one for each class) that you can iterate through.

As you retrieve each Type object, you can check for instances of your attribute on the class by calling the Type's GetCustomAttributes method. Rather than retrieving all the attributes, you can pass the type of your attribute as the method's first parameter to limit the attributes returned to just your attribute. (In order to use your attribute's type, you'll need to add a reference to your attribute to your code-generation project.) The second parameter passed to the method should be False to indicate that you don't want any of the base classes that the class inherits from to be searched.

The `GetCustomAttributes` method returns an array of objects, so you'll need to process the return value of this method in a loop. This example retrieves all the classes in an assembly and then, for each class, retrieves an attribute named `ClassAttribute` in the namespace `MyAttributes`:

```
foreach (Type typ in asb.GetTypes())
 {
   object[] classAtts;
   classAtts =  typ.GetCustomAttributes(
                   typeof(MyAttributes.ClassAttribute), false);

   foreach(MyAttributes.ClassAttribute att in classAtts)
   {
     ...process attributes on the class ...
   }
 }
```

If you are allowing your attributes to be used on members of the class (fields, methods, etc.), you can use a similar process to retrieve a specific class member. The `Type` object that represents your class has methods that allow you to retrieve a single member by name and type (e.g., `GetMethod`, `GetEvent`). However it's more likely that you'll simply want to process all the members in a class, looking for any members with one of your attributes. You can retrieve members by type by using the `Type` object's methods `GetFields`, `GetEvents`, `GetMethods`, and so on. Again, however, it may be just as easy to use the `GetMembers` method to retrieve all members and process them.

When retrieving members you'll also have to deal with the variety of members: private, public, static, and so on. All of the `Type` object's `Get*` methods accept as a parameter members of the `BindingFlags` enumeration, which allows you to control which types of members you will retrieve. (By default, for instance, the `Get*` methods don't retrieve private members.)

BEST PRACTICE Unless you're expecting developers to restrict themselves to using your attribute on specific types of members (e.g., only on public members), the best practice is to combine all the `BindingFlags` members (using `Or` in Visual Basic or `|` in C#).

This example gets all the members of `MyWindowsForm.Form1` by using a combination of `BindingFlags` that ensures that all members are retrieved. Once the members have been retrieved, the code then checks each member for an attribute called `MyAttributes.MemberAttribute`:

```
Type typ = asb.GetType("MyWindowsForm.Form1");

 foreach (MemberInfo mi in typ.GetMembers(BindingFlags.Instance |
          BindingFlags.Public | BindingFlags.NonPublic |
          BindingFlags.Static | BindingFlags.DeclaredOnly))
  {
    object[] memberAtts;
    memberAtts = mi.GetCustomAttributes(
              typeof(MyAttributes.MemberAttribute), false);
    foreach (MyAttributes.MemberAttribute att in memberAtts)
    {
      ...process attributes on members of the class
    }
  }
}
```

Once you've retrieved an attribute, it is instantiated (i.e., the attribute is instantiated when the `GetCustomAttributes` method executes) and any properties specified in the developer's code are set from the values passed in the code file. If the developer has passed bad values to the attribute's constructor or properties, any error-handling code you've placed in the attribute will execute as part of the `GetCustomAttributes` call.

BEST PRACTICE   Wrap your `GetCustomAttributes` code in a `try...catch` block to catch errors thrown because the developer passed bad values to your attribute.

This example uses a `try...catch` block to catch errors and then displays them in Visual Studio's status bar:

```
object[] memberAtts;
try
{
  memberAtts = mi.GetCustomAttributes(
            typeof(MyAttributes.MemberAttribute), false);
```

```
}
catch (Exception ex)
{
 _applicationObject.StatusBar.Text = ex.Message;
 return;
}
```

Although you can set an attribute's property from your code-generation code, it doesn't accomplish much because the attribute will be re-created (and its properties reset) with the next `GetCustomAttributes` call.

Documenting with Attributes

In addition to processing attributes, you may want to add attributes to code that you generate in order to record information to be used in the next code generation (adding attributes was discussed in Chapter 3 along with the other tools available through the `FileCodeModel`). Remember, however, that attributes are only available after the application is compiled. If you need to record information to use in subsequent generations, it may make more sense to record them in XML documentation (if the language supports it) or embedded comments, which can be inserted either as objects using the `FileCodeModel` or as text using the `Document`/`TextDocument` objects (discussed in Chapter 4).

Generating Code from Custom File Formats

Rather than have the developer enter his or her inputs into an existing file in the project (e.g., a code file or a configuration file), you can have the developer enter his or her inputs into a new file using a format you define and process the resulting file with a custom tool. Your custom tool will be invoked each time the developer saves the file (or switches away from the editing window in Visual Studio 2008/2010). In Solution Explorer, the resulting file will be nested under the file with the developer's input (see Figure 8-8). By using a Visual Studio template, you can provide the developer with a start point for this file. You can also create a visual designer (described in Chapter 11) that allows the developer to create an input document by dragging and dropping visual components onto a design service.

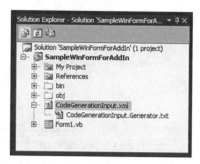

FIGURE 8-8   The file CodeGenerationInput.xml has had its Custom Tool property set to
SiteProcessor. When the developer switches away from the file, the SiteProcessor custom
tool adds the CodeGenerationInput.Generated.cs file using content from the original file.

Custom tools are also known as "single file generators," which better
describes their function: They take as input text from a file and generate a
second file. Developers can associate a custom tool with any file in a project just by setting the file's Custom Tool property to the name of your custom tool (you can also specify the custom tool to be used with a file as part
of a file's template, or you can set the CustomTool property from an add-in).
After a custom tool is associated with a file, every time the file is saved (or,
in Visual Studio 2008/2010, every time the file is changed or the window
deactivated), your custom tool will be invoked and the contents of the file
passed to your custom tool, and any output from your custom tool will
be saved as a new file with the same name as the original file but with a
different extension.

While this sounds like a great feature for code generation there are a
couple of wrinkles in the process. Although you create your custom tool in
.NET, because Visual Studio is a COM application and your custom tool is
being invoked by Visual Studio directly, you must both register your tool
with Windows and install it in the Global Assembly Cache. Because your
tool is being installed in the GAC, you must also assign your custom tool a
strong name. Fortunately, with the right project settings, all you'll have to
do is select Build from Visual Studio's menus to generate your DLL, register it with Windows, and install it in the GAC.

Setting Up the Project

Over the various versions of .NET, Microsoft has provided a number of tools
for implementing custom tools. The method I describe here is to implement the `Microsoft.VisualStudio.Shell.Interop.IVsSingleFileGenerator`

interface. Therefore, the first step in creating a custom tool (after creating a new class library) is to add a reference to the `Microsoft.VisualStudio.Shell.Interop` library, which holds the interface.

To support registering in the Project Properties, find the Register for COM Interop option (on the Build tab in C# or the Compile tab in Visual Basic) and check it (if you change your configuration from Debug to Release, you may need to reset this option). In the Application tab, click the Assembly Information button and check the Make Assembly COM-Visible option.

Installing to the GAC

To support installing your project into the GAC, you'll first need to give your project a strong name, which is held in an .snk file. Still in Project Properties, go to the Signing tab and check the Sign the Assembly option. Then, from the Choose a Strong Name Key File drop-down list, select <New...> (see Figure 8-9). In the resulting dialog, enter a filename (I use the name of the project) and uncheck the password option.

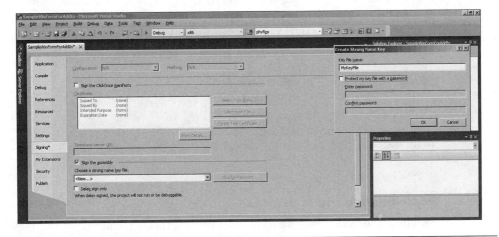

FIGURE 8-9 In the Signing tab of the Properties dialog, you can create a new file to hold a strong name for your project. The file (and its key) will automatically be included in your application when it is built.

To install your custom tool to the GAC, you'll need to call the gacutil utility after your tool is compiled. Still in Project Properties, add the following lines to the `PostBuild` event to remove the current version of the tool from the GAC and add the new version (note that the first line uses `TargetName`—the

project name—and the second version uses `TargetPath`—the name of the
DLL). You'll have to determine where the gacutil is installed on your computer and use that path to complete this code:

```
"<full path to gacutil>\gacutil.exe" -u "$(TargetName)"
"<full path to gacutil>\gacutil.exe" -i "$(TargetPath)"
```

Set the drop-down list under the postbuild events to "When the build
updates the project output."

Your project is now configured to do most of the necessary utility tasks
every time the project is compiled. You may find you get error messages
when you compile your tool that say that one or more of your referenced
DLLs (e.g., `Microsoft.VisualStudio.Shell.Interop`) is "not registered for
COM interop." You can ignore those messages.

Setting Up the Class

The class that will be your custom tool must implement the
`IVsSingleFileGenerator` interface. Each class must also have a unique
GUID assigned to it using the `Guid` attribute. (This GUID is the identifier
that COM uses for your class.)

This class has a GUID generated using Visual Studio's Create GUID
tool on the Tools menu and then copied and pasted into the code:

```
[System.Runtime.InteropServices.Guid(
            "2890B999-71C7-4997-8DA6-27408064EBD8")]
public class TextGenerator :
   Microsoft.VisualStudio.Shell.Interop.IVsSingleFileGenerator
(
```

Implementing the Interfaces

Much of the code that goes into the two methods required by the interfaces is boilerplate code that is almost identical from one custom tool to
another.

When Visual Studio calls your custom tool, it calls the
`IVsSingleFileGenerator` interface's `GetDefaultExtension` method to determine what file extension to put on the file generated by the tool. Although
this code may vary from one custom tool to another, it's very simple: All you
need to do is return a string with a valid file extension, as this example does:

```
public int DefaultExtension(out string pbstrDefaultExtension)
{
  pbstrDefaultExtension = ".Generated.cs";
  return 0;
}
```

The `IVsSingleFileGenerator` interface's `Generate` method is called by Visual Studio whenever the content file is saved. Visual Studio passes to this method the name of the file, the namespace for the project, the contents of the file, and a progress bar. You must return, through two parameters on the method, your generated code as an array of bytes and the length of the array. If your code generation fails, you should return an empty array and 0 as the length of the array.

BEST PRACTICE If your code generation process takes more than a second or two, you should update the progress bar passed to your `Generate` method during your processing.

I put my code-generation code in a method called `GenerateCode` in a separate class and call that method from the `Generate` method inside a `try...catch` block. In my `GenerateCode` method, I throw an error if anything goes wrong. As a result, my `Generate` method looks very similar in every custom tool—only the name of the class holding my `GenerateCode` method changes:

```
byte[] generatedCode;
try
{
  SiteGenerator cg = new SiteGenerator;
  cg.generatedCode = GenerateCode(wszInputFilePath, wszDefaultNamespace,
                     bstrInputFileContents, pGenerateProgress);
  rgbOutputFileContents[0] = System.Runtime.InteropServices.Marshal.
                             AllocCoTaskMem(generatedCode.Length);
  System.Runtime.InteropServices.Marshal.Copy(
     generatedCode, 0, rgbOutputFileContents[0], generatedCode.Length);
  pcbOutput = generatedCode.Length;
}
catch
{
  pcbOutput = 0;
  rgbOutputFileContents[0] = IntPtr.Zero;
}
```

BEST PRACTICE Separate the code that's unique to your custom tool from the standard code used in all custom tools.

The following code is the simplest possible version of the GenerateCode method: It checks to see that there is something in the file contents and returns a string containing a single space. In this version, I first initialize the progress bar to show 0 steps out of a potential 100 steps completed; then, at the end of the method, I set the progress bar to show 100 steps out of 100 completed:

```
using System;
using System.Collections.Generic;
using System.Text;
namespace CustomToolGenerators
{
 public class SiteGenerator
  {
   protected byte[] GenerateCode(string FilePath,
                          string Namespace,
                          string FileContents,
                          Microsoft.VisualStudio.Shell.
                            Interop.IVsGeneratorProgress Progress)
   {
    if (FileContents == "")
    {
     throw new Exception("No content");
    }
    Progress.Progress(0, 100);
    string generatedCode = " ";
    Progress.Progress(100, 100);
    return System.Text.Encoding.UTF8.GetBytes(generatedCode);
   }
  }
}
```

Visual Studio takes care of generating the new filename by taking the full name of the file that the developer assigned the custom tool to, stripping off the file's extension, and appending the extension returned by your GetDefaultExtension method. Visual Studio then deletes any existing version of the file, creates a new version of the file, and puts the content returned by the Generate method in the file.

Registering Your Custom Tool for Visual Studio

Your custom tool must not only be registered with Windows, it must also have a registry entry for every language in Visual Studio that the tool supports. One way to handle that requirement is add two methods to your tool that add (and remove) the keys each time that the tool is registered (or unregistered) with Windows.

The following code adds the key for C# when the class is being registered or unregistered. To make the code reusable, I've broken the material that varies from one custom tool to another out into a set of static variables. To use these methods, you may need to update the Visual Studio version number (the version number in the example is for Visual Studio 2008). You will always need to update the tool's name, the tool's description, and the tool's GUID (this must be the same GUID you assigned to your tool in the Guid attribute on the class declaration):

```
static string VSVersion = "9.0";
static string CSLangGUID = "fae04ec1-301f-11d3-bf4b-00c04f79efbc";
static string ToolName = "TextGenerator";
static string ToolDesc =  "Generates a class from text input";
static string ToolGUID = "2890B999-71C7-4997-8DA6-27408064EBD8"

[System.Runtime.InteropServices.ComRegisterFunction]
public static void RegisterClass(Type typ)
{
 Microsoft.Win32.RegistryKey key;
 key = Microsoft.Win32.Registry.LocalMachine.CreateSubKey(
        @"SOFTWARE\Microsoft\VisualStudio\" + VSVersion +
        @"\Generators\{" + CSLangGUID + @"}\" + ToolName + @"\");
 key.SetValue("", ToolDesc);
 key.SetValue("CLSID", "{" + ToolGUID +"}");
 key.SetValue("GeneratesDesignTimeSource", 1);
}


[System.Runtime.InteropServices.ComUnregisterFunction]
public static void UnregisterClass(Type typ)
{
   Microsoft.Win32.Registry.LocalMachine.DeleteSubKey(
        @"SOFTWARE\Microsoft\VisualStudio\" + VSVersion +
        @"\Generators\" + CSLangGUID + @"\" + ToolName + @"\",
        false);
}
```

Here's a list of the GUIDs to use:

- **C#**—fae04ec1-301f-11d3-bf4b-00c04f79efbc
- **VB**—FAE04EC1-301F-11d3-BF4B-00C04F79EFBC
- **J#**—E6FDF8B0-F3D1-11D4-8576-0002A516ECE8

BEST PRACTICE Depending on what version of Visual Studio and .NET you have installed, you may be able to use the enumerated values in `ProvideCodeGeneratorAttribute` instead of hard-coding these GUIDs.

Testing Your Custom Control

Because Visual Studio caches code generators when it opens, to test your custom tool you must open a new version of Visual Studio. Once you've started Visual Studio and opened a project, find (or create) a file with suitable text for your tool, and, in the Properties List, set its Custom Tool property to the name of your custom tool. You can run your custom tool by

- Saving the file.
- Right-clicking the file in Solution Explorer and selecting Run Custom Tool.
- In Visual Studio 2008/2010 just switching away from the window after making a change.

If you get a message that your custom tool cannot be found, here are the most likely causes:

- A mismatch between the GUID used in the attribute on your class declaration and the GUID used for the CLSID in the `SetValue` method that adds the Visual Studio registry entries.
- Bad keys generated for Visual Studio either because you've specified the wrong version number for the version of Visual Studio you're testing in or the wrong GUID for the language you're testing in. You can check your entries using RegEdit and navigating to the key specified in your code under `HKEY_LOCAL_MACHINE`.

- The custom tool was not moved to the GAC or an older version was not removed from the GAC. You can manually move your tool to the GAC by opening the Visual Studio command prompt and navigating to the folder containing your DLL. To install your tool in the GAC, use

```
gacutil -i <nameofyourtool>.DLL /f
```

  The `/f` option ensures that this installation overwrites any existing version. To remove any previous versions, use `gacutil -u <nameofyourproject>`.
- The tool failed to register in Windows. You can manually register your tool by opening the Visual Studio command prompt, navigating to the folder with your custom tool's DLL, and running the regasm utility, passing the name of the DLL: `regasm <nameofyourdll>.dll`. You can unregister a component by passing the `/u` parameter to regasm: `regasm /u <nameofyourdll>.dll`.

BEST PRACTICE You won't be able to debug your custom tool when it's called from Visual Studio. Instead, create a test harness that will feed dummy file contents to your generation class's `GenerateCode` method (placing your code-generation code in a separate class facilitates this).

To test your application when called in Visual Studio, you can use the minimal custom tool code from the previous example. Just set the return value from your method to the text from your input file that will be passed to your method—this will also let you check that the text Visual Studio is handing to your routine matches the text you're using to test your custom control. As discussed in the next section, you can access the Visual Studio IDE from your custom tool so you can write messages to the status bar or one of the Visual Studio windows.

Integrating Custom Tools

You have two mechanisms for further integrating your custom tool into Visual Studio: You can access the Visual Studio object model from your custom tool and you can manage the Portable Execution file that is generated from the code that your custom tool creates.

Accessing Visual Studio

To access Visual Studio from your custom tool, you'll need to add references to the `envdte` and `Microsoft.VisualStudio.OLE.Interop` libraries to your custom tool project. With those references added, you can retrieve a reference to the Visual Studio object model using code like this example, which puts a reference to the DTE object in a variable called `dte`:

```
EnvDTE.DTE dte = null;
dte = (EnvDTE.DTE)Microsoft.VisualStudio.
        Shell.Package.GetGlobalService(typeof(EnvDTE.DTE));
```

Working with the information available inside a custom tool is restrictive, however, because you're only passed the full path to the file holding the input and the namespace for the project. Typical code in your custom tool to retrieve the `ProjectItem` for the input file will do so by looping through all the `Projects` and then through all the `ProjectItems` in each `Project` to find the one with a matching pathname. That code would look like this:

```
foreach (EnvDTE.Project prj in dte.Solution.Projects)
{
  foreach(EnvDTE.ProjectItem prji in prj.ProjectItems)
  {
   if (FilePath.EndsWith(prji.Name))
   {
     ...code to work with ProjectItem
   }
  }
}
```

Managing the Compiled Version of Your Code

When a custom tool generates content, that code is compiled into a Portable Executable (PE) file to generate the types and other class information that IntelliSense requires. For Visual Basic, Visual C#, and Visual J# projects, you can use the `BuildManager` object to monitor when your custom tools produce output. You can also use the `BuildManager` object to retrieve information that you can use to manage the PE file. The `RunCustomTool` method will also force code to be generated, allowing you to ensure that all code in a project is up to date.

By accessing the compiled PE file using Reflection, your custom tool can instantiate any objects defined by the generated code. It's easier, however, to set up two events in your add-in to use the `BuildManager` to monitor when custom tool output is produced or deleted. You can then use the `BuildManager` to access the PE information. I describe the basics of this process in this section; however, as I discuss at the end of the next section, a solution that would support multiple projects in a Visual Studio solution would be more complicated.

Monitoring Custom Tool Activity The Build Manager provides two events that can be used to monitor custom tool activity:

- **DesignTimeOutputDirty**—Raised when the custom tool generates new output. You use this event to trigger retrieving information about the output.
- **DesignItemOutputDeleted**—Raised when the output file is deleted. You use this event to discard information previously retrieved about the custom tools' output.

The first step monitoring custom tool activity is to declare a `BuildManagerEvents` object at the top of your add-in's `Connect` class:

```
private VSLangProj.BuildManagerEvents bme;
```

The second step is to add code to wire up the `BuildManager` events. This code would be placed in the `Open` event of the `SolutionEvents` object, as described in the section "Simple Events" in Chapter 2.

The following code retrieves a `VSProject2` reference to the first project in the solution. (`VSProject2` and the rest of the `VSLangProj` objects are discussed in detail in Chapter 5, "Supporting Project-Specific Features.") The code then retrieves, from the `VSProject2` object, a reference to the `BuildManager` for the project. Using the reference to the `BuildManager`, the code attaches an event handler to each of the `DesignTimeOutputDeleted` and `DesignTimeOutputDirty` events:

```
VSProject2 bmPrj;
BuildManager bm;
bmPrj = (VSProject2)
            _applicationObject.Solution.Projects.Item(1).Object;
bm = bmPrj.BuildManager;

bme = bmPrj.Events.BuildManagerEvents;
bme.DesignTimeOutputDeleted +=
    new _dispBuildManagerEvents_DesignTimeOutputDeletedEventHandler(
        bme_DesignTimeOutputDeleted);
```

```
bme.DesignTimeOutputDirty +=
    new _dispBuildManagerEvents_DesignTimeOutputDirtyEventHandler(
        bme_DesignTimeOutputDirty);
```

The two event handlers have identical signatures: Both are passed the moniker (effectively, the name of the generated file) that can be used to retrieve information about the output of the custom tool. Here's what the two event handlers would look like (their names must match the names used in the previous example):

```
void bme_DesignTimeOutputDirty(string Moniker)
{
}

void bme_DesignTimeOutputDeleted(string Moniker)
{
}
```

In the `SolutionEvent` object's `Closed` event, you should disconnect the event handlers, as this code does:

```
bme.DesignTimeOutputDeleted -= new
    _dispBuildManagerEvents_DesignTimeOutputDeletedEventHandler(
        bme_DesignTimeOutputDeleted);
bme.DesignTimeOutputDirty -= new
    _dispBuildManagerEvents_DesignTimeOutputDirtyEventHandler(
        bme_DesignTimeOutputDirty);
```

As I said earlier, to support a solution that contains multiple projects, you need more complicated code. To begin with, you need to create a collection of `BuildManagerEvent` objects with a separate `BuildManagerEvent` object for each project. You would also create the event routines as methods in a separate class and instantiate one instance of that class for each project in the solution. Finally, the code to wire up the events at the end of the example would attach the events to methods in the instance of the class created for each project.

Retrieving Information about Custom Output   In the `DesignTimeOutputDirty` event, you can retrieve information about the output file whose moniker is passed to the event. Because all custom tool events are processed by the single event routine for the project, you'll need to examine the moniker passed to the event routine to determine if you want to take action. A simple moniker looks like a filename (e.g., CodeGenerationInput.Generated.cs); if the output file is nested in a folder, then the folder name is also included in the moniker (e.g., Folder1\\CodeGenerationInput.Generated.cs).

Because your custom tool manages the extension of the output file, you can use that to determine if this is a file you're interested in. This code, for instance, checks to see if the moniker ends with "Generated.cs":

```
if (Moniker.EndsWith("Generated.cs"))  {
```

Once you've determined that the event has been triggered by a custom tool you're interested in, you can then use the FileCodeModel to retrieve a reference to the file to work with it, using the moniker. (The FileCodeModel objects are discussed in Chapter 3.)

Using the moniker, you can also retrieve information about the PE. The information is returned in an XML document that contains the path to the PE (the Application element's private_binpath attribute) and the name of the DLL (the Assembly element's codebase attribute). The name of the output file is also included. Here's a typical example:

```
<root>
   <Application private_binpath =
          "C:\Projects\MySoln\MyApp\\MyApp\obj\Debug\TempPE\"/>
   <Assembly codebase = "CodeGenerationInput.Generated.cs.dll"
             name = "CodeGenerationInput.Generated.cs"
             version = "0.0.0.0"
             snapshot_id = "1"
             replaceable = "True"/>
   </root>
```

If you wanted to hold the PE information for a number of custom tools, you might begin by declaring, at the top of the add-in, a collection to hold the moniker and PE information:

```
private Dictionary<string, string> csOutput =
                    new  Dictionary<string, string>();
```

In the DesignTimeOutputDirty event, after determining that you were interested in the custom tool that triggered the event, you would retrieve a reference to the project's BuildManager (this code continues to assume that there is only a single project in the solution):

```
VSProject2 bmPrj;
BuildManager bm;
bmPrj =
 (VSProject2)_applicationObject.Solution.Projects.Item(1).Object;
bm = bmPrj.BuildManager;
```

PE information can be retrieved from the BuildManager by calling its BuildDesignTimeOutput method, passing the moniker. This code checks to see if the moniker is already in the collection and, if it isn't, adds the moniker along with the PE information. If the moniker is in the collection, this code just updates the entry with the PE information:

```
string res = bm.BuildDesignTimeOutput(Moniker);
if (!csOutput.ContainsKey(Moniker))
{
  csOutput.Add(Moniker, res);
}
else
{
  csOutput[Moniker] = res;
}
```

Processing All Output in a Project Using the BuildManager's DesignTimeOutpuMonikers property, you can also process all the monikers for output currently generated in the project. This property returns an object that, if not null, can be cast into an Array object. The resulting Array object has an entry for each output file in the project. This example builds the collection in the previous example by iterating through the array of monikers:

```
Array mkrs = null;
Object obj = bm.DesignTimeOutputMonikers;
if (obj != null)
{
  mkrs = (System.Array)obj;
  foreach(String mkr in mkrs)
  {
    csOutput.Add(mkr, bm.BuildDesignTimeOutput(mkr));
  }
}
```

Running a Custom Tool   For any VSProjectItem, you can cause its custom tool to regenerate its output by calling the VSProjectItem's RunCustomTool method. This example iterates through all the ProjectItems in a Project, checking each ProjectItem's CustomTool property. If the property is not a zero-length string, the code casts the ProjectItem to a VSProjectItem and calls its RunCustomTool method to regenerate the code:

```
foreach (ProjectItem csPji in
    _applicationObject.Solution.Projects.Item(1).ProjectItems)
{
 if (csPji.Properties.Item("CustomTool").Value.ToString() != "")
 {
  VSProjectItem vspji = (VSProjectItem) csPji.Object;
  vspji.RunCustomTool();
 }
}
```

Reviewing the Tools

In this chapter, you've seen three sets of tools you can use as part of your code-generation solution. Templates can be used to reduce the code you need to generate code by including boilerplate material in a Visual Studio template. To give the developer a structured way of providing input to your code-generation process, you can create attributes. Finally, a custom tool provides a way to process a file of input information and create a file of code.

PART II

CASE STUDIES

CASE STUDY: GENERATING A CONNECTION STRING MANAGER

In this chapter:

- Defining the Problem
- Setting Up the Add-In
- Creating the Code Generator
- Customizing the Template
- Generating Code
- Reading Input
- Notifying the Developer
- Supporting Customization
- Tying Generation to Events
- Generating a Simple Class

In this chapter, I walk through an end-to-end solution for code generation that concentrates on integrating with Visual Studio and working with the `CodeElement` objects. The code for this solution is kept purposely simple to avoid involving other tools. (For example, I only make minimal use of the code editor object.) The case study in the next chapter includes a wider range of tools, including the CodeDom.

I've also assumed that there will be only one configuration file open at a time—because you can only have one app.config or web.config in a project, that's not an unreasonable assumption. However, because a Visual Studio solution can include multiple projects, it's at least conceivable that a developer could have two or more configuration files open at a time. The case study in the next chapter shows a more sophisticated process for handling events to support scenarios where multiple files that trigger code generation could be open.

This solution does demonstrate how to do the following:

- Support all project types, including ASP.NET websites, without using the `VsWebsite` objects (or, at least, only having to use them once)
- Support customization by the developer
- Read existing files in the project to get the input specifications
- Create a page in the Tools | Options dialog to allow the developer to configure code generation
- Tie code generation to events in Visual Studio

As part of this solution, I include some utilities that you can use in other code-generation solutions. One caveat: To simplify the code in this example, I assume that I'm only generating C# code, although I discuss where the solution would be different when supporting Visual Basic.

Finally, within those self-imposed limitations, I've tried to demonstrate a variety of techniques to show the range of options available to you when generating code. My goal for this chapter is to demonstrate a process for developing an add-in, along with some of my best practices and design patterns I follow.

Defining the Problem

The problem I want to address is relatively simple: handling the connection strings in an application's configuration file. A typical example of the separate section available for holding connection strings in an app.config or web.config file looks like this:

```
<connectionStrings>
  <add name="Northwind" connectionString="..."
      providerName="System.Data.SqlClient" />
</connectionStrings>
```

When retrieving the connection string, you access the connection strings as named members of a collection. To retrieve the connection string from the previous example in a non-ASP.NET application, you'd use this code:

```
string MyConnection = ConfigurationManager.
        ConnectionStrings["Northwnd"].ConnectionString;
```

Here is the syntax for an ASP.NET application:

```
return System.Web.Configuration.WebConfigurationManager.
          ConnectionStrings["Northwnd"].ConnectionString;
```

This syntax creates problems for developers. The absence of IntelliSense support when specifying the connection string means that you have to switch back to your configuration file in order to find what connection strings you have and what you called them; if you mistype the name of the connection string, you won't find that mistake until that line of code executes (probably when someone who has input into your job appraisal is looking over your shoulder). You don't have to take my word that this syntax is error-prone: Did you catch the misspelling of "Northwnd" in the sample code? It should have been "Northwind" to match the `connectionString` example—but if you don't spot that problem when reading the code, you won't find it until the code executes.

A Model Solution

ASP.NET provides a better model for handling connection strings in the way that the personalization provider handles properties. As with connection strings, you define personalization properties by entering XML tags into your website's configuration file. A typical example looks like this:

```
<properties>
    <add name="LinesPerPage" type="int" defaultValue="0"/>
</properties>
```

Unlike connection strings, however, at runtime, you don't access your personalization properties as members of a collection. Instead, you access the properties you defined in the Web.config through properties on the Profile object, like this:

```
Profile.LinesPerPage = 15;
```

When entering this code you get full IntelliSense support for all the Profile properties (see Figure 9-1). If you ask for a property that doesn't exist, your problem is found at compile time, not runtime. Overall, personalization delivers a solution that provides better support to developers than is available with connections strings, even though the input to both processes is the same.

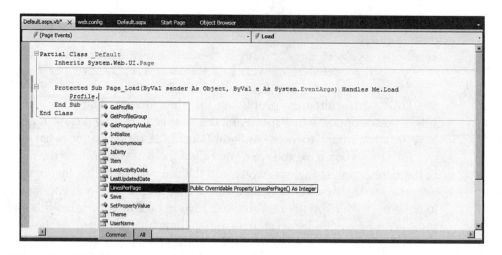

FIGURE 9-1 Although personalization properties are defined in an application's
configuration file, access to those properties is handled through specific properties on the
Profile object.

The personalization solution is made possible through the magic of
code generation: By analyzing the entries in the configuration file, Visual
Studio and ASP.NET generate a `Profile` object with all the properties
specified in the Web.config file's XML tags. Because the data type for each
property is specified in the XML tags, the generated code isn't "general-
purpose" code with multiple `if` statements checking the data type or with
all variables declared as type Object—you get the specific code you need
for the properties you defined in the configuration file.

A similar solution for connection strings lets the developer write code
like this:

```
string MyConnection = ConnectionManager.Northwind;
```

In this solution, the `ConnectionManager` object is a static class that isn't
instantiated and has a property for each connection string. This solution
gives the developer full IntelliSense support and compile-time checking
when accessing a connection string.

The code for my `ConnectionManager` object looks something like this for
Northwind property in a non-ASP.NET project:

```
public static partial class ConnectionManager
{
  public static string Northwind
```

```
    {
      get
      {
        return ConfigurationManager.
                        ConnectionStrings["Northwind"].ConnectionString;
      }
    }
  }
```

Supporting Customization

The ConnectionManager solution also allows the developer to introduce custom code to support those instances where a full connection string isn't stored in the configuration file. For instance, one of my clients provides data gathering and storage services to their customers. To support scalability (and to help ensure privacy), each customer's data is kept in a separate database. As a result, my client stores a template connection string in the application's configuration file. The template contains replaceable components that support tailoring the connection string for each customer. In my client's application, whenever a connection string is retrieved, code in the application modifies the template and tailors the string to work with a specific customer's database. The ConnectionManager solution supports this kind of modification by allowing the developer to step in and add his or her own code to the process.

Setting Up the Add-In

Practical code-generation solutions should seamlessly integrate with the developer's normal activities. I begin this project by creating the add-in that will trigger code generation whenever the config file is closed (or whenever the developer chooses to generate code by selecting a menu option).

Defining the Add-In

I start a new code-generation project either by extending an existing add-in with similar functionality or creating a new one. For this project, I start a new add-in. I always begin with the simplest possible interface for triggering the code generation: a single menu item that runs the solution. This simplifies testing and debugging. Near the end of the project, I convert this add-in to run when the project is built or when the configuration file is closed.

From the File menu, I select New Project and, in the New Project dialog, under Extensibility, I select the Visual Studio Add-In template. After giving my add-in a name (I used "ConnectionManager") and specifying a folder to keep it in, I click the OK button to start the wizard. In the wizard, I take the following actions:

- Select C# as the language.
- Deselect Microsoft Visual Studio Macros.
- Replace the default name and description for the add-in with my own text.
- Select all three choices on the fourth page:
  - Add a command to the Tools menu.
  - Have the add-in load with Visual Studio.
  - Promise not to put up a modal dialog.
- Add some information for the About dialog.

Once the project is created, I modify the project's properties (as described in Chapter 2, "Integrating with Visual Studio"):

- Set the assembly name (and make the same change in the `<Assembly>` element of the two .addin files).
- In the Build Events tab (C#) or on the Compile tab after clicking the Build Events button (Visual Basic), I add these two lines to the Pre-build event command line. (This code is spread over two lines to fit on the page, but the second and third line should be entered as one line in the Pre-build text box.)

```
if exist "$(TargetPath).locked" del "$(TargetPath).locked"
if exist "$(TargetPath)" if not exist "$(TargetPath).locked" move
              "$(TargetPath)" "$(TargetPath).locked"
```

Creating the Menu

Once the project is generated, my next step is to modify the code in the Connect.cs file. One of my goals when designing the Connect.cs file is to create a version that doesn't require many changes when setting up a new add-in. To support that, in the Connect.cs file I add four fields (named `menuName`, `menuItemName`, `menuItemCaption`, and `menuTooltip`) at the top of the class. If all that's required in an add-in is a single menu item on a menu (and that's always my start point for any solution), the only changes required are to the values of these four fields:

```
string menuName = "Tools";
string menuItemName = "ConStrGentr";
string menuItemCaption = "Generate Connection String Class";
string menuToolTip = "Create a class for managing connection strings";
```

I then replace all the code in the OnConnection method with the following code in Visual Studio 2005/2008, which uses my fields to find the menu specified in my four fields:

```
public void OnConnection(object application, ext_ConnectMode
                        connectMode, object addInInst,
                        ref Array custom)
{
 _applicationObject = (DTE2)application;
 _addInInstance = (AddIn)addInInst;

 if (connectMode == ext_ConnectMode.ext_cm_UISetup)
 {
  object[] contextGUIDS = new object[] { };
  Commands2 commands = (Commands2)_applicationObject.Commands;

  string FoundMenuName;

  try
  {
   System.Resources.ResourceManager resourceManager = new
     System.Resources.ResourceManager(
       _addInInstance.ProgID + ".CommandBar",
       System.Reflection.Assembly.GetExecutingAssembly());
   System.Globalization.CultureInfo cultureInfo = new
       System.Globalization.CultureInfo(_applicationObject.LocaleID);
   if (cultureInfo.TwoLetterISOLanguageName == "zh")
   {
    System.Globalization.CultureInfo parentCultureInfo =
                                        cultureInfo.Parent;
    FoundMenuName = resourceManager.GetString(
            String.Concat(parentCultureInfo.Name, menuName));
   }
   else
   {
```

```
    FoundMenuName = resourceManager.GetString(String.Concat(
            cultureInfo.TwoLetterISOLanguageName, menuName));
  }
}
catch (Exception e)
{
 FoundMenuName = menuName;
}
if (FoundMenuName == "")
{
 FoundMenuName = menuName;
}
```

The equivalent code in Visual Studio 2010 looks like this:

```
CommandBar cb;
bool MainMenu = true;
string MenuBarName = "Menubar";

if (MainMenu)
{
 cb = ((CommandBars)_applicationObject.CommandBars)[MenuBarName];
 cb = ((CommandBarPopup)cb.Controls[FoundMenuName]).CommandBar;
}
else
{
 CommandBars cbs = (CommandBars)_applicationObject.CommandBars;
 cb = cbs[FoundMenuName];
}
```

In Visual Studio 2008/2010, the next code adds a new menu item (with
the name specified in `menuItemName`) to the menu I just found, with the caption and tooltip specified in `menuItemCaption` and `menuToolTip`:

```
Commands2 cmds = (Commands2)_applicationObject.Commands;
CommandBars cbs = (CommandBars)_applicationObject.CommandBars;
CommandBar cb = cbs[FoundMenuName];

Command NamedCommand = null;
try
{
 NamedCommand = _applicationObject.Commands.Item(
            _addInInstance.ProgID + menuItemName, 1);
}
catch
```

```
{
  try
  {
   NamedCommand = cmds.AddNamedCommand2(_addInInstance,
              menuItemName, menuItemCaption, menuToolTip,
              true,50, ref contextGUIDS
              (int) vsCommandStatus.vsCommandStatusSupported +
              (int) vsCommandStatus.vsCommandStatusEnabled,
              (int) vsCommandStyle.vsCommandStylePictAndText,
              vsCommandControlType.vsCommandControlTypeButton);
  }
  catch {}

  try
  {
   CommandBarControl cbc =
              cb.Controls[menuItemCaption];
  }
  catch
  {
   NamedCommand.AddControl(cb, 1);
  }
 }
}
}
```

In Visual Studio 2005, I would need to replace the code that uses AddNamedCommand2 with code that uses AddNamedCommand:

```
Command command = cmds.AddNamedCommand(_addInInstance,
              menuItemName,menuItemCaption, menuToolTip,
              true,59,ref contextGUIDS,
          (int) vsCommandStatus.vsCommandStatusSupported) +
              (int) vsCommandStatus.vsCommandStatusEnabled);
```

In addition to replacing the code in the OnConnection method, I also need to modify the code in the QueryStatus method to allow me to use any menu item created by this add-in:

```
public void QueryStatus(string commandName,
              vsCommandStatusTextWanted neededText,
              ref vsCommandStatus status,
              ref object commandText)
```

```
{
 if(neededText ==
        vsCommandStatusTextWanted.vsCommandStatusTextWantedNone)
 {
  if (commandName.StartsWith(_addInInstance.Name + ".Connect"))
  {
   status = (vsCommandStatus)vsCommandStatus.
                                vsCommandStatusSupported
             |vsCommandStatus.vsCommandStatusEnabled;
   return;
  }
 }
}
```

Calling the Solution

To make the Connect.cs class as portable as possible, I put my code-generation solution in a separate class. This means that the only change required to the Exec method of Connect.cs is the name of the class and method that implements the solution.

For this solution, I have the Exec method instantiate a class called DatabaseUtilities and call a method named GenerateConnectionManager. I pass the DTE2 object that provides access to Visual Studio to the constructor for this code-generation class. As a result, the code in this Exec method to create the DatabaseUtilities class, pass the _applicationObject variable that holds the DTE2 object, and call the GenerateConnectionClass method looks like this:

```
public void Exec(string commandName,
                vsCommandExecOption executeOption,
                ref object varIn, ref object varOut,
                ref bool handled)
{
 handled = false;
 if(executeOption == vsCommandExecOption.
                                vsCommandExecOptionDoDefault)
 {
  if (commandName == _addInInstance.ProgID + "." + menuItemName)
  {
   DatabaseUtiltiies dbu = new
                        DatabaseUtiltiies(_applicationObject);
   dbu.GenerateConnectionClass();
```

```
   handled = true;
   return;
  }
 }
}
```

Creating the Code Generator

With the framework for calling my code-generation solution in place, I'm ready to start creating the code-generation code in my DatabaseUtilities class. The constructor for the class accepts the reference to the DTE2 object and moves it to a field in the class. The initial version of the class also contains the GenerateConnectionManager method that's called from my add-in:

```
using System;
using System.Collections.Generic;
using System.Text;
using EnvDTE;
using EnvDTE80;

namespace ConnectionStringGenerator
{
    class DatabaseUtiltiies
    {
        DTE2 applicationObject;

        public DatabaseUtiltiies(DTE2 ApplicationObject)
        {
            applicationObject = ApplicationObject;
        }

        public void GenerateConnectionManager()
        {

        }
    }
}
```

At this point, I've got enough code to start testing my solution by adding a line of code to my `GenerateConnectionManager` method that writes to the status bar:

```
applicationObject.DTE.StatusBar.Text = "Code generator called.";
```

I can now check that the menu item appears (with all the text spelled correctly), that I can load my generation class, and that I can successfully call the generation method. If all that works, I'm ready to start thinking about what the solution will do.

Finding the Project

The first step in this code-generation project is to retrieve a reference to the project that the developer wants to modify. At this point, it's worthwhile to think about the problem from the point of view of the developer for whom you're generating the code. When the developer clicks the menu item that starts the code-generation process, what project will the developer expect your code to work with?

For a code-generation solution run from a button on a menu, my first choice is to work with the project for the currently open document. This code retrieves the project for that document:

```
Project prj = null;
if (applicationObject.ActiveDocument != null)
{
  prj = applicationObject.ActiveDocument.
                          ProjectItem.ContainingProject;

}
```

However, if there is no open document, my second choice is to work with the project for the item currently selected in Solution Explorer. This code checks to see if an item is selected in Solution Explorer and if the item has an associated `ProjectItem`. Then, if both of those conditions are true, it retrieves the associated `Project`:

```
else
{
  if (applicationObject.SelectedItems.Count > 0)
  {
    if (applicationObject.SelectedItems.Item(1).ProjectItem
                                        != null)
    {
```

```
    prj = applicationObject.SelectedItems.Item(1).
                            ProjectItem.ContainingProject;
  }
  else
  {
    prj = applicationObject.SelectedItems.Item(1).Project;
  }
}
```

Unfortunately, there is a possibility that no document is open, that nothing is selected in Solution Explorer, or that the selected item doesn't return a `Project` reference. If I can't determine the `Project`, I give up and exit. However, the decent thing to do in that situation is to tell the developer that no code has been generated. It's tempting to pop up a form telling the developer that no code was generated, but when working through the Add-In Wizard, I promised never to display a modal dialog. So, instead I just update Visual Studio's status bar with code like this. (In the section "Notifying the Developer" later in this chapter, I enhance the messaging to use the `TaskList` for more serious messages.)

```
if (prj == null)
{
  applicationObject.DTE.StatusBar.Text =
                        "Please select a project item.";
  return;
}
```

Assuming that I get a reference to the `Project`, I now get references to the `Project`'s `ProjectItems` collection and the `Solution` it's part of—I'll need both of these objects later in the solution:

```
ProjectItems pjis = prj.ProjectItems;
Solution2 sln = (Solution2) applicationObject.Solution;
```

Does Anything Need to be Done?

In the process I recommended in Chapter 1, "Introducing Code Generation," as part of reading your inputs you should determine whether any code needs to be generated. In this case, that means retrieving the web.config file and determining if it contains any `connectionString` elements.

This code attempts to retrieve the project's web.config file and, if that fails, the project's app.config file. If neither exists, the code exits:

```
ProjectItem cfg = null;
try
{
 cfg = pi.Project.ProjectItems.Item("web.config");
}
catch
{
 try
 {
  cfg = pi.Project.ProjectItems.Item("app.config");
 }
 catch {}
}
if (cfg == null)
{
 return;
}
```

With a configuration file found, the code loads its contents into an XML document by passing the full pathname to the configuration file to an XmlDocument object. The code then uses an XPath expression to search the document for connectionString elements. If none are found, the code exits:

```
System.Xml.XmlDocument dom;
dom = new System.Xml.XmlDocument();

dom.Load(@cfg.Properties.Item("FullPath").Value.ToString());
System.Xml.XmlNode ndCons =
     dom.SelectSingleNode("//connectionStrings");
if (ndCons == null || ndCons.ChildNodes.Count == 0)
{
 return;
}
```

Segregating Generated Code

I'm almost ready to start adding code, but I need to decide how to handle the files containing my generated code. Although many code generators attempt to hide generated classes from the developer, my preference is to leave the code visible. (Among other benefits, this makes it easier for me to check that I'm generating the right code during development and debugging.)

However, I do segregate my generated code into special folders. Using the reference to the `ProjectItems` collection, I can add that folder to hold my generated code using the `AddFolder` method. For most projects, I create a folder called "Generated Code" to put the class file in. However, for ASP.NET projects, I place the class file in the App_Code folder.

These folders may already be present. (Even my own Generated Code folder may already exist if the developer has run this add-in, or another one of my code-generation utilities, before.) Adding the folder a second time will raise an error; however, rather than check that the folder already exists, I just catch the error and discard it. I'll need to access the folder again, so after adding it I retrieve a reference to the new folder through the `ProjectItems`' `Item` method (unfortunately, the `AddFolder` method doesn't return a reference to the new folder) and store it.

I begin by declaring a field to hold the reference to the folder with the generated code:

```
ProjectItem codeFolder;
```

In the following code, I first check to see what kind of project I have by looking at the GUID in the `Project` object's `Kind` property. If it's an ASP.NET project, I attempt to add the App_Code folder. For any other kind of project, I add a folder named "Generated Code." As I noted before, if the folders already exist, I just catch the error and discard it. After attempting to add the folder, I get a reference to it:

```
if (prj.Kind == "{E24C65DC-7377-472b-9ABA-BC803B73C61A}")
{
 try
 {
  pjis.AddFolder("App_Code",
             "{6BB5F8EF-4483-11D3-8BCF-00C04F8EC28C}");
 }
 catch { };
 codeFolder = pjis.Item("App_Code");
}
else
{
 try
 {
  pjis.AddFolder("Generated Code",
             Constants.vsProjectItemKindPhysicalFolder);
```

```
    }
    catch {};
    codeFolder = pjis.Item("Generated Code");
}
```

I could simplify the code required to add the App_Code folder by using the `VsWebSite` objects (described in Chapter 5, "Supporting Project-Specific Features"). However, for this case study, one of my goals is to use as few tools as possible, which means avoiding using the project-specific objects described in that chapter.

With the folder in place, I add the class file that will eventually contain my ConnectionManager code. At this point I have to decide how I want to handle regeneration when the developer is generating the code for the second (or subsequent) time. The simplest strategy for supporting regeneration is to find the file containing the code from the previous generation and delete it. The alternative is to attempt to reconcile the previously generated code against the current environment, a process that is both difficult to implement and error-prone. (One solution is demonstrated in the case study in Chapter 10, "Case Study: Generating Validation Code," where I selectively replace methods in a class to leave the developer's methods in place while replacing my generated methods.)

In a well-designed solution, you should only need to update an existing file occasionally. Typically, solutions end up having to reconcile old code with new code because the solution didn't provide a clean separation between the generated code and the developer's custom code. For this example, I keep most of the generated code in one file and provide a separate file for the developer's custom code.

For this solution, both of the files will have their names begin with "ConnectionManager." The file that holds the generated code will be named "ConnectionManager.Generation," the file holding the developer's code will be named "ConnectionManager.Customization." Initially, all I build into the solution is the ConnectionManager.Generation file.

In this solution, if the ConnectionManager.Generation file already exists, I don't want to try adding it again and catching the error: I always want to delete any existing version of the file in order to start generating the code from a blank slate. To ensure that I'm deleting the right file, I use the full pathname to the file by concatenating together the path to the project and name of the folder I added. The code looks like this:

```
string ProjectPath;
ProjectPath = System.IO.Path.GetDirectoryName(prj.FullName);
```

```
ProjectItem prji = sln.FindProjectItem(@ProjectPath + @"\" +
        codeFolder.Name + @"\ConnectionManager.Generation.cs");
if (prji != null)
{
  prji.Delete();
}
```

Adding the Template

After ensuring that the file doesn't exist, I now add the Visual Studio template that provides the base for my generation class: a class file in C#. To get this file in the right folder, I use the reference to the folder where I'm going to keep my generated code, which I retrieved earlier. This example adds the template for a non-ASP.NET project:

```
string ItemTemplatePath = sln.GetProjectItemTemplate(
                                    "Class.zip", "CSharp");
ProjectItem pji = codeFolder.ProjectItems.AddFromTemplate
        (ItemTemplatePath,"ConnectionManager.Generation.cs");
```

To enable my add-in to support ASP.NET, I need to add a different template. This code checks the project's Kind property and, when the project is a website, adds the correct class. Revising the previous code to handle ASP.NET projects produces the following code:

```
string ItemTemplatePath;
if (prj.Kind == "{E24C65DC-7377-472b-9ABA-BC803B73C61A}")
{
  ItemTemplatePath = sln.GetProjectItemTemplate("Class.zip",
                                        @"Web\CSharp");
}
else
{
  ItemTemplatePath = sln.GetProjectItemTemplate("Class.zip",
                                        "CSharp");
}
ProjectItem pji = codeFolder.ProjectItems.AddFromTemplate
        (ItemTemplatePath,"ConnectionManager.Generation.cs");
```

It's possible, for a number of reasons, that the AddFromTemplate method will successfully add the class file but not return a ProjectItem. (For instance, if the template is a wizard, you won't get a return value because wizards don't return `ProjectItems`.) So, after adding the item, I check to see if the reference is null; if it is, I use `FindProjectItem` to get a reference to the class file. (This also provides a check that the class file was successfully added.)

```
if (pji == null)
{
 pji = sln.FindProjectItem(@ProjectPath + @"\" +
          codeFolder.Name + @"\ConnectionManager.Generation.cs");
}
if (pji == null)
{
   applicationObject.DTE.StatusBar.Text =
                             "Unable to add class file.";

   return;
}
```

Customizing the Template

Because the input to any code-generation solution controls the output, it's time to consider what the input for this code-generation solution looks like. I assume that the config file for the application contains a `ConnectionStrings` element, like this:

```
<connectionStrings>
    <add name="MainDB" connectionString="..." providerName="..."/>
</connectionStrings>
```

The solution should generate a class that looks like this:

```
using System;
using System.Collections.Generic;
using System.Linq;
using System.Text;

namespace MyProject
{
  class ConnectionManager
  {
    string MainDB
```

```
    {
      get
      {
        return System.Configuration.ConfigurationManager.
                    ConnectionStrings["MainDB"].ConnectionString;
      }
    }
  }
}
```

Unfortunately, the result of adding the template for a new class in a non-ASP.NET project looks like this:

```
using System;
using System.Collections.Generic;
using System.Linq;
using System.Text;

namespace MyConsoleProject.Generated_Code
{
    class ConnectionManager
    {
    }
}
```

In a projectless web application, the class looks like this:

```
using System;
using System.Collections.Generic;
using System.Linq;
using System.Web;

/// <summary>
/// Summary description for ConnectionManager
/// </summary>
public class ConnectionManager
{
    public ConnectionManager()
    {
        //
        // TODO: Add constructor logic here
        //
    }
}
```

A number of differences exist between the template file and the class file for which I'm aiming. To get the class file I want, I must do the following:

- **Simplify the namespace.** For many projects, I will have added the class to a subfolder named Generated Code. By default, in a C# project, the folder name will be included in the class's namespace (e.g., MyProject.Generated_Code). I'd prefer not to force developers to have to drill down through the Generated_Code namespace; instead, I will have the ConnectionManager be in the project's root namespace.
- **Make the class static/shared.** Making this change allows the developer to call properties on the class without having to instantiate it.
- **Delete the constructor.** Static/shared classes are not allowed to have constructors.
- **Make the class a partial class.** Because this is created as a partial class, developers can customize ConnectionManager's behavior by adding code to a separate file.

In addition, I want to ensure that the project has a reference to the `System.Configuration` DLL. Web projects will have this reference by default but other types of project won't.

Had I used a custom template (as described in Chapter 8, "Other Tools: Templates, Attributes, and Custom Tools," and demonstrated in the case study in Chapter 10), I could omit much of the following code. However, using custom templates does make your code-generation solution dependent on having the right template installed on the developer's computer. Although the following solution requires more code, it does mean that my solution is more self-contained.

Fixing the Namespace

To simplify the `Namespace`, I first retrieve the `FileCodeModel` for the class file. If the project is a "projectless" website, I must cast the `ProjectItem` as a `VSWebProjectItem` and call its `Load` method before I can access its `FileCodeModel`. For other project types, I can just access the `FileCodeModel`; therefore, once again, the code checks to see if this is an ASP.NET project and does the right thing:

```
FileCodeModel fcm;
if (prj.Kind == "{E24C65DC-7377-472b-9ABA-BC803B73C61A}")
{
 VsWebSite.VSWebProjectItem tmpWPI;
 tmpWPI = (VsWebSite.VSWebProjectItem) pji.Object;
 tmpWPI.Load();
 fcm = tmpWPI.ProjectItem.FileCodeModel;
}
else
{
 fcm = ConnMgr.FileCodeModel;
}
```

Once the `FileCodeModel` is retrieved, I iterate through the top-level items until I find the `Namespace`. Once I find the `Namespace`, I set it to the project's `DefaultNamespace`, which I retrieved from the `Project`'s `Properties` collection. For Visual Basic projects, a `Namespace` typically isn't included in the file, but that's not a problem—if the `Namespace` isn't found, the code does nothing:

```
CodeElement2 codeClass;
foreach (CodeElement2 ce in fcm.CodeElements)
{
  if (ce.Kind == vsCMElement.vsCMElementNamespace)
  {
    ce.Name = prj.Properties.Item(
                "DefaultNamespace").Value.ToString();
```

Because my code resets the `Namespace`'s name, there's a very real possibility that my reference to the `Namespace` may be corrupted after the change. So, after changing the `Namespace`'s name, I use this code to reacquire the reference to the `Namespace`:

```
CodeElement2 ceNamespace = (CodeElement2) fcm.CodeElements.Item
      (prj.Properties.Item("DefaultNamespace").Value.ToString());
```

Modifying the Class

To modify the class, I now find the `Class` by iterating through the `CodeElements` collection within the `Namespace` I just changed and store the reference in a variable named `codeClass`:

```
foreach (CodeElement2 ceClass in ceNamespace.Children)
{
  {
   if (ce.Kind == vsCMElement.vsCMElementClass)
   {
    codeClass = ce;
   }
  }
}
```

If there is no Namespace in the Class (the typical scenario for a Visual Basic file), the code acquires the reference to the Class and puts it in codeClass inside the loop that looks for the Namespace:

```
if (ce.Kind == vsCMElement.vsCMElementClass)
{
 codeClass = ce;
}
```

With the Namespace corrected (if present) and a reference to the class held in the codeClass variable, I now look for the class's constructor inside codeClass's Children collection and delete it. Because I've added a C# file, I can identify the constructor by looking for a function with the same name as the class ("ConnectionManager"). For a Visual Basic application, I'd be looking for a method named New:

```
foreach (CodeElement2 ce in codeClass.Children)
  {
   if (ce.Kind == vsCMElement.vsCMElementFunction &&
       ce.Name == "ConnectionManager")
   {
    fcm.Remove(ce);
   }
}
```

I also need to modify the class's definition to make the class partial and shared/static. A CodeClass2 object has the necessary functionality to make those changes. Because the code has already retrieved a reference to the class as a CodeElement, all that I have to do is to cast my codeClass reference to a CodeClass2 object to get the functionality I need:

```
CodeClass2 cc = (CodeClass2) codeClass;
```

Now that I have a reference to a `CodeClass2` object, I make the class a partial class by setting its `ClassKind` property and a static/shared class by setting its `IsShared` property:

```
cc.ClassKind = EnvDTE80.vsCMClassKind.vsCMClassKindPartialClass;
cc.IsShared = true;
```

Adding a Reference

In order to access the `ConnectionStrings` element in the application's configuration file, non-web projects will need a reference to the `System.Configuration` assembly (website projects already have the necessary reference). To add this reference, the first step is to cast the reference to the `Project` object to a `VSLangProj.VSProject` type. Once the project is cast, a reference to the `System.Configuration` assembly can be added by name using the `References` collection's `Add` method (if the reference is already present, no error is raised):

```
VSLangProj.VSProject vsPrj;
vsPrj = (VSLangProj.VSProject) prj.Object;
vsPrj.References.Add("System.Configuration");
```

Generating Code

With the template fully customized, I can start generating the code for the properties I want to add to the class. For now, I'm going to assume that I've retrieved a single connection string name from the application's configuration file and put the connection string's name in the variable `PropertyName`. I'm also going to assume that the single line of code that the property requires is in the variable `PropertyReturnCode`. In the next section, "Reading Input," I look both at retrieving the information from the configuration file and handling multiple connection strings. The code for this example is sufficiently simple that using the CodeDom to generate the code is overkill. In the next chapter, I look at a case study where the code is sufficiently complex to justify the CodeDom.

The following code adds a property using whatever name is in the variable `PropertyName` (I omit the name for the property's setter in order to create a read-only property):

```
CodeProperty cp;

cp = cc.AddProperty(PropertyName, null,
                    vsCMTypeRef.vsCMTypeRefString, -1,
                    vsCMAccess.vsCMAccessPublic,null);
```

The design for the ConnectionManager requires the method to be static/shared. In theory, to make that change all I need to do is set the IsShared property on the CodeProperty2 object that represents my newly added property. Unfortunately, in some versions of Visual Studio, the AddProperty method returns a CodeProperty object that doesn't support the IsShared method and can't be cast to a CodeProperty2 object.

The solution is to use the CodeProperty object's Getter property to retrieve the CodeFunction object for the new property's getter, and because CodeFunctions do have an IsShared property, I can use that to make the property static/shared:

```
cp2.Getter.IsShared = true;
```

Now that the property has been added, I insert the code for the property using the CodeEditor object. The first step is to retrieve the StartPoint for the body of the property's Getter and, from it, create an EditPoint. Once the EditPoint is created, my next step is to delete any default code inserted into the property by the AddProperty method (in C#, for instance, the AddProperty method inserts a line of code that throws an exception):

```
EditPoint epGetter = cp.Getter.GetStartPoint(
                vsCMPart.vsCMPartBody).CreateEditPoint();
epGetter.Delete(cp.Getter.GetEndPoint(vsCMPart.vsCMPartBody));
```

After clearing any default code, the final step is to insert any new code:

```
epGetter.Insert(PropertyReturnCode);
```

Reading Input

So far, I've just assumed that I've retrieved the inputs to the process: the names of the connections string in the app.config or web.config file. In this section, I look at retrieving that input and integrating it into the solution.

I've kept the code for this case study purposely simple to concentrate on the structure of a code-generation solution. For a case study that generates more complex code, see Chapter 10.

Processing the Configuration File

The connection strings are kept in the configuration file for the application, so my first step is to retrieve either the web.config file (for ASP.NET projects) or app.config file (for all other project types). Rather than check the project type, I use the ProjectItems collection to try and retrieve the app.config file; if I don't find it, I try to retrieve the web.config file. If neither is found, there are no connection strings to generate so I display a status message and exit.

Because failing to find an item in the ProjectItems collection raises an error, I use a try...catch block to determine if the configuration files are found:

```
ProjectItem cfg;


try
{
 cfg = prj.ProjectItems.Item("web.config");
}
catch
{
 try
 {
   cfg = prj.ProjectItems.Item("app.config");
 }
 catch
 {
  if (prj == null)
  {
   applicationObject.DTE.StatusBar.Text =
                            "No configuration file.";
   return;
  }
 }
}
```

Once I've found the configuration file, the next step is to read it. The
`Properties` collection for a `Project` item includes the `FullPath` to the item.
Using that value, I can load the configuration file into an `XMLDocument`, as this
code does:

```
System.Xml.XmlDocument dom;
dom = new System.Xml.XmlDocument();

dom.Load(@cfg.Properties.Item("FullPath").Value.ToString());
```

Adding Property Code

With the document loaded, the next step is to loop through the children of
the `connectionStrings` element. For each child element, I retrieve the
name attribute from the element and use that to create the property:

```
System.Xml.XmlNode ndCons =
dom.SelectSingleNode("//connectionStrings");
foreach (System.Xml.XmlNode ndCon in ndCons)
{
  string PropertyName = ndCon.Attributes["name"].Value;

  CodeProperty cp;
  cp = cc.AddProperty(PropertyName, null,
                      vsCMTypeRef.vsCMTypeRefString,
                      -1, vsCMAccess.vsCMAccessPublic, null);
  cp.Getter.IsShared = true;

  EditPoint epGetter = cp.Getter.GetStartPoint(
                       vsCMPart.vsCMPartBody).CreateEditPoint();
  epGetter.Delete(cp.Getter.GetEndPoint(vsCMPart.vsCMPartBody));
  epGetter.Insert("return " +
          "System.Web.Configuration.WebConfigurationManager." +
          "ConnectionStrings[\""+ PropertyName +
          "\"].ConnectionString;");
}
```

For a non-ASP application, the last line of code looks like this:

```
epGetter.Insert("return ConfigurationManager.ConnectionStrings[
                \"" + PropertyName + "\"].ConnectionString;");
```

Notifying the Developer

So far, in notifying the developer, I've simply written a message to the status bar. However, that's only really appropriate for messages that provide information about ongoing processing. Where the add-in is unable to continue processing, it's more appropriate to write the message to the TaskList, where it will appear in the Add-In and Macros category.

Defining the Output Utility

To handle output, I use a single method that, when passed a message and a severity level, either updates the status bar or adds an item to the task list, depending on the severity level. Updating the status bar not only lets the developer using your utility know what's going on, it's also helpful in debugging—if your add-in abends, the status bar will display the last message sent to it, giving you a clue as to where in your add-in you stopped processing. Because I use this method in a variety of code-generation projects, I put it in its own class library project called CodeGenerationUtilities (this project needs references to both EnvDTE and EnvDTE80).

My utility also includes an enumeration, which I call GenerationLevel. I use it to specify the error level of the message. As a minimum, you need to support two severity levels: one for messages to be written to the status bar and one for messages to be written to the Task List. The two levels that I use are called "information" and "severe":

```
namespace CodeGenerationUtilities
{
 public enum GenerationLevel
 {
  information,
  severe
 }
```

In order to update the status bar and the Task List, my utility needs to access the DTE2 object used by the add-in. I pass that reference to the utility in its constructor.

Handling the Task List

In the utility's constructor, I delete all related messages that may be in the Task List from previous code generations. In order to avoid deleting messages created by other code-generation utilities, I use the TaskList's SubCategory: When adding messages I set the SubCategory to a value unique to the particular code-generation solution. (All my code-generation solutions set the TaskList's Category to "Code Generation.") As a result, I can use the SubCategory to delete messages from previous executions of this code-generation solution. I pass the SubCategory to be used when adding or deleting messages into the utility's constructor and store it in a field. As a result, the constructor for the utility looks like this:

```
string subcategory;

public Utilities(DTE2 ApplicationObject, string SubCategory)
{
  applicationObject = ApplicationObject;
  subCategory = SubCategory;
  TaskList tl = applicationObject.ToolWindows.TaskList;
  foreach (TaskItem ti in tl.TaskItems)
  {
    if (ti.SubCategory == SubCategory)
    {
      ti.Delete();
    }
  }
}
```

My utility includes a WriteOutput method that accepts the message text to display and a GenerationLevel flag. If GenerationLevel is set to severe, the message is added to the TaskList; if GenerationLevel is set to information, the message is used to update the status bar:

```
public class Utilities
  {
    public void WriteOutput(string Message, GenerationLevel Level)
    {
      if (Level == GenerationLevel.severe)
      {
        TaskList tl = applicationObject.ToolWindows.TaskList;
        TaskItems2 tis = (TaskItems2)tl.TaskItems;
```

```
    TaskItem ti = tis.Add2("Code Generation",
                            subCategory, Message,
                            (int)vsTaskPriority.vsTaskPriorityHigh,
                            (int)vsTaskIcon.vsTaskIconCompile,
                            true,"",0,true,true,false);
    }
    else if (Level == GenerationLevel.information)
    {
      applicationObject.DTE.StatusBar.Text = Message;
    }
}
```

Using the Output Method

With the `CodeGenerationUtilities` object created, I can add a reference to the add-in so that it can use the class. To simplify code, the add-in will need a `using` statement (or an `Imports` statement in Visual Basic) that points to the new project:

```
using CodeGenerationUtilities;
```

My code-generation solution also needs a class-level variable that can hold a reference to the utility:

```
Utilities util;
```

In my add-in's constructor, I create a reference to the `CodeGenerationUtilities` object:

```
util = new Utilities(applicationObject,
                        "ConnectionStringGenerator");
```

With that work done, I can use the `WriteOutput` method to send messages to the developer running the code-generation solution. As an example, the following call adds a message to the Task List:

```
util.WriteOutput("Unable to create Connection Manager",
                    GenerationLevel.severe);
```

Supporting Customization

As I noted at the start of this case study, part of this solution includes giving the developer the ability to modify the connection string retrieved from the configuration file. There are at least two ways to provide this option:

- Add a second partial class (the "customization" class) where the developer can add code to modify the connection string. The class holding the generated code calls methods in this second class before returning the connection string to the calling application. The developer can add code inside these methods to modify the connection string.
- Allow the developer to inherit from our generated class. Again, our generated code would call methods that allow the developer to modify the connection string before the string is returned. However, with this design, the developer would override those methods to add his or her own code.

For this case study, I use the first strategy. As part of that strategy, I add a second file to the project (named ConnectionManager.Customization) where developers can put their custom code.

I also allow the developer to turn customization on and off so that when the developer doesn't need to modify the connection string through Visual Studio's Options dialog, the customization support (e.g., the ConnectionManager.Customization file) won't be generated.

Customizable Code

When customization is turned on, the property generated calls a method and passes it the connection string. The property then returns whatever is passed back by the method. A typical example of the generated code with customization support looks like this:

```
public static string Northwind
{
  get
  {
   return NorthwindCustomization(
        System.Web.Configuration.WebConfigurationManager.
          ConnectionStrings["Northwind"].ConnectionString);
  }
}
```

The corresponding customization class contains stubs for the customization methods:

```
public static partial class ConnectionManager
{
 public static string NorthwindCustomization(string ConnectionString)
 {
  return ConnectionString;
 }
}
```

Developers can now put any code to modify the connection string in these stubs. To ensure that the developer never loses any code, my code never deletes the customization class. If a customization stub doesn't exist, the code-generation process will add the stub. However, no compile error is raised if a developer renames (or deletes) a connection string that he or she has written customized code for. Unfortunately, the customized code will never be called.

The add-in offers one other customization option. Although the add-in's default implementation is a static/shared class, developers may find that too restrictive when they start adding their custom code. In order to give the developers more options, I also allow them to turn off the static/shared option.

Accepting Input

Rather than expect the developer to specify these options for each generation, I let the developer set the customization options in the Tools | Options dialog. For a complete solution, the options should be stored on a project-by-project basis so the dialog for these choices should be a list of projects showing the choice for each option. However, that would take the focus of this case study into the realm of Windows Form programming and away from creating an effective code-generation implementation, so this example just supports a global setting that applies to all projects.

Defining the Options Dialog

My first step in adding to the Tools | Options dialog is to create a separate project (named ConnectManagerUI) to hold the user control that becomes part of the Tools | Options dialog. Because, even for testing purposes, this project's DLL must go into the Add-Ins library, I create a new class library

project and set the output path on the Tools | Options | Build dialog to
...\Visual Studio *version*\Addins\.

In order to have the user control loaded by Visual Studio, I add the following elements to my add-in project's .Addin files (this code assumes that
the user control will be called ConnectionManagerOptions). The Tools |
Options dialog uses the values in the `Category` and `SubCategory` elements to
create the TreeView on the left side of the dialog that lets the developer
navigate to my user control. I also use the `Category/SubCategory` values in
my add-in's code to retrieve the options the developer sets:

```
<ToolsOptionsPage>
 <Category Name="Code Generation">
  <SubCategory Name="Connection Manager">
   <Assembly>ConnectionManagerUI.dll</Assembly>
    <FullClassName>ConnectionManagerUI.ConnectionManagerOptions
    </FullClassName>
  </SubCategory>
 </Category>
</ToolsOptionsPage>
```

Saving Developer Choices

It's my responsibility to save and retrieve the choices entered by the devel-
oper in the Tools | Options dialog. To support that, I add a class to my
CodeGenerationUtilities project with methods that save and retrieve string
values to and from the Windows registry. That class looks like this:

```
namespace CodeGenerationUtilities
{
 public class Utilities
 {
  public static string GetValue(string Name)
  {
   Microsoft.Win32.RegistryKey key;

   key = Microsoft.Win32.Registry.CurrentUser.OpenSubKey(
              @"SOFTWARE\Microsoft\VisualStudio\9.0", false);
   return key.GetValue(Name, "").ToString();
  }

  public static void SaveValue(string Name, string value)
  {
```

```
Microsoft.Win32.RegistryKey key;

key = Microsoft.Win32.Registry.CurrentUser.OpenSubKey(
                @"SOFTWARE\Microsoft\VisualStudio\9.0", true);
key.SetValue(Name, value,
                Microsoft.Win32.RegistryValueKind.String);

    }
}
```

Option Manager Class

Before creating the user control, I also create a class in the same project as the user control to manage the values entered by the developer. In addition to simplifying the code in the user control, this option manager class is required if I'm going to pass the values saved by the user control to the add-in that generates the code.

The option manager class has one property for each value I allow the developer to set in the user control and uses the SaveValue and GetValue methods in my Utilities class to save data in the Windows registry as strings. The code in the option manager class sets the names that these values will be saved under in the Windows registry. The naming convention that I use is the word "Generate," followed by the name of the code-generation solution, followed by the property name.

This option manager class for this case study has properties for turning customization support on or off (SupportCustomization, which saves its value under the name GenerateConnectionManagerSupportCustomization) and specifying whether the class and property should be static/shared (IsStatic, which saves its value under the name GenerateConnectionManagerIsStatic):

```
namespace ConnectionManagerUI
{
 public class ConnectionStringProperties
 {
  public string SupportCustomization
  {
   get
   {
    return Utilities.GetValue(
        "GenerateConnectionManagerSupportCustomization");
   }
   set
   {
```

```
        Utilities.SaveValue(
            "GenerateConnectionManagerSupportCustomization", value);
      }
    }

  public string IsStatic
  {
   get
   {
    return Utilities.GetValue(
        "GenerateConnectionManagerIsStatic");
   }
   set
   {
    Utilities.SaveValue(
        "GenerateConnectionManagerIsStatic", value);
   }
  }
 }
}
```

Creating the User Control

I'm finally ready to add the user control that will appear in the Tools | Options dialog (see Figure 9-2). The user control has two check boxes, one for each of the two options offered by this add-in: whether a customization file will be generated and whether the generated classes should be static/shared.

I must add two attributes to the user control to have it work well with the Tools | Options (ComVisible and ClassInterface). In addition, the user control must implement the EnvDTE.IDTToolsOptionsPage interface. This code shows the resulting definition for the user control for this case study:

```
namespace ConnectionManagerUI
{
  [System.Runtime.InteropServices.ComVisible(true)]
  [System.Runtime.InteropServices.ClassInterface(
      System.Runtime.InteropServices.ClassInterfaceType.AutoDual)]
public partial class ConnectionManagerOptions: UserControl,
                                       EnvDTE.IDTToolsOptionsPage
  {
```

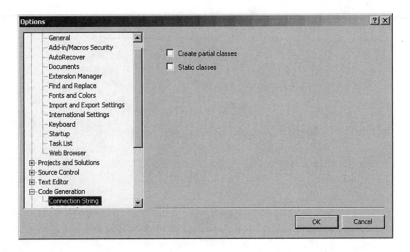

FIGURE 9-2 The user control for the case study allows the developer to turn support for customization on or off and to specify whether the generated class is static/shared.

In the user control, I take advantage of the option manager class that I created earlier to do most of the user control's work. I instantiate that class in my user control's constructor:

```
public ConnectionManagerOptions()
{
 InitializeComponent();
 opts = new ConnectionStringProperties();
}
```

Implementing the User Control Interface

The IDTToolsOptionsPage interface adds several methods to the user control, but I only need to put code in four of them. I add code to the OnAfterCreated event to retrieve the current values for the property and to the OnOk event to save the current values. In these events, I just call the appropriate methods on my option manager class (with a little extra code to initialize the page when the user control is called for the first time):

```
public void OnAfterCreated(EnvDTE.DTE DTEObject)
{
 if (opts.IsStatic == "true"|| opts.IsStatic == "")
 {
```

```
    this.StaticCheckbox.Checked = true;
  }
  else
  {
    this.StaticCheckbox.Checked = false;
  }

  if (opts.SupportCustomization == "true")
  {
  this.CustomizationCheckbox.Checked = true;
  }
  else
  {
    this.CustomizationCheckbox.Checked = false;
  }
}

public void OnOK()
{
  if (this.StaticCheckbox.Checked)
  {
   opts.IsStatic = "true";
  }
  else
  {
   opts.IsStatic = "false";
  }

  if ( this.CustomizationCheckbox.Checked)
  {
   opts.SupportCustomization = "true";
  }
  else
  {
   opts.SupportCustomization = "false";
  }
}
```

Because I intend to pass the values collected in the user control to an
add-in running in Visual Studio, I also implement the interface's
GetProperties method. All that I have to do is to set the PropertiesObject
passed to this routine to an instance of my option manager class:

```
public void GetProperties(ref object PropertiesObject)
{
  PropertiesObject = opts;
}
```

Integrating with the Add-In

With the work on the user control complete, the developer can choose his or her options in the Tools | Options page. I access the developer's choices by retrieving a `Properties` object from the `applicationObject`, specifying the `Category` and `SubCategory` I set in the .add-in file's `ToolsOptionsPage` element. I typically end up using these options throughout my add-in, so I usually declare the `Properties` object at the class level:

```
Properties props;
```

I then retrieve the options in the add-in's constructor. To retrieve the options set through the user control, I pass the `Category` and `SubCategory` I set in the `ProvideOptionPage` attribute on the user control to the `get_Properties` method on the `applicationObject`. (In Visual Basic, you read the `Properties` property.) In the `get_Properties` method, the `SubCategory` value is passed to a parameter called `PageName`. For this case study, the `Category` is "Code Generation" and the `SubCategory` is "Connection Manager":

```
props = applicationObject.get_Properties["Code Generation",
                                "Connection Manager"];
```

To retrieve any particular property, I pass the property name from my data manager object to the `Properties` object's `Item` method. This example, for instance, retrieves my `IsStatic` method from my option manager class and, because the value returned by the property is a string, converts it into a Boolean value:

```
bool IsStatic;

if (props.Item("IsStatic").Value.ToString() == "true")
{
  IsStatic = true;
}
else
{
  IsStatic = false;
}
```

The resulting values can be used to control code generation. For instance, this example uses the IsStatic value to control whether the class is declared as static/shared:

```
if (!IsStatic)
{
  cc.IsShared = true;
}
```

Generating Custom Code

Working with a file that holds code written by the developer requires a different strategy than a file holding only code you generate. In general, it's *never* okay to delete a developer's code, but it is okay to make the code invalid or irrelevant.

As an example, in this case study the developer may add custom code to work with the Northwind property that is tied to the Northwind connection string. If the developer then deletes the connection string named "Northwind" from the configuration file and ConnectionManager is regenerated, my solution will re-create the ConnectionManager.Generation file without the Northwind property.

Without the Northwind property in place, the developer's custom code is orphaned and will never be called—but that's not a problem (at least, it's not *your* problem). Even if removing the generated Northwind property prevents the solution from compiling because of problems with the custom code (not the case with this solution), the problem is—from the developer's point of view—solvable: When the compile fails, the developer will get a message pointing to the offending custom code. The developer can then modify or delete the code.

What would not be a good idea would be to "helpfully" delete the developer's custom code. After all, the developer may intend to move his or her orphaned custom code to another custom routine—if my solution deletes the code, that option is no longer available to the developer.

In the customization file, the general strategy is to first check before adding any custom code to see if it's already present. If the code is present, the solution should leave the code alone; if the custom code isn't present, the solution should generate whatever support code is part of the code-generation solution. If the developer wants to have any support for custom code regenerated, all the developer has to do is delete the relevant custom code. With the custom code gone, the solution will regenerate any necessary support code.

Adding Custom Code

In the case study, the first place where I implement this strategy is in adding the customization file. For the file holding the generated code, the file is always deleted and re-created. For the customization file, on the other hand, if the file is present, the solution just retrieves a reference to it; only if the customization file isn't already present does my solution generate the customization file. This code checks to see if customization is being supported and, if it is, implements that strategy:

```
if (IsCustomized)
{
 pjic = sln.FindProjectItem(@ProjectPath + @"\" +
      codeFolder.Name + @"\ConnectionManager.Customization.cs");
 if (pjic == null)
 {
   if (prj.Kind == "{E24C65DC-7377-472b-9ABA-BC803B73C61A}")
   {
    ItemTemplatePath = sln.GetProjectItemTemplate("Class.zip",
                                                @"Web\CSharp");
   }
   else
   {
    ItemTemplatePath = sln.GetProjectItemTemplate("Class.zip",
                                                "CSharp");
   }
   pjic = codeFolder.ProjectItems.AddFromTemplate(
      ItemTemplatePath, "ConnectionManager.Customization.cs");
 }
}
```

The same process is followed when adding the support stubs inside the customization file: Stubs are only added if they're not already present.

Tying Generation to Events

Rather than use a menu item to trigger code generation, a better solution for this case study is to tie the code generation to events in Visual Studio. The obvious choice for this case study is to check for changes in the configuration file: Whenever the configuration file is closed, for instance, the code could check for the presence of connection strings and regenerate the ConnectionManager. This is the strategy used for generating the code behind the .NET DataSet designer: The code is generated when the designer is closed (and, in Visual Studio 2008 and 2010, when the focus shifts away from the DataSet's visual designer).

However, the developer also needs a way to force the ConnectionManager to be regenerated if only for those situations where the developer wants to make a change and leave the configuration file open. You could leave the menu item in place (or add a button to the ConnectionManager's Tools | Options dialog). However, a better solution is to tie the code generation into the build process.

Integrating with Builds

Integrating with the build process is the easier of the two events to set up, so I look at that option first. The first step is to declare a class-level variable to hold a reference to the events package that references build events. For a build-related event, that variable is declared with the `BuildEvents` data type, as this code does:

```
EnvDTE.BuildEvents BuildE;
```

In order to tie the code-generation property into Visual Studio events, I have to wire up the events when the add-in is loaded by Visual Studio. I have a couple of choices here: I can either use the add-in's constructor (called from the `Connect` method in C# or the `New` method in Visual Basic) or the `OnConnection` method. I use the `OnConnection` method because I can check the `connectMode` parameter passed to the method to ensure that the method is being called in setup mode. Just to be safe, though, I also check that I haven't already set up the event by seeing if my class-level variable is set to null.

This code retrieves the `BuildEvents` package and then ties a method in the connect class (which I've named `BuildE_OnBuildBegin`) to the `OBuildBegin` event:

```
if (connectMode == ext_ConnectMode.ext_cm_UISetup)
{
 if (BuildE == null)
 {
  BuildE = _applicationObject.Events.BuildEvents;
  BuildE.OnBuildBegin += new
      _dispBuildEvents_OnBuildBeginEventHandler(BuildE_OnBuildBegin);
 }
```

In my `OnBuildBegin` method, I need to create my generation class (`DatabaseUtilities`) and call my code-generation method

(GenerateConnectionManager) whenever the project is being rebuilt. To determine whether the project is being rebuilt, I can check the two flags passed into the event handler:

- **BuildScope**—Reports the scope of the build (batch, project, or solution)
- **BuildAction**—Type of build (Clean, Build, Rebuildall, Deploy)

If I created temporary files or folders that I didn't automatically delete as part of the code-generation process, I should remove those when the event is called with BuildAction set to Clean. However, for this solution, the Clean action is the one BuildAction where I don't want to regenerate ConnectionManager:

```
void BuildE_OnBuildBegin(vsBuildScope BuildScope,
                         vsBuildAction BuildAction)
{
 if (BuildAction != vsBuildAction.vsBuildActionClean)
 {
   DatabaseUtiltiies dbu;
   dbu = new DatabaseUtiltiies(_applicationObject,
                              _addInInstance);
   dbu.GenerateConnectionManager();
 }
}
```

Integrating with Documents

To catch the events that fire when the configuration file is opened or closed, I first have to catch the events fired when any document is opened or closed. I add another field (named docMaster) to my class to hold the DocumentEvents package for this "master" document event routine. Eventually, I'm going to need a reference for the event that ties to my configuration file, so I also add a field (named docConfig) to hold that reference:

```
EnvDTE.DocumentEvents docMaster;
EnvDTE.DocumentEvents docConfig;
```

In the OnConnection method, when the method is called in setup mode, I check to see if I've set the event package; if I haven't, I set the reference. Once I've set the reference, I attach a method (which I've called docMaster_DocumentOpened) to the DocumentOpened event. The DocumentOpened event is a filtered event: Because I pass a reference to a document to this

event, the event will only fire when that specific document is opened. For
my "master" event handler, however, I want to catch events for all documents, so I pass a null as part of wiring up the event:

```
if (docMaster == null)
{
 docMaster = (EnvDTE.DocumentEvents)
            _applicationObject.Events.get_DocumentEvents(null);
 docMaster.DocumentOpened +=new
              _dispDocumentEvents_DocumentOpenedEventHandler(
                                    docMaster_DocumentOpened);
}
```

In my docMaster_DocumentOpened event handler, I want to wire up an event
routine that will fire when the configuration file is closed. (This may be just
the initial version of this handler: If I expand this solution, I can add more
code in this handler to check for other documents that I'm interested in and
wire up events for them also.) I first check to see if I've already set an event
for the configuration file by checking the field where I hold the reference
(docConfig). If that field is null, I then check the Document parameter passed to
the event handler to see if the document being opened is either the web.con-
fig or app.config file:

```
void docMaster_DocumentOpened(Document Document)
{
  if (docConfig == null && Document.Name == "app.config")
  {
```

If the document being opened is either of the configuration files, I get
a reference to the DocumentEvents package as I did in setting up the master
event handler. This time, however, I filter the event by passing the Document
object that represents the configuration file. In this case study, I want to
capture the DocumentClosing event so I wire up the DocumentClosing
EventHandler to a routine I've named docConfig_DocumentClosing:

```
 docConfig = (EnvDTE.DocumentEvents)
          _applicationObject.Events.get_DocumentEvents(Document);
 docConfig.DocumentClosing +=new
          _dispDocumentEvents_DocumentClosingEventHandler(
                                docConfig_DocumentClosing);
 }
}
```

In my `docConfig_Closing` event handler, as before, I create my code-generation class and call the method that creates the connection manager. In addition, at the end of the routine, I set the reference for this handler to null:

```
void docConfig_DocumentClosing(Document Doc)
{
 DatabaseUtilities dbu;
 dbu = new DatabaseUtiltiies(_applicationObject, _addInInstance);
 dbu.GenerateConnectionManager();
 docConfig = null;
}
```

Generating a Simple Class

This chapter has demonstrated a complete—though simple—code-generation solution. Principally, this solution hasn't dealt with having multiple config files open at the same time, and I've deliberately restricted the objects I've used to keep the toolkit required for understanding this chapter small. I've also assumed that the generated code will always be in C#. (Although, because the solution generates so little code, extending it to handle Visual Basic—or any other language—would be very simple.) I also haven't spent much time on structuring code—the focus of the project is to concentrate on the code-generation process. The case study in the next chapter goes beyond this solution to handle multiple documents, using a larger toolkit, generating more complex code, and supporting both C# and Visual Basic through the CodeDom.

You can download the code for this case study from my website (www.phvis.com) and www.informit.com.

CHAPTER 10

CASE STUDY: GENERATING VALIDATION CODE

In this chapter:

- Defining the Problem
- Starting the Code-Generation Project
- Wiring Up the Add-In
- Starting the Generation Utility
- Defining a Template
- Generating Code
- Specifying Code with the CodeDom
- Generating Code in the Target Language
- Supporting "Projectless" Websites
- Handling Errors
- Building a Complete Code-Generation Solution

ASP.NET provides a range of validation controls, but noticeable by its absence is a control that validates data by checking it against a value in a table. This case study uses code generation in combination with an ASP.NET validation control to fill that gap. At the end of this chapter, I also use some of the project-specific objects described in Chapter 5, "Supporting Project-Specific Features."

In this case study, I develop an ASP.NET validation control that the developer would use like any other validator: The developer would add it to a WebForm by dragging it from the toolbox onto a WebForm and then configure it by setting properties on the control. However, the code that validates data entered by the user at run time will be generated at design time. The generated code will be kept in a separate file from the rest of the WebForm's code. That code will, however, be in a partial class so that it will be incorporated into the code for the WebForm when the application is built.

In addition to the properties required to support generating the validation code, the control will also have a property (called `SuppressGeneration`) that allows the developer to prevent code from being generated—this will allow the developer to modify the automatically generated code and persist it through subsequent generations.

In this case study, in addition to some of the tools from the first case study, I use four other tools:

- Visual Studio templates
- CodeDom
- CodeEditor
- VSWebSite

Because a project can have multiple .aspx files, this case study shows how to support generating code for multiple files that are open simultaneously. I also use the `UndoContext` to support the developers who want to back out the changes made by this code-generation solution. Finally, this case study will be putting the generated code in a file that could, potentially, include both generated and developer-written code. As a result, when it comes time to insert the code, I need to manage which code I replace and which code I leave in place.

Defining the Problem

To handle checking a value against a field in a table, ASP.NET developers typically use a CustomValidator and write custom code in the CustomValidator's `ServerValidate` event. The `ServerValidate` event is passed two parameters, the second one of which (called `args`) passes the data to be checked in its `Value` property. The developer can implement the event using any code at all but, typically, the code the developer uses tends to look very similar from one `ServerValidate` event to another.

The Dedicated Code Solution

Here's what the generated code might look like—an example of the dedicated code to handle checking an EmployeeId against the Employees table in the Northwind database. As you'll see, the code is relatively straightforward. The first step in checking a value against the EmployeeId in the

Employees table of the Northwind database is to create a `SqlConnection` object. To perform this check from a CustomValidator the developer would create the code in a `ServerValidate` event as in this example:

```
public void CustomValidator1_ServerValidate(
        object sender, WebControls.ServerValidateEventArgs args)
{
 SqlConnection conn;
 conn = new SqlConnection(
        System.Web.Configuration.WebConfigurationManager.
          ConnectionStrings["Northwind"].ConnectionString))
```

The code would then create a parameterized `SqlCommand` object that would count the number of rows with a matching EmployeeId:

```
SqlCommand cmd = conn.CreateCommand();
cmd.CommandText =
  "Select Count(*) From Employees Where EmployeeId = @EmployeeId;";
cmd.Parameters.Add("@EmployeeId", System.Data.SqlDbType.Int);
```

The next step would be to set the value of the parameter in the `SqlCommand` using the EmployeeId passed to the event in the `Value` property of the `args` parameter (if the value isn't an integer, we can automatically assume that it isn't a valid EmployeeId):

```
int result;
if (!int.TryParse(args.Value, out result))
{
 args.IsValid = false;
 return;
}
else
{
 cmd.Parameters[0].Value = result;
}
```

The final step is to execute the command and see how many matching rows are returned—a return value of 0 indicates that the EmployeeId doesn't exist in the table and the value is invalid. The result of the test is passed back to the CustomValidator control through the `IsValid` property of the `args` parameter:

```
conn.Open();
result = Convert.ToInt32(cmd.ExecuteScalar());
```

```
conn.Close();

if (result == 0)
{
 args.IsValid = false;
}
else
{
 args.IsValid = true;
}
```

The Generalized Code Solution

It's possible to create a LookupValidator control with generalized code that would be able to handle this problem. However, generalizing this code would require at least three If or Select...Case statements:

- Selecting the right object type for the connection. Ideally, for Oracle databases the code would use the OraConnection and OraCommand objects.
- Setting the data type on the Parameter object. Not all fields will be integers, for instance.
- If the value being looked up is a string value, the conversion to a string value (and the corresponding test) is not required.

In addition, the Select statement would have to be assembled by concatenating together the table name and the field name with the constant parts of the SQL statement. As I noted in Chapter 1, "Introducing Code Generation," whenever SQL commands are being assembled in code, it's worth investigating whether a code-generation solution could be used to create the correct SQL statement at design time.

The Generated Code Solution

Looking at the dedicated and generalized code solutions, it's obvious that the code varies depending on three values that change from one implementation to another. Those three values are the names of

- The connection string to draw from the connectionStrings element in the Web.config file
- The table
- The field

In addition, the code varies depending on the data type of the field being looked up, which is also known at design time. With all the values known at design time and a SQL statement that must be assembled, this problem is an excellent candidate for a code-generation solution.

Rather than generate a custom LookupValidator for each set of values, this case study uses the CustomValidator as model for implementing a code-generation solution. Like the CustomValidator, the LookupValidator will fire an event that will be handled by code in the page that the validator is used on. Instead of the developer writing the code in the event, however, the code generator will generate the event handler code. Because the generated code is part of the application—rather than being part of the LookupValidator—the developer will be able to review the code and alter it on a control-by-control basis, if necessary. And, because the validator is represented in the .aspx page as an XML-compliant tag, it's easy to parse the control's tag to pull values from it making it easy to extract the input values for the code-generation process.

The code generation will execute whenever an .aspx page is closed (or when the developer clicks the Generate LookupValidator menu choice). The code-generation solution will check the current page for instances of the LookupValidator control and, for every LookupValidator found, will wire up an event routine and generate the code for the event. The code will be driven by property values the developer has set on the LookupValidator either in the Properties window or in Source view.

For this case study, I have the developer provide the data type of the lookup field. An alternative solution would have the code generator use the connection string, table, and field name to retrieve the data type from the database at design time.

The generated code will be placed in a partial class for the WebForm with the LookupValidator. When the application is compiled, the partial class containing the generated event code will be combined with the other code for the WebForm.

One of the features of this solution is that this model can be used as a template for other "code-generated" validators. The LookUpValidator itself just provides a place to hold the input values required by the code-generation process and to tie the generated code into the ASP.NET validation framework. As a result, creating other "code-generated" validators just consists of defining the properties that the validator will accept and generating the code that uses those properties.

The initial version of this solution will only work as described in a web application project and not in a "projectless" web application. In a "projectless" web application, each .aspx file is allowed only one code file; as a result, a partial class file in a separate file will not be integrated with the rest of the code in the page. However, at the end of this chapter, I include a workaround that allows this solution to work in "projectless" web applications.

Creating the Validator

The first step in this solution is to create a LookupValidator that accepts as property values the five values that drive code generation: the connection string name, the table name, the field name, the field's data type, and a flag to turn off code generation. In addition, like the CustomValidator, the LookupValidator must fire an event that passes a parameter (called `args`) with two properties: one called `value` that holds the data to be tested and another called `IsValid` that accepts a Boolean value indicating whether the data being tested is valid.

Creating the validation control is relatively straightforward: You create a new project, from the Web tab select ASP.NET Server Control, and give your project a name (I used "PHVValidators"). Once the project is created, rename the default ServerControl1.cs file to the name you want for your control (I used "LookupValidator") and have it inherit from `BaseValidator`. The `BaseValidator` provides most of the functionality that a validator control needs: a `ControlToValidate` property to tie the validator to another control on the page, an `ErrorMessage` property to set the message to be displayed if the data is invalid, and support for the ASP.NET validation framework. All that needs to be added to the BaseValidator is a test for valid data and any properties required to support the test.

The code at the top of the validator's class can be simplified to what I have here:

```
using System;
using System.ComponentModel;
using System.Web.UI;
using System.Web.UI.WebControls;
namespace PHVValidators
{
  [DefaultProperty("ControlToValidate")]
  [ToolboxData("<{0}:LookupValidator runat=server>
               </{0}:LookupValidator>")]
  public class LookupValidator :
                System.Web.UI.WebControls.BaseValidator
  {
```

Within the class, I need five fields to hold the names of the connection string, the table, the field, the field's data type, and a Boolean field to support the property that allows the developer to suppress code generation.

Following are the declarations for the five fields I need in the LookupValidator. For the data type field, I use the same enumerated data type that the CompareValidator uses for its Type property:

```
string connectionStringName = "";
string tableName = "";
string fieldName = "";
ValidationDataType type = ValidationDataType.Integer;
bool suppressValidation = false;
```

Using the ValidationDataType enumerated value provides the developer using the control with more support than, for instance, defining the field as a string. At design time, in the Properties window, the property that manages my type field will have a drop-down list showing the five values in the ValidationDataType enumeration: String, Integer, Double, Date, and Currency.

The next step is to define the event that the generated code will go in. The delegate for that event will pass a reference to the LookupValidator and a specialized EventArgs object (to be defined shortly):

```
public delegate void ServerValidateHandler(
                Object sender, ServerValidateEventArgs args);
```

With the delegate defined, I can declare an event, named ServerValidate, using the delegate. Because I'm going to generate the code for the LookupValidator's event, I'd prefer that developers didn't use the event themselves. To prevent that, I decorate the event with two attributes that prevent the event from appearing in the Properties Windows (Browsable) and in IntelliSense (EditorBrowsable):

```
[System.ComponentModel.Browsable(false)]
[System.ComponentModel.EditorBrowsable(
                System.ComponentModel.EditorBrowsableState.Never)]
public event ServerValidateHandler ServerValidate;
```

The only method in the BaseValidator class that must be overridden is the EvaluateIsValid method. This method must return False if the value in the control being validated is invalid and True if the value is valid. In the EvaluateIsValid method, I just want to raise the event that will be caught by the generated code and pass the EventArgs parameter to the event. When I create the EventArgs, I pass it the current value from the control that LookupValidator is tied to. (This value is retrieved through the base class's

GetControlValidationValue and ControlToValidate members.) The method should only raise the event if the event has been wired up, as in this example:

```
protected override bool EvaluateIsValid()
{
 if (ServerValidate != null)
 {
  ServerValidateEventArgs args;
  args = new ServerValidateEventArgs(
          this.GetControlValidationValue(this.ControlToValidate));
  ServerValidate(this, args);
  return args.IsValid;
 }
 return true;
}
```

Written this way, the LookupValidator will also check the data even if there is no data in the related control. If you want to restrict the LookupValidator to check the value only if there is data present, the EvaluateIsValid method would look like this:

```
string ValueToTest;
ValueToTest = this.GetControlValidationValue(this.ControlToValidate);
if (ValueToTest.Length > 0)
{
 args = new ServerValidateEventArgs(ValueToTest);
 ServerValidate(this, args);
 return args.IsValid;
}
else
{
 return true;
}
```

Testing for empty controls could be made configurable by adding another property to the LookupValidator that would allow the developer to turn this behavior on and off (the CustomValidator, for instance, has a ValidateEmptyText property that allows the developer to decide if empty controls should be checked).

In order to support the developer setting the field values in the Properties window, I need a property for each field. The properties for TableName and FieldName are similar to the ConnectionStringName property, shown here:

```
[Default("")]
public string ConnectionStringName
{
 get
 {
  return connectionStringName;
 }
 set
 {
  connectionStringName = value;
 }
}
```

The only differences for the Type property are the return value and, as a result, the default value:

```
[Default(ValidationDataType.Integer)]
public ValidationDataType Type
{
 get
 {
  return type;
 }
 set
 {
  type = value;
 }
}
```

For the SuppressGeneration property, I specify a default value of False:

```
[DefaultValue(false)]
public bool SuppressGeneration
{
 get
 {
  return suppressGeneration;
 }
 set
 {
  suppressGeneration = value;
 }
}
```

A number of other enhancements and features could be incorporated into the validator, but this is enough code to enable the solution. Still to be created, however, is the EventArgs object that is passed between the LookupValidator and the event-handling code in the WebForm.

The EventArgs Parameter

In order to communicate between the LookupValidator and the WebForm, the control will pass an object that inherits from System.EventArgs. The object will have two fields to hold the value of the control being tested and to hold the results of testing that value:

```
public class ServerValidateEventArgs : System.EventArgs
{
 string value;
 bool isValid = false;
```

The constructor for the EventArgs object accepts the value to be tested and uses that to set a private field:

```
public ServerValidateEventArgs(string Value)
{
 value = Value;
}
```

The object will also have two properties, supporting the properties of the args parameter passed to the ServerValidate event of the CustomValidator:

- **Value**—This property is set in the LookupValidator and is passed to the generated code application. It is the value held in the control being validated.
- **IsValid**—This property is set in the WebForm to indicate whether the data passed in the Value property is valid. Its initial value will be False.

A read-only property exposes the field that holds the value to be tested (the property is read-only to prevent the application from changing the value):

```
public string Value
{
 get
 {
```

```
    return value;
  }
}
```

The `IsValid` property on the `EventArgs` object will be a read/write property to allow the WebForm to set it and the LookupValidator to read it:

```
public bool IsValid
{
 get
 {
  return isValid;
 }
 set
 {
  isValid = value;
 }
}
```

Creating Other Code-Generated Validators

That's all the code required for the validator. To create other dedicated validators, here's all you would need to do:

- Change the name of the validator.
- Remove the properties used in this case study, except for the `SuppressGeneration` property.
- Add any other properties required by your validator to support code generation.
- Optionally, pass additional data to the event by creating a different `EventArgs` object.

Adding the Validator to the Toolbox

After compiling the validator, you should add it to your Visual Studio toolbox so that you can use it in your ASP.NET project. Here are the steps to add the validator to the toolbox:

1. Open an .aspx page in any ASP.NET project.
2. After displaying the toolbox, right-click in the Validation tab and select Choose Items.

3. In the resulting dialog, click the Browse button and navigate to the DLL holding your validator.
4. Double click the DLL.
5. Close the Choose Toolbox Items dialog.

The validator will appear in the Visual Studio toolbox in the Validation tab. Dragging the validator onto an .aspx page will generate a Register tag at the top of the page, like this one:

```
<%@ Register assembly="PHVValidators"
    namespace="PHVValidators" tagprefix="cc1" %>
```

Further down, near where you dropped the validator on the page, you'll have the tag for the LookupValidator itself:

```
<cc1:LookupValidator ID="LookupValidator1" runat="server">
</cc1:LookupValidator>
```

A developer using the LookUpValidator can now set the properties on the validator using the Properties window. After the developer sets the `ConnectionStringName`, `TableName`, `FieldName`, `ControlToValidate`, and `ErrorMessage` properties, the tag would look like this:

```
<cc1:LookupValidatorControl ID="LookupValidatorControl1" runat="server"
  ConnectionStringName="Northwind"
  ControlToValidate="TextBox1"
  ErrorMessage="Employee Id not valid"
  FieldName="EmployeeId"
  TableName="Employees">
</cc1:LookupValidatorControl>
```

The next step is to create the add-in that will recognize when the validator is added to a page and generate the code for the event raised by the validator, based on the values in the control's properties.

Starting the Code-Generation Project

With the validator created and added to the Visual Studio toolbox, it's time to start working on the code generator's add-in. The first step is to create a Visual Studio add-in from the Extensibility section in the Other Project

Types tab. After working through the wizard's pages (as described in Chapter 2, "Integrating with Visual Studio," and Chapter 9, "Case Study: Generating a Connection String Manager"), only three steps are required to finish configuring the project.

First, in Project Properties, set the assembly name to match your project name. Make the same change to the `<Assembly>` tags in your two .addin files.

Second, in the Build Events tab, this code should be added to the Pre-build Event Command Line text box (the last two lines in this code example must be on a single line):

```
if exist "$(TargetPath).locked" del "$(TargetPath).locked"
if exist "$(TargetPath)" if not exist "$(TargetPath).locked"
      move "$(TargetPath)" "$(TargetPath).locked"
```

Finally, you need to add to your Code Generation projection references to `System.XML`, `System.Web`, and the DLL holding your LookupValidator.

The next task is to modify the code in the Connect.cs file in the project to trigger code generation. I support two triggers: a menu item that the developer can use to generate the code on demand and a Visual Studio event to generate the code automatically when an .aspx page is closed in the Visual Studio editor. (See Chapter 2 for more information on creating an add-in.)

Wiring Up the Add-In

Even when I have a code-generation solution that will be run automatically from an event, I prefer to also have a menu choice that will run the utility. When testing and debugging my code-generation solution, I initially test by using the menu choice and only at the end of the development phase wire up the code-generation methods to an event. Because I typically have multiple code-generation solutions, I create a menu header on the Tools menu called "Code Generation" and attach the methods for specific code-generation solutions to the submenus on that menu header.

In this case study, supplying a button to run code generation also provides better support for the developer. I'm only going to wire up my code-generation solution to the `Closing` event for .aspx files. Providing a menu choice lets developers generate code without having to close the file, just by clicking the menu choice.

Creating a Submenu

The first step in adding submenus to a menu header is to check to see if the menu header is present (the menu header may have been added by another one of my code generation solutions). This code, in OnConnection event of the Connect.cs class, checks to see if the menu header already exists on the menu held in the cb variable. (See the section "Creating the Menu" in Chapter 9 for the code to find the Tools menu.) If the item is not found, the code creates the header as a CommandBarPopup and adds it to the menu:

```
try
{
 cbp = (CommandBarPopup)cb.Controls["Code Generation"];
}
catch
{
 cbp = (CommandBarPopup)cb.Controls.Add(MsoControlType.msoControlPopup,

                                        System.Type.Missing,

                                        System.Type.Missing,

                                        System.Type.Missing,

                                        System.Type.Missing);
 cbp.Caption = "Code Generation";
}
```

The next step is to create a NamedCommand that will trigger the code-generation utility. As shown in Chapter 2, I first set some values in variables and then use them when creating the NamedCommand:

```
string menuName = "Tools";
string menuItemName = "lkupvdGentr";
string menuItemCaption = "Generate LookupValidator";
string menuToolTip =
        "Create a class for integrating with an ASP.NET validator";
```

Because of the values I've set in the variables, the code that I use to create my NamedCommand is the same in all my add-ins. I first check to see if the NamedCommand already exists and, if it does not, create it:

```
Command NamedCommand = null;
try
{
 NamedCommand = _applicationObject.Commands.Item(
                    _addInInstance.ProgID + menuItemName, 1);
}
catch
{
 try
 {
  NamedCommand = cmds.AddNamedCommand2(_addInInstance,
                                menuItemName, menuItemCaption,
   menuToolTip,
                                true, 50, ref contextGUIDS,
                    (int)vsCommandStatus.vsCommandStatusSupported +
                    (int)vsCommandStatus.vsCommandStatusEnabled,
                    (int)vsCommandStyle.vsCommandStylePictAndText,
                    vsCommandControlType.vsCommandControlTypeButton);
 }
 catch { }
```

With the `NamedCommand` created, I check to see if the corresponding menu item is already present and, if not, attach it to the menu header created earlier and held in the `cbp` variable:

```
try
{
 CommandBarControl cbc = cbp.Controls[menuItemCaption];
}
catch
{
 NamedCommand.AddControl(cbp.CommandBar, 1);
}
```

The final step is to attach some code to the submenu. When the submenu is clicked, the `Exec` method in the Connect.cs file is called, so that method should contain the code to check which menu item was clicked, create my code-generation utility (passing the DTE2 and AddIn objects), and call the method that generates the code. This code takes care of that and sets the `handled` parameter passed to the `Exec` method:

```
if (executeOption == vsCommandExecOption.vsCommandExecOptionDoDefault)
{
 if (commandName == _addInInstance.ProgID + "." + menuItemName)
 {
  WebFormUtilities wfu;
  wfu = new WebFormUtilities(_applicationObject, _addInInstance);
  wfu.GenerateValidator();
  handled = true;
  return;
 }
}
```

To run this code, you need to add a class called WebFormUtilities to your add-in project with a method called GenerateValidator. The section "Starting the Code-Generation Utility" later in this chapter covers this. Before looking at that code, however, I finish the changes required in the Connect.cs file.

Handling Multiple Documents in Events

Although I wouldn't tie code generation to an event until I had the utility working, I cover the code that wires up the events here because it also goes in the Connect.cs file. This code is more complex than the version in the first case study because, although a project can have only one configuration file, a single project could have multiple .aspx files open. In order to support tracking events for multiple files open in multiple projects, I have to hold onto the objects related to the events for each document. To support that, I use two separate Dictionary objects: one for the DocumentEvents object for each document and one for each event handler created for each object.

The first step is to catch the event fired when a solution is open. This code goes in the OnConnection method of the Connect.cs file. (Wiring up Visual Studio events is covered in detail in Chapter 2.)

```
if (slnE == null)
{
 slnE = _applicationObject.Events.SolutionEvents;
 slnE.Opened +=
     new _dispSolutionEvents_OpenedEventHandler(slnE_Opened);
}
```

I use the Solution object's Opened event to wire up an event to execute when any document is opened. The code creates the DocumentEvents object and then wires up a method named docMaster_DocumentOpened to the object's DocumentOpened event. I pass a null when retrieving the DocumentEvents object so that the docMaster_DocumentOpened event will be called when any document is opened:

```
EnvDTE.DocumentEvents docMaster;
void slnE_Opened()
{
 docMaster = _applicationObject.Events.get_DocumentEvents(null);
 docMaster.DocumentOpened +=
    new _dispDocumentEvents_DocumentOpenedEventHandler(
                                docMaster_DocumentOpened);
}
```

In my docMaster_DocumentOpened event I check to see what kind of file the developer is working on and wire up any additional events to that file. Because I'm only interested in WebForms, I check to see if the file that's just been opened is an .aspx file. If it is, because I generate code when the file is closed, I get the DocumentEvents object for the Document. To support having multiple documents open at the same time, I add the Document and the associated DocumentEvents to a generic Dictionary of Documents and DocumentEvents. I also check that Dictionary object at the start of the routine to retrieve the DocumentEvents object if it's already been created (if I don't find the Document in the Dictionary, I create it):

```
System.Collections.Generic.Dictionary<Document,
  _dispDocumentEvents_DocumentClosingEventHandler>
 docEventDict =
        new System.Collections.Generic.Dictionary<Document,
               _dispDocumentEvents_DocumentClosingEventHandler>();

EnvDTE.DocumentEvents docMaster;

void docMaster_DocumentOpened(Document Doc)
{
 _dispDocumentEvents_DocumentClosingEventHandler docEvent = null;

 EnvDTE.DocumentEvents docEvents = null;
 if (Doc.Name.EndsWith(".aspx"))
 {
```

```
if (!docEventsDict.TryGetValue(Doc, out docEvents))
{
  docEvents = (EnvDTE.DocumentEvents)
      _applicationObject.Events.get_DocumentEvents(Doc);
  docEventsDict.Add(Doc, docEvents);
}
```

I next create a `DocumentClosingEventHandler` and wire it to a method called `docWebForm_DocumentClosing`:

```
docEvent = new _dispDocumentEvents_DocumentClosingEventHandler(
                        docWebForm_DocumentClosing);
```

Finally, I wire up the `DocumentClosingEventHandler` to the `DocumentEvents` object for the `Document`. I also put the handler in a `Dictionary` with the `Document`:

```
if (docEvent != null)
{
  docEvents.DocumentClosing += docEvent;
  docEventDict.Add(Doc, docEvent);
}
```

In the `docWebForm_DocumentClosing` method, I disconnect the events for the document just closed and call my code-generation method. First, I retrieve the `DocumentEvents` object from the `Dictionary` using the `Document` object passed to the closing event:

```
void docWebForm_DocumentClosing(Document Doc)
{
    WebFormUtilities wfu;
    DocumentEvents docEvents;
    _dispDocumentEvents_DocumentClosingEventHandler docEvent;
    if (docEventsDict.TryGetValue(Doc, out docEvents))
    {
```

I then retrieve the `DocumentClosing` object from the second `Dictionary`, again using the `Document` object passed to the event. With both of those objects retrieved, I can disconnect the event and remove the `Document` from the list:

```
if (docEventDict.TryGetValue(Doc, out docEvent))
{
```

```
docEvents.DocumentClosing -= docEvent;
docEventDict.Remove(Doc);
```

With the housekeeping taken care of, I create the object that holds my code-generation code, passing a reference to the DTE2 object and the AddIn object. I then call the method that generates the code, passing the Document object:

```
wfu = new WebFormUtilities(_applicationObject, _addInInstance);
wfu.GenerateValidator(Doc);
```

By storing the event-related objects in dictionaries, the add-in can support multiple open documents, even if those documents are in separate projects.

Starting the Generation Utility

With the add-in wired up to Visual Studio's menu and event system, I can start writing the code that manages the code-generation process.

Responding to the Add-In

For this case study, the add-in expects to call a method named GenerateValidator on a class library project called WebFormUtilities. The first step in creating the code-generation portion of this solution, therefore, is to provide a minimal implementation of the method so that the add-in code can be tested.

The add-in expects the class's constructor to accept two objects: one of type DTE2 and one of AddIn. In the constructor, I move the values passed to the constructor into fields in the class. In the constructor, I also initialize an instance of my CodeGenerationUtilities class (described in Chapter 9). The add-in can call two versions of the GenerateValidator method: one that accepts no parameters (called from the menu) and one that accepts a Document (called from the event code). A minimal implementation of the class looks like this (all but the last three using statements will be added for you—the final using statement refers to the Namespace for my LookupValidator control):

```
using CodeGenerationUtilities;
using System.Xml;
using System;
```

```csharp
using System.Collections.Generic;
using System.Text;
using System.Data;
using EnvDTE;
using EnvDTE80;
using System.CodeDom;
using System.CodeDom.Compiler;
using PHVValidators;

namespace LookupValidatorGenerator
{
 class WebFormUtilities
 {
  readonly DTE2 applicationObject;
  readonly AddIn addInInstance;
  readonly CodeGenerationUtilities.Utilities cgu;

  string ProjectLanguage;
  string FileType;
  Project prj;

  public  WebFormUtilities(DTE2 ApplicationObject,
                          AddIn AddInInstance,
                          ProjectItem Pji)
  {
   applicationObject = ApplicationObject;
   addInInstance = AddInInstance;
   pji = Pji;

   cgu = new Utilities(applicationObject, "Lookup Validator");
  }

  public void GenerateValidator()
  {

  }

  public void GenerateValidator(Document Doc)
  {

  }
 }
}
```

At this point, I would want to test my code to make sure I've successfully wired it into Visual Studio. The easiest way to do that is to write a short message to Visual Studio's status bar in the `GenerateValidator` methods using the `WriteOutput` method of my `Utilities` object:

```
cgu.WriteOutput("Running successfully", GenerationLevel.Information);
```

I can now press F5 in Visual Studio, navigate to my Code Generation menu, and select my Generate LookupValidator menu choice. If I've done everything right, "Running successfully" will appear in Visual Studio's status bar. If I've added the event-driven code, I should get the same message if I open an .aspx file and then close it.

Two of the three components of this case study are in place: the add-in and the base code generation class. The third component is the template for the class that will hold the generated code.

Defining a Template

In this case study, I reduce the amount of code required in my code-generation methods by using a Visual Studio template. The template will ensure that I have the following:

- A `Namespace` and `Class` (with their names set correctly—or as close as I can get to being set correctly)
- All the necessary `using` statements added
- All required references added to the project

I begin creating the template by creating a skeleton class in a test web application project. A typical skeleton class would look like this (I would give the file the name LookupTest.Generation.cs):

```
using System;
using System.Collections.Generic;
using System.Web;
using System.Data;
using System.Data.SqlClient;

namespace LookupTest
{
  public partial class WebFormTest : System.Web.UI.Page
```

```
    {

    }
}
```

Once the skeleton class is created, from the File menu in Visual Studio 2008/2010, I select Export Template and work through these pages in the wizard:

1. Choose Item Type. Select Item Template and the project containing the sample solution.
2. Select Item to Export. Select my skeleton class file.
3. Select Item References. Check off the references that the sample solution requires (in this case study, those are `System`, `System.Data`, and `System.Web`).
4. Select Template Options. Enter a name for the template (I used "LookupValidatorBase") and a description (I used "The base for generating code to handle the LookupValidator's event in a Web Application Project").

In Visual Studio 2005, you must create a .zip file containing the skeleton class file, a .vstemplate file using the template provided in Chapter 8, "Other Tools: Templates, Attributes, and Custom Tools," and an .ico file.

In Visual Studio 2008 and 2010, when the wizard finishes running, the ZIP file will be placed in the My Exported Templates folder and an Explorer window will open to show the folder. In Visual Studio 2005, you should place the ZIP file in the *documents*\Visual Studio 2005\Templates\ItemTemplates folder.

Both the skeleton class and the .vstemplate file need some customization. In the skeleton file you should make these two changes:

- Remove the namespace and put in the replaceable parameter `$rootnamespace$`.
- Remove the class name and put in one of the replaceable parameters `$safeitemname$` or `$fileinputname$`—I've found `$fileinputname$` to be more reliable.

The resulting code file in the template would look something like this:

```
using System;
using System.Collections.Generic;
```

```
using System.Web;
using System.Data;
using System.Data.SqlClient;

namespace $rootnamespace$
{
  public partial class $fileinputname$ : System.Web.UI.Page
  {

  }
}
```

In the .vstemplate file, in the `ProjectItem` tag, you should set these three attributes:

- **TargetFileName**—Use one of the replaceable filenames plus an extension that identifies the file as containing generated code (e.g., `$safeitename$.Generation.cs` or `$fileinputname$.Generation.cs`).
- **OpenInEditor**—Set this attribute to False to prevent the file from being shown to the developer automatically after it's added.
- **ReplaceParameters**—Set this attribute to True.

The name inside the `ProjectItem` element must match the name of your skeleton class. A typical `ProjectItem` tag would look like this:

```
<ProjectItem
       SubType="ASPXCodeBehind"
       TargetFileName="$fileinputname$.Generation.cs"
       OpenInEditor="false"
       ReplaceParameters="true">LookupTest.Generation.cs</ProjectItem>
```

If you're working in Visual Studio 2008 or 2010, after making your changes in the My Exported Templates folder, you'll need to copy the ZIP file to the *documents\Visual Studio folder*\Templates\ItemTemplates folder.

After creating your template, you should test it by adding the template from the Project menu's Add New Item menu. Your templates will appear at the bottom of the Add New Items dialog in the My Templates section. Adding the example I showed earlier to MyProject, using the name _Default for the file, would result in a file called _Default.Generation.cs being added to the project and containing this code:

```
using System;
using System.Collections.Generic;
```

```
using System.Web;
using System.Data;
using System.Data.SqlClient;

namespace MyProject
{
 public partial class _Default
 {

 }
}
```

You can now confirm that your application will compile when a copy of your template has been added to it.

Generating Code

The code-generation process consists of five steps:

1. Extracting project information. For this case study, I need to determine what kind of project I'm running in and what language should be used for the generated code.
2. Checking conditions. Does code need to be generated? For this case, this means checking to see if the file contains any LookupValidator controls.
3. Generating the code.
4. Creating the necessary folders and files to hold the code.
5. Adding the code to the file, taking into account that some code in the file may have been added by the developer.

Starting the Process

There are two versions of the method that generates the code:

- A version that is called from the menu and accepts no parameters
- A version called from the `DocumentClosing` event for an .aspx file and accepts the `ProjectItem` that represents the .aspx file to be processed

For the version called from the menu, I must decide which file to generate code for. There are several options available (process all .aspx files in the project, process just the file currently selected in Solution Explorer, etc.). For this case study, I'm going to generate code for the file currently open in the editor, provided it's an .aspx file. This code retrieves the Document currently open in the editor, provided it's an .aspx file, and passes it to the version of the GenerateValidator method that expects a Document:

```
public void GenerateValidator()
{
  if (applicationObject.ActiveWindow.Document != null &&
      applicationObject.ActiveWindow.Document.Name.EndsWith(".aspx"))
  {
    GenerateValidator(
             applicationObject.ActiveWindow.ProjectIem.Document);
  }
}
```

In the event that is to be passed the Document object, I check to see if the Document is open in a Window. If the Document isn't open (and it probably isn't), I must open it in a Window in order to access it through the TextDocument object. If I do open the Document, I track that information in a variable called isNewWindow:

```
public void GenerateValidator(Document Doc)
{
  bool isNewWindow = false;
  Document doc;
  if (Document.Windows.Count > 0)
  {
    doc = pji.Document.Windows.Item(1).Document;
  }
  else
  {
    isNewWindow = true;
    Window win = pji.Open(Constants.vsViewKindTextView);
    doc = win.Document;
  }
```

Now that the Document to be processed has been determined, I can also extract information about the related Project to determine the language and file type to use when generating code. I store that information in a structure of my own called `ProjectInfo`, declared at the class level:

```
public struct ProjectInfo
{
   public Project Project;
   public string LanguageType;
   public string FileType;
}
```

To retrieve that information, I have a method called `SetProjectInformation` that, when passed a `Document` object, returns an instance of my `ProjectInfo` structure (`SetProjectInformation` is described later in this chapter in the section "Utility Methods"):

```
ProjectInfo pi = SetProjectInformation(Doc)
```

Looking ahead to when the code-generation process is complete, I need to consider how I want to finish processing. If I opened the document in a new `Window` (recorded in my variable `isNewWindow`), I close the `Window` before exiting the method, saving any changes. If the save fails, I write a message to the Visual Studio user interface using my `CodeGenerationUtilities` class:

```
if (isNewWindow)
{
   doc.Windows.Item(1).Close(vsSaveChanges.vsSaveChangesYes);
   if (!doc.Saved)
   {
    cgu.WriteOutput("Unable to save changes", GenerationLevel.severe);
   }
}
```

Managing the Code-Generation Process

The next step in the process is checking that code needs to be generated. That breaks down into two steps:

- Retrieving the `TextDocument` associated with the file.
- Checking the contents of the `TextDocument` to see if there is a tag for the LookupValidator control. If there is, I check that all the necessary values are present and that the tag's `SuppressGeneration` attribute, if present, is set to False.

I now convert the `Document` into a `TextDocument` and check to see if any `LookupValidator`s exist in the document. To check for the existence of a `LookupValidator` tag, I create an `EditPoint` object positioned at the start of the `TextDocument` and then use the `EditPoint`'s `FindPattern` method to see if any matching text exists. (The `EditPoint` object is covered in detail in Chapter 4, "Modifying Code in the Editor.")

```
TextDocument td = (TextDocument)
              applicationObject.ActiveDocument.Object("TextDocument");

EditPoint edStart = td.StartPoint.CreateEditPoint();
EditPoint edFound = null;
TextRanges txts = null;
if (edStart.FindPattern(":LookupValidator", (int)
    vsFindOptions.vsFindOptionsFromStart, ref edFound, ref txts))
{
```

If a `LookupValidator` tag does exist in the document, I can move on to generating code and inserting it into a file. First, I call the method that retrieves the `Project` for the `ProjectItem`, the project's language, and the file extension to use for my generated code file. I keep that information in a structure called `ProjectInfo`. I then call the method that generates the code, passing the `TextDocument` containing the `LookupValidator` tags and the `ProjectInfo` structure. This method may not return any code: The `LookupValidator`s may be missing values or have their `SuppressGeneration` attribute set to False.

If that method does successfully generate code, I then set the name for the file that will hold the generated code. With that name in hand, I call a method that adds the folder and the file that will hold the generated code, passing the `ProjectInfo` structure, the name of the template to use, and the name of the file to create. With all the infrastructure in place, I finally call the method that puts the code into the file:

```
string code = ProcessValidators(td, pi);
if (code != "")
{
  string FileName = doc.Name.Substring(0,doc.Name.IndexOf("."))
                    + "generation" + pi.FileType;
  ProjectItem CodeFile = AddFolderAndFile(pi,
            "LookupValidatorBase.zip", FileName);
  AddCode(code, CodeFile);
}
```

Utility Methods

This solution uses two helper methods. The first is the `SetProjectInformation` method described earlier that returns an instance of my `ProjectInfo` structure with the language and file type to use when generating code. The second helper function adds the file that the generated code will be put into.

Determining Project Information

For most project types, I can retrieve the related `Project` object through the `Document` object's `ProjectItem` property. However, in a "projectless" website, the `Document` has no `ProjectItem` associated with it. So this code first attempts to retrieve the `ProjectItem` for the `Document` inside a `Try...Catch` block. If that succeeds, the code uses the `ProjectItem` to retrieve the `Project` object. If that attempt fails, the code then iterates through all the `Project`s in the `Solution` until it finds a `Project` with a location that matches the path for the `Document`:

```
private ProjectInfo SetProjectInformation(Doc)
{
  ProjectInfo pi = new ProjectInfo();
  try
  {
    pi.Project = Doc.ProjectItem.ContainingProject;
  }
  catch
  {
    foreach (Project proj in applicationObject.Solution.Projects)
    {
      if (System.IO.Path.GetDirectoryName(Doc.FullName) ==
            System.IO.Path.GetDirectoryName(proj.FullName))
      {
        pi.Project = proj;
        break;
      }
    }
  }
  return pi;
}
```

Now that the `Project` for the object has been retrieved, I can use the GUID stored in the `Project`'s `Kind` property to determine the correct language and file type to use. For a website, the code uses the `CurrentWebsiteLanguage` entry from the `Project` object's `Properties` collection to determine language and file type. I store that information in the `ProjectInfo` structure also:

```
switch (pi.Project.Kind)
{
  case "{F184B08F-C81C-45F6-A57F-5ABD9991F28F}":
    pi.ProjectLanguage = "VisualBasic";
    pi.FileType = ".vb";
    break;
  case "{FAE04EC0-301F-11D3-BF4B-00C04F79EFBC}":
    pi.ProjectLanguage = "CSharp";
    pi.FileType = ".cs";
    break;
  case "{E24C65DC-7377-472b-9ABA-BC803B73C61A}":
    switch (pi.Project.Properties.Item(
            "CurrentWebsiteLanguage").Value.ToString())
    {
      case "Visual C#":
        pi.ProjectLanguage = "CSharp";
        pi.FileType = ".cs";
        break;
      case "Visual Basic":
        pi.ProjectLanguage = "VisualBasic";
        pi.FileType = ".vb";
        break;
    }
    break;
}
```

This process isn't foolproof: For a "projectless" website, each page can be in a different language. If you intend to support sites with multiple languages, you may need to generate code based on the current file's language rather than the project's language.

Adding the Code-Generation File

The method for adding the folder and file doesn't handle "projectless" websites because the workaround I provide at the end of the chapter doesn't require adding a new folder or file. The pattern for adding the folder in standard projects is simple: The code attempts to add the folder and discards the error if the folder already exists. Regardless of whether the folder was already present or the code created it, the method then finds the ProjectItem that represents the folder:

```
public ProjectItem AddFolderAndFile(ProjectInfo pi,
        string TemplateName, string FileName)
{
```

```
ProjectItems pjis = pi.Project.ProjectItems;

cgu.WriteOutput("Adding code folder", GenerationLevel.information);
try
{
 pjis.AddFolder("Generated Code",
                Constants.vsProjectItemKindPhysicalFolder);
}
catch { };
ProjectItem CodeFolder = pjis.Item("Generated Code");
```

The next part of the method returns a reference to the file that the code will be added to. The code first assumes that the file exists and attempts to return it. If that fails, the code retrieves the template to be used, using the name passed into the method. The code then adds the file using the AddFromTemplate method on the code-generation folder's ProjectItems collection. The AddFromTemplate method is passed the filename and language type from the ProjectInfo structure. After the file is added, the method finds the added file and returns it (when adding a custom template, the AddFromTemplate method does not return a reference to the new class):

```
cgu.WriteOutput("Adding code file", GenerationLevel.information);
try
{
 return CodeFolder.ProjectItems.Item(FileName + ".generation" +
                                     pi.FileType);
}
catch
{
 string ItemTemplatePath = ((Solution2)applicationObject.Solution).
     GetProjectItemTemplate(TemplateName, pi.ProjectLanguage);
 CodeFolder.ProjectItems.AddFromTemplate(ItemTemplatePath, FileName);
 return CodeFolder.ProjectItems.Item(FileName + ".generation" +
                                     pi.FileType);
}
}
```

You may have noticed that these methods won't change from one code-generation project to another. In practice, I keep this method (and the method for setting the ProjectInfo structure) in the CodeGenerationUtilities project I described in Chapter 9.

Processing the Validators

At this point, I can start processing all the validators in the `TextDocument`. It would be convenient to load the whole page as an XML document and process it. Unfortunately, an .aspx file (even one that's XHTML compliant) is only "mostly" XML compliant. The various ASP.NET directives at the top of the file defeat any XML processor, for instance. That doesn't mean I have to abandon using XML—it just means that a hybrid approach that combines XML and the code editor objects is required. (The code editor objects are discussed in Chapter 4.)

My first step is to create an `EditPoint` at the start of the document and use that `EditPoint`'s `FindPattern` method to find the first `LookupValidator` tag in the document. Because there may be multiple `LookupValidator` tags in the `TextDocument`, I do this search as part of a loop. Once the first `LookupValidator` tag is found, the `edStart` `EditPoint` will be positioned on the *L* of the tag name and `edEndFound` will be positioned on the *r* at the end of the tag name:

```
string ProcessValidators(TextDocument td)
{
  EditPoint edStart = td.StartPoint.CreateEditPoint();
  StringBuilder code = new StringBuilder();
  EditPoint edEndFound = null;
  TextRanges txts = null;
  while (edStart.FindPattern("LookupValidator", (int)
         vsFindOptions.vsFindOptionsNone, ref edEndFound, ref txts))
  {
```

To retrieve the whole tag, I need to position an `EditPoint` on the ">" at the end of the tag—another call to `FindPattern`, searching for ">" will do that. With an `EditPoint` positioned at the start of the tag name and an `EditPoint` positioned on the tag's closing ">," I can extract the tag's text using the `GetText` method of the starting `EditPoint`, passing it the `EditPoint` that marks the end of the tag. By wrapping this text fragment between the "<" character and a valid `LookupValidator` closing tag, I turn the text into a valid XML document. The result looks like this:

```
<LookupValidator ID=\"LookupValidator1\" runat=\"server\" \r\n ...>
</LookupValidator>
```

Here is the code that creates that XML document:

```
EditPoint edElementEnd = null;
edEndFound.FindPattern(">", (int)
        vsFindOptions.vsFindOptionsNone, ref edElementEnd, ref txts);
string element = "<" + edStart.GetText(edElementEnd) +
                "</LookupValidator>";
```

I can now load this document into an XmlDocument object, making it easy to parse out the parameters I need. The first attribute I want to check is the SuppressGeneration attribute. If it's absent or set to False, I can go on and retrieve the values I want: ID, ConnectionStringName, TableName, and FieldName. Because I can only be sure that the ID attribute exists, I have to check each attribute to ensure it's not null before retrieving it. Because the Type attribute has a default value of Integer, if the Type attribute is not present, I assume a value of Integer:

```
XmlDocument xdoc = new XmlDocument();
xdoc.LoadXml(element);
XmlNode nd = xdoc.ChildNodes[0];
if (nd.Attributes["SuppressGeneration"] == null ||
    nd.Attributes["SuppressGeneration"].Value == "false")
{
 string Id = nd.Attributes["ID"].Value;
 string ConnectionName = "";
 string TableName = "";
 string FieldName = "";
 string DType = "";
 if (nd.Attributes["ConnectionStringName"] != null)
 {
  ConnectionName = nd.Attributes["ConnectionStringName"].Value;
 }
 if (nd.Attributes["TableName"] != null)
 {
  TableName = nd.Attributes["TableName"].Value;
 }
 if (nd.Attributes["FieldName"] != null)
 {
  FieldName = nd.Attributes["FieldName"].Value;
 }
 if (nd.Attributes["Type"] != null)
 {
  DType = nd.Attributes["Type"].Value;
 }
```

```
else
{
  DType = "Integer";
}
```

If all the values are present, I can go on to generate the event code—beginning with the event's name. If the name of the event handler has already been assigned, I can retrieve it from the onServerValidate attribute; if that attribute isn't present, I can create the event name and assemble a complete attribute. Once I've assembled the attribute, I insert it before the last character in the tag using the ending EditPoint's Insert method:

```
if (ConnectionName != "" && TableName != "" &&
    FieldName != "" && DType != "")
{
  string EventName;
  if (nd.Attributes["onServerValidate"] == null)
  {
    edElementEnd.CharLeft(1);
    string eventAttribute;
    EventName = Id + "_ServerValidate";
    eventAttribute = "onServerValidate=\"" + EventName + " \"";
    edElementEnd.Insert(" " + eventAttribute + " ");
  }
  else
  {
    string EventName = nd.Attributes["onServerValidate"].Value;
  }
```

With all the parameters retrieved or created, I can call the method that will generate the code. I append the resulting string to the StringBuilder created at the start of this method that will hold all the code generated for this TextDocument:

```
code.Append(GenerateCode(EventName, Id, ConnectionName, TableName,
                         FieldName, DType, pi));
```

Because there might be multiple instances of my LookupValidator tag in a TextDocument, I reposition the EditPoint that I searched from at the start of this loop to the last ">" in the current tag's closing element. If there are no more tags, the loop ends and I return the string of generated code:

```
edElementEnd.FindPattern("LookupValidator>", (int)
    vsFindOptions.vsFindOptionsNone, ref edStart, ref txts);
}
return code.ToString();
```

Inserting Code

For now, I skip over the method that generates the code to look at inserting the code into the file. For this case study, in addition to the adding code, I need to perform two other tasks:

- When the template was added to the project, the Namespace was automatically updated in the resulting code file. However, because the file is kept in a subfolder, the subfolder's name will have been included in the namespace (e.g., MyProject.Generated_Code). The folder name must be removed from the Namespace to ensure that this code file will be combined with the WebForm's code.
- Normally, I would simply delete all the code from any previous code generation and then insert the new code. However, if the developer has modified some code from a previous generation and suppressed generation for that LookupControl, I don't want to delete that code.

Dealing with both problems is relatively straightforward. After opening the file, I loop through all the code elements. When I find the Namespace, I reset it to the part of the name before the first period:

```
void AddCode(string code, ProjectItem CodeFile)
{
  FileCodeModel fcm = CodeFile.FileCodeModel;
  foreach (CodeElement ce in fcm.CodeElements)
  {
    if (ce.Kind == vsCMElement.vsCMElementNamespace)
    {
      if (ce.Name.IndexOf(".") > 0)
      {
        ce.Name = ce.Name.Substring(0, ce.Name.IndexOf("."));
      }
```

Now that I've found the Namespace, I know that, in my template, the first element inside the Namespace is the Class. I retrieve the Class and then loop through all of the `Class` members, checking each method to see if I've generated code for it. If I have, it means that code generation was not suppressed for that LookupValidator, and I should delete the member in order to replace it with the generated code:

```
CodeClass cc = (CodeClass) ce.Children.Item(1);
foreach (CodeElement md in cc.Children)
{
  if (md.Kind == vsCMElement.vsCMElementFunction)
  {
   if (code.Contains(md.Name))
   {
    cc.RemoveMember(md);
   }
  }
}
```

I'm now ready to insert the generated code. I use the `CodeClass`'s `GetStartPoint` method to get an `EditPoint` at the end of the `CodeClass`'s body and then use that `EditPoint`'s `Insert` method to add my code (inserting generated code at the end of the `Class` ensures that the developer's custom code bubbles to the start of the `Class`):

```
EditPoint codePoint = cc.GetEndPoint(vsCMPart.vsCMPartBody).
                    CreateEditPoint();
codePoint.Insert(code);
```

Specifying Code with the CodeDom

All that's left to show is the code that generates the event-handler routines. In this case study, that's handled in a method I've called `GenerateCode`. This method is passed the names of the event, the Id of the LookupValidator, the connection string, the table, and the field to be used. The method's opening looks like this:

```
string GenerateCode(string EventName, string Id, string ConnectionName,
                string TableName, string FieldName, string DType,
                ProjectInfo pi)
{
```

Inside the `GenerateCode` method I use the CodeDom objects to generate a `ServerValidate` event handler for the LookupValidator passed to the method. (The CodeDom objects are covered in detail in Chapter 6, "Generating Language-Neutral Code.")

Generating the Lookup Methods

This section walks through the unique parts of the roughly 300 lines of CodeDom code required to generate these two dozen lines of code that go in the LookupValidator control's `ServerValidate` method:

```
protected void LookupValidator1_ServerValidate(
        object sender, PHVValidators.ServerValidateEventArgs args)
{
 int result;
 System.Data.SqlClient.SqlConnection conn;
 System.Data.SqlClient.SqlCommand cmd;

 conn = new System.Data.SqlClient.SqlConnection(
        System.Web.Configuration.WebConfigurationManager.
          ConnectionStrings["Northwind"].ConnectionString);

 cmd = conn.CreateCommand();
 cmd.CommandText =
   "Select Count(*) From Employees Where EmployeeId = @EmployeeId";
 cmd.Parameters.Add("@EmployeeId", System.Data.SqlDbType.Int);

 if ((int.TryParse(args.Value, out result) == false))
 {
  args.IsValid = false;
  return;
 }
 else
 {
  cmd.Parameters[0].Value = result;
 }

 conn.Open();
 result = ((int)(cmd.ExecuteScalar()));
 conn.Close();

 if ((result == 0))
 {
```

```
  args.IsValid = false;
}
else
{
  args.IsValid = true;
}
}
```

If writing 300 lines of code in order to generate 24 lines of code seems like a poor use of your time, remember that you don't need to use the CodeDom when creating a code-generation solution. Most shops don't need the ability to generate code in a variety of languages, which is the primary purpose of the CodeDom. Much can be done, for instance, by inserting strings using the Code Editor objects or by using search-and-replace to replace tokens in a template's code. You can also copy in text from files using the `FileCodeModel`.

However, if you need to generate code in any language, you need the CodeDom. This section of the case study demonstrates a typical application of the CodeDom. In the following sections I look at several parts of that code that are unique. (For example, I show only one example of creating an `If` statement even though the generated code has two `If` statements.) The full routine is available for download from my website.

Initializing

At the start of the code-generation method, I retrieve the connection string from the Web.config file, using the name of the connection string that was passed to the generation method. The code in the `GetConnectionElement` method is similar to the code from the case study in Chapter 9 that retrieves connection strings from the project's config file. The major difference is that this version returns the complete XML node. If `GetConnectionElement` doesn't find a matching tag in the `connectionStrings` element, the method returns null and I exit without generating any code:

```
XmlNode connNd = GetConnectionElement(pi, ConnectionName);
if (connNd == null)
{
  return "";
}
```

At the top of my `GenerateCode` method, I create some utility variables I use throughout the generation method. For instance, many methods require that an array of code statements be passed to them. I create two arrays at the start of the process and reuse them throughout the method. This code creates a single-position array and a two-position array:

```
CodeExpression[] parms1 = new CodeExpression[1];
CodeExpression[] parms2 = new CodeExpression[2];
```

I also need references to standard data types. This example creates a reference to the int data type:

```
CodeTypeReference intType;
intType = new CodeTypeReference(typeof(int));
CodeTypeReferenceExpression intRef;
```

Similarly, I use `CodePrimitiveExpression` objects to represent some standard literal values such as True, False, 0, and 1. This example creates a reference to False:

```
CodePrimitiveExpression falseValue;
falseValue = new CodePrimitiveExpression(false);
```

Creating the Event-Handler Method

With my utility variables initialized, I can start generating the code for the event handler. The event-handler method accepts two parameters, one of type `Object` (called `sender`) and one of `ServerValidateEventArgs` (called `args`). This code creates the `args` parameter:

```
string argsName = "args";
CodeTypeReference argsType;
argsType = new CodeTypeReference(typeof(ServerValidateEventArgs));
CodeVariableReferenceExpression argsRef;
argsRef = new CodeVariableReferenceExpression(argsName);
```

I also need a reference to the `Value` and `IsValid` properties on the `args` object. Here is the code that creates a reference to the `IsValid` property:

```
string isValidName = "IsValid";
CodePropertyReferenceExpression isValidRef;
isValidRef = new CodePropertyReferenceExpression(argsRef, isValidName);
```

With all the components created, the following code creates the event-handler method. The settings for the `Attributes` property suppress the default attribute of `virtual` and gives the method a scope of `protected`. I then create parameters from the `sender` and `args` objects and attach them as parameters to the method:

```
CodeMemberMethod cmm = new CodeMemberMethod();
cmm.Name = EventName;
cmm.Attributes = MemberAttributes.Family | MemberAttributes.Final;

CodeParameterDeclarationExpression sender =
    new CodeParameterDeclarationExpression(senderType, senderName);
cmm.Parameters.Add(sender);
CodeParameterDeclarationExpression args =
    new CodeParameterDeclarationExpression(argsType, argsName);
cmm.Parameters.Add(args);
```

Generating ADO.NET Objects

With the method header created, the first code I want to generate is the declarations for the ADO.NET objects, which will vary depending on the database being accessed. I determine what type of objects to create by checking either the connection string or the `providerName` in the element returned from my `GetConnectionElement` method.

This code generates objects for a `SqlClient` provider. In addition to creating the `SqlConnection` and `SqlCommand` objects, the method sets the prefix to be used in parameters. Based on the `Type` parameter set in the LookupValidator (passed into this generation method in a parameter called `DType`), I also set a reference to the correct enumerated value for the parameter's data type:

```
string parmPrefix = "";
CodeTypeReference connType = null;
CodeTypeReference cmdType = null;

if (connNd.Attributes["providerName"].Value == "System.Data.SqlClient")
{
  connType = new
    CodeTypeReference(typeof(System.Data.SqlClient.SqlConnection));
  cmdType = new
    CodeTypeReference(typeof(System.Data.SqlClient.SqlCommand));
```

```
parmPrefix = "@";
CodeTypeReferenceExpression sqlDbType;
sqlDbType = new CodeTypeReferenceExpression(typeof(SqlDbType));

switch (DType)
{
  case "Integer":
   parmType =  new CodeFieldReferenceExpression(sqlDbType,"Int");;
   break;
  case "String":
   parmType = new CodeFieldReferenceExpression(sqlDbType, "NText");
   break;
  ...more options...
 }
}
```

With the correct data type defined for the ADO.NET objects, I can create the declarations for the objects using the type I just created. Following is the code to create the declaration for the connection object, add it to the `Statements` collection for the method, and define a reference to the newly created declaration:

```
string connName = "conn";
CodeVariableDeclarationStatement conn;
conn = new CodeVariableDeclarationStatement(connType, connName);
cmm.Statements.Add(conn);
CodeVariableReferenceExpression connRef;
connRef = new CodeVariableReferenceExpression(connName);
```

Creating the line of code that instantiates the connection object, passing the connection string, and assigning the result to the connection object variable is complex. First, I create a reference to the `WebConfigurationManager` (this is why the add-in needs a reference to the `System.Web` library):

```
CodeTypeReference configMgrRef;
configMgrRef = new CodeTypeReference(
        typeof(System.Web.Configuration.WebConfigurationManager));
CodeTypeReferenceExpression configMgrExp;
configMgrExp = new CodeTypeReferenceExpression(configMgrRef);
```

The next step adds a reference to the ConnectionStrings property on the WebConfigurationManager:

```
CodePropertyReferenceExpression connStrings;
connStrings = new
    CodePropertyReferenceExpression(configMgrExp, "ConnectionStrings");
```

Now I add an index to the ConnectionStrings property. This is an occasion when I use one of the arrays I created at the start of the generation method: I set the first position in the array to the name of the connectionStrings element passed to the generation method. After adding the index to the ConnectionStrings parameter, I add the ConnectionString property to it:

```
parms1[0] = connStringName;
CodeIndexerExpression configIndex;
configIndex = new CodeIndexerExpression(connStrings, parms1);
CodePropertyReferenceExpression connStringAccess;
connStringAccess = new CodePropertyReferenceExpression(
        configIndex, "ConnectionString");
```

Having created the indexed access to the ConnectionStrings collection, I use it as a parameter for the code that instantiates the connection object. I then use the instantiated object in an assignment statement to assign the instantiated object to the connection variable. Finally, I add the resulting assignment statement to the method's Statements collection:

```
CodeObjectCreateExpression connCreate;
parms1[0] = connStringAccess;
connCreate = new CodeObjectCreateExpression(connType, parms1);
CodeAssignStatement connAssign;
connAssign = new CodeAssignStatement(connRef, connCreate);
cmm.Statements.Add(connAssign);
```

I use a similar process to create the code that adds a parameter to the command's Parameters collection.

Building the Parameterized Select Statement

The ADO.NET objects will, eventually, need a SQL statement. This code creates the SQL statement, using the `Format` method to insert the values passed into the generation method into the appropriate position in a SQL statement:

```
string selectStatement;
selectStatement = string.Format(
 "Select Count(*) From {0} Where {1} = {2}{1}",
 TableName, FieldName, parmPrefix);
select = new CodePrimitiveExpression(selectStatement);
```

Now that the `select` statement is created, I add a reference to the `CommandText` property on the command object and create an assignment statement to set the property to the `select` statement. The assignment statement gets added to the method's `Statements` collection:

```
CodePropertyReferenceExpression cmdText;
cmdText = new CodePropertyReferenceExpression(cmdRef, "CommandText");
CodeAssignStatement cmdTextAssign;
cmdTextAssign = new CodeAssignStatement(cmdText, select);
cmm.Statements.Add(cmdTextAssign);
```

The `select` statement accepts a parameter that must also be added to the command object. I first create a reference to the parameter name by concatenating the prefix and the field name:

```
parmName = new CodePrimitiveExpression(parmPrefix + FieldName);
CodePropertyReferenceExpression cmdParms;
```

The next step is to create a reference to the `Parameters` property on the command object and a reference to the `Add` method on that property:

```
cmdParms = new CodePropertyReferenceExpression(cmdRef, "Parameters");
CodeMethodReferenceExpression cmdParmsAdd;
cmdParmsAdd = new CodeMethodReferenceExpression(cmdParms,"Add");
CodeMethodInvokeExpression cmdParmsAddInvoke;
```

To call the `Add` method, I must create an object that generates an `invoke` statement. Again, I use one of my parameter arrays to hold the parameters to be passed to the method when it is invoked. Once I've created the `invoke` statement, it gets added to the method's `Statements` collection:

```
parms2[0] = parmName;
parms2[1] = parmType;
cmdParmsAddInvoke =
        new CodeMethodInvokeExpression(cmdParmsAdd, parms2);
cmm.Statements.Add(cmdParmsAddInvoke);
```

Handling Data Conversions

In the generated code, if the value passed to the method isn't a string value, I need to convert it to the correct data type and use an `If` statement to check to see if the conversion was successful. After checking the data type passed into the generation method to see if the conversion code is required, I create an array that will go into the True part of the `If` statement. Into that block, I put an assignment statement that sets the command object's parameter to the result of the conversion:

```
if (DType != "String")
{
 CodeStatement[] canConvertBlock = new CodeStatement[1];
 CodeAssignStatement assignParms;
 assignParms = new CodeAssignStatement(parmsIndexedValue, resultRef);
 canConvertBlock[0] = assignParms;
```

I create another array to hold the statements when the conversion fails. That block has two lines—one statement to set the `IsValid` property on the `args` object to False and a `Return` statement:

```
CodeStatement[] noConvertBlock = new CodeStatement[2];
noConvertBlock[0] = setIsValidFalse;
noConvertBlock[1] = new CodeMethodReturnStatement();
```

The `TryParse` statement must be called from the correct data type as specified in the LookupValidator. This code creates `TryParse` statements called from int and DateTime data types:

```
CodeMethodReferenceExpression tryParse = null;
switch(DType)
{
 case "Integer" :
   tryParse = new CodeMethodReferenceExpression(intRef,"TryParse");
   break;
```

```
case "DateTime":
  tryParse = new CodeMethodReferenceExpression(dateRef, "TryParse");
  break;
...more options...
}
```

The second parameter to the `TryParse` statement is an `out` parameter. This code creates that parameter and then places it, along with a value to convert, in the two-position array that I created at the start of the generation method:

```
CodeDirectionExpression outResultRef;
outResultRef =
    new CodeDirectionExpression(FieldDirection.Out,resultRef);
parms2[0] = argsValue;
parms2[1] = outResultRef;
```

I can now create the invoke code that calls the `TryParse` method, passing the array with the parameters. I use that invoke object to create a test that compares the output of the `TryParse` statement to the False value I defined at the start of the generation method. With the condition and the two blocks of code created, I create the `If` block and add it to the method's `Statements` collection:

```
CodeMethodInvokeExpression tryParseInvoke;
tryParseInvoke = new CodeMethodInvokeExpression(tryParse,parms2);
CodeBinaryOperatorExpression testTryParse;
testTryParse = new CodeBinaryOperatorExpression(tryParseInvoke,
    CodeBinaryOperatorType.ValueEquality, falseValue);
CodeConditionStatement ccs;
ccs = new CodeConditionStatement(testTryParse,
    noConvertBlock, canConvertBlock);
cmm.Statements.Add(ccs);
```

Casting a Method Result

Near the end of the event handler, I call the `ExecuteScalar` method on the command object. The output of the `ExecuteScalar` needs to be cast to an integer value. This code first creates an invoke statement for the `ExecuteScalar` and then creates a cast that converts the `ExecuteScalar` statement to an integer. I use that cast statement in an assign statement to set my `result` variable. I then add that assignment statement to the method's `Statements` collection:

```
CodeMethodInvokeExpression executeScalar;
executeScalar = new CodeMethodInvokeExpression(cmdRef,
                        "ExecuteScalar");
CodeCastExpression castScalar;
castScalar = new CodeCastExpression(intType,executeScalar);
CodeAssignStatement setResult;
setResult = new CodeAssignStatement(resultRef,castScalar);
cmm.Statements.Add(setResult);
```

Generating Code in the Target Language

Once you've created all those CodeDom objects, you'll want to convert them into actual code. I use a standard method that accepts a `CodeMemberMethod` and returns a string holding the code (the code providers are discussed in Chapter 6):

```
string CodeGenerationMember(CodeMemberMethod cmm, ProjectInfo pi)
{
 StringBuilder generatedCode;
 System.IO.StringWriter codeWriter;

 generatedCode = new StringBuilder();
 codeWriter = new System.IO.StringWriter(generatedCode);
 switch (pi.ProjectLanguage)
 {
  case ("CSharp"):
   Microsoft.CSharp.CSharpCodeProvider csProv =
          new Microsoft.CSharp.CSharpCodeProvider();
   csProv.GenerateCodeFromMember(cmm, codeWriter, null);
   break;
   ...other languages...
 }
}
```

Supporting "Projectless" Websites

As I mentioned at the start of this chapter, this case study won't support what I've been calling "projectless" websites. In a website, a WebForm's partial class can't be spread over multiple files: All the application-related code for the WebForm must be in the file specified in the `CodeFile` attribute of the .aspx file's `Page` directive. Because of that, the code placed in the Generated Code folder used in this solution doesn't have access to the controls specified in the .aspx file.

There is, however, a solution: Insert the code into the same file as the rest of the WebForm's code. It's still possible to keep the generated code separate from the developer's own code by creating a partial class and adding it to the end of the code file for the WebForm. This requires jumping through a few hoops but extends the solution to an important class of ASP.NET applications. To implement this solution, you need to add references to the `VsWebSite.Interop` and `VsWebSite.Interop90` libraries.

Adding Code

The only other changes required are in the part of the utility that actually inserts the code into a file. In the project's mainline, I need to check the `Project` object's `Kind` property again and call a different routine to handle the WebForm:

```
if (pi.Project.Kind == "{E24C65DC-7377-472b-9ABA-BC803B73C61A}")
{
 AddCodeWebSite(code, pji);
}
else
{
 ProjectItem CodeFile = cgu.AddFolderAndFile(pi,
                  "LookupValidatorBase.zip", FileName);
 AddCode(code, CodeFile);
}
```

The `AddCodeWebSite` method first casts the `ProjectItem` into a `VSWebProjectItem2` object. This gives me access to the `RelatedFiles` collection that holds a reference to the code file for the WebForm. Having retrieved the `ProjectItem` for the code file, I then convert it to a `VSWebProjectItem2` so that I can call its `Load` method to access the `FileCodeModel` for the code file.

```
void AddCodeWebSite(string code, ProjectItem pji)
{
 VSWebProjectItem2 vspji = (VSWebProjectItem2) pji.Object;
 ProjectItem codeFile = vspji.RelatedFiles.Item(1);
 VSWebProjectItem2 vsCodeFile = (VSWebProjectItem2) codeFile.Object;
 vsCodeFile.Load();
 FileCodeModel fcm = vsCodeFile.ProjectItem.FileCodeModel;
```

The next step is to determine if the file already contains the partial class that I want to insert the validation code into. The problem is that both the original class and the class to hold my generated code will have identical signatures: They're both partial classes with the same name. The convention I use is to insert the class file with the generated code as the last item in the file. Alternatives would be to add an attribute or a comment to the class with the generated code or enclose it in a region.

This code loops through all the class elements in the file and, if there's only one class, sets the bolNotFound variable to True. If there's more than one class, I store a reference to the last one in my lookupClass variable:

```
CodeClass lookupClass = null;
bool bolNotFound = false;
foreach (CodeElement ce in fcm.CodeElements)
{
  if (ce.Kind == vsCMElement.vsCMElementClass)
  {
    if (bolNotFound)
    {
     lookupClass = (CodeClass) ce;
     bolNotFound = false;
    }
    else
    {
     bolNotFound = true;
    }
  }
}
```

If I don't find the second class file, I must add it. This is made awkward because of the way that the FileCodeModel handles partial classes: I can only create a partial class by inserting a standard class and then setting its ClassKind property. Fortunately though, the FileCodeModel doesn't do much error-checking when inserting a class, it does check to ensure that you don't add a second class with the same name as an existing class.

My solution is to assign the class with a dummy name (the name of the class with the string "_New" added to the end). After the class is added, I set the ClassKind property to make it a partial class and then rename the class to the name that I wanted originally:

```
if (bolNotFound)
{
 string className;
 className = pji.Name.Substring(0,pji.Name.IndexOf("."));
 string tempClassName = className +  "_New";

 object[] bases = { "System.Web.UI.Page" };
 lookupClass = fcm.AddClass(tempClassName, -1, bases, null,
          vsCMAccess.vsCMAccessPublic);
 CodeClass2 lookupClass2 = (CodeClass2)lookupClass;
 lookupClass2.ClassKind =
          EnvDTE80.vsCMClassKind.vsCMClassKindPartialClass;
 lookupClass2.Name = className;
}
```

It's important to note that using the AddClass method like this limits this solution to C# projects. (In a Visual Basic application, the AddClass method doesn't support passing base classes in the third parameter.) The simplest alternative that would support Visual Basic is, in the method that generates the code using the CodeDom, to check the Project object's Kind property and generate a whole new class. This solution has some costs: You would have to delete the existing class before adding the new class, preventing you from maintaining the developer's code from one generation to another. If a developer wanted to use the SuppressGeneration option and keep any generated code, the developer would have to copy the code out of your class and into the original class in the code file before the next generation run. Another solution would be to add the class using the AddClass method, as shown but without a base class. You could then use an EditPoint or a CodeSnippet to insert the Inherits System.Web.UI.Page statement.

Once the class is added, the code to insert the code is similar to what I used for the web application project. As in my original method, I would iterate through all the existing methods, deleting any that I've generated code for. The only real difference in this version is that, after inserting the code, I have to unload the VSWebProjectItem2 that I loaded at the start of the method:

```
EditPoint codePoint = lookupClass.GetEndPoint(vsCMPart.vsCMPartBody).
CreateEditPoint();
codePoint.Insert(code);
vsCodeFile.Unload();
```

Handling Errors

Until you've used your add-in in every possible scenario, it's only realistic to recognize that the add-in will, occasionally, produce output that you don't want. Most of the changes that this add-in makes fall into the "no harm, no foul" category. For instance, the add-in adds a new folder and a new file to the project—changes that are unlikely to prevent the application from compiling or running successfully.

However, once you start inserting and deleting code, there is a real possibility that you'll prevent the application from compiling. The appropriate approach is to wrap up all the changes you make to an application's code into a single UndoContext so that the developer can back out of your changes (and restore any methods you deleted) with a single Undo.

Wrapping the methods that insert the code in an UndoContext does the trick. As discussed in Chapter 4, using the UndoContext requires defensive programming. Because only a single UndoContext can be open at a time, I always check to see if the context is already open and I only close the UndoContext if I opened it. Leaving an UndoContext open can disable the Undo function for the developer, so I include a Try...Catch block that ensures any context I open is closed.

To implement the UndoContext, I wrap the calls to the two methods that insert code inside a Try block along with the code that checks to see if the context is open (and opens it if it is not). In the corresponding Finally block, I check to see if the context is open. If I opened it, I close it:

```
bool CreatedUndo = false;
UndoContext undo = applicationObject.UndoContext;

try
{
 if (!undo.IsOpen)
 {
  undo.Open("Fixing Name", true);
  CreatedUndo = true;
 }
```

```
string FileName = doc.Name.Substring(0, doc.Name.IndexOf("."));
if (pi.Project.Kind == "{E24C65DC-7377-472b-9ABA-BC803B73C61A}")
{
   AddCodeWebSite(code, pji);
}
else
{
  ProjectItem CodeFile = cgu.AddFolderAndFile(pi,
                "LookupValidatorBase.zip", FileName);
  AddCode(code, CodeFile);
}
}
finally
{
 if (undo.IsOpen && CreatedUndo)
 {
  undo.Close();
 }
}
```

Building a Complete Code-Generation Solution

This chapter has demonstrated the techniques required to implement a full-featured code-generation solution including handling events from multiple documents in multiple projects. In this case study, I also showed how the objects in the CodeDom can be used together to generate typical code constructs.

Although the case study in this chapter and the previous chapter have used two separate add-ins, in practice you probably don't want to have multiple add-ins, with each generating events for—potentially—the same documents. Instead, you should create a single "code generation master" add-in that you can easily extend to implement new code-generation solutions. The structure for that add-in is discussed in Appendix C, "A Code-Generation Add-In."

As with the case study in Chapter 9, the code for this utility (and the LookupValidator control) can be downloaded from my website (www. phvis.com) and from www.informit.com.

CHAPTER 11

CASE STUDY: GENERATING DATA-CONVERSION CODE

In this chapter:
- Defining the Problem
- Creating the Designer
- Enhancing Model Validation
- Generating Code
- Distributing Your Designer
- Visual Studio 2010 Additions
- Capturing Inputs

This case study looks at creating a class that parses a string of data consisting of a variable collection of items and converts that data into .NET data types. This case study uses T4 templates, but primarily you'll see how to create a visual designer that developers use to generate the input specifications for code generation. Effectively, then, this chapter looks at one of the first steps in the code-generation process: How the developer enters the inputs to the code-generation process. At the end of this chapter, you'll see how to associate a custom tool with your template so that code is automatically generated when the developer closes the visual designer. Although this chapter assumes that the custom tool will generate code using a T4 template, you could associate any custom tool (as described in Chapter 8, "Other Tools: Templates, Attributes, and Custom Tools,") with the designer's output.

Visual Studio's Tools for Domain-Specific Languages includes a visual designer generator that allows you to create a drag-and-drop interface that developers can use to create the inputs for the code-generation process. This chapter walks you through how to create a simple visual designer, how to drive T4 code generation from your visual designer, and how to deploy your designer so that developers can use it to create solutions.

This technology is available as a download for all versions of Visual Studio from 2005 on up:

- For Visual Studio 2005, you need both the Visual Studio 2005 Software Development Toolkit and the Domain-Specific Language Toolkit for Visual Studio 2005.
- For Visual Studio 2008, you only need the Visual Studio 2008 Software Development Toolkit.
- For Visual Studio 2010, you need both the Visual Studio 2010 Software Development Toolkit and the Domain-Specific Language Toolkit for Visual Studio 2010.

Two differences between Visual Studio 2005/2008 and Visual Studio 2010 are relevant to this chapter:

- In Visual Studio 2005/2008, for other developers to use your designer they must either download and install the DSL Tools on their computer, or you have to get a package load key (PLK) from Microsoft (which is not hard to do, as I describe at the end of this chapter).
- The process for deploying your designer is much simpler in Visual Studio 2010. (I describe both methods near the end of this chapter.)

Be aware: If you create a designer in Visual Studio 2005/2008, you will need to migrate the project that defines the designer to Visual Studio 2010 using a migration tool provided with Visual Studio 2010.

Defining the Problem

When creating a visual designer, you're responsible for creating the graphical components that a developer can drag onto your editor to create a graphic representation of the code to be generated. Typically, this is a set of classes and connectors for joining the classes together. On the classes (and, occasionally, on the connectors), you provide properties where the developer can enter values that you use in generating code.

For this case study, I'm drawing on one of my clients who created an application that reads data from Radio Frequency Identifier (RFID) tags attached to trucks. Any particular RFID tag, when activated, sends a string of bytes to a reader. The format of those bytes will vary from one tag to another. For instance, one tag will send a string of bytes that represents a single piece of data: the number of miles the truck has travelled since the tag was attached to the truck. Another more sophisticated tag will send two pieces of data: the number of miles the truck has travelled since the tag was attached (life mileage) and the number of miles travelled since the tag was last reset (trip mileage). A different kind of tag might send a string of bytes representing tire pressure information: the current tire pressure, the low/high pressure limits, a flag signaling that the tire pressure is currently outside those limits, and the length of time that the tire pressure has been wrong. There are, potentially, an infinite number of tags, some of which will be created by third-party tag manufacturers.

Each tag requires a custom program that parses the data coming from the tag and decodes it. Parsing the string of bytes consists of separating the byte stream into segments. Let's use a tire pressure tag as an example:

- The first two bytes of the string are a code indicating which tire on the truck is being reported on.
- The next four bytes in the string represent the tire pressure.
- The byte in position 6 is either all 0s (tire pressure OK) or all 1s (tire pressure not OK).

The framework for the application includes a class (called Decoder) with methods for converting a string of bytes into a .NET data type. A tag manufacturer, therefore, has to write a program that splits up the string of bytes from its tag and passes each segment to the correct Decoder method.

This "tag-parsing" class that a tag manufacturer must create must have a single method (called ParseTag) that accepts the complete string of bytes. For various reasons (most of them historical but also related to working with embedded code), these strings are passed through the application as .NET Strings (rather than as, for instance, byte arrays). The tag manufacturer's class must have a unique name (usually based on the name of the tag manufacturer's company and the tag's model number). Here's a skeleton of a typical tag parsing class:

```
public class PHVISTagParse
{
  public void ParseTag (string TagData)
  {
  }
}
```

Within the method, the string must be broken into segments and passed to the correct method on the `Decoder` class. (All the methods on the `Decoder` class are shared/Static methods.) For the tire pressure example, the code to extract the data would look something like this:

```
string Position;
Position = Decoder.TirePosition(TagData.Substring(0,2));
long Pressure;
Pressure = Decoder.Long4Byte(TagData.Substring(2,4));
bool OutOfLimit;
OutOfLimit = Decoder.Boolean(TagData.Substring(6,1));
```

Of course, `Decoder` methods as well as segment start points/length would change from one tag to another.

Rather than ask tag manufacturers to write this code, a better solution would be to provide a visual designer that generates the code. This would ensure, for instance, that the code created matched whatever specifications or restrictions we wanted to place on it (e.g., the signature for the `ParseTag` method). To use our visual designer, a developer would do the following:

1. Open Visual Studio.
2. Create a new project.
3. Add our designer to his or her project by using Project | Add New Item and selecting the TagParse template from the Add New Item dialog.
4. When the designer opens, the developer would drag a `ParseManager` object onto the design surface and set its `TagName` property (this is used to generate the class name) and its `MessageLength` (this is used to check that `Decoder`s are processing all of the message).
5. The developer would then drag three `Decoder` objects onto the designer. For each `Decoder`, the developer would set the `DecoderName`, `StartPoint`, `Length`, `DecodeMethod`, and `DataType` properties. The `DecoderName` would be used in error messages, and the other four properties are used in generating the code in the method. The designer will check that there are no gaps or overlaps between the end point of one `Decoder` and the start of another, and that the whole message has been assigned to one of the `Decoder`s.
6. The developer would add connections between the `ParseManager` and the `Decoder`s.
7. The developer would close the designer, causing code for this tag's parse class to be generated.

The term used to refer to the graphic that the developer creates (and that drives code generation) is "model." The model for the tag with life and trip mileage might look like Figure 11-1.

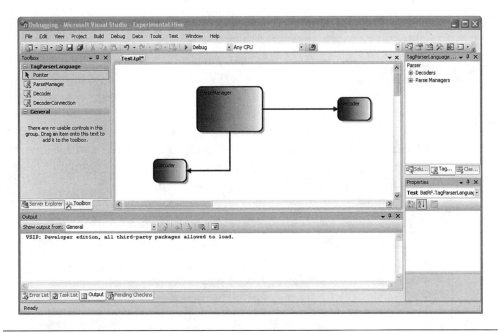

FIGURE 11-1 A simple code-generation model in a custom visual designer.

There's more to the application than this (for instance, storing the data in the database, supporting standard validation routines, and configuring error-handling). However, this is a "good enough" scenario to demonstrate how to create a visual designer and drive code generation from any model a developer creates in the designer.

BEST PRACTICE Don't confuse the visual components in your designer (and their properties) with the classes and members you will be generating. The purpose of the visual designer is to

- Provide a graphic representation of the problem that makes sense to the developer.
- Allow the developer to enter the necessary data for the code-generation process.

To avoid confusion between the components of an application and the components used in the designer, I use the term "items" for the designer's components
rather than using "objects," "classes," "components," or "XML elements."

Creating the Designer

You create your designer as a separate project that you then deploy to
other developers as a Visual Studio package (a `VsPackage`—a successor to
Visual Studio add-ins). Your first step, then, is to create a project that
contains your designer.

To create the project, choose File | New Project | Extensibility |
Domain-Specific Language Designer and enter a name and location for
your project (I named my project TagParse.) The Domain-Specific
Language Designer Wizard will appear (see Figure 11-2).

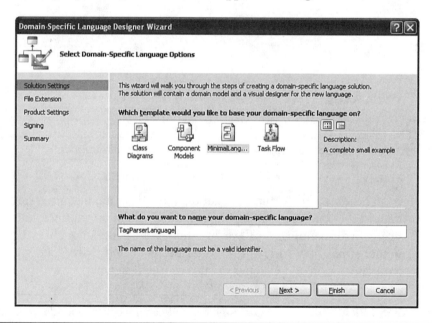

FIGURE 11-2   The wizard gathers the initial information used to generate the projects you
need to create a visual designer.

On the first page of the wizard, you'll select the kind of model you want
to use to have the wizard preload some typical components. As you'll see

shortly, the best solution with the current version of the DSL tools is to pick the Minimal Language option from the window in the middle of the page. On this page, you can also assign a name to the system of components you create. (I named my language TagParseLanguage, or TPL for short.)

BEST PRACTICE Often the best name for your language is just to add the word "Language" to the end of the project name.

On the next page of the wizard (see Figure 11-3), you'll specify the file extension for the text file your designer will generate (I used tpl). An association will be set up in the Windows registry for the file extension you select, so you should avoid any well-known extensions. The wizard will check to see if any application on your computer is already associated with that extension and allow you to deregister it. You can also select an icon that represents your file when it's displayed in Solution Explorer.

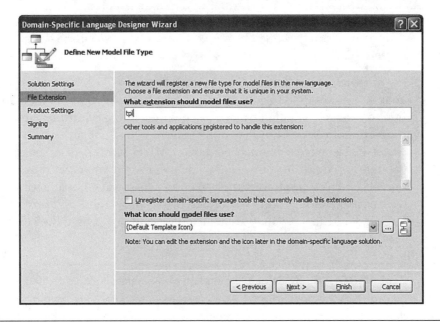

FIGURE 11-3 The designer you create will store its information in a file with the extension specified on this page of the wizard.

On the next page of the wizard (see Figure 11-4), you enter information about your company and the project that will be using your language.

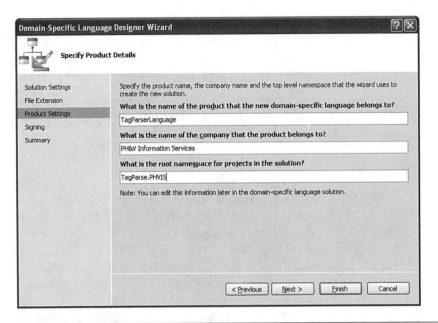

FIGURE 11-4 The namespace generated here is used by the code within the designer, not the code you generate.

Your entries are used to generate the namespace for your designer. You are free to change the default namespace either in the wizard or later in the properties of your designer, so don't panic if you're not sure what your best choice is. Do avoid using unacceptable XML characters (e.g., ampersands, greater-than signs) in your company name, even if you don't intend to use those characters in your designer's namespace—your company name is still incorporated into the XML generated by the wizard and your project won't build if, for instance, you've used an ampersand in it. I used the namespace `TagParse.PHVIS`.

BEST PRACTICE   By default, the portion of the namespace up to the first period is all that will appear in the Add New Item dialog in Visual Studio, so you should use that part of the namespace to create a name that will be meaningful to developers.

On the fourth page of the wizard (see Figure 11-5), you select a strong name to be used to sign your assembly. If you have a strong name key file,

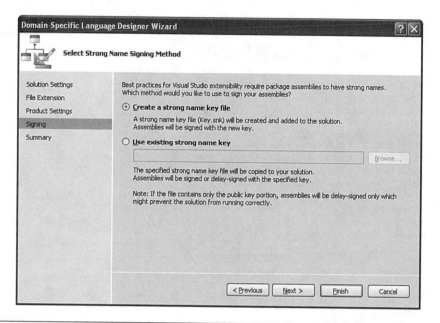

FIGURE 11-5 If you have a strong name key file, the second option on this page of the wizard will let you navigate to it.

you can select it, but the simplest solution is to use the default option and let the wizard generate a strong name for you.

The final page of the wizard (see Figure 11-6) shows the choices you made on the previous page. Click the Finish button to create your project. The result should be a project similar to the one in Figure 11-7.

Building the Designer

You're now ready to start creating your designer. A visual designer has three interrelated sets of items you need to specify:

- **Logical items**—These items drive the code-generation process.
- **Graphical items that represent those components**—These control the appearance of items in the designer.
- **Entries for your designer's toolbox**—These represent the graphical items a developer can drag and drop onto the design surface.

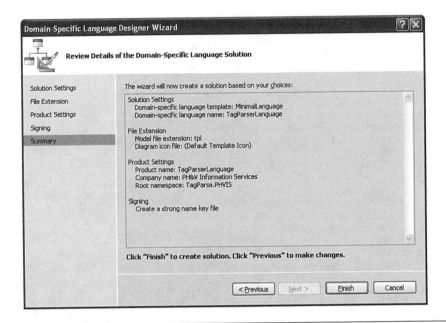

FIGURE 11-6   Most of the options you select on this page can be changed from the Properties window of your visual designer project.

FIGURE 11-7   In addition to the two projects shown here (Dsl and DslPackage), the wizard has generated a third project that is loaded when you test your designer.

When a developer drags an item from the toolbox onto the visual designer, the graphical representation of the item appears on the screen while a set of XML elements representing the logical item is added to the designer's file. This file will have the file type you specified in the wizard. (I refer to this as "the designer's file.") As the developer sets properties on the graphical objects in your designer, those values are stored in the elements in the designer's file.

Eventually, your code generation will be driven by the XML elements and values stored in them in the designer's file. The developer, however, is insulated from the XML, any T4 templates, and the generated code: The developer just drags components onto a designer, creates connections between them, and sets properties on them.

Once again, you're going to have to deal with the "writing code to write code" conceptual problem. To create your visual designer, you use a visual designer—specifically, the DslDefinition.dsl file that is included in your designer project. To try and reduce some of the confusion around "using a designer to create a designer," I refer to the DslDefinition.dsl file as the "DSL Editor" and the designer you're creating as "your visual designer" or "your designer."

If you double-click that designer, you'll see something like the display shown in Figure 11-8. The DSL Editor has two panes (called "swimlanes"). The swimlane on the left shows the logical items. In this lane, you also define any relationships that the developer will be able to create between your logical items in your designer. For instance, in the case study, I want the developer to be able to create connections between the ParseManager and Decoders. To support that, in the DSL Editor, I have to create a relationship between the ParseManager and the Decoder item.

The swimlane on the right shows the visual items that developers will drag onto your visual designer when creating their model.

In addition to working with the DSL Editor, you'll also need to work with the DSL Explorer that appears whenever the DSL Editor is open (see Figure 11-9). The default location for this Explorer is tabbed with Solution Explorer. In the DSL Explorer, for instance, you'll create the toolbox entries for the items that developers will use in your designer.

Because it's unlikely you'll use the default components shown in Figure 11-9, you should begin by deleting all of them except for the LanguageDiagram. (By default, the name for this item is created from your project name—mine is called TagParseLanguageDiagram.) Don't attempt to start fresh by deleting the default .dsl file—with the current set of tools there's no easy way to add a new one. This is why, in the wizard, it's best to start with the Minimal Language template: There's less to delete when you get to this stage.

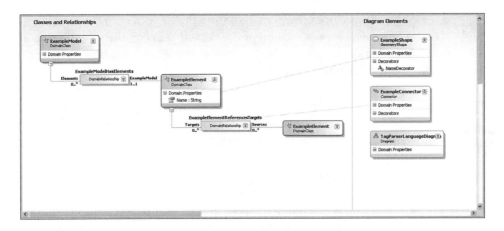

FIGURE 11-8   The default designer generated when you select the Minimal Language
project type in the wizard.

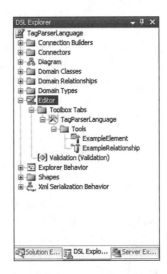

FIGURE 11-9   The DSL Explorer provides a treeview for exploring and changing your
designer.

After cleaning out the DSL Editor, switch to the DSL Explorer. Drill
down from the Editor node through the Toolbox Tabs node, the node with
the name of your language, and the Tools node to get to the list of default
items to be added to your designer's toolbox. Delete them also.

Adding Items to Your Designer

You're now ready to start creating the logical items that developers use to specify what code is to be generated. For the case study, I need three:

- **Parser**—The container element for the XML generated by your designer. Although I don't take advantage of this container in the case study, you can assign properties to this item to hold design-time values that apply to the whole model rather than to individual items. (I refer to this item as the "root item.") Every designer has a root item.
- **ParseManager**—The developer adds one of these to your designer for any TagParse model. The ParseManager item has two properties: TagName and MessageLength. Graphically, the ParseManager is displayed as a rounded rectangle in red with the text "ParseManager."
- **Decoder**—Developers add at least one and, potentially, many Decoders for any ParseManager—one for each piece of data in the tag's string of bytes. A Decoder has five properties: DecoderName, StartPoint, Length, DecodeMethod, and DataType. Graphically, Decoders are displayed as a rounded rectangle in blue with the text "Decoder."

Begin by adding the root item for your designer to the DSL Editor. To add an item, return to the DSL Editor and, from Visual Studio's toolbox, drag a DomainClass onto the page and assign it a name. (I named mine Parser.) If you wanted to give developers the ability to assign names to the items in your designer, you would use a named domain class. After dragging on the Parser item, I added a second domain class that I named ParseManager.

Each item that developers will use in your designer must have an embedded relationship with the root item. To create that relationship, return to the toolbox and click the Embedding Relationship tool. Then click (don't drag) the root item and click the item you just added to the DSL Editor. The editor automatically creates a DomainRelationship item between the two items and assigns the DomainRelationship a name. The editor also creates a copy of the second item. The editor will ensure that any changes you make to one copy of your item will appear in the other copy (see Figure 11-10).

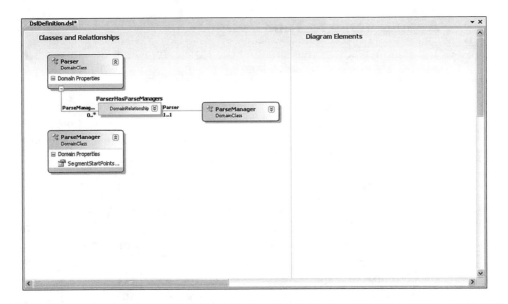

Figure 11-10   After adding a relationship between items in your designer, you'll have two copies of your "child" item (one in the relationship and one standalone copy) as with the ParseManager shown here.

Adding Domain Properties

With a logical item added to your designer and with an embedded relationship with the root item, your next step is to add domain properties to your item. Domain properties are the properties that appear on your items when a developer is using them to create a model; you will also have access to these properties (with the values that the developer entered) when generating code. To put it another way, domain properties are where developers will record the values you will use to customize the code you generate.

If the item isn't expanded (if you can't see the line "Domain Properties" in the item), click the chevron in the upper-right corner of the item to expand it. To add a Domain Property to your item, right-click the Domain Properties line and select Add New Domain Property. When your new domain property appears in the item, assign it a name in the Properties window. You can also assign your domain property a default value (I used "MyTag") and change the Type setting. (I left this domain property's Type property at the default value of String.)

To finish defining your logical items, add the rest of the items that developers will need to create a model. In my case, I added another item named `Decoder` and created an embedded relationship between it and my root item (`Parser`). I added these domain properties to the item:

Name	Type	Default Value
DecoderName	String	Zero-length string
StartPoint	Int32	0
Length	Int32	1
DecodeMethod	String	Long4Byte
Type	String	String

Adding an Enumerated Data Type

Leaving the DecodeMethod as a string would allow the developer to enter any text. However, the only valid entries for this property are the static/shared methods on the system's Decoder class. To prevent bad values from being entered, the developer should be limited to a list of enumerated values that include the names of the methods on the Decoder class. Fortunately, you can add new data types to your designer, including lists of enumerated values.

The first step is to add a new enumerated data type to the DSL Editor: In the DSL Explorer, right-click the top line and select Add New Domain Enumeration. The new enumeration will be added to the Domain Types folder. After renaming the domain enumeration (I used ValidDecoderMethods), right-click it and select Add New Enumeration Literal. The new literal will be added in the Literals folder below your enumeration—just change the Name property of the literal to create a new value. (For the case study, I added three literal values: Boolean, Long4Byte, and TirePosition.)

With your new enumerated data type in place, in the DSL Editor set the Type property of your domain property to the name of your enumerated data type. For the case study, on the Decoder item, I changed the Type property on my DecodeMethod domain property to my new enumeration: ValidDecodeMethods.

Adding Relationships to Support Connections

If you're going to allow the developer to create connections between items in the designer, you must define those relationships in the DSL Editor. In the case study, developers will be able to create connections between the

ParseManager and Decoders, so I have to add that relationship to the DSL Editor. I can create this relationship as a reference relationship rather than an embedded relationship—the relationship between ParseManager and Decoder items mimics the relationship between objects when one object has a reference variable that points to another object. Because the ParseManager holds multiple references to Decoders, the ParseManager is the parent in the relationship and the Decoder item is the child.

To define that relationship, I click the ReferenceRelationship tool in the toolbox, click the parent item in the relationship (ParseManager, in this case) and then the child item (Decoder). As with the embedded relationship, the DSL Editor creates a relationship item and a copy of the child item.

In the DSL Editor, I can use these relationships to control how many of each item can be added to a model and to associations between the items. For instance, there should be one and only one ParseManager in a model. So I select the line leading from the root item to the relationship object for the ParseManager relationship and, in the Properties window, set its Multiplicity property to 1..1. The line leading from the relationship object to the ParseManager already has its Multiplicity property set to 1..1, so I don't have to change it.

I can have one or more Decoders in a model, so I select the line leading from the root item to the relationship that joins it to the Decoder. I then set its Multiplicity property to 1..*.

Because a ParseManager can also have multiple Decoders (and will always have at least one), I also set the Multiplicity property for the line on the left side of ParseManager's relationship to Decoders to 1..*. However, because a Decoder belongs to exactly (and at least) one ParseManager, I set the Multiplicity property for the line on the right side of the relationship to 1..1 (see Figure 11-11).

Adding Graphical Items

With all the items added, you can start creating the graphical items that the developer will interact with when working with your designer. I usually start by creating any connectors I'll need. I first create a connector called DecoderConnector, which developers will use to join the model's ParseManager to Decoders. Graphically, DecoderConnections will be displayed as black arrows with a single arrow at the Decoder end of the line.

To add a connector to the DSL Editor, drag a connector from the toolbox onto the DSL Editor. (The connector will appear in the right swimlane, as shown in Figure 11-12.) After adding the connector, set its name and (optionally) its RoutingStyle, SourceEndStyle, TargetEndStyle, or any

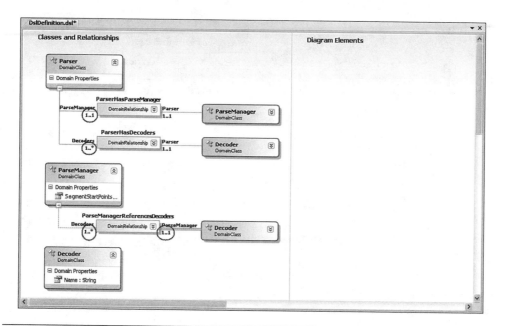

FIGURE 11-11 The circled Multiplicity settings have been changed from their default values.

other properties that allow you to control how the connector will be displayed. The only connector I require connects the ParserManager in a diagram to its Decoders, so I call it ParseManagerToDecoderShape. I just set the TargetEndStyle to FilledArrow.

The next step is to associate the graphical connector with a relationship in the left swimlane. To do that, in the toolbox, click the Diagram Element Map, click the relationship, and then click the connector. (The result can be seen in Figure 11-13.) The Diagram Element Map tool is used to connect all logical elements in the left swimlane to graphical items in the right swimlane.

I don't really need the ParseManager-to-Decoder connectors for the case study—I could generate the necessary code from the ParseManager and Decoders without connecting them. You only need to add connectors when their presence or absence will control code generation. That's true in at least two cases:

- When relationships between items can't otherwise be determined. (In this case study, all Decoders are automatically part of the single ParseManager in any model.)
- When there is design-time information that is best recorded by the developer on the connector rather than one on of the other items.

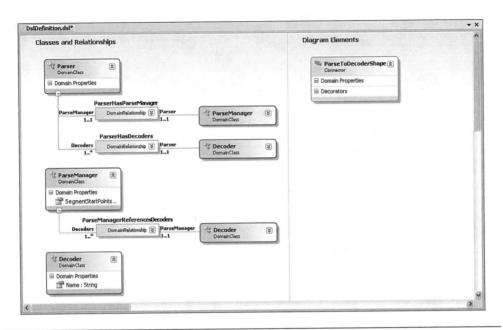

FIGURE 11-12 Connectors are graphical items and appear in the right swimlane of the DSL Editor.

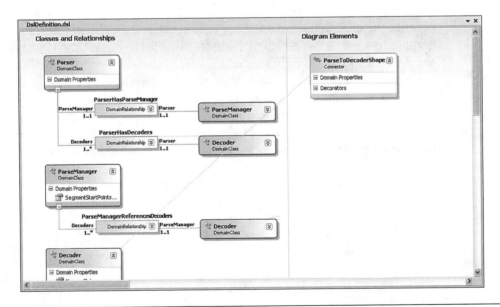

FIGURE 11-13 After adding a connector, you must use the diagram element map to assign it to a relationship.

If I was going to allow multiple ParseManagers in a solution (in order to support multiple tags in a single class, for instance), the DecoderConnectors would be essential. Without connectors, I wouldn't be able to determine which Decoders to use in generating each ParseManager class. Because I'm allowing only a single ParseManager in each model, the DecoderConnectors function purely as a visual tool for expressing the design (and, of course, also let me discuss how to add connectors to a project and use those connections when generating code).

BEST PRACTICE When creating a visual designer, don't ignore that, in addition to generating code, you are creating a *visual* designer. The graphical models created by the developer also act as documentation for how the code will work and should be easily understood by the developer and other stakeholders.

The next step is to add graphical components to represent each logical item that a developer will be able to add to your designer. To add a graphical component, drag a Geometry shape from the toolbox onto the DSL Editor and assign it a name (it will also appear in the right swimlane with your connectors). The naming convention I use for the graphical items is the name of the logical item the shape will be assigned to with the suffix "Shape." My first shape will be associated with the ParseManager, so I gave it the name ParseManagerShape. To associate a logical item with a graphical item, click the Diagram Element Map in the toolbox, then click the logical item (ParseManager, in my case) and, finally, click the graphical item (ParseManagerShape).

Once the graphical item has been added, you can control its appearance. I set the ParseManagerShape's Geometry property to RoundedRectangle and its FillColor to Red. In order to identify the shape when it's displayed in your designer, you can also add a text decorator (to display a label on the shape) or an icon decorator (to have a graphic displayed). I added a text decorator to the ParseManagerShape and set it to "Parse Master."

Finally, double-click the line that joins your graphical shape to the logical shape. This will display the DSL Details window (by default, the DSL Details window will appear below the DSL Editor window). All three drop-down lists in this dialog should be filled in. However, on occasion, I've found that the Parent Element Path is empty. From the Parent Element Path's drop-down list, drill down through the relationship that this item has with the root item (in my case, ParserHasParseManager) and double-click the root item (see Figure 11-14).

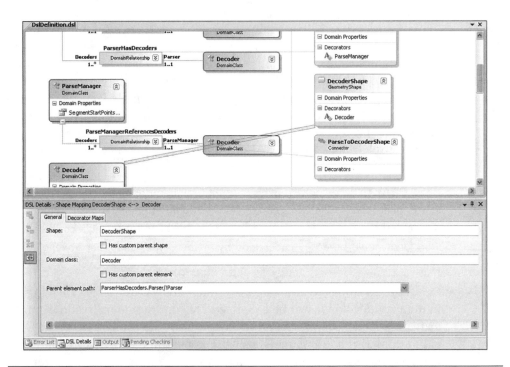

FIGURE 11-14 You may need to set the Parent Element Path of a mapping between a logical item and a graphical item.

To complete the graphical items for the case study, I added a second Geometry graphical item and tied it to the Decoder logical item. I set its properties as I did for the ParseManagerShape but set the FillColor to Blue and the value in the text decorator to "Decoder." I also checked the Parent Element Path by double-clicking the line that joined my graphical item to my logical item.

Because my root item (Parser) isn't going to appear in the visual designer when developers are creating a model, I don't bother to create a graphical element for it.

Adding Toolbox Items

The final step in creating your designer is to add items to your designer's toolbox. In my case, I want to add the three logical items to my toolbox: ParseManager, Decoder, and the reference relationship between ParseManager and Decoder (called ParseManagerReferencesDecoders).

You add toolbox items in the DSL Explorer. First, drill down through the Editor node to the node named for your language under the Tools node. (In my case, the node is called TagParseLanguage.) Now, right-click the language node and select Add New Element Tool. When the item is added, set the following properties:

- **Name**—The convention I use for naming toolbox items is to use the name of the related logical item with the suffix "Tool" (ParseManagerTool, in this case).
- **Class**—Set this to the logical item that the tool represents (ParseManager, in my case).
- **ToolTip Icon**—Any 16×16 bitmap will do—some default bitmaps are provided with the toolkit download.

You should also consider setting the Caption and ToolTip properties because they are displayed in Visual Studio's user interface. Set them to values that will make sense to developers using your designer. (I used "Parse Master" for both.)

Repeat this process for each logical item that the developer will need to add to your designer.

To add a connector to the toolbox, right-click the language node and select Add New Connection Tool. You must set the following properties:

- **Name**—The convention I use for connection tools is to use the name of the parent item (in this case, "ParseManager"), the word "To," the name of the child item ("Decoder"), and the suffix "Tool." This produces ParseManagerToDecoderTool as the name.
- **ConnectionBuilder**—This is the ConnectionBuilder that the DSL Editor has generated for the relationship. (You'll be able to select the ConnectionBuilder from a drop down list.) In my case, that is the ParseManagerReferencesDecoderBuilder.
- **Toolbox Icon**

The final result should look like Figure 11-15.

Validation, Generation, and Test

There are some tasks left before your designer is ready to test.

You need to tie your root item into your designer. First, in the DSL Editor, select the LanguageDiagram element and set its ClassRepresented property to your root item (in my case, that is "Parser"). Then, in the DSL Explorer, select the Editor node and set its RootClass property to your root item (still "Parser").

You can now let the DSL tools check for errors. Right-click anywhere in the DSL Editor and select Validate All. If your validation fails,

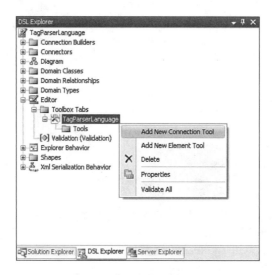

FIGURE 11-15 Toolbox items are added in the DSL Explorer under the Editor node.

you'll get a list of errors—double-clicking them will usually take you to the error's site where, hopefully, you can figure out what step you've missed.

DSL Tools makes extensive use of T4 to generate the code for your designer from your entries in the DSL Editor and the DSL Explorer. Before testing your editor, you must generate the code. To generate the code, return to Solution Explorer and, at the top of the window, click the Transform All Templates button.

Once you've generated your code, press F5 to test your designer. Visual Studio will launch a new version of itself (with the title "Experimental Hive") and open a project called Debugging (see Figure 11-16). You may get a dialog stating that an add-in failed to load. If so, just click No and continue.

This Debugging project was generated when you created the project. In addition to allowing you to test your designer, this project is a good place to develop the T4 code that will generate code from the model a developer creates in your designer. The Debugging project will contain two blank instances of your designer file (your designer's file has the file type you specified when you created your designer project): one called "sample" and one called "test" (in my case, for instance, they were called "sample.tpl" and "test.tpl"). The "sample" file is tied to two T4 templates (discussed later) and is the version you should use to see if you can successfully generate code.

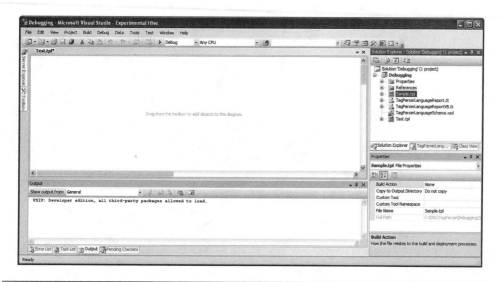

FIGURE 11-16   The Debugging project that is opened when you debug your designer project was also generated by the wizard when you created your designer project.

BEST PRACTICE   The "test" file is not tied to any templates, so it won't generate any code—use it to see if developers can drag and drop components from the Toolbox to build diagrams the way you envisioned without having to worry about the code-generation process.

When you double-click either of these files, you'll open a visual editor with a toolbox on the left listing all the logical items you created toolbox items for. As you drag items onto the design surface, an Explorer view (tabbed with Solution Explorer by default) provides a TreeView display of the items added to your designer (see Figure 11-17).

You can add a new instance of your designer file to the project: Just select Project | Add New Item and scroll to the bottom of the Add New Item dialog. You will find your designer listed in the My Templates section. Adding your designer will give you a new instance of your designer, but with no T4 template file attached to it. Therefore, although you'll be able to create a new visual model, no code will be generated. You'll be able to fix that when you create the deployment package for your application by converting your template into a custom tool. (I cover that later in the chapter in the "Distributing Your Designer" section.)

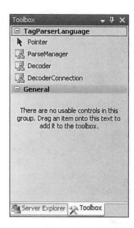

FIGURE 11-17   Your designer's toolbox lists all the logical items that you added to the toolbox in the DSL Editor.

Enhancing Model Validation

As part of creating a T4 solution, you can insert code to execute when a developer chooses to validate the model he or she creates. You add validation by extending your DomainClass with a partial class containing methods that check for problems in the model. When you do find an error, you can call the LogErrors method to record your error. (The LogErrors method was discussed in Chapter 7, "Generating Code from Templates with T4.") Within your code, you can also call any methods described in earlier chapters. (For example, you could use the IsValidId method of the CodeModel objects described in Chapter 3, "Manipulating Project Components," to determine if the value the developer set a property to is a valid identifier in your target language.)

Enabling Validation

Because validation can be time consuming (especially if the number of items to check in the model is large), validation is turned off by default in your designer. You can decide if your validation methods will be called for any models created with your designer by turning on options in the DSL Explorer. To set when your validation will be called, drill down through the Editor node and click the Validation node (see Figure 11-18). The Properties window for the Validation nodes lists the five options for triggering validation:

FIGURE 11-18   To enable validation, you need to set the options on the Validation node in the DSL Explorer that control when validation will be invoked.

- **Uses Save, Uses Load, Uses Open**—Setting these to True will cause your validation methods to be executed whenever the model is saved, loaded, or opened.
- **Uses Menu**—Setting this property to True causes your validation code to execute only when the developer selects Validate or Validate All from the designer's context menus (if you don't set this property to True, the context menu won't have any validation choices).
- **Custom**—Setting this property to True causes validation to occur only when triggered by code in your model. You can also create groups of validation methods to execute validation selectively.

After setting these properties, you need to transform all templates before building your designer. For this chapter, I ignore the Custom option.

BEST PRACTICE   Remember that your validation methods will be called for every *instance* of the DomainClass you add your validation code to. If your validation method takes time to complete, validation can substantially slow down the developer who is using your designer. Setting the validation options to Menu ensures that your validation code will be called only when the developer expects to stop working in order to validate the model.

Adding Validation Code

To add validation code to your designer, you create a partial class for the DomainClass that you want to hold your validation code and decorate the class with the `Microsoft.VisualStudio.Modeling.Validation.ValidationState` attribute, passing the `Microsoft.VisualStudio.Modeling.Validation.ValidationState.Enabled` enumerated value to the attribute.

For this case study, I want to ensure that there is a Decoder for each part of the message (i.e., no gaps exist between Decoders, and the last Decoder includes the end of the message). I also want to ensure that no two Decoders overlap (i.e., that the start point for any Decoder is after the end point of the previous Decoder). To do that I add a partial class to the ParseManager with code that will iterate through all the ParseManager's children. If I supported having multiple ParseManagers in a model, this would let the developer validate each ParseManager separately by right-clicking a ParseManager and select Validate from the context menu.

I begin by declaring the partial class and decorating it with the `ValidationState` attribute:

```
using Microsoft.VisualStudio.Modeling.Validation;

namespace TagParse.PHVIS
{
  [ValidationState(ValidationState.Enabled)]
  partial class ParseManager
  {
```

BEST PRACTICE In general, put validation methods on the object they are to validate or, where you're validating groups of objects, as low in the model's hierarchy as possible. This reduces the number of instances of any object that will be processed when the developer chooses to validate an object. Put as little validation in the "root item" as possible because it will cause the validation code for every item in the model to be run.

Within the partial class, you can now add your validation methods, decorating them with the `Microsoft.VisualStudio.Modeling.Validation.`

ValidationMethod attribute. You can control when your method is called by passing the attribute entries from the Microsoft.VisualStudio.Modeling. Validation.ValidationMethod.ValidationCategories enumeration. (These values correspond to the options in the Validation node of the DSL Explorer: Save, Load, etc.) By OR'ing these attributes together, you can have the method called at several points in the model's life cycle.

This example causes a method call CheckForGap to be called when the model is loaded or opened and when the Validate choice is selected from the menu. The method must accept a ValidationContext object, which gives you access to the LogMessage method (among other features). This is the declaration for my method that checks that there are no gaps or overlaps in the Decoders attached to a ParseManager:

```
[ValidationMethod(ValidationCategories.Load |
                ValidationCategories.Open |
                ValidationCategories.Menu)]
private void CheckForGap(ValidationContext vc)
{
```

The code for this particular validation method is straightforward. The code first accesses all the Decoders associated with the ParseManager through ParseManager's Decoders collection and sorts them by their StartPoint using a LINQ query. The code then iterates through the collection, checking that each Decoder begins immediately after the previous one. If there is a gap or overlap between two Decoders, I use the ValidationContext object passed to the method to write an informative message to the Errors list. (For more on the LogMessage, see Chapter 7.) After finishing the loop, I check that the last decoder in the collection includes the last character in the message:

```
var decs = from Decoder dec in this.Decoders
           orderby dec.StartPoint
           select dec;
Decoder lastDec = decs.First();

foreach (Decoder dec in decs)
{
  if (dec != lastDec &&
      dec.StartPoint != lastDec.StartPoint + lastDec.Length)
  {
   vc.LogMessage(dec.DecoderName + "'s start point is after " +
                 lastDec.DecoderName + "'s end point(" +
```

```
                (lastDec.StartPoint + lastDec.Length).ToString() + ")",
                "TP001");
    }
    lastDec = dec;
}

if (decs.Last().Length + decs.Last().StartPoint !=
        this.MessageLength)
{
    vc.LogMessage("A gap exists between the end of " +
                decs.Last().Id + " and the end of the message",
                "TP002");
}
```

BEST PRACTICE   Generally speaking, you should avoid raising exceptions or preventing the user from saving their work when your validation code finds a problem. Most developers will not build a complete model in one session. As a result, developers will often be saving incomplete models that will not pass your validation tests. You should raise an exception only for validation errors that can be corrected without forcing the designer to build a complete model (e.g., ensuring that the Id property of a DomainClass is not blank).

Other Options

The DSL Toolkit offers several other ways of managing validation. For instance, you can also extend the ValidationController that is generated for you to take complete control of the validation process (this is enabled through the Uses Custom option on the Validation node in the DSL Explorer). This enables you to override events in the model and determine which objects you want to validate. You can also create and assign rules that will fire only when changes are made to items in the model.

Generating Code

You're now ready to add T4 template code to your Debugging project and see if you can generate valid code from any models created in your designer. In the Debugging project, two T4 templates are tied to the "sample" designer file:

- *nameofyourlanguage***Report**—In this template, no language is specified in the template directive at the top of the file, so you must use C# as the processing code in this template. My version was called TagParseLanguageReport.tt.
- *nameofyourlanguage***ReportVB**—This template has VB specified as the processing language in the template directive at the top of the file. You must use Visual Basic as the processing language in this template. My version was called TagParseLanguageReportVB.tt.

When you open either of these T4 templates, you'll notice that the default code refers to the sample items you deleted out of the DSL Editor when you created your project. That's the result of the Debugging project being generated when you created your project: The changes you've made to your designer since then aren't reflected in the Debugging project's T4 templates. You should delete all the code following the last directive at the top of the file.

I've already discussed T4 in detail in Chapter 7. In this chapter, I concentrate on how you link a T4 template to the output of a visual designer and how to drive your code generation from the items the developer has added to your designer. Any feature of T4 used in this chapter but not discussed is covered in detail in Chapter 7.

BEST PRACTICE   If you're using a third-party T4 editor in Visual Studio 2005/2008, you should add a reference in the Debugging project to the *.Dsl.Dll file in the bin folder of your DSL project. This will give you some IntelliSense support when editing your T4 code.

Configuring the Template

The first lines in the template use T4 directives to establish the base class that the template will use and the file type for the output file:

```
<#@ template inherits=
"Microsoft.VisualStudio.TextTemplating.VSHost.
              ModelingTextTransformation" #>
<#@ output extension=".cs" #>
```

The next line in the template is a custom directive whose name will vary from one designer to another. T4 templates are always processed inside a host. When you use a designer, a custom processor with the same name as your language is generated for you. The convention I use when setting the language name in the wizard is to add the suffix "Language" to the name of the project where I created my designer. Because I had called my project TagParse, my naming convention led me to naming my language "TagParseLanguage" when the option came up in the wizard. The custom directive also has an attribute named `processor`, which is set to a string made up of the name of your language with the suffix "DirectiveProcessor."

The custom directive also has an attribute called `requires`, which is used to tie your template to a designer. The `requires` attribute is passed the string `filename='nameofyourdesignerfile.yourfileextension'`. In my case, I had set the file type for my designer to "tpl." Therefore, when the wizard added the "sample" designer file to my project, it named the file sample.tpl. In the case study, therefore, the directive that ties a T4 template to the "sample" designer file looks like this:

```
<#@ TagParseLanguage processor="TagParseLanguageDirectiveProcessor"
    requires="fileName='Sample.tpl'" #>
```

Your next step is to add code to your T4 template to access the items added to the "sample" designer file. Tying a T4 template to a designer file does *not* cause the template to generate code when the designer file is updated. It does mean that, when the T4 template generates code (when the template is saved, for instance), the template will have access to classes based on the logical items added to the designer file by the developer. These classes are created by the designer from the items the developer added to the model and have a full range of properties for navigating between the items in the model that allow you to retrieve all the items the developer added to the model.

You are guaranteed there will be an object generated from your root item in the designer file (in the case study, the root item is called Parser). Through the root item you can access collections for each item that has an embedded relationship with the root item. Because I created embedded relationships for both the ParseManager and Decoder items, I can access both of those through the root item (assuming that the developer added any to the file).

This code, for instance, iterates through all the Decoders added to the designer by the developer by using the `Decoders` property on the root item:

```
<#foreach (Decoder dcd in this.Parser.Decoders)
    {
```

```
#>
 ...generated code...
<#
   }
#>
```

To demonstrate the results, first assume that the developer has added a single Decoder to the designer and set its properties as follows:

- **DecodeName**—Long4Byte
- **StartPoint**—2
- **Length**—4
- **DataType**—int

Also assume that a T4 template associated with this template contains this code that iterates through all the Decoder objects in the ParseManager's Decoders collection. For each Decoder object, the following T4 template generates code that defines a variable of the DataType specified in the Decoder and calls the DecodeMethod specified in the Decode class:

```
<# int i = 0;
   string varName = "var";
   foreach (Decoder dcd in this.ParseManager.Decoders)
   { i++;
#>
   <#=dcd.DataType#> <#= varName#><#=i#>;
   <#= varName#><#=i#> =
       Decoder.<#= dcd.DecodeMethod#>(TagData.Substring(
       <#= dcd.StartPoint#>,<#=dcd.Length#>));
<#
   }
#>
```

When the T4 template is saved, it would generate code that looks like this:

```
int var1;
   var1 =
       Decoder.Long4Byte(TagData.Substring(
       2,4));
```

In addition to the collections on the root item, the other logical items you defined have navigation properties based on the relationships you defined. The names and functionality generated for these "navigation" properties are based on the Multiplicity settings in your model.

For instance, when I added the Decoder item to the DSL Editor, I set the Multiplicity property on its relationship with the root item to allow for multiple Decoders. As a result, the `Parser` class in my example has a property called `Decoders` (with an *s* at the end) that returns a collection of `Decoder` objects. On the other hand, when I created the relationship between the root item and the `ParseManager`, I set the Multiplicity so that there could be, at most, one `ParseManager` in the relationship. As a result, the `Parser` class has a singular property called `ParseManager` (with no *s* at the end) that returns a single `ParseManager` object. This code, for instance, retrieves the value of the `TagName` property on the single `ParseManager` allowed in the designer:

```
<#= this.Parser.ParseManager.TagName #>
```

Because I created a reference relationship between the `ParseManager` and any `Decoder`s, the resulting `ParseManager` object has a `Decoders` property that gives access to any `Decoder`s the developer has connected to the `ParseManager`. This code would retrieve the `ParseManager` and process all (and only the) `Decoder`s connected to that `ParseManager`:

```
foreach (Decoder dcd in this.TagParse.ParseManager.Decoders)
```

Any enumerated values you created in your designer project can be used in your T4 project. This code is valid in the case study template, for instance, because of the enumerated value I added to the designer:

```
dcd.DecodeMethod = TagParse.PHVIS.ValidDecodeMethods.Boolean;
```

Distributing Your Designer

Once you've created your designer, you'll want to distribute it to other developers. You'll also want to integrate your T4 template into your designer so that developers won't have to open and close the template to generate their code.

I first look at integrating your template with your designer and then look at creating a deployment package for distributing the designer. The deployment process is different in Visual Studio 2005/2008 compared to Visual Studio 2010, so I cover both processes separately.

Converting the Template to a Custom Tool: Visual Studio 2005/2008

As your designer works now, to generate code from your template the developer would have to open and close your template. That step can be eliminated by converting your template into a custom tool and setting the CustomTool property on the designer's file. (Custom tools are discussed in Chapter 8.) As part of converting your template into a custom tool, you can move your T4 template into a resource file and out of Solution Explorer so it won't clutter up the developer's project. Although the custom tool used here uses a T4 template, you could use this process to associate any custom tool you create (as described in Chapter 8) with your visual designer.

Distributing your template as part of a resource file means developers won't be able to modify your templates. (I regard that as a benefit.) However, if you haven't met the developer's needs or provided sufficient opportunities for the developer to customize your solution and the developer can't change your template, it's likely that the developer will attempt to "fix" your generated code and abandon your code-generation solution. If the developer can change your template, then they are more likely to continue to use your solution. If you're comfortable with letting the developer "enhance" your templates, don't insert them into the resource file as described here. You can, instead, install the templates into the same folder as the tool and let the developer modify the templates there.

To set up your template as a custom tool, you need to enhance your DslPackage project. The first step is to add a folder to your project called CodeGeneration. Use Add | Existing Item to add your T4 template, created in the Debugging project, to this folder. If you haven't changed the names of the files generated by the wizard, this file will either have a file called *nameofyourlanguage*Report (if you used C#) or *nameofyourlanguage*ReportVB (if you used VB) in the folder. You should change the name of your T4 template to something more meaningful (the convention I use is the name of my project with the suffix "Generation"— TagParseGenerator). Once you've added the template and changed its name, erase the CustomTool property on the T4 template.

In the custom directive that ties the template to a particular designer file, you need to update the file name with the name of the designer file (otherwise the template will all be looking at the "sample" file from the Debugging project). To support that, put an arbitrary placeholder in place of the file name. I use %INPUTFILENAME% to create a template like this (in your T4 template, the custom directive's name will be the name of the language you specified in the wizard rather than my "TagParseLanguage"):

```
<#@ TagParseLanguage processor="TagParseLanguageDirectiveProcessor"
                requires="fileName='%INPUTFILENAME%'" #>
```

Next, put your T4 template into a resource file. First, add a resource file to the same folder as your template: Right-click the CodeGeneration folder, select Add | New Item, and add a Resources file. The naming convention I use for the resource file is the name of my project with the suffix "Resources" (TagParseResources.resx, in this case). When the resource file opens, drag your template file from Solution Explorer into the resource file.

Finally, you'll need to add the code that will generate the code using your template. Add to the CodeGeneration folder a class file to hold that code. The naming convention I use for this class is the name of my designer project with the suffix "CustomTool." (For the case study, this produces TagParseCustomTool.) Put the following code in the class file making these changes:

- Replace the namespace in the `using` clause with the namespace for your designer project. You can retrieve this namespace by double-clicking the DslDefinition.dsl file, switching to the DSL Explorer, and clicking the top line. The namespace you entered is listed in the Properties window.
- Set the namespace for the class to the namespace you created for your designer project.
- Change the name of the class to the name of your language with the suffix "Package." The name of your language appears in the Properties window in the Name property above the Namespace property described earlier.
- Set the second property of the ProvideCodeGenerator attribute to the name you gave your template file when you added it to the resource file.
- Set the third property of the ProvideCodeGenerator attribute to some description of your language.
- Use the Tools | Create GUID menu option to generate a new GUID and paste it into the GUID attribute.

Here is the template for your code using the values for this case study:

```
using Microsoft.VisualStudio.TextTemplating.VSHost;
using BatRF.TagParseLanguage.CodeGeneration;
```

```
namespace TagParse.PHVIS
{
   [ProvideCodeGenerator(typeof(CodeGenerator), "TagParseGenerator",
       "Generates tag parsers", true, ProjectSystem=
             ProvideCodeGeneratorAttribute.VisualBasicProjectGuid))]
    internal sealed partial class TagParseLanguagePackage
    {
    }

   [System.Runtime.InteropServices.Guid(
       "4B041800-E61B-4738-8D92-986152F448A7")]
    public class CodeGenerator :
       Microsoft.VisualStudio.TextTemplating.
                     VSHost.TemplatedCodeGenerator
    {
      protected override byte[] GenerateCode(string InputFileName,
                                     string InputFileContent)
      {
        ...more code to go here...
      }
    }
}
```

A custom tool must be registered for each language it will be used in. This example registers the custom tool for C# using the `ProvideCodeGeneratorAttribute.CSharpProjectGuid` enumerated value. To register for another language, you'll need to change the value used. (You can register your custom tool for multiple languages by adding multiple `ProvideCodeGenerator` attributes.)

Within the `GenerateCode` method, add the following code to invoke your template. (You need to change the name of the resource `TagParseResources.TagParseGenerator` to the names you gave your resource file and your template file.) This code also checks for my designer filename marker (`%INPUTFILENAME%`) and replaces it with the correct value for the file being generated. This code also supports replacing an `%INPUTNAMESPACE%` token so that you can insert a namespace into your generated code—I retrieve the namespace for the current project from the `FileNamespace` property of the `TemplateCodeGenerator` class that my `CodeGenerator` class inherits from. However, you could also just retrieve the namespace for the current project in your T4 code:

```
System.IO.FileInfo fi = new System.IO.FileInfo(InputFileName);
if (fi.Length < 10)
{
 return null;
}
InputFileContent = System.Text.ASCIIEncoding.UTF8.GetString(
                     TagParseResources.TagParseGenerator);
InputFileContent = InputFileContent.Replace(
                     "%INPUTFILENAME%", InputFileName);
InputFileContent = InputFileContent.Replace(
                     "%INPUTNAMESPACE%", this.FileNamespace);

byte[] data = base.GenerateCode(InputFileName, InputFileContent);
byte[] ascii = new byte[data.Length - 3];
System.Array.Copy(data, 3, ascii, 0, data.Length - 3);
return ascii;
```

The `GenerateCode` method is discussed in more detail in Chapter 8 as part of creating custom tools. Be aware that this code silently exits without generating code if the designer file hasn't been saved yet (that's the code that checks the file's length).

You can now test your custom tool by pressing F5 to open the Debugging project. Delete or exclude your TestLanguageReport/TestLanguageReportVB file—because the template is now in the resource file and called as a custom tool, you don't need it as a standalone file any more. Set the CustomTool property on your designer file to the name you used in the second parameter of the `ProvideCodeGenerator` attribute in your `CodeGeneration` class file. To generate your code, just open and close your designer (or right-click your designer file and pick Run Custom Tool).

Preloading the Custom Tool Property

Finally, you'll need to have the CustomTool property on the designer file automatically set to the name of your custom tool when the developer uses Add New Item to add your designer to a project. That's handled by adding a key to the Windows registry. You can have those entries made when your designer is installed (and removed when your designer is uninstalled) by adding the following two methods to the class file in your CodeGeneration file. (These methods are covered in more detail in Chapter 8.)

To use this code, you need to change the following:

- VSVersion to the version of Visual Studio that you're using. The example is set to use Visual Studio 2008.
- LangGUID to the GUID for the language of your choice. The example has the GUID for C#.
- GeneratorExtension to the file extension for your designer file.
- GeneratorName to the name of your custom tool. This is the same value you passed to the second property of the PrivateCodeGenerator attribute.

```
static string VSVersion = "9.0";
static string LangGUID = "{fae04ec1-301f-11d3-bf4b-00c04f79efbc}";
static string GeneratorExtension = ".tpl2";
static string GeneratorName = "TclFileCodeGenerator";

[System.Runtime.InteropServices.ComRegisterFunction]
public static void RegisterClass(System.Type typ)
{
 Microsoft.Win32.RegistryKey key;
 string keyname = @"SOFTWARE\Microsoft\VisualStudio\" + VSVersion +
                  @"\Generators\" + LangGUID + @"\" +
                  GeneratorExtension + @"\";
 key = Microsoft.Win32.Registry.LocalMachine.CreateSubKey(keyname);
 key.SetValue("", GeneratorName);
}


[System.Runtime.InteropServices.ComUnregisterFunction]
public static void UnregisterClass(System.Type typ)
{
 string keyname = @"SOFTWARE\Microsoft\VisualStudio\" + VSVersion +
                  @"\Generators\" + LangGUID + @"\" +
                  GeneratorExtension + @"\";
 Microsoft.Win32.Registry.LocalMachine.DeleteSubKey(keyname,false);
}
```

To have these methods executed when your designer is installed, you must make the DslPackage project visible to Windows. In the Application tab, click the Assembly Information button and check the Make Assembly COM-Visible option.

NON–BEST PRACTICE   Using these registration functions isn't the best way to
go—you'd be better off to let your registry entries be made directly by the
Windows Installer. (In fact, with Visual Studio 2010, if you deploy as a Visual
Studio extension, these entries will be ignored.) In addition, setting the COM-
Visible option generates some annoying messages during debugging (but doesn't
seem to interfere with testing or debugging your designer), so you should only
set the option as part of creating your deployment package. But having said all
that, this will work in Visual Studio 2005 and later.

Create a Deployment Project: Visual Studio 2005/2008

To create a deployment project, you must add a Domain-Specific
Language Setup project to your designer solution. Right-click the solution
in Solution Explorer, select Add | New Project, and, in the Add New
Project dialog's Other Projects | Extensibility section, select Domain-
Specific Language Setup project. The convention I use for naming the
Setup project is the name of my project with the suffix "Install" (in this case,
"TagParseInstall").

You now need to get a PLK and embed it into your DslPackage project:

1. Open your designer, switch to DSL Explorer, and click the top line.
2. From the Properties window, follow the directions at http://msdn.
   microsoft.com/en-us/library/bb165395.aspx to get to the request
   form. Enter the following information in the Properties window:
   - Company name.
   - Package name. (Called just "Name" in the Properties window.)
   - Package GUID.
   - Package version. (Must be entered as Major.Minor.Build.
     Revision—not the order that the values appear in the Properties
     window.)
3. Click the Request PLK button on the form.
4. Copy the generated PLK from the bottom of the form.
5. In the DslPackage project, double-click the VsPackages.resx file to
   open it.
6. Add a string resource with a name of "1" and paste your PLK into
   the value.
7. Still in the DslPackage project, expand the Generated Code folder
   and double-click the Package.tt file to open it.

8. Uncomment this line:

```
[VSShell::ProvideLoadKey("Standard", Constants.ProductVersion,
        Constants.ProductName, Constants.CompanyName, 1)]
```

You're now ready to create your MSI file:

1. Click the Transform All Templates button in Solution Explorer to regenerate code from your templates (including templates in the setup project). If you don't transform your templates, your MSI file will not be generated.
2. Build your setup application.
3. Navigate to the setup project's bin folder to find your MSI file.

You can distribute your designer to other developers by giving them the MSI file. If you run the installation on your own computer (to make sure it works), uninstall it before attempting to debug your designer project again. The temporary registry entries created when you start debugging from your designer project will conflict with the more permanent entries generated by the installation. You may need to reboot your development computer after removing the installation, transform all your templates, and rebuild your designer before you will be able to debug it again.

Deploying: VS2010

In Visual Studio 2010, creating a deployment package no longer requires adding a special setup project to your solution. Instead, everything you need to deploy your designer is generated every time you test your designer. To deploy your application, you just need to double-click the DslPackage.vsix file you'll find in the Debug folder of your DslPackage project.

Visual Studio 2010 Additions

Visual Studio adds three new features that are useful when using a visual designer that go beyond the scope of this book's focus on code generation:

- **ModelBus**—Adding a ModelBus adapter to your template allows you to reference one model from another model.
- **DslLibrary**—You can store and retrieve portions of your model in a common library.

■ **Databinding**—Supports using a WPF or WinForms surface for
your designer.

Capturing Inputs

This case study has focused primarily on creating a visual designer that a
developer can use to provide the inputs for a T4 code-generation template.
The chapter has only touched on some of the features of the DSL Editor.
The editor supports the following features, for instance:

■ Customizing what happens when the developer drops an item into
the designer.
■ Items can be configured as derived classes.
■ Inheritance relationships can be created among items in the model.
■ Text decorators, instead of displaying a fixed string, can display the
value of a domain property.
■ Icon decorators can be configured so that the icon is updated
depending on a value in a domain property.
■ The Generates Double Derived property on a graphical component
supports creating two partial classes when the code is generated for
the logical item represented by this graphical item.

Even with this short look at the DSL Designer project, you're ready to
create your own graphical designer for developers to use to specify their
inputs to the code-generation process. This, coupled with T4 templates,
allows you to create a powerful (and easy-to-use) way to create code-
generation solutions. However, you're not obliged to use T4 templates with
your designer: Even a cursory look at the contents of the designer file
shows that the XML generated by the designer is relatively easy to read
and process. You can use your own tools to process the designer file and
still let developers use a visual designer to specify their inputs.

As with the case studies in Chapter 9, "Case Study: Generating a
Connection String Manager," and Chapter 10, "Case Study: Generating
Validation Code," the code for this utility can be downloaded from my
website (www.phvis.com) and from www.informit.com.

APPENDIXES

GENERATING MENU NAMES

The following code, run from an add-in, gives you a list of all the menus you can attach your menu items to:

```
CommandBars cbs;
cbs = (CommandBars) _applicationObject.CommandBars;

for(int ing = 1; ing < cbs.Count; ing++)
{
   System.Diagnostics.Debug.WriteLine(cbs[ing].Name);
}
```

This code generates a list of the context menus in the Project and Context menus (these are the context menus you are most likely to want to add your own menu items to):

```
cbs = (CommandBars) _applicationObject.CommandBars;
CommandBarPopup cbp;
for(int ing = 1; ing < cbs.Count; ing++)
{
    if (cbs[ing].Name == "Project and Solution Context Menus")
    {
        for (int ing2 = 1; ing2 < cbs[ing].Controls.Count; ing2++ )
        {
            cbp = (CommandBarPopup)cbs[ing].Controls[ing2];
            System.Diagnostics.Debug.Print(cbp.Caption);
        }
    }
}
```

OPTIONS DIALOG CATEGORIES, SUBCATEGORIES, AND PROPERTIES

Given the name of a category and a subcategory, the following code will display all the property items within the the subcategory. This example shows all the entries in the category "TextEditor" and the subcategory "Basic":

```
Properties     props =
        _applicationObject.get_Properties("TextEditor","Basic");
for (int ing = 1; ing < props.Count; ing++)
{
    Property prop = props.Item(ing);
    System.Diagnostics.Debug.Print(prop.Name);
}
```

You can get the list of categories and subcategories from the Windows registry under the key HKEY_LOCAL_MACHINE\SOFTWARE\Microsoft\VisualStudio*MajorVersion.MinorVersion*\AutomationProperties.

A CODE-GENERATION ADD-IN

In the case studies in Chapter 9, "Case Study: Generating a Connection String Manager," and Chapter 10, "Case Study: Generating Validation Code," I built separate, standalone solutions for each problem. In both instances, a significant part of the case study was devoted to developing the Visual Studio add-in that integrated the code generator into the application. In practice, I don't actually build my code-generation solutions that way.

Rather than have multiple code-generation solutions that I load into Visual Studio, I have one add-in project with multiple class files. Each class file (e.g., `DatabaseUtilities`, `WebFormUtilities`) contains several related code-generation solutions. Because I have only one code-generation solution, I also keep my `CodeGenerationUtilities` class in this project rather than in a separate project.

The major benefit of this design is that I have only one `connect` class (in the Connect.cs file) to modify when I create a new code-generation solution. Having a single, easily extensible `connect` class makes it easier to add new code-generation solutions—I don't have to spend much time working on my Visual Studio integration code and can concentrate on the class containing my code-generation solution. To that end, I've standardized the way my code-generation classes interact with the code in the `connect` class.

If you're considering building a single code-generation project to hold all your code-generation solutions, this appendix discusses my approach.

Integrating Code-Generation Classes

Each of my code-generation classes interacts with the `connect` class in the following areas:

- The `OnConnection` method, where a menu item is added to my Generate Code submenu on the Tools menu

- The DocumentOpened event, where the code-generation class checks any recently opened file to see if it should be handled
- At least one custom event that triggers code generation
- The Exec method, where the method on my code-generation class that begins code generation is called when the user clicks the menu item added to the submenu

Adding the Submenu Button

To support adding to the Generate Code submenu, I add three public, static, read-only properties to each code-generation class. These three properties return the MenuItemName, MenuItemCaption, and MenuToolTip values I use to create the menu item added to the Generate Code submenu. (The code for adding the Generate Code menu item itself remains in the Connect class.) The values here are the ones for the LookupValidator case study in Chapter 10.

```
public static string LookupVMenuItemName
{
 get
 {
  return "lkupvdGentr";
 }
}


public static string LookupVMenuItemCaption
{
 get
 {
  return "Generate LookupValidator";
 }
}


public static string LookupVMenuToolTip
{
 get
 {
  return "Create a class for integrating with an ASP.NET validator";
 }
}
```

In the Connect.cs class, I have a method (called AddToSubmenu) that adds a menu item to the submenu:

```
void AddToSubMenu(CommandBar cb, Commands2 cmds,
                 ref Object[] contextGUIDS,
                 string menuItemName, string menuItemCaption,
                 string menuToolTip)
{
 Command NamedCommand = null;
 try
 {
  NamedCommand = _applicationObject.Commands.Item(
             _addInInstance.ProgID + menuItemName, 1);
 }
 catch
 {
  try
  {
   NamedCommand = cmds.AddNamedCommand2(
       _addInInstance, menuItemName, menuItemCaption, menuToolTip,
       true, 50, ref contextGUIDS,
       (int)vsCommandStatus.vsCommandStatusSupported +
       (int)vsCommandStatus.vsCommandStatusEnabled,
       (int)vsCommandStyle.vsCommandStylePictAndText,
       vsCommandControlType.vsCommandControlTypeButton);
  }
  catch { }

  try
  {
   CommandBarControl cbc = cb.Controls[menuItemCaption];
  }
  catch
  {
   NamedCommand.AddControl(cb, 1);
  }
 }
}
```

To support adding menu items both to menus and submenus, AddToSubMenu accepts, as its first parameter, a CommandBar object. If the menu item is being added directly to a menu, I can just pass the menu to the method; if the menu item is being added to a submenu (as it is in this example), I pass the CommandBar property for the submenu header.

To support adding my menu choice to some menu other than the Tools menu (to add to one of Visual Studio's context menus, for instance), I have another routine that, when passed a menu name, returns the corresponding menu in Visual Studio 2008 and earlier:

```
CommandBar GetMenu(string proposedMenuName)
{
 string FoundMenuName;
 try
 {
  System.Resources.ResourceManager resourceManager =
        new System.Resources.ResourceManager(
                  _addInInstance.ProgID + ".CommandBar",
                System.Reflection.Assembly.GetExecutingAssembly());
  System.Globalization.CultureInfo cultureInfo = new
    System.Globalization.CultureInfo(_applicationObject.LocaleID);
  if (cultureInfo.TwoLetterISOLanguageName == "zh")
  {
   System.Globalization.CultureInfo parentCultureInfo =
                                    cultureInfo.Parent;
   FoundMenuName = resourceManager.GetString(
              String.Concat(parentCultureInfo.Name, menuName));
  }
  else
  {
   FoundMenuName = resourceManager.GetString(String.Concat(
        cultureInfo.TwoLetterISOLanguageName, menuName));
  }
 }
 catch
 {
  FoundMenuName = menuName;
 }

 if (FoundMenuName == "")
 {
  FoundMenuName = menuName;
```

```
}
CommandBars cbs = (CommandBars)_applicationObject.CommandBars;
return cbs[FoundMenuName];
}
```

In Visual Studio 2010, use the following code to find a menu. (Don't forget to set the `MainMenu` variable to True, as in this example, to find menus on the main menu bar.)

```
CommandBar GetMenu(string proposedMenuName)
{
CommandBar cb;
bool MainMenu = true;
string MenuBarName = "Menubar";

if (MainMenu)
{
  cb = ((CommandBars)_applicationObject.CommandBars)[MenuBarName];
  cb = ((CommandBarPopup)cb.Controls[FoundMenuName]).CommandBar;
}
else
{
  CommandBars cbs = (CommandBars)_applicationObject.CommandBars;
  cb = cbs[FoundMenuName];
}
}
```

The code for finding the Tools menu, adding the Generate Code submenu, and then adding the menu item for the LookupValidator code generator looks like this:

```
object[] contextGUIDS = new object[] { };
Commands2 commands = (Commands2)_applicationObject.Commands;

CommandBar cb = GetMenu("Tools");
CommandBarPopup cbp;

try
{
  cbp = (CommandBarPopup)cb.Controls["Code Generation"];
```

```
}
catch
{
 cbp = (CommandBarPopup)cb.Controls.Add(
                        MsoControlType.msoControlPopup,
                        System.Type.Missing,
                        System.Type.Missing,
                        System.Type.Missing,
                        System.Type.Missing);
                    cbp.Caption = "Code Generation";
}

Commands2 cmds = (Commands2)_applicationObject.Commands;
AddToSubMenu(cbp.CommandBar, cmds, ref contextGUIDS,
           WebFormUtilities.LookupVMenuItemName,
           WebFormUtilities.LookupVMenuItemCaption,
           WebFormUtilities.LookupVMenuToolTip);
}
```

In those cases where I'm adding a new code-generation solution to my Generate Code submenu, the only change I have to make is to add another call to my `AddToSubmenu` method.

Responding to Events

The pattern I follow for wiring up code-generation solutions is to catch the opening event fired for every file and handle that event in a method named `docMaster_DocumentOpened`. In that method, I check to see if the file is to be processed by one of my code-generation solutions and wire up the event that will trigger code generation. Depending on the design for the solution, I wire up to an event related to the following items:

- **Document window**—This allows me to generate code whenever the developer switches away from the window.
- **Document**—This supports generating code when the document is closed.
- **Build**—This supports generating code when the project is built.

To support having multiple documents open, I create a `Dictionary` object to hold the `DocumentEvents` object plus an additional `Dictionary` for each type of event I'm tracking. This example creates the Dictionary objects for the DocumentEvents object and the document-closing events:

```
Dictionary<Document, DocumentEvents> docEventsDict = null;
Dictionary<Document,
    _dispDocumentEvents_DocumentClosingEventHandler> docEventDict = null;
```

The code generator for the LookUpValidator case study demonstrates the pattern I use in the document-opened event. Because the LookUpValidator only tracks .aspx files, my code in docMaster_ DocumentOpened first checks to see if the just-opened document is worth tracking. If it is, I check the relevant Dictionary to see if the DocumentEvents object for this Document has already been created. If it hasn't, the code creates the object and adds it to the Dictionary with the Document as the key value:

```
EnvDTE.DocumentEvents docEvents = null;
if (Doc.Name.EndsWith(".aspx"))
{
  if (!docEventsDict.TryGetValue(Doc, out docEvents))
  {
    docEvents = (EnvDTE.DocumentEvents)
      _applicationObject.Events.get_DocumentEvents(Doc);
    docEventsDict.Add(Doc, docEvents);
  }
```

The final step is to create the appropriate event handler, wire it up to the DocumentEvents object, and store it in the appropriate Dictionary. This example handles the document-closing event:

```
  docEvent = new _dispDocumentEvents_DocumentClosingEventHandler(
             docWebForm_DocumentClosing);
}
if (docEvent != null)
{
  docEvents.DocumentClosing += docEvent;
  docEventDict.Add(Doc, docEvent);
}
```

The event handlers wired up in the `docMaster_DocumentOpened` event look very similar for all my code solutions: I retrieve the related `DocumentEvents` object and the event handler object from their respective `Dictionary` objects where they were stored when created. Once they're retrieved, I disconnect the event from the `DocumentEvents` object and call the code-generation solution. Although it's not essential to do it here, this is also where I typically call the utility method that determines the project's language and file type, which I then pass to my code-generation method:

```
void docWebForm_DocumentClosing(Document Doc)
{
 WebFormUtilities wfu;
 DocumentEvents docEvents;
 _dispDocumentEvents_DocumentClosingEventHandler docEvent;
 if (docEventsDict.TryGetValue(Doc, out docEvents))
 {
  if (docEventDict.TryGetValue(Doc, out docEvent))
  {
   docEvents.DocumentClosing -= docEvent;
   docEventDict.Remove(Doc);
   wfu = new WebFormUtilities(_applicationObject, _addInInstance);
   ProjectInfo pi =
    GenerationUtilities.SetProjectInformation(Doc, _applicationObject);
   wfu.GenerateValidator(Doc, pi);
  }
 }
}
```

Because developers may close one solution and open another without shutting down Visual Studio, I use the solution-opening event to disconnect any events that are already wired up and re-create my `Dictionary` objects. This is also the event where I wire up the handler to catch all document-opening events:

```
void slnE_Opened()
{
 if (docEventsDict != null)
 {
```

```
foreach (KeyValuePair<Document, DocumentEvents>
                docEvents in docEventsDict)
{
  foreach (KeyValuePair<Document,
           _dispDocumentEvents_DocumentClosingEventHandler> docEvent
                in docEventDict)
  {
   if (docEvents.Key == docEvent.Key)
   {
    docEvents.Value.DocumentClosing -= docEvent.Value;
   }
  }
 }
}
docEventsDict = new Dictionary<Document, DocumentEvents>();
docEventDict = new Dictionary<Document,
           _dispDocumentEvents_DocumentClosingEventHandler>();

docMaster = _applicationObject.Events.get_DocumentEvents(null);
docMaster.DocumentOpened +=
    new _dispDocumentEvents_DocumentOpenedEventHandler(
                docMaster_DocumentOpened);
}
```

One last task remains: to wire up the solution-open event. I do that in the OnConnection method when the method is passed ext_ConnectMode. ext_cm_UISetup in its connectMode parameter. That code looks like this:

```
if (connectMode == ext_ConnectMode.ext_cm_UISetup)
{
    if (slnE == null)
    {
     slnE = _applicationObject.Events.SolutionEvents;
     slnE.Opened += new
            _dispSolutionEvents_OpenedEventHandler(slnE_Opened);
    }
}
```

Responding to the Menu Button

The third place that the `connect` class interacts with a code-generation class is in the `Exec` method. All that's necessary in that method is to add an `If` block for each code-generation solution and, in the block, instantiate the code-generation class and call the method that starts generating code. To support the LookupValidator solution, the `If` block looks like this:

```
if (commandName ==
    _addInInstance.ProgID + "." + WebFormUtilities.LookupVMenuItemName)
{
WebFormUtilities wfu;
wfu = new WebFormUtilities(_applicationObject, _addInInstance);
wfu.GenerateValdiator();
}
```

An Extensible Solution

With this framework in place, adding a new code-generation solution consists of adding the following items:

- A class to my code-generation project to hold the code-generation code. This class also has static, read-only properties that return the information required by the `connect` class to create the menu.
- A call to the `AddToSubMenu` method in the `OnConnection` method of the `connect` class to add the solution to the Code Generation submenu (assuming that I want the solution to be available from Visual Studio's menu system).
- An `If` block in the `Exec` method to call the solution when the user selects it from the menu.
- An `If` block to the `docMaster_DocumentOpened` event handler to wire up an event to call the code-generation method (and, potentially, a new `Dictionary` if this is an event type that hasn't been used in the add-in before).
- An event handler to call the code generation solution.

By keeping all your code-generation solutions in a single project, you can avoid having to create a custom connect class for each solution. Using my framework, I can extend my connect class to handle a new solution in less than 10 minutes.

A copy of the current version of my code-generation skeleton can be downloaded from my website (www.phvis.com) and www.informit.com. (Be aware: I'm constantly "enhancing" this skeleton to reduce the work required to add a new solution, so the version that you get may not correspond to what you see in this appendix.)

DISTRIBUTING CODE-GENERATION SOLUTIONS

The easiest way to distribute a code-generation solution—at least, easiest for developers who are installing your solution—is to distribute it as a VSI file. Just by double-clicking the VSI file, a developer can install one or more Visual Studio add-ins, project item templates, or toolbox controls.

A VSI file is a ZIP file (with its extension changed to .vsi) that contains the following items:

- A .vscontent file
- All items required by your add-in (its DLL and AddIn file plus any supporting files—e.g., Visual Studio template files and toolbox controls)

Unfortunately, there is no wizard or project template for creating a VSI file from within Visual Studio, so you'll have to assemble it yourself.

Creating the .vscontent File

The .vscontent file can have any name you want but the file type must be "vscontent". The file consists of a vsContent element containing one or more Content elements. Each Content element describes one item to be added to Visual Studio: an add-in, a project item template, or a toolbox control (you can also use the VSI file to add macros and code snippets if they're part of your code-generation solution).

To avoid conflicts with XML encoding, you should not have an XML directive (the line beginning <?xml) at the start of your .vscontent file.

Adding Add-Ins

A `Content` element describes one add-in, using these elements:

- **Two `FileName` elements**—One with the name of the DLL and one with the name of the add-in's Addin file
- **`DisplayName`**—A human-readable name for your add-in, which will be displayed in the template installer and Visual Studio's Add-In Manager
- **`Description`**—A human-readable description of your add-in, also displayed in the installer and Add-In Manager
- **`FileContentType`**—Holds the string "Addin"
- **`ContentVersion`**—Set to "2.0" to install the add-in in Visual Studio 2008 or later (the only option)

A .vscontent file for an add-in called PHVGenerators looks like this:

```
<VSContent
  xmlns="http://schemas.microsoft.com/developer/vscontent/2005">
  <Content>
    <FileName>PHVGenerators.Addin</FileName>
    <FileName>PHVGenerators.dll</FileName>
    <DisplayName>Implements code generation solutions</DisplayName>
    <Description>Code Generation Add-In from PH&VIS</Description>
    <FileContentType>Addin</FileContentType>
    <ContentVersion>2.0</ContentVersion>
  </Content>
</VSContent>
```

Adding Templates

You can add templates to Visual Studio's Add New dialog by using these elements inside a `Content` element:

- A single `FileName` element specifying the name of the ZIP file containing the template.
- A `FileContentType` element set to "VSTemplate."

- A `ContentVersion` element set to "1.0" to install in Visual Studio 2005 or later. To install in Visual Studio 2008 or later, set the element to "2.0".
- An `Attributes` element containing three `Attribute` elements that specify where the VSTemplate will appear in the Visual Studio Add New Item dialog.

An `Attribute` element has two attributes: `name` and `value`. The three `Attribute` elements you need should have their `name` and `value` attributes set as follows:

- **name: "Project"**—The `value` attribute must be set to one of the project types listed in the treeview in Visual Studio's Add New Item dialog (e.g., "Visual C#" or "Visual Basic").
- **name: "ProjectSubType"**—The `value` attribute must be set to one of the subtypes listed under the project type you specified in the Project Attribute (e.g., "Web")
- **name: "TemplateType"**—The `value` attribute must be set to "Item."

This example adds a template contained in a file called LookupValidator.zip (creating a template file is described in Chapter 8, "Other Tools: Templates, Attributes, and Custom Tools"). The `Attribute` elements specify that the template should appear in the C# part of the Add New Item dialog, in the Web Section and that this is a project item template. The `ContentVersion` element specifies that this template can be installed in Visual Studio 2005 or later:

```
<VSContent
  xmlns="http://schemas.microsoft.com/developer/vscontent/2005">
  <Content>
    <FileName>LookupValidator.zip</FileName>
    <DisplayName>Template for LookupValidator</DisplayName>
    <Description>Item template: Supports LookupValidator</Description>
    <FileContentType>VSTemplate</FileContentType>
    <ContentVersion>1.0</ContentVersion>
    <Attributes>
      <Attribute name="ProjectType" value="Visual C#"/>
      <Attribute name="ProjectSubType" value="Web"/>
      <Attribute name="TemplateType" value="Item"/>
```

```
    </Attributes>
  </Content>
</VSContent>
```

Adding a Toolbox Control

To add a toolbox control, you need to ensure the `Content` element contains the following items:

- Single `FileName` element containing the name of the control's DLL
- A `ContentVersion` element set to either "1.0" to install in Visual Studio 2005 (or later) or "2.0" to install in Visual Studio 2008 or later
- A `FileContentType` set to "Toolbox Control"

This example adds a DLL called LookupValidator control:

```
<VSContent
    xmlns="http://schemas.microsoft.com/developer/vscontent/2005">
  <Content>
    <FileName>LookupValidator.dll</FileName>
    <DisplayName>Lookup Validator </DisplayName>
    <Description> A Validator for doing lookup on a table</Description>
    <FileContentType>Toolbox Control</FileContentType>
    <ContentVersion>2.0</ContentVersion>
  </Content>
</VSContent>
```

Adding Files

Having created a .vscontent file, your next step is to create a ZIP file or a Windows compressed folder and add your .vscontent file to it. Once you've added the .vscontent file, you must add to the ZIP file all the files specified in the `FileName` elements of your .vscontent file. When adding files to the ZIP file, you must add the files without any subfolder information. Once you've added all the necessary files, you can change your ZIP file's extension to .vsi.

A Complete Example

Putting this altogether, deploying a code-generation solution that installs a single add-in that implements both of the case studies (the connection manager and the lookup validator) requires three `Content` elements, one for each of the following:

- The add-in that contains the code for both solutions
- The template used by the LookupValidator
- The toolbox control used by the LookupValidator

If the two case studies had been built separately as two separate add-ins, I'd need two `Content` elements: one for each add-in. The resulting .vscontent file would look like this:

```
<VSContent
    xmlns="http://schemas.microsoft.com/developer/vscontent/2005">
    <Content>
        <FileName>PHVGenerators.dll</FileName>
        <FileName>PHVGenerators.Addin</FileName>
        <DisplayName>Code generation manager</DisplayName>
        <Description>Code Generation Add-In from PH&VIS</Description>
        <FileContentType>Addin</FileContentType>
        <ContentVersion>2.0</ContentVersion>
    </Content>
    <Content>
        <FileName>LookupValidator.zip</FileName>
        <DisplayName>Template for LookupValidator</DisplayName>
        <Description>Item template: Supports LookupValidator</Description>
        <FileContentType>VSTemplate</FileContentType>
        <ContentVersion>1.0</ContentVersion>
        <Attributes>
            <Attribute name="ProjectType" value="Visual C#"/>
            <Attribute name="ProjectSubType" value="Web"/>
            <Attribute name="TemplateType" value="Item"/>
        </Attributes>
    </Content>
    <Content>
        <FileName>LookupValidator.dll</FileName>
        <DisplayName>Lookup Validator</DisplayName>
```

```
   <Description> A Validator for doing lookup on a table</Description>
   <FileContentType>Toolbox Control</FileContentType>
   <ContentVersion>1.0</ContentVersion>
  </Content>
</VSContent>
```

The VSI file would also need to contain the following:

- The DLL for the add-in (PHVGenerators.dll)
- The Addin file for the add-in (PHVGenerators.Addin)
- The ZIP file for installing the template (LookupValidator.zip)
- The DLL for the toolbox control (LookupValidator.dll)

Installing the Solution

To install your solution, the developer must shut down Visual Studio and double-click your VSI file. This will start the Visual Studio Content Installer. On the first page of the installer, the developer can select which components to install before clicking the Next button. The developer will next get a warning that the file has not been signed and, after clearing that message, be taken to the second page of the installer where clicking the Finish button will install your solution. As part of the installation, the installer will start and shut down Visual Studio.

INDEX

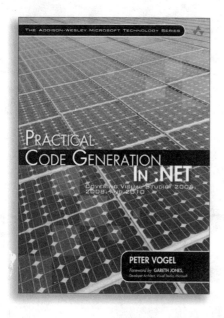

FREE Online Edition

Your purchase of **Practical Code Generation in .NET** includes access to a free online edition for 45 days through the Safari Books Online subscription service. Nearly every Addison-Wesley Professional book is available online through Safari Books Online, along with more than 5,000 other technical books and videos from publishers such as Cisco Press, Exam Cram, IBM Press, O'Reilly, Prentice Hall, Que, and Sams.

SAFARI BOOKS ONLINE allows you to search for a specific answer, cut and paste code, download chapters, and stay current with emerging technologies.

Activate your FREE Online Edition at www.informit.com/safarifree

R.C.L.

NOV. 2010

G

> **STEP 1:** Enter the coupon code: GWPDKFH.

> **STEP 2:** New Safari users, complete the brief registration form.
> Safari subscribers, just log in.

If you have difficulty registering on Safari or accessing the online edition, please e-mail customer-service@safaribooksonline.com